James Anthony Froude

The English in Ireland in the Eighteenth Century

Vol. III

James Anthony Froude

The English in Ireland in the Eighteenth Century
Vol. III

ISBN/EAN: 9783742868282

Manufactured in Europe, USA, Canada, Australia, Japa

Cover: Foto ©ninafisch / pixelio.de

Manufactured and distributed by brebook publishing software (www.brebook.com)

James Anthony Froude

The English in Ireland in the Eighteenth Century

THE ENGLISH IN IRELAND.

VOL. III.

LONDON: PRINTED BY
SPOTTISWOODE AND CO., NEW-STREET SQUARE
AND PARLIAMENT STREET

THE ENGLISH IN IRELAND

IN THE

EIGHTEENTH CENTURY.

BY

JAMES ANTHONY FROUDE, M.A.

IN THREE VOLUMES.

Vol. III.

LONDON:
LONGMANS, GREEN, AND CO.
1874.

All rights reserved.

CONTENTS.

BOOK VIII.

CHAPTER I.

THE UNITED IRISHMEN.

SECTION		PAGE
I.	Meaning and causes of Democracy	1
	Philosophy of progress	4
	Increase of discontent in Ireland . . .	6
II.	Wolfe Tone	8
	United Irishmen	11
	Tone's Programme	12
III.	Effects on Ireland of the French Revolution . .	17
	Celebrations at Belfast	18
	Mr. Pitt and Catholic Emancipation . . .	21
	Supposed conservative character of the Catholic religion. Views of Edmund Burke . . .	22
	Two parties in the Catholic Committee . . .	25
IV.	Skirmishes in the Irish Parliament	27
	The Dublin Foundling Hospital	29
V.	Richard Burke and the Government . . .	33
	Administration of Lord Westmoreland . . .	36
	Catholic policy of the Cabinet	38
VI.	Grattan on Reform of Parliament	44
	Petition of the Catholic Committee	46
	Rash proceeding of Richard Burke	49
	Debate on Emancipation	51
	Catholic Petition rejected	53

SECTION		PAGE
VII.	The Catholic Committee and the United Irishmen	56
	Wolfe Tone and his friends	59
	Alliance of the Catholics with the Revolution	63
	Effects of the Battle of Valmy	65
	The Catholic Convention	67
	National Guards	69
	Mission of Delegates from the Convention to England	71
	Remonstrance of the Irish Government against the reception of the Delegates	73

CHAPTER II.

THE FITZWILLIAM CRISIS.

		PAGE
I.	Opinion of the Cabinet	75
	Letter of Lord Westmoreland	77
	Arthur Wellesley in the Irish Parliament	80
	Lord Edward Fitzgerald	82
	Catholic Relief Bill	84
	Dr. Duigenan	86
	Speech of Sir Lawrence Parsons	90
	The Oligarchy	93
	Fitzgibbon in the House of Lords	96
II.	Catholics admitted to the franchise	104
	The Defenders in arms	105
	Disturbances in Belfast	106
	The Catholic Committee	109
	Civil War in Limerick	111
	Convention Bill	113
III.	Lord Moira	114
	The French Directory and Mr. Jackson	117
	Escape of Hamilton Rowan	118
	Trial and suicide of Jackson	120
IV.	Recall of Lord Westmoreland and nomination of Lord Fitzwilliam	122
	Policy of religious equality	126
	Bill of Mr. Grattan	128
	The King interferes	131
	Recall of Lord Fitzwilliam	134
	Confusion in Dublin	136
	Lord Camden appointed Viceroy	137
	The Duke of Portland's instructions to him	138

SECTION		PAGE
V. Reception of Lord Camden in Dublin	. . .	141
Catholic Relief Bill		145
Grattan's manner as a speaker	. . . .	147
Defeat of the Catholic Bill	. . . .	150
VI. Spirit of the North .	. . . . .	151
Battle of the Diamond	. . . . .	154
The Orangemen	. . . . .	155

BOOK IX.

CHAPTER I.

THE FRENCH AT BANTRY.

I. Alternative Policies	156
Overtures of Ireland to France . . .	158
Mission of Wolfe Tone	159
II. Union of the United Irishmen and the Defenders .	161
Plans for Insurrection	163
Views of the Duke of Portland	165
III. Conspiracy Bill	167
Strength of the Orangemen	170
Insurrection Bill	171
Lord Edward Fitzgerald and Arthur O'Connor in Switzerland	173
Secret informations	174
Formation of the Yeomanry	178
The Opposition in Parliament	180
IV. Inclination of the Cabinet towards the Catholics .	183
Dr. Hussey and the Militia	184
The potato-diggers	188
V. Wolfe Tone in Paris	190
Communications with the Directory . .	192
Plans for Invasion	194
General Hoche	199
Preparations at Brest	201
French expedition sails	203
Bantry Bay	205
French troops unable to land	206

SECTION	PAGE
Fleet returns to Brest	207
VI. Effect in Ireland of the appearance of the French on the coast	209
Peasantry apparently well-disposed	211
English negligence	214
Explanation of the apathy of the people	217

CHAPTER II.

THE SECESSION OF THE OPPOSITION.

I. Theory of a Parliamentary Opposition	220
Irish popular tendencies	222
Probable views of Grattan	223
Address of Arthur O'Connor	225
II. Debates in Parliament on the French Invasion	229
Proposed Absentee Tax	231
Associations for murder	233
The disarming of Ulster	234
III. Denunciations of General Lake	239
Vacillation of the Cabinet	243
Fresh murders in Ireland	246
Mutiny of the Nore	246
Effects of concession in Ireland	249
IV. Plot to assassinate Lord Carhampton	250
Secession of the Irish Opposition	255
Proclamation for the disarming of the Insurgents	256
Divided counsels among the Rebel leaders	259
Fresh applications to France	260
Lord Cornwallis declines the command of the Irish army	261
V. Plan for invasion from Holland	262
Battle of Camperdown	265
Irish incendiary Newspapers	268
Tyrannicide	269
Agrarian murders	271
Lord Moira in the British Parliament	274
VI. Character of the Irish conspirators	277
Curious communication made to Lord Downshire	278
Lady Edward Fitzgerald	283

CHAPTER III.

THE EVE OF '98.

SECTION PAGE
I. Situation of the Irish Government 285
   Irish gentry wavering 287
   'The Press' 288
   Lord Moira's speech in Ireland . . . 291
   Reply of Lord Clare 294
   Historical treatment of Clare 301
II. Fresh information 303
   Thomas Reynolds 304
   The army and Sir Ralph Abercrombie . . 306
   Resignation of Abercrombie 310
III. Arrests at Margate 312
   Arrests in Dublin on March 12 . . . 315
   Trial of O'Coigley and Arthur O'Connor . . 318
   Conduct of the English Whigs . . . 320
   Execution of O'Coigley 323
IV. The Orangemen 324
   Resolution to disarm the South . . . 327
   Fresh murders 328
   Intended confiscation of the property of the Irish gentry 330
V. General Lake in Munster 333
   Severities exercised on the Irish . . . 336
   Judkin Fitzgerald 337
VI. The Brothers Sheares 340
   Arrest of Lord Edward Fitzgerald . . . 342
   Arrest of John and Henry Sheares . . . 346
   Strength and weakness of the Irish conspiracy . 349

BOOK X.

CHAPTER I.

THE REBELLION.

I. Meaning of the Rebellion 352
   Military force in Ireland 354
   Calculated treachery of the rebels . . . 356
   The rising round Dublin 357

CONTENTS.

SECTION		PAGE
	Massacre at Prosperous	360
	Fight at Clane	364
	Attack on General Dundas	365
	Attack on Carlow	366
	Disposition of the Irish gentry	367
	Anxiety of Lord Camden	369
	Apologists for the Rebellion	371
	Fight at the Curragh of Kildare	373
II.	Rising in Wexford	375
	The beacon-fire on Corrigrua Hill	378
	Father John Murphy	380
	Attack on Enniscorthy	385
	Camp on Vinegar Hill	388
	First massacres there	390
III.	Danger of Wexford	392
	Battle of Three Rocks	394
	Evacuation of Wexford by the troops	395
	Plan of the rebel campaign	398
IV.	State of Ulster	399
	Battle at New Town Barry	401
	Defeat of General Walpole	403
	Appeal of Lord Camden	404
V.	Attack on New Ross	406
	Battle in the streets	409
	Defeat of the rebels	410
VI.	Scullabogue	412
VII.	Dublin again in danger	416
	Fresh discoveries	418
	Battle of Arklow	422
VIII.	Partial rising in Ulster	425
	Change of temper in the Presbyterians	427
	Letter from Camden to the Duke of Portland	429
	Regiments sent from England	430
IX.	State of Wexford	431
	Scenes on Vinegar Hill	433
	Concentration of troops	436
	Advance of the army	437
	Massacre on Wexford Bridge	439
	Panic in the town	440
X.	Capture of Vinegar Hill by General Lake	443
	The rebels evacuate Wexford	445
	Retribution	447
	Execution of Father John Murphy	449

CHAPTER II.

LORD CORNWALLIS AND THE UNION.

SECTION	PAGE
I. The Opposition in the British Parliament	451
The Whig Peers	453
Recall of Lord Camden	456
II. Lord Cornwallis Viceroy	458
Mistakes of Lord Cornwallis	459
Ignorance of Irish history and character	460
The Irish gentry	462
Remedies, real and unreal	466
True need of Ireland	472
III. Trials and executions in Dublin	473
Confessions of the leading conspirators	478
Unsent letter from the Duke of Portland	479
IV. The French at Killala	482
Defeat of Lake at Castlebar	483
Surrender of Humbert	484
Capture, trial, and death of Wolf Tone	485
V. Character of the Rebellion	488
The Union	490
Reasons why it had become necessary	491
Means by which it was carried	492
Speech of Lord Clare in the Irish House of Lords	494

THE ENGLISH IN IRELAND

IN THE

EIGHTEENTH CENTURY.

BOOK VIII.

CHAPTER I.

THE UNITED IRISHMEN.

SECTION I.

The Dungannon Volunteers had asserted that freedom was the indefeasible birthright of man, and they defined freedom to consist in the consent of the governed to the laws which they were required to obey. They might as well have said that their consent was required to the law which would break their necks if they fell over a precipice. The conditions under which human society will cohere harmoniously are inherent in the nature of things; and human laws are wise or unwise, just or unjust, so far as they are formed on accurate discernment of the purpose of the Maker of the world. To live well is the most difficult of arts. The rules to which individuals must conform, if the State is to prosper, can be discerned only by men of practical intellect and nobleness of character; and in growing and vigorous nations the functions of government are, therefore, entrusted not to those persons only who have given proof of energy and ability, but to those who by birth and station are raised above the temptations of self-interest.

Strength brings security, and security negligence. Civilization and prosperity introduce luxurious habits and extravagant expenditure. The high persons and privileged classes to whom the care of the Commonwealth has been entrusted forget their duties in their pleasures. They believe that the State exists only for themselves. They pass unequal laws, and the people are oppressed, and clamour naturally to share the powers which can be no longer trusted in the old hands.

Hence come reforms and revolutions, the shaking off of rulers who have become incompetent and mischievous. The change is called progress, and is admired and applauded as some grand political achievement, a thing excellent in itself, an entrance into a new era of universal happiness. Many times in the world's history these glorious hopes have been entertained, but always to be disappointed. Only at critical moments, when some patent wrong has to be redressed, will the better kind of men leave their proper occupations to meddle with politics. The peasant and the artisan, the man of business and the man of science, all of all sorts who are good in their kind, give themselves to their own work, caring only to do well what nature has assigned to them to do. The volunteer politicians in every class, those who put themselves forward in elections to choose or to be chosen, are usually the vain, the restless, the personally ambitious ; and therefore the same causes which undermine aristocracies destroy even more rapidly popular Governments. Democracies are proverbially short-lived. They can destroy class privileges, they can overthrow institutions, but their function ends in destruction; and when the generations pass away which, under a sterner system, had learnt habits of self-command, and could therefore for a time dispense with control, they pass away to give place usually to despotism. Private character degenerates. Individuals forget their country to care only for themselves, and therefore dwindle to their personal level. The men of the first French Revolution and the American Revolution were greater than any which either country has produced in the days of universal suffrage, equality, and miscalled liberty.

The aristocracy in these islands lost the confidence of the people in the last century. Their power and privileges have melted from them and are still melting, and we have again committed ourselves to the enthusiastic beliefs of which the Dungannon resolutions were no more than a crude expression. We have a new philosophy to gild a phenomenon which would look less pretty were its character confessed. Once more we have made an idol of spurious freedom, and we are worshipping it duly with unflinching devotion and the inexorable logic of faith. Universal happiness waits to appear where the rights of man shall have been completely recognised. Battle after battle is fought and won. Paradise is still unattained, but we do not doubt the truth of our theory ; we conclude only that the process of destruction is incomplete. The enemy still lets, and will let, till he be taken out of the way. When all men shall be free to think, free to speak, free to act at their own secret wills, and prejudice and tyranny cease to interfere with them, then at length the universal brotherhood will be a fact, and misery will cease out of the land. All men are by nature equal and free. All men being free have a right to share in the making of the laws. Being alike interested in the results, we assume that they will choose the best representatives to make them, and will become themselves elevated and ennobled in the exercise of their lofty prerogative. The propositions are as false as the anticipation is delusive. Men are not equal, but infinitely unequal. No man is free by nature, and becomes free only by the discipline of submission, by learning to command himself, or by submitting to be commanded by others. The multitude, who are slaves of their own ignorance, will choose those to represent them who flatter their vanity or pander to their interest. Emancipation from authority cannot elevate, but can only degrade those who are not emancipated by nature and fact.

False though it be, however, in its principles, the philosophy of progress pushes its way towards its goal with unflinching confidence and logical coherence. That which is unsound must fall before it; that which is untrue must be seen to be false; that which is unjust must perish. Then at length the wheel will have come full round, and finding ourselves not in Paradise at all, but sitting in arid desolation amidst the wrecks of our institutions, we shall painfully wake from our dream and begin again the long toil of reconstruction.

The history of Ireland in the concluding years of the last century forms a remarkable episode in this yet uncompleted drama. The degeneracy of authority which precipitates civil convulsions had developed itself in Ireland more rapidly than in the rest of the empire. The executive Government was unequal to the elementary work of maintaining peace and order. The aristocracy and legislature were corrupt beyond reach of shame. The gentry had neglected their duties till they had forgotten that they had duties to perform. The peasantry were hopelessly miserable; and finding in the law not a protector and a friend, but a sword in the hands of their oppressors, they had been taught to look to crime and rebellion as the only means of self-defence. Never anywhere were institutions more ripe for destruction than those which England had planted in the unfortunate island which to their common misfortune nature had made part of her dominions. For ten years the Irish people had been fed, chameleon-like, with promises of immediate redemption. The Parliament had achieved its independence. Volunteer battalions had celebrated the triumph with the music of musketry and cannon. Platform and newspaper and flying placard had echoed and repeated the florid rhetoric of Grattan and his friends. Liberty had not prevented rents from rising, landlords from multiplying whisky stills, or whisky stills and middlemen and tithe proctors from driving the people into lower depths of misery and madness. The most enthusiastic patriots were inclining to lie down and despair, when before the astonished eyes of Ireland, as of all Europe, rose the portent of the French Revolution, preaching on scaffold and at cannon's mouth the long waited for emancipation of mankind. Young Ireland, fed from boyhood on Grattan's declamation, passionately believing in freedom, and mad with disappointment at the failure of the Constitution of '82, responded with ecstasy. The cause of Ireland's, as of all other misery, was the tyranny of classes who, by chicanery and fear, had made the masses of mankind their slaves. France was pointing the way for all who had hearts to follow. Grattan had obtained the independence of Parliament; the independence was a shadow without political equality. Let Irishmen recover their personal rights, and independence would become a fact, and the long-waiting era of blessedness would at last arrive. The soil was unequally prepared. The Catholic religion assimilates ill with visions of political liberty, and except occasionally and for immediate objects disclaims connection with theories to which it is naturally an enemy. The special grievances of which Irish Catholics complained might incline them, however, to make common cause with those whose aim was universal emancipation. Meanwhile the northern Presbyterians were hereditary republicans. Smarting with the additional wrongs which had been inflicted on them in Ireland, they had sympathised ardently with the revolt of the American colonies, and in the American success they had seen an earnest of the ultimate success of their principles. They had furnished the strength of the Volunteer movement, they had been clamorous for Parliamentary reform, and though baffled so far, had lost no atom of their faith or their enthusiasm. No less strong were the liberal emotions of the rising generation of educated Irish gentlemen. Trinity College was a hotbed of liberal sentiment. Every clever Irish lad was a born orator, and the orator everywhere is the natural champion of wild imaginations. Among the lawyers, the younger men of business, the aspiring tradesmen, the men of letters, the poets, the artists, the feeling was the same. Grattan was the universal idol, while in the lower stratifications, among the houghers and the tarring and feathering committee, the city mob was in perfect enmity against the authors of the tyrannous Police Bill.

In union alone was there to be found strength. The Protestant reformers who were in earnest felt that they were nothing without the Catholics. Paris had abolished distinctions of creed. Ireland's first cry was to recall three million fellow-citizens to the national standard. Catholic and Protestant were to shake hands over the buried memories of ancient quarrels, and combine in a glorious struggle against the common foe.

SECTION II.

BOOK VIII.
1790.

THE character of the new movement may be conveniently studied in the person of its most celebrated representative. Theobald Wolfe Tone was born on the 20th of June, 1763. His grandfather was a farmer at Naas; his father a coachmaker in Dublin. Theobald was the eldest son. He was educated at a good school, where he showed talents, but was incurably idle. His fancy was for the army, but his father, ambitious for him of a higher career, sent him instead to Trinity College, where, though the idleness was uncured, he maintained his reputation for ability. When he was nineteen he was second in a duel between two fellow-students, where his friend killed his antagonist. Such a misfortune was too common to attract notice. Tone finished his college career as if nothing had happened, and immediately after he fell in love. His fair one returned his affection. As neither of them possessed a sixpence, they feared their parents might interpose delays, so they shortened the road to happiness by an elopement. This, too, was in keeping with the general recklessness of the time. The young couple were forgiven, but Theobald, leaving his airy ways, was condemned to a profession. The wife remained in Dublin. The husband was sent to London, according to Irish custom, to study law for two years at the Temple. The responsibilities of matrimony failed to steady so mercurial a temperament. Young Tone hated law as he hated all regular studies. He never opened his Blackstone. He eked out his resources by writing articles for newspapers. He meditated emigration to the South Sea Islands, and addressed a memorial to Pitt on the propriety of founding a military college there. His communication being left unnoticed, he vowed that he would make Pitt smart for neglecting him. He returned to Dublin to be called to the bar in 1789, 'knowing,' he says, 'as much of law as he knew of necromancy.' He went circuit and paid his expenses; but preferring to conquer fame and fortune by a less tedious process, he turned to politics, composed a patriotic pamphlet on the Round Robin, and attracted the favourable notice of the Opposition leaders. George Ponsonby smiled upon him. The Northern Whig Club, the brother society of the club in Dublin, established by Lord Moira and Lord Charlemont, elected him a member.

Tone, however, had already outgrown the Whig philosophy. He had found a friend in the gallery of the House of Commons of more congenial temperament, a retired ensign, who had been in India, named Russell. These two, with Tone's young wife, spent the summer of 1790 together by the sea. They had little hopes of their own country. Tone turned his thoughts again to emigration, a second time he drew an outline of his colonial scheme, and sent it, not again to Pitt, but to Lord Grenville. The project was not without sense, for Lord Grenville sent him a courteous acknowledgment, and promised to bear his overtures in mind.

'If the plan had been followed,' says Tone, 'Russell and I were both going instead of planning revolutions in Ireland;' but Lord Grenville thought no more of the matter, and confessing frankly that personal resentment was the explanation of his subsequent conduct, he renewed his vow to make the Cabinet repent. In the winter he founded a rival club in Dublin, composed of spirits like his own. Among the members were Mr. Stack, a clerical fellow of Trinity; Whitly Stokes, the dean, keeper of the college lions, as Tone nicknamed him; Dr. Drennan, a physician; Peter Burrowes, a rising barrister; Thomas Addis Emmett, a barrister also, elder brother of Robert, all of whom left their mark in the development of the Irish drama.

Of this party, Tone liked Whitly Stokes the best, their opinions most nearly coinciding; the sole fault of Stokes being that he was not for lawless measures. 'What he would highly that he would holily.' A reservation which Tone early concluded it would be impossible to allow.

The Bastile fell in July 1789; in 1790, Burke published his letters on the French Revolution, to which Tom Paine replied with ' The Rights of Man.' Tone and his friends were for Tom Paine, and young Ireland was of the same way of thinking. In Tone's own words, ' oppressed, plundered, insulted Ireland ' was electrified into life.[1] The Northern Whig Club, spite of its aristocratic connections, was scarcely less sympathetic. The Irish Parliament was dissolved in the summer, and the members spared neither their fortunes nor their energies to defeat the Castle candidates. Robert Stewart,[2] then an ardent patriot, carried Down in the popular interest after a struggle of fifty-four days. Sir Hercules Rowley and Mr. O'Neil, both members of the club, were returned for

---

[1] *Memoirs of Theobald Wolfe Tone, by himself.*
[2] Afterwards Lord Castlereagh, then twenty-one years old.

Antrim. They were carried through Belfast in a triumphal car with cannons firing. Volunteers revived for the occasion, marched at their side; and Hibernia walked before them with a wreath in one hand and a pole with a cap of liberty in the other. The town was illuminated at night. Fires blazed on all the adjoining hill tops, and the Volunteer Light Dragoons met on Bunker's Hill, name of significant omen, to swear that they would never lay down their arms till their country was free.[1] The city determined that in the ensuing year it would observe the 14th of July with becoming solemnity as the anniversary of the fall of the Bastile.

Fired with these scenes, and seeing, as he supposed, the fields ripening rapidly for the harvest, Ensign Russell, who was now living at Belfast, invited Tone to sketch an outline of policy to be ready for the celebration. Tone replied with composing a singular and characteristic paper, which, however extravagant and absurd it may appear, yet must be read also with the recollection that it kindled a fire in Ireland which a hundred thousand men scarcely sufficed to extinguish, and which cost sixty thousand Irish lives.

The object was to form a society of 'United Irishmen.' It was to be instituted 'with the secrecy and something of the ceremonial of Freemasonry; secrecy to pique curiosity; ceremonial to strike the soul through the senses, and addressing the whole man, animate his philosophy by the energy of his passions.'

'Secrecy,' writes Tone, 'is expedient and necessary. It will make the bond of union more cohesive and the spirit of

[1] *History of Belfast*, p. 345.

union more ardent and more condensed. It will envelope the dense flame with a cloud of gloomy ambiguity that will not only facilitate its own agency, but will confound and terrify its enemies by their ignorance of the design, the direction, or the consequences. It will throw a veil over those individuals whose professional prudence might make them wish to lie concealed. . . . A country so great a stranger to itself as Ireland, where North and South and East and West meet to wonder at each other, is not yet prepared for the adoption of one political faith; while there may be individuals from each of these quarters ready to adopt such a profession, to propagate it with their best abilities, and, when necessary, with their blood. Our provinces are ignorant of each other; our island is connected; we ourselves are insulated, and distinctions of rank and property and religious persuasion have hitherto been not merely lines of difference, but brazen walls of separation. We are separate nations, met and settled together, not mingled but convened—uncemented, like the image which Nebuchadnezzar saw, with a head of fine gold, legs of iron, feet of clay—parts that do not cleave to one another.

'In the midst of an island where manhood has met and meets with such severe humiliation, where selfish men and classes have formed a malignant conspiracy against public good, let our beneficent conspiracy arise—one plot of patriots pledged by solemn adjunction to each other in the service of the people—the people in the largest sense of that momentous word. Let the cement of this constitutional compact be a principle of such strong attraction as completely to overpower all accidental and temporary repulsions, and thus consolidate the scattered and shifting sand of society into an adhesive and immovable caisson, sunk beneath the dark and troubled waters.

'Our society will not call itself a Whig Club or a Revolution Society. It will not be an aristocracy affecting the language of patriotism. . . . It will not by views merely retrospective stop the march of mankind, or force them back into the lanes and alleys of their ancestors. Let its name be the "Irish Brotherhood." Let its aim be to make the light of philanthropy—a pale and ineffectual light—converge, and by converging kindle into ardent, energetic, enthusiastic love for Ireland that genuine, unadulterated enthusiasm which descends from a luminous head to a burning heart, and impels the spirit of man to exertions unequivocally great. What is our end? The rights of man in Ireland! The greatest happiness of the greatest numbers in this island; the inherent and indefeasible claims of every free nation to rest in this nation; the will and power to be happy; to pursue the common weal as an individual pursues his private welfare, and to stand in insulated independence an imperatorial people.

'The greatest happiness of the greatest number! On the rock of this principle let this Society rest; by this let it judge and determine every political question; and whatever is necessary for this end let it not be counted hazardous, but rather our interest, our duty, our glory, our common religion.... Let every member wear, day and night, an amulet round his neck, containing the great principle which unites the brotherhood, in letters of gold on a ribbon striped with all the original colours, and enclosed in a sheath of white silk, to represent the pure union of the mingled rays and the abolition of all superficial distinctions, all colours and shades of difference, for the sake of an illustrious end. Let this amulet of union, faith, and honour depend from the neck, and be bound about the body next to the skin, and close to the heart.... This is enthusiasm! It is so. And who has a spark of Hibernicism in his nature who would not feel it kindle into a flame of generous enthusiasm? Who that has a drop of sympathy in his heart, and sees how happiness is heaped up in mounds, how misery is diffused and divided among the millions, does not exclaim, "Alas for the suffering, and oh for the power to redress it!" Who is there that has enthusiasm sufficient to such an exclamation that would not combine with others as honest as himself to make the will live in the act, and to swear he will redress it?

'Let the Society meet four times a year, and an acting committee once a month. Let these meetings be convivial, but not the transitory patriotism of deep potations. Confidential — the heart open, but the door locked. Conversational — not a debating society. There is too much haranguing in this country already—a very great redundance of sound. Would that we spoke more laconically and acted more emphatically! and we shall do so when our aim is at something nobler and fairer than even the sublime and beautiful of Mr. Burke—the sublimity of common-sense, the beauty of common weal.

'Our Society should be chaste and cautious in the selection of members, shunning equally the giddiness of the boy and the sullen indifference to the public good which comes with decline of years. They should be honest Irishmen, of whatever rank, of whatever religion, who know liberty, who love it, who wish to have it, and who will have it.

'The external business of the Society will be—

'1. Publications to propagate their principles, and effect their ends.

'2. To keep up communication with the different towns, and to use every exertion to accomplish a national convention of the people of Ireland.

'3. To communicate with similar societies abroad, as the Jacobin Club in Paris, the Revolution Society in England, the Committee for Reform in Scotland. Let the nations go abreast. Let the interchange of sentiment among mankind concerning the rights of man be as immediate as possible.

'Eulogies of such men as have deserved well of their country *until death* should be from time to time delivered by one of the brotherhood. Their works should live in a library, to be founded by the Society, and dedicated to liberty; and the portraits of such men should adorn it. Let the shades of the mighty dead look down and consecrate our meetings. The Athenians fastened their edicts on the statues of their ancestors. Let our laws and liberties have a similar attachment, taking heed always to remember what has been too much forgotten, that we are to be ancestors ourselves; and as our bodies moulder down after death, merely to pass into new forms of life, let our spirits preserve a principle of animation to posterity, and germinate from the grave.

'What time is most applicable for the establishment of this institution? Even now. Le grand art est dans l'apropos. Why is administration so imperious? Because the *nation* does not act. The Whig Club is not a transfusion from the people. We do not understand that club, and they do not feel for us. When the aristocracy comes forward, the people fall backward. When the people come forward, the aristocracy, fearful of being left behind, insinuate themselves into our ranks, and rise into timid leaders or treacherous auxiliaries. They mean to make us their instruments. Let us rather make them our instruments. One of the two must happen. . . . On the 14th of July, which shall ever commemorate the French Revolution, let this Society pour out their first libation to European liberty, eventually the liberty of the world, and with their hands joined in each other, and their eyes raised to heaven, in His presence who breathed into them an everliving soul, let them swear to maintain the rights and prerogatives of this nation as men, and the rights and prerogatives of Ireland as an independent people. "Dieu et mon droit" is the motto of kings. "Dieu et la liberté," exclaimed Voltaire, when he first beheld Franklin. "Dieu et nos droits," let Irishmen cry aloud to each other—the cry of mercy, of justice, and of victory.'[1]

Accompanying this singular production were a series of resolutions for Parliamentary reform and Catholic emancipation, adopted and printed immediately afterwards in the programme of the society,[2] and a private letter evidently addressed to Russell, in which the writer explained his views more fully than in a paper intended for wider circulation.[3]

---

[1] Abridged from a copy in the State Paper Office.—Irish MSS., June 1700, privately furnished to the Government, and transmitted by Lord Westmoreland.

[2] '*Acts of the Society of United Irishmen.*' Dublin, 1704, pp. 3, 4.

[3] A copy of this letter also fell into the Viceroy's hands, probably by treachery, and was enclosed to the Cabinet in the same packet.

'The foregoing resolutions,' said the writer, 'contain my true and sincere opinion of the state of this country, so far as in this present juncture it may be advisable to publish it. They fall short of the truth, but truth itself must sometimes condescend to temporise. My unalterable opinion is that the bane of Irish prosperity is the influence of England. I believe that influence will ever be extended while the connection between the countries continues. Nevertheless, as I know, that opinion is for the present too hardy, though a little time may establish it universally, I have not made it a part of the resolutions.

'The Whig Club are not sincere friends to the popular cause. They dread the people as much as the Castle does. I dare say that my Lord Charlemont, and I am pretty sure that Mr. Grattan, would hesitate at the resolutions which I send. I beg you will dismiss the respect for great names. Read them, and read what I have now said,[1] and determine impartially between us. I have alluded to the Catholics, but so remotely as not to alarm the most cautious Protestant. It is, indeed, nonsense to talk of a reform in Ireland in which they shall not have their due share. To fear the Catholics is a vulgar and ignorant prejudice. Look at France and America; the Pope burnt in effigy at Paris; the English Catholic at this hour seceding from his Church; a thousand arguments crowd on me; but it is unnecessary here to dwell on them. The opportunity for publishing the resolutions will be the 14th of July, at the commemoration of the French Revolution—that morning-star of liberty to Ireland.'

---

[1] The resolutions were three:—
'1. That the weight of English influence was so great as to require a *cordial union of all the people of Ireland* to maintain liberty.
'2. That the only constitutional method of opposing that influence was by Reform of Parliament.
'3. That no Reform was practicable which did not include Irishmen of every religious persuasion.'

SECTION III.

As a preparation for the celebration of the taking of the Bastile at Belfast, the Northern Whig Club held a preliminary meeting on the 15th of June, the anniversary of the signature of Magna Charta. The aristocratic composition of that body was unsatisfactory to the ardent reformers. Its sentiments were considered timid and hesitating. Liberal public opinion nevertheless must have been far gone, even in those circles, when a society which contained Charlemont, Moira, Lord Clifford, Robert Stewart,[1] and Sir Hercules Rowley could accept as toasts, and drink with wild enthusiasm, 'the Revolution,' 'the National Assembly of France,' 'the Majesty of the People,' 'Tom Paine,' and 'the Rights of Man.'[2] In the fête which followed on the 14th Belfast rivalled Paris in extravagance. The event of the day was described as the grandest in human history. The heart that could not sympathise with it was declared depraved. The ceremonial commenced with a procession. The Volunteer companies, re-filled to their old numbers, marched first, with banners and music. A battery of cannon followed, and behind the cannon a portrait of Mirabeau. Then a gigantic triumphal car, bearing a broad sheet of canvas, on which was painted the opening of the Bastile dungeons. In the foreground was the wasted figure of the prisoner who had been confined there thirty years, melting all eyes to tears; in the near

---

[1] Afterwards Lord Castlereagh.
[2] *History of Belfast*, pp. 347–8.

distance the doors of the cells flung back, disclosing the skeletons of dead victims or living wretches writhing in chains and torture. On the reverse of the canvas Hibernia was seen reclining, one hand and one foot in shackles, and a Volunteer artilleryman holding before her radiant eyes the image of Liberty.

The Whig Club brought up the rear, walking two-and-two, in green cockades, the entire Society except Charlemont being present to do honour to the occasion, and among them, therefore, Lord O'Neil, Moira, and Castlereagh.

In the evening three hundred and fifty patriots sat down to dinner in the Linen Hall. They drank to the King of Ireland. They drank to Washington, the ornament of mankind. They drank to Grattan, Molyneux, Franklin, and Mirabeau—these last two amidst applause that threatened to shake the building to the ground.

Belfast evidently was in fine revolutionary condition, and was therefore well-selected by Tone as the scene of his first operations. In his diary he informs the world 'that he was determined to subvert the tyranny of an execrable Government, and make Ireland free.' He was sure of the Catholics. 'He knew that there existed, however it might be concealed, in the breast of every Irish Catholic an inextinguishable abhorrence of the English name and power.' He was sure, too, of sympathy from the Presbyterian Liberals of the Ulster towns. He hoped to gain all the Presbyterians, seeing how long they had suffered from the proud Establishment. But the Catholic question was a difficulty, both in town and country. There were unpleasant rumours of the Peep-of-Day Boys, of farmers in the Down and

Antrim hills so far behind their age as to think more of the defence of Derry than the taking of the Bastile, to hate Popery worse than they hated England. To them he addressed himself in a pamphlet which his friends in the North printed and circulated. In October he went down to Belfast with his friend Russell, to inaugurate there the first lodge of the society which he had succeeded at last in founding, and to contend against anti-Catholic prejudice. In his diary he has drawn the portraits of the two bold youths who were setting forth to measure swords with the British Empire, and of the dreams which inspired them.

'October. Belfast.—Secret Committee. Dined with Sinclair.[1] Politics and wine. Paine's book. P. P.[2] very drunk.

'October 16 (Sunday).—Vile sermon against smuggling and about loyalty, and all that. Put the question to D. relative to Ireland's existence independent of England. D.'s opinion decidedly for independence. France would help, and Ireland without debt would spring up like an air-balloon and leave England far behind.

'October 21.—Dinner with D. Battle on the Catholic question. They agree to the justice of emancipation, but boggle at expediency—damned nonsense. Russell eloquent. Ready to fight. Arguments over a bottle foolish.

'October 23.—Dinner at A. Stewart's, with a parcel of squires from Down. Persuaded myself and Russell afterwards that we were hungry. Went to Donegal Arms. Supped on a lobster. Drunk; ill-natured to Russell. Mem., to do so no more.

'October 24.—Woke sick. Couldn't eat.

---

[1] A leading Belfast Republican. [2] His friend Russell.

'October 25.—Dinner at ——. Furious battle on the Catholic question. Neither party convinced. Damned stuff. Home early. Russell well on, but not quite gone,' &c., &c.

Under such auspices, and by such men, the Society of United Irishmen was launched at Belfast; and a start thus made, the two apostles of liberty returned to Dublin, to found a sister lodge in the metropolis. Simon Butler, younger brother of Lord Mountgarret, was the first chairman. Napper Tandy, ' with the frenzy-rolling eye,' volunteered as secretary. On the 9th of November the first meeting was held, at the Eagle, in Eustace Street, when the three resolutions already accepted in the North were adopted as principles of action: to emancipate Ireland from English influence, to reform the Parliament, and to unite the people of Ireland of all creeds and races in a common bond. The third resolution was essential to the first and second, yet to obtain its acceptance proved a harder task than Tone anticipated. He was assured of the hatred of the Catholics to England. The hatred was rather to Protestants, Presbyterian as well as Anglican, and a signal illustration of it had just shown itself in Ulster. Mr. Jackson, of Armagh, who died in 1787, had left an estate to maintain schools where there was to be no distinction of religion. These schools were condemned by the priests. The trustees were repeatedly fired at. In the spring of 1791 the house of one of the masters, Alex. Barclay, was broken open. Three men rushed in, twisted a cord about his neck till they pressed his tongue out, and cut it off. They cut off the fingers and thumb of his right hand. They seized his wife, cut out her tongue, and cut off her fingers. They then cut out her child's tongue, and slashed away the calves of his legs. The one offence which the man had committed was the teaching in a school of which the priests disapproved. They made no concealment. They went with torches along the road to their work as if for a public purpose. This act was the admiration of the barony, and it was said openly that unless the schools were abandoned all concerned in them should suffer in the same way.[1]

The mutilation of Barclay was a spurt from the old fire of 1641. There were other Catholics of course who, as in 1641 also, abhorred the cruelties which brought discredit on their cause, who represented themselves as eager for an opportunity of showing their loyalty, who undertook, if Government would trust them with arms, to be the first to repress and punish the atrocities of their wilder brethren. For their sakes the penal code had been relaxed. The Castle had been long on kindly terms with their prelates. Liberal opinion in England had long been working in their favour. Pitt, an advocate for Reform, was an advocate equally for Catholic Emancipation. He had sought the opinion of the Universities of France and Spain, on the charges generally alleged against Catholics, that their allegiance to their sovereign was subordinate to their allegiance to the Pope; that they held that heretics might be lawfully put to death, and that no faith was to be kept with them. The Universities had unanimously disavowed doctrines which they declared at once inhuman and unchristian, and on the strength of the disavowal the

---

[1] 'Report of the Trustees of the Jackson Charity,' February 1, 1791.—Musgrave's *History of the Irish Rebellion*, vol. i.

BOOK VIII.
1791.

British Parliament repealed the Penal Acts of William for England and Scotland, restored to the Catholics the free use of their chapels, and re-admitted them to the magistracy.

Which of the two parties among the Catholics of Ireland would direct the action of the general body, if similar confidence was extended to them in that island, might still be uncertain. Pitt believed, on the whole, that the Liberal policy would be the safest policy; that the savage spirit was sustained by the disabilities, and that the hatred on which Irish faction relied would disappear before judicious conciliation. The Belfast demonstration made him the more anxious to anticipate the projected union of disaffection. As affairs in France assumed a darker aspect, the great antagonist of the Revolution desired to rally to the side of order every influence which could be called Conservative. Of such influences the most powerful was religion, and where could he find a surer friend than in the ancient Church which the Jacobins were trampling under their feet? He saw before him a certain struggle with the potent, overcrowing spirit which was shaking Europe to its foundations, and with such a prospect the Irish problem became of pressing consequence. Disaffection in Ireland had been a most mischievous factor in the war with America. A union of Irishmen in the interest of nationality and revolution might prove incomparably more dangerous, while there never could be a fairer occasion to recover the loyalty of the respectable portion of the Irish Catholic community, and to give them an opportunity of washing out the stains which clung to them in the traditions of the past.

In these views Pitt had an ardent supporter in
Edmund Burke. Swept as he was into the stream
of English politics, identified with English states-
manship, and occupied with the great questions of
the imperial and internal policy of the British dominions, Burke had never forgotten the land of his
birth, and had never missed an opportunity of being
of service to her. He read her history with a prejudiced affection, which saw the wrongs which she
had suffered, and was blind to the crimes which had
provoked them. He had been her advocate in the first
Whiteboy insurrection. He had braved the anger of
his Bristol constituents by reprobating the restrictions
on her trade. He had denounced the Irish Penal Laws
as without example for inhumanity and cruelty, although they were almost a transcript from the laws
passed in France on the revocation of the Edict of
Nantes, although the laws against Protestants in
Papal Italy and Spain were more cruel by far than
the laws in Ireland against Catholics. His opinions
on these subjects had long been openly expressed.
The conviction became more keen with the progress
of the French Revolution. Welcome as it had been
to him at its dawn, when it appeared only to be the
rising of an oppressed people against aristocratic
tyranny, the Revolution became an object of abhorrence to him when it declared war against priests.
Burke was not himself a Catholic, but as little was
he a Protestant. His sympathies were with the old
faith. His most intimate friends were Catholics to
the end, and at the end even more than at the beginning. His advice to Pitt, his advice to the world,
was to save his countrymen from the revolutionary

tempter by restoring to them the privileges of citizenship.

Thus the Irish Catholics, who in the eyes of Swift were hewers of wood and drawers of water, doomed to immediate extinction, and protracting their waning existence by the condescending toleration of the Government, found themselves with two roads opening before them, either of which might restore them to the ascendancy which they had lost at the Boyne and at Aghrim. Tone was doubtless right in saying that at the bottom they all hated England; but some of them hated the Revolution worse, and dreaded besides the possible consequences to them of another war; while the fiercer spirits, identifying religion with nationality, dreaming of the recovery of their lost estates, and of revenge on the old oppressors, looked, like Phelim O'Neil and Roger Moore, in 1641, to a general overthrow of authority. Let the invader be swept first out of the island with any help that offered itself; other accounts could be settled afterwards, when they had the island to themselves.

The Catholic Bishops and clergy, Irish at heart, yet terrified at the aspect of France, were inclined rather to order and to the English connection, if England would give them what they asked. By them the Catholic Committee in Dublin had hitherto submitted to be guided. In 1790 they prayed Parliament for a further removal of their disabilities. Not a member of the House of Commons could be found to present their petition. Confident in Pitt's disposition towards them, the Catholic prelates published a letter condemning revolutionary principles. At the beginning of 1791 a sub-committee advised another attempt of the same kind, not to ask for definite measures of relief, but mildly to express a hope that they were not to continue strangers in their own land, to declare their confidence in the benignity of their Sovereign, and their willingness to submit their claims to the wisdom and benevolence of the Legislature. The leaven of the new spirit had by this time penetrated the Catholic organisation. A majority in the General Committee refused to sue any longer for rights which they were entitled to demand; and relying on promises from Belfast, exclaimed against an attitude which would encourage a continuance of tyranny.

The line of division became thus definitely apparent. Lord Kenmare, Lord Fingal, Lord Gormanstown, and sixty prelates and gentlemen, withdrew from an association with whose views they were no longer in harmony. The Government accepted the seceders as the true representatives of Catholic sentiment. In September, after the Belfast demonstration, John Keogh, a Dublin merchant, a man of some ability and in the Bishops' confidence, went to London, and had an interview with Pitt. He was told generally that England would make no objection if the Irish Parliament would admit Catholics to the Bar and to the Commission of the Peace. The franchise was a future question which would be open to consideration. Lord Westmoreland was instructed to smoothe the way towards concessions, and on the 21st of November he was able to inform Dundas 'that he had pretty well reconciled most of the friends of Government to the policy of following the example of England.'[1]

[1] 'Lord Westmoreland to Dundas, November 21, 1791.' S. P. O.

SECTION IV.

BOOK VIII.
1790.

THE plot was now rapidly thickening. Before proceeding with the story attention must be recalled to the proceedings of the Irish Parliament during the first two years of Lord Westmoreland's administration.

Lord Buckingham had shown the agitators of the House of Commons that Government was too strong for them. They revenged themselves by abusing Lord Buckingham's memory, and worrying, though they could not control, his successor. In the debate on the Address at the opening of the session of 1790, when Mr. Grattan produced as usual the list of Ireland's grievances, Egan, a blunt, humorous barrister, spoke of Buckingham as 'our late execrated Chief Governor;' of Ireland as 'the political Botany Bay of Great Britain;' of the Irish Parliament as being, 'like the Temple of Jerusalem, polluted with money-changers.'[1]

Grattan denounced Buckingham's corruption. The friends of Government were insolent in their majority. Dennis Browne spoke of the complaints of undue influence as 'the clamour of jobbers and peculators, who had been repelled by the Viceroy with contempt, and who therefore reviled and abused him.' Toler ridiculed the Opposition as apostles of revolution, whose language in plain English meant, 'Swallow our faith, and it shall make you whole, and damn him everlastingly who will not thus think of our politics.' Beresford, the new Commissioner of Revenue, carried the war into the enemy's camp. He

[1] *Irish Debates*, January 22, 1790.

admitted that 'there was a certain influence in the State;' and 'it was better placed,' he said, 'in a known and responsible power than in the indentured apprentices of English faction.'

The inglorious battle raged from day to day, the patriots dashing themselves against the chains, and flinging into words the passion for which they could find no escape in action.

Beresford's defence brought up George Ponsonby. 'Good God, sir,' said the future Chancellor, 'how long shall we be told that influence is not too great; we who saw in the last session the very members who joined in the censure of the Viceroy go up ten days after to him cringing and crawling with an address of congratulation? If the House does not resist such a system, there will be a day when the contest will rest between the people and them, and the nation as a nation will do themselves justice.' 'Let Ministers beware,' said Lawrence Parsons, 'how they teach the people that nothing short of separation will attain for them good government. Will any minister of England dare to say to the people of Ireland, You are an independent kingdom, the laws of England no longer bind you? You have gained all that you asked. But I will make you feel that you have gained nothing. I will increase my influence over you and your Parliament, and I will keep you to the end of time a degraded and depressed dependency.'

'Modern patriotism,' said Mr. Johnson, with a sarcasm which might have come from the Dean of St. Patrick, 'is to the political what a modern infection is to the animal constitution. They are equally the children of licentiousness, equally manifest their vigour by their venom, and nothing but the application of a metallic poison can stop the progress of either. Gold is to the political what mercury is to the animal constitution, and the ministers and physicians who apply them are equally justified by the necessity.'[1]

'The sale of peerages,' said Curran, with a counter-thrust, 'is as notorious as that of the cast horses in the Castle Yard; the publicity the same, the terms not very different, the horses not warranted sound, and the other animals warranted rotten. When arguments fail we are threatened! A million will be expended in bribing the country at the next election —to make us what? A catacomb of ministerial mummies—not a scene of honest contest, not a temple of liberty, but a den of thieves.'

Among gentle recriminations such as these the session of 1790 passed away, some natural misgiving never, it appeared, occurring to the patriot orators that among a people so willing to be bribed, what they called liberty was for ever impossible.

Early in the summer there was a dissolution and a general election. The patriots carried Dublin and a few counties in Ulster, but on the whole Curran's prophecy was fulfilled. The owners of property were frightened by the revolution, and the Castle majority was rather increased than diminished. The novel feature in the new House was the introduction into it of three men who, in their several ways, were to become notable. Robert Stewart, the future Castlereagh, was returned, as was said above, for Down; Arthur Wesley, or Wellesley, for Trim; and Arthur O'Connor for Philipstown.

[1] *Irish Debates*, February 4, 1790.

A short session was held in July to choose a Speaker. The strength of parties was exhibited in the selection of John Foster against William Ponsonby, who was put forward by the patriots. In the succeeding January the House assembled for business in a mood conspicuously sobered by the events on the Continent. Grattan, as the day seemed going against him, was more than usually magnificent, but his oratory failed of its effect. Mervyn Archdall said, and the House seemed to agree with him, that the public owed more to the practical motions of honourable gentlemen who usually sate in silence [1] than to invective and brilliant rhetoric which died as it flashed and left no mark behind it. To bid Grattan cease his oratory was to bid him cease to be, for there was nothing else which he could do. How little Grattan knew of the real needs of Ireland, how careless he could be on subjects which furnished no room for appeal to political passion, he had now a remarkable opportunity of showing.

There was in Dublin an institution called the Foundling Hospital. It had large private funds, and was assisted liberally by grants from Parliament. Three hundred peers and gentlemen were the governors, and twenty-one at least were required to be present at the periodical meetings of the board. Sir John Blaquiere, in bringing the condition of the Hospital before the House, stated that from the day of its foundation as many as twenty-one governors had never been in attendance save when some office was to be given away. They had delegated their authority to the treasurer. The treasurer had been bedridden

---

[1] He was referring particularly to Mr. La Touche, who had moved for a committee of enquiry into the increase of whisky-shops.

for six years. In consequence Sir John had to mention circumstances 'too horrible for the ear,' which the reporter, for the honour of his country, thought it necessary to conceal.[1] In substance he stated that the number of infants received in the past year into the Hospital was 2,180, and that of that number as many as 2,087 were dead or unaccounted for. A story so startling was received with outcries of incredulity. Ireland's character was at stake before the world. The Corporation of Dublin met and made enquiries, and reported that the charge was utterly without foundation. Blaquiere had moved for leave to introduce a Bill to remodel the governing body. Grattan, as member for the city, presented a petition that leave be refused, and spoke warmly in vindication of the existing management. Blaquiere was too sure of his ground to be beaten from it by clamour. He was surprised, he said, that so eminent a person as Mr. Grattan should have become the advocate of abuses which disgraced the society of men. He repeated that out of 2,187 children introduced in one year into the establishment more than 2,000 had disappeared. He held in his hand, he said, a return for the last ten years which had been given upon oath. In that time 19,368 children had been entered on the books, and almost 17,000 were dead or missing.

A committee of enquiry was appointed. The condition of the Hospital was sifted to the bottom. The result was laid before the House by Blaquiere in the ensuing year. The average annual number of infants who survived admission to this beautiful institution, taken on a large number of years, was 130. The

[1] *Irish Debates*, March 2, 1791.

annual expenses were 16,000*l.* Each child, therefore, who was saved from death was costing the public 110*l.* He expected to find, he said, that his original information had understated the frauds, but had exaggerated the cruelty. He had been sorry to find that although the robbery was, as he anticipated, greater, the murders were no fewer than he had before declared. The wretched little ones were sent up from all parts of Ireland, ten or twelve of them thrown together into a 'kish,' or basket, forwarded on a low-backed car, and so bruised and crushed and shaken at their journey's end that half of them were taken out dead and were flung into the dungheap.

The Irish members were not especially soft-hearted, but they could not listen without emotion to so horrible a tale. One speaker appealed to his fox-hunting friends whether they would not be more careful in transmitting the whelps of their hounds. Dennis Browne said truly that of all stories he had ever read or heard of, the report of the committee was the most horrible.[1]

Such was the actual discharge of the common duties of humanity in Dublin in the days when Ireland had her own Parliament, and patriotic hearts were at white heat to raise their country in the scale of nations. But the popular tribunes, who were so busy with the removal of ideal grievances, had no leisure for the petty details of crime and misery. Sir John Blaquiere was no political saint, but he could see the horrors of wholesale infanticide. Grattan preferred to rave against corruption, and even in his raving was but half-sincere. When he divided the House upon

---

[1] *Irish Debates*, March 12, 1792.

the mode in which the Castle influence was exerted, Arthur O'Connor, the most advanced Radical in the House, voted against him. The Castle majority had been created only to overcome the yet grosser monopoly of power and patronage by the Boyles and Ponsonbies. O'Connor refused to assist Grattan in re-invigorating an aristocracy 'who had misgoverned Ireland from the day of the Conquest.'[1]

[1] *Irish Debates,* March 19, 1791.

SECTION V.

THE session of 1791 was as barren as its predecessor. The working forces of the drama were no longer in the Parliament. Could the Catholics be kept from dangerous courses, they had a prospect of immediate and perhaps complete emancipation from the English Cabinet. The more disturbing, therefore, to their moderate friends in both countries was the institution and rapid growth of the United Irishmen. At Beaconsfield especially they were watched with an emotion which became at last unbearable. Mr. Richard Burke, as often happens with the children of men of genius, resembled his father in the form and manner of his mind. The intellect only was absent, and the place of it was supplied by vanity. In his own family his defects were invisible. Edmund Burke regarded Richard as immeasurably his own superior. They had met and spoken with Keogh when he was in London on the business of the Catholic Committee. It was then perhaps that Richard Burke offered his services to reconcile the two Catholic factions, and secure for both the confidence of the British Government.

No time was to be lost. The Dublin Lodge of United Irishmen contained already many Catholics. It was even spoken of as a Catholic society.[1] Napper Tandy, the noisiest of the demagogues, was its secretary, and the violence of its manifestoes was fast neutralising the efforts of the Viceroy to reconcile influential Protestants to emancipation.

---
[1] 'Lord Westmoreland to Dundas, November 21, 1791.'

Describing himself as the agent of the Catholic Committee, young Burke waited on Pitt and Dundas. They expressed their pleasure that the Irish Catholics should have chosen a representative whose name was a security that they did not mean to join with the revolutionists. They acknowledged their own general wish to see the Catholics restored to their rights as citizens. But Pitt, it is likely, saw the character of the person with whom he was dealing—he declined to say anything specific till he knew the sentiments of the Irish Government. Richard Burke said that he was going himself to Dublin. He asked to be allowed to correspond privately with the Cabinet. Pitt declined to communicate with him except through the Secretary at the Castle. He begged to be allowed to take over with him 'a confidential communication of the sentiments which Mr. Pitt had expressed,' that he might show it to his friends. Pitt told him positively 'he could not gratify him in that matter.' He asked whether Mr. Pitt would recommend him to go. Pitt said that he must judge for himself, and declined to advise. He consented, however, to give Burke a letter of introduction to the Lord-Lieutenant. 'From the anxiety which Mr. Burke expressed that the Catholics and Dissenters should not form a union together, the Cabinet had no desire to restrain though they could not hinder his journey.'[1]

Such was the account given by Dundas of this interview, and had he told the whole truth, Westmoreland would have had no cause of complaint. But in the unguarded freedom of a private conversation the

---

[1] 'Dundas to Westmoreland, January 29, 1792. Private.' S. P. O.

Ministers had evidently gone further than Dundas acknowledged. They had allowed Burke to talk at length to them on the history of Ireland, to dilate on the penal laws, to represent the Catholics as the harmless victims of Protestant tyranny, and perhaps unconsciously they had permitted these views to influence their policy. The same packet which carried Burke to Dublin carried a public and a private letter from Dundas to Westmoreland. The public letter instructed him to recommend to the Irish Parliament the concessions which had been already made in England, the admission of the Catholics to the bar and the magistracy, the repeal of the Intermarriage Act, and the repeal of the law which forbade them to possess arms. On the franchise, too, the language was scarcely ambiguous. The Viceroy was not formally directed to make enfranchisement a Government measure. It was admitted to be dangerous. But he was informed that 'the Cabinet considered that the risk to the Protestant interest would be greater by the total exclusion of the Catholics than by their admission.'[1]

Such instructions were, to say the least of them, extremely serious. The franchise was a point on which Protestant opinion in Ireland was passionately sensitive, and on which the Catholic Committee was itself divided. It was still withheld even in England, and at that very moment Fingal, Kenmare, Gormanstown, and the other moderate Catholics who had seceded from the more violent faction, were sending in addresses, in which they deprecated the premature agitation of so critical a question,[2] and desired to leave

[1] 'Dundas to Westmoreland, December 26, 1791.'
[2] December 27, 1791. Printed in *Plowden*.

their pretensions to the discretion of the Legislature. For the Cabinet to make itself the advocate of immediate action and to throw the responsibility of refusal on the Irish Parliament was ungenerous and ill-advised. But this was not all. The secret communication which accompanied the official despatch was of a far more serious character.[1] 'In your private letter,' Lord Westmoreland wrote in reply,

> 'I am directed to impress on the minds of leading people, *as a guide for their decision in the present discussion,* that they must not expect the power and resources of England to be exerted in any contest that may arise for pre-eminence or power between religious distinctions of Irishmen; that it is your decided opinion all such differences, as far as regards political considerations, should be done away. I must tell you the inevitable results of communicating these sentiments of yours. The fears and jealousies that universally affect the Protestant mind are not confined to Parliament, but affect almost every individual and every public body. The steadiest friends of British government apprehend that indulgence will give the Catholics strength to press for admission to the State. In this they see the ruin of political power to the Protestants, and—trifling as you may consider the danger—a total change of the property of the country. The final consequence will be a confederacy of the Protestants, with very few exceptions, to resist every concession. They will resolve to support their own situation by their own power. You will lose for the Catholics the very indulgence which you desire to procure. You will cause the conviction which it is your object to prevent. The Catholic body can only act against the Protestant by outrage and intimidation, and you will be obliged by the necessary principles of government to spill the blood of the very people whom the expectation of your indifference may have raised to a state of ferment. The next consequence

---

[1] This letter is not in the State Paper Office, but the substance of it can be gathered from Lord Westmoreland's reply.

will be a general confederacy against the present Administration, the Protestant interest considering themselves made a sacrifice to false policy or resentment. What is the state of this country? The Government strong; the Parliament well-disposed; the country quiet; the Catholics of respectable landed property and clergy disavowing every turbulent sentiment, stepping forward and separating themselves from the agitators. Some concession is due to them, but the publication of your sentiments would at once shut the door. Why sacrifice our present strength? Why sacrifice an old and established policy which has for a century maintained the Government of Ireland, to the intimidation of Napper Tandy and his associates at the head of the lower rank of Catholics in Dublin unconnected with the nobility, landed gentry, or clergy of their communion?

'If I am to understand that I am directed to endeavour to reconcile the minds of Protestants to the English concessions, or admission to the franchise, by an information or intimidation that England will not interfere in any contest produced by refusal, and that even those concessions are to *be considered as a prelude to the abolition of all religious distinctions*, I must request you will again take the sense of his majesty's confidential servants, and if they continue of the mind that such language shall be held, that you will send me positive directions how I am to proceed, that I may not be counted as responsible.'[1]

The writing of the private letter had, unfortunately, not been the limit of Dundas's rashness. What he had written to Westmoreland he had said to the impetuous youth who was coming forward as the Catholic champion. Young Burke had rushed over open-mouthed, declaring himself empowered to inform the Catholic Committee of the real intentions of Mr. Pitt's Administration. He called on the Secretary, Major Hobart, at the Castle, and presented Pitt's

[1] 'Westmoreland to Dundas, January, 1792. Private.' Abridged. S. P. O.

letter. Hobart invited him to his house, and talked freely with him on the subject of his mission, but soon found 'he would not continue on that footing,' but insisted that he had separate authority from the Cabinet.[1] The introduction from the Prime Minister gave a quasi countenance to this strange pretension. Mr. Burke's next proceeding was to furnish Hobart with a dissertation on the rebellion of 1641, and to protest, in the Committee's name, against the reception or publication of any more moderate addresses from the loyal Catholics. 'If such a step was persevered in,' he said, 'it would lay the foundation of a complicated and incurable civil war.'[2]

Hobart wrote to Dundas, enclosing this production, and informing him of the behaviour of his protégé. 'I should undervalue your understanding,' he said, 'if I troubled you with a comment upon this composition: the folly and insolence of it is in keeping with the whole of his conduct. There is not a man in the country with whom he has conversed, except those belonging to the Catholic Committee, that does not consider him the most barefaced incendiary that ever hazarded the peace of the country. He has made many people believe that the English Cabinet has determined to sacrifice the Protestants of Ireland to the Catholics.'[3]

Dundas savagely disclaimed having given Burke authority to speak for the Administration,[4] but he could not dispel the impression already created, nor did the disclaimer arrive in time to prevent most serious

---

[1] 'Major Hobart to Dundas, January 17.' S. P. O.

[2] Alluding perhaps to the difference between the Kilkenny Parliament and the native Irish.

[3] 'Major Hobart to Dundas, January 17, 1792. Private.' S.P.O.

[4] 'To Westmoreland, January 20. Private.' S. P. O.

confusion. The Catholic Committee, relying on Burke's language, denounced the Kenmare address. Dr. McKenna, a prominent member of the advanced faction, issued a counter-manifesto. Burke called on Fitzgibbon to inform him that all communications of the Castle with the Catholics must pass through the Committee, and to tell him 'that if at some early period the Catholics were to be admitted to seats in Parliament,' the Committee would for the present be contented with the English concessions.[1] On reflection he felt that he had been too modest. Preparatory to the meeting of Parliament he conveyed to Hobart the Committee's ultimatum. Their present demand was for admission to the Bar, to the magistracy, to the grand and petty juries, and for a right of voting at the county elections. 'I shall be happy,' he said, 'to receive the answer of Government as soon as is convenient on these points. If I am not favoured with it before next Saturday, I shall conclude that your silence proceeds from a natural reluctance to employ your pen in conveying to me the disagreeable intelligence that the representations made to Government by the Catholics of Ireland have failed of success, and I shall inform my clients accordingly.'[2]

Never was Irish Viceroy in such a situation as Lord Westmoreland. Parliament was to meet on the 19th of January, and as yet there had been no time to receive from England a retractation of the ill-considered language of Dundas. A son of Edmund

[1] 'Edward Cooke to Bernard Scrope, January 11. Private.' S. P. O.
Fitzgibbon spoke of McKenna's manifesto, and called it conceited bombast. Burke said that for himself he highly approved of it, and that Grattan, who had seen it before it was printed, approved of it also.

[2] 'Richard Burke to Major Hobart, January 11, 1792.' S. P. O.

Burke had appeared in Dublin as the agent of a revolutionary body, yet introduced by the Prime Minister, declaring himself in the confidence of the Cabinet, and insisting on measures unhappily identical with those recommended in the private letters of the Home Secretary. It was hardly possible to doubt that he was speaking the truth. He was telling the Catholics that if they chose to rebel they had nothing to fear from England. Dundas had said the same thing, and had not yet unsaid it. The most moderate Catholics were beginning to ask 'how it was to be expected that they should desist from pressing the point of suffrage, when it was thrown at their heads by the Ministers of England?'

'If you suppose,' wrote Major Hobart to Dundas,

'That the Protestants will yield without a struggle, be assured you are misinformed. Let me impress upon your mind that the connection between England and Ireland rests absolutely on Protestant ascendency. Abolish distinctions, and you create a Catholic superiority. If ever the Catholics are persuaded that the Protestants are not certain of English support, they will instantly think it worth while to hazard a conflict. It may be said, What is it to England whether Protestants or Catholics have the preeminence in Ireland? It is of as much consequence as the connection between the two countries, for on that it depends. While you maintain the Protestant ascendency the ruling powers in Ireland look to England as the foundation of their authority. A Catholic Government could maintain itself without the aid of England, and must inevitably produce a separation of the Executive, to be followed by a separation of the countries. You must be aware of all the property which Englishmen possess in Ireland. It will be forfeited on the first appearance of success on the part of the Catholics. Are you prepared to meet the clamours of those who have an interest in property in Ireland? You will never

have the country quiet till strong and decided language is
held by the British Government on the principle of exclusion from the suffrage—the language which would have answered every purpose before Mr. Burke's arrival. He has so completely impressed an opinion that the British Cabinet has acquiesced, that nothing short of a positive declaration to the contrary will remove the alarm of the Protestants, or check the threatening importunity of the Catholics.'[1]

1792.
January.

On the eve of the session the Viceroy called a meeting of such of the servants of the Crown as he could best depend on—Fitzgibbon,[2] Wolfe,[3] Beresford, the Archbishop of Cashel, Charles Agar,[4] Sir John Parnell,[5] and Prime Serjeant Fitzgerald. He laid before them the instructions of the Cabinet, and invited their opinion. They agreed unanimously that neither 'the point of arms nor of the franchise' could be carried in the present humour of Parliament, and that the attempt to force them would be as impolitic as it would be useless. Beresford objected to the principle of concession, but under the circumstances was inclined to yield unimportant points. The Archbishop was for maintaining the existing law in its fullest stringency.

Westmoreland suggested that if trouble followed on the refusal of the relaxation which the British Parliament had granted, the English Government might decline to support the Protestant party.

The Archbishop said truly that the situations of England and Ireland were totally different. In Ireland the private fortune of every Protestant was at stake. Parnell was scarcely less determined, but

---

[1] 'Major Hobart to Dundas, January 17. Private.' S. P. O.
[2] The Chancellor.
[3] Attorney-General, afterwards Lord Kilwarden, and murdered in Emmett's insurrection.
[4] Afterwards Lord Somerton.
[5] Chancellor of the Exchequer.

considered it might be prudent to give way in trifles till ' the Reform frenzy ' had burnt itself out in France. The conclusion at last arrived at was, follow the English model, open the professions, and repeal the Intermarriage Act. The object of Napper Tandy and the Committee was to prevent moderate concessions, to keep up the ferment. Some effort, it was thought, must be made by the Government to prevent the better-disposed Catholics from falling under their control.

The Council, nevertheless, though admitting the necessity, were still strongly opposed to the mention of the subject from the Throne. Dundas had insisted that the matter should be so handled 'that the grace of the suggestion should belong to Government.' But it was felt that the announcement of concessions in the Speech would confirm the misgivings which had been excited by Burke's language, 'that Ministers had resolved to abandon the Protestant cause.' The Address would commit Parliament before the subject had been discussed.

' Instead of the relaxation of the penal laws having tended to unite Protestants and Catholics,' wrote Westmoreland, as if it was something to be surprised at, 'it has increased the apprehension and hatred.'

It was decided that a Relief Bill should be entrusted to Edmund Burke's friend, Sir Hercules Langrishe, and that Major Hobart should speak in its favour. At the last moment, before the opening of Parliament, the Viceroy called a meeting of the supporters of Government; and to quiet their alarms assured them that neither the suffrage nor the right to arms would be conceded, however violently the Catholics might demand them. Finally, Lord Westmoreland wrote for leave to contradict officially the pretensions to authority which young Burke had advanced. If the Cabinet would 'play fair,' he undertook for the quiet of the country. The only dangers to be apprehended would arise from a belief that the Home Government was irresolute, and that Burke and not the Viceroy was the true exponent of their sentiments.

Dundas's answer was the strongest condemnation of his past precipitancy, for it showed that neither he nor Pitt had formed any real policy for Ireland, although he had gone so far as to threaten that England might be a passive spectator of a civil war. He deprecated and resented the supposition that the Cabinet 'intended to play what was called a Catholic game.' 'The Cabinet,' he said, 'urged nothing which the Irish Council might think unsafe.' 'They had no bias.' 'They had no interest separate from that of Ireland.' On second thoughts, they considered after all that it was 'inexpedient' to license the Catholics to possess arms; and as for the franchise, they wished only 'that the Protestants should decide for themselves how far a slight concession might safely be made.'[1]

---

[1] 'Dundas to Westmoreland, January 20, 1792.' S. P. O.

In 'a most private,' separate, and autograph letter of the same date, Dundas adds:—

'I have nothing further to say, except that I and all his Majesty's Ministers have some reason to complain of the spirit and temper which have manifested themselves among our friends in Ireland on this business. If they had made no advances to us on the matter, we should have left it to their own judgment. But all through the summer and autumn they were expressing their fears to us of a union between the Catholics and the Dissenters. They asked for our opinion, and we gave it. What motive could we have except an anxious concern for the security of the Irish Establishment? Whether we are right or wrong time will show; but there is no imaginable reason why this opinion should have been received with jealousy.

'Mr. Pitt concurs in every thing I have said. He and I have not had a shade of difference in our opinion.'

SECTION VI.

BOOK VIII.
1792.
January.

On the 19th of January the session began which at Pitt's bidding was to open the sluices and make rebellion eventually inevitable. The Speech was silent, as the Council advised, on the great subject. Mr. Grattan, had he dared, would have at once challenged the omission and have entered notice of a Bill to give the Catholics the franchise. But his constituents of Dublin, though their politics were revolutionary, had not divested themselves of Protestant prejudice. The Corporation had insisted that he should take no part in assailing the ascendency. He could not afford to quarrel with them, and when he rose, as usual, to attack the Address, he confined himself to general invective. In an oration which was considered one of his most splendid efforts he demanded Parliamentary Reform, taking as the ground of his argument the events of the past ten years.

'There was a time,' he said, 'when the vault of liberty could hardly contain the flight of your pinions. Some of you went forth like a giant rejoicing in his strength. You now stand like elves at the door of your own Pandemonium. The armed youth of this country like a thousand streams thundered from a thousand hills and filled the plain with congregated waters, in whose mirror was seen for a moment the image of the British Constitution. The waters subside, the torrents cease, the rill ripples within its own bed, and the boys and children of the village paddle in the brook. By the traffic of Parliament the King is absolute. These Houses are as much an instrument in his hand as a bayonet in the hands of a regiment. Like a regiment, we have an adjutant who sends to the infirmary for the old and to the brothel for the young, and men thus carted to their places to vote for the Minister are called the representatives of the people.'

The oratory flowed for several hours. When the trick of rhetoric is once mastered it may stream for ever. The Irish Parliament was growing weary of it. Sir Hercules Langrishe gave notice, when Grattan sate down, of his intended Catholic Relief Bill. The vexation of the Viceroy was hourly increasing at the gratuitous embarrassment which had been forced upon him. 'I am sure,' wrote Edward Cooke, the Army Secretary, 'that in point of real dignified policy nothing at all ought to be done for the Catholics this session. There is but one mind in the House of Commons. The Administration is obliged to canvass for measures which must weaken Government and lay the groundwork of perpetual discord.'[1] 'Mr. Burke's stories,' wrote Major Hobart, 'are hourly gaining ground. The effect of them already has produced a determination against all concession however trifling, so I fear we shall carry nothing.'[2] The knot might well have proved insuperable but

[1] 'This country is not known,' Cooke continued. 'It is the most easily governed in the world, if the true line is proceeded upon. How are you now? The British Government and Grattan coinciding in the same measures with different views, the one to strengthen, the other to abolish English influence; the Irish Ministry in opposition to the English in principle, and with them in acquiescence; the supporters of Government seeing ruin to themselves in standing by administration, the Ponsonbies on the watch to defeat administration by gaining the confidence of the Protestant interest.'—'Edward Cooke to Bernard Scrope, January 21, 1792.' S. P. O.

[2] 'January 22.' S. P. O.

for the fervid enthusiasm of the English agent of the Catholic Committee. So long as he was supposed to be in the confidence of Pitt, the Irish Radicals had endured Richard Burke for the sake of the advantages which they looked to gain through him. A character less congenial with the Hibernian temperament could not easily have been found. Though sometimes ridiculous themselves, the Irish have the most acute perception of absurdity in others. Richard Burke supposed himself a person of extraordinary genius. His letters and essays show nothing but impassioned commonplace and unbounded vanity. He was brought in contact with men in Dublin who were as much his intellectual superiors as he conceived himself to be theirs. He tried their patience severely, and at times overstrained it. Receiving no reply to the ultimatum which he had addressed to Hobart, he had prepared a petition in the name of the Committee for a full measure of enfranchisement. He was looking for a member of the House of Commons to whom he could entrust it, to be levelled as a thunderbolt at the expected imperfect Bill which was to be introduced by Langrishe. The Opposition members met at Leinster House to hear it read. They liked neither the petition nor its author. He said, as if he was conferring a favour, that he was willing to entrust it to any one of them, excepting only to Mr. Egan, who had before objected to expressions in it. Egan, a big coarse man, with a red face, whose wit was as sharp as Curran's, rose amidst general laughter, walked across the room to where Burke was sitting, looked him in the face and bowed deeply. 'Sir,' he said, 'with the highest reverence for your derivation, I entertain none whatever for the modesty of your vocation.'¹ The supposed representative of Pitt was a person with whom it was imprudent to quarrel. Mr. O'Hara at length took charge of the petition, touching it, however, as if it was red-hot iron.

On all grounds it was undesirable to prolong the suspense. On the 25th of January Langrishe's measure was brought in. He spoke with studied moderation. He spoke of the harshness of the penal laws. He sketched the successive removals of their most oppressive features in 1778 and 1782. He considered that the Catholics ought to be grateful for the concessions which were then made, and he believed, he said, that they were not insensible to the generosity which in so many important respects had replaced them on a level with their fellow-citizens. Other claims were now advanced in their behalf in the name of the rights of man. Mr. Paine might know of such rights. To him the word was without meaning. There might be natural rights in a state of nature, but there were none in political society. His interest in the Catholics had been diminished by recent publications which professed to express their sentiments. If the Catholics embraced those opinions the State could not embrace them in the Constitution ; and if the House of Commons yielded to intimidation it would betray the country. He was able to say, however, that the influential Catholics, laity and clergy alike, repudiated and denounced these extravagant pretensions. They had been tempted to combine with the Dissenters for revolution, but they had refused to taste the cup of sedition. Neither he nor

---

¹ *Life of Grattan*, vol. iv. p. 57.

they were advocates for a sudden extravagant transfer of power and authority. He would ask the House merely to admit them to the practice and profession of the law, to remove the remaining restrictions which interfered with their education, to repeal the Intermarriage Act, and abolish the limitations on the number of apprentices which they might take into their houses or places of business.

If this had been all, if these few concessions would have closed an angry controversy, the House would have been mad to hesitate at them. But they knew well that it was not all. Even Langrishe had spoken of a *sudden* transfer of power as if a transfer still lay ahead of them which should be effected gradually. Major Hobart did not relieve their anxieties. He seconded the motion, but did not speak upon it. Mr. Cuffe, a Privy Councillor, expressed the general sentiment when he said that any indulgence granted now to the Catholics must be accompanied by an intimation to the Committee that Government would not be intimidated either by them or by their English agent. The Establishment in Church and State should be protected on the principles of the Revolution of 1688, and men of any or all religions who sought to disturb the peace of the country should be made to know that they would be punished.

A desultory conversation followed. Allusions were made to the good conduct of the Catholics during the American war. Presently up rose Mr. O'Hara, with Burke's petition in his hand.

The House, he said, seemed uncertain what the Catholics really desired. He was in a position to tell them from authority. He had been requested to lay before the House a statement which completely expressed their wishes and their expectations. It was not drawn by themselves. It was drawn by an individual a particular friend of his own, who was not himself a Catholic. Mr. O'Hara offered it for consideration, but begged he might not be understood to be its particular patron.

Charles Sheridan was observing that a paper not sanctioned by any public body, and written by a Protestant, was a curious authority for the views of the Catholics, when there was a rush at the doors, a noise, and agitated movement. Richard Burke, who had been listening in the gallery, and was unable to endure to hear his performance ironically handled, plunged down into the body of the House and was about to speak. Amidst shouts of 'Custody' and cries for the Sergeant-at-Arms the daring young gentleman retreated as fast as he entered. Disgust with his impertinence might easily have taken a serious form, when Toler, now Solicitor-General, rose and, with happy adroitness, said he feared the House could not accept the petition. It was a strange affair. He had never seen or heard the like of it, save in a cross-reading in a London newspaper. 'On such a day a most violent petition was presented to the House of Commons; it missed fire and the villain made off.' Amidst shouts of delighted laughter leave was given to bring in Langrishe's Bill. Richard Burke had helped the Government out of the mire, while he had ruined his own mission.[1] No one can survive in

---

[1] 'Mr. Burke is certainly the most unaccountable animal ever employed in any mission. It was a chance whether he produced unexampled mischief and ruined the Government. I am inclined to think his folly and madness have been beneficial to us. His imprudence has been beyond expression, and has given general offence. The stories about the petition are hardly credible. This composition was

Ireland being made publicly ridiculous. The Catholic Committee gave him 2,000 guineas, sent him about his business, and resumed the management of their own affairs. The present Bill being now likely to be passed, as a complete settlement of the Catholic question, the revolutionary factions of both creeds were earnest to show that it would be no settlement at all, to frighten the House into rejecting it, and so to leave the sore open. Mr. O'Neil presented a petition from the Belfast Presbyterians for the complete removal of all Catholic disabilities. The Catholic Committee in Dublin drew a similar one of their own, which, with an evident slight to Burke, they entrusted to Egan. The Belfast petition was rejected on the motion of Mr. Latouche, the House refusing to receive it. They had consented against their own judgment to accept Langrishe's Bill, but 'the alarm being still universal that Government had ulterior views,' they desired to mark emphatically that they would go no further.[1] On whether the Catholic petition should be received there was a sharp debate, the supporters of the Catholic clauses insisting

shown to Egan, Curran, and Grattan, who were inclined to support it, but they struck out some objectionable words. They must be pretty strong that this trio would object to. Mr. Burke would not permit an iota to be altered. Of course these gentlemen declined to present it. Burke proposed sending a challenge to Egan for his refusal, upon pretence that he had promised. Mr. O'Hara was next pitched upon. He begged leave to read it, but Burke would not consent to that, and O'Hara agreed. Upon what passed in the House of Commons, Burke called a meeting of his committee, to verify their signatures before Mr. O'Hara. They wished to alter the objectionable parts of the petition. Burke would not consent. The Catholics refused to acknowledge their signatures, and the Catholics and Burke parted with mutual criminations. We have heard no more of the petition; so whether it will be presented or not seems doubtful. I am in hopes this Republican and factious committee, a species of Parliament most excessively dangerous, will now lose their consequence. An advantage already derived is the universal dislike to the levelling spirit, and the ruin of Napper Tandy and his associates.—Westmoreland to Dundas, January 28.' S. P. O.

[1] 'Westmoreland to Dundas, February 13.' S. P. O.

on being heard. Prominent among their champions was Colonel Hutchinson, the Provost's son,[1] who inherited his father's eloquence without his shrewdness. He talked the Liberal cant of the day, which may be compared instructively with the modern Papal syllabus. The sentiments of mankind on religion, he said, were altogether changed. The spirit of Romanism was softened, the influence of the Pope was feeble as the decrepit hand which wielded it. Catholics loved liberty as much as Protestants, and would cease to be bigots when the Protestants ceased to be persecutors.

In the same spirit George Ponsonby maintained that modern enlightenment had exploded the old superstitions. Mankind were now content with the great truths of the Gospel, unperplexed with the mystic jargon of school theology. Religious mysteries had fallen into the contempt which they deserved, and it would be the fault of the Legislature if by submitting to threadbare prejudice they allowed the public mind to be again disturbed by such 'despicable nonsense.'

Francis Hutchinson, the Provost's second son, soared into nationalist rhetoric. 'When the pride of Britain was humbled in the dust,' he said, 'her enemies led captive, the brightest jewel of the Imperial crown torn from her diadem, at the moment when the combined fleets of the two great Catholic powers of Europe threatened a descent upon our coasts, from whom did we derive our protection then?' Truth would have answered from Rodney and from Howe, who sent the combined fleets of France and Spain to the bottom of the sea. Ireland

---

[1] Afterwards General Lord Hutchinson, who succeeded Abercrombie in Egypt.

would have answered, ten years before, from her glorious Protestant Volunteers. Francis Hutchinson said, 'We found it in the support of three millions of our fellow-citizens, in the spirit of our national character, in the virtue of our Catholic brethren.'

The burning eloquence of the House was all on the side of emancipation, but it was based as usual upon illusion. There was no longer Fitzgibbon to show folly its proper figure. The defence of truth and common sense was left to less articulate advocates. General Cunningham said it was as plain as any proposition in Euclid that to give the franchise to Catholics implied a Catholic Parliament, and that a Catholic Parliament meant a revolution.' The Catholic Committee offered pledges on dangerous subjects. They renounced all claim to the forfeited estates. They promised that they would not meddle with the Protestant Establishment. Mr. Ogle, of Wexford, pointed out that such engagements would bind none but those who made them. The Catholics must become supreme in the State by mere weight of numbers, and when the power was in their hands it was idle to suppose that they would not use it in their own interest. 'The House had heard much,' said Mr. Pery, 'of the enlightened liberality of the time— what was it but a wild democratic spirit aiming at universal impossible equality?'[1]

---

[1] 'Sir Boyle Roche was the buffoon of the Conservative party. He amused the House with analysing the signatures to the Catholic petition. The first name was that of Mr. Edward Byrne, one of the largest merchants in Dublin, who paid 100,000*l.* a year to the revenue. Roche described him as "a sugar baker, seller of wine and other commodities." Keogh, the Committee's ambassador to Pitt, he called "a retailer of poplins in Dame Street." In this not eminently wise spirit he went through the list, and enquired whether a meeting of turbulent shopkeepers and shoplifters, a repetition of the tarring and feather-

The House refused to receive the Catholic petition by 208 voices to 23, so heavy was the preponderance of opinion against granting political power to a body whom the nature of things forbade to be other than their enemies. Langrishe's Bill was passed unwillingly to please the English Cabinet, but the friends of order in Ireland flattered themselves that they had heard now the last of concession, and Charles Sheridan gave a definition of Protestant ascendancy which was universally accepted, and which the immense majority of the members declared themselves determined to uphold. 'By Protestant ascendancy he meant a Protestant King, to whom only, being Protestant, they owed allegiance; a Protestant House of Peers, composed of Protestant Lords Spiritual in Protestant succession; of Protestant Lords Temporal with Protestant inheritance; and a Protestant House of Commons elected by Protestant constituents, a Protestant legislature, a Protestant judiciary, a Protestant executive, in all and each of their varieties, degrees, and gradations.'

Three days after the Bill had been read the last time, the House of Commons itself, the building which had witnessed Grattan's triumph, and 'for beauty had been the admiration of Europe,' was burnt to the ground. The session in consequence came to a premature end, and closed in the middle of April. Before the curtain fell there was a mock-heroic passage at arms with the United Irishmen. Napper Tandy, not liking the language in which the society and

ing committee of 1784, was to be taken as a representation of the Catholic nobility and gentry of Ireland.'—*Irish Debates*, February 1792.

himself had been spoken of, sent Toler, the Solicitor-General, a challenge. The Irish laws of honour allowed a gentleman to refuse such invitations from a tradesman. Toler brought the letter before the House, and an officer was sent to arrest the offender and bring him to the bar for breach of privilege. Napper slipped through a window and escaped. The society was on its trial. To show the white feather would be fatal. Tone, who had been watching over its progress, himself keeping in the background, saw the moment come when he must act. He consulted Hamilton Rowan, a young hot-blooded associate who had become lately a member. They extemporised an irregular meeting. Rowan took the chair, with Tone for secretary. They passed a resolution that the House of Commons had treated them 'with insolence,' printed five thousand copies of it, which they sent flying through the country, with their names attached, and they gave notice that if they were again interfered with they would challenge the Speaker. In other countries such proceedings would have passed for idle bombast. In Ireland Tone and Rowan became the heroes of the hour. As the session approached its end Napper, too, appeared to challenge martyrdom when it would be unattended with inconvenience. The authority of the House would determine with the prorogation. On the last day he was seen strutting through the streets towards College Green, intending to present himself to the House. He was encountered by the Sergeant-at-Arms, and was brought to the bar, Tone and Rowan sitting conspicuous in the uniform of the Whig Club in the front of the gallery. At the motion of the Attorney-

General, Napper was committed to Newgate, to which he was escorted by an adoring crowd. His imprisonment lasted but an hour or two. On his release he commenced a prosecution against the Viceroy, by which Dublin was entertained and excited for the remainder of the year.

SECTION VII.

BOOK VIII.
1792.

So far the Catholic Committee had trusted to expectations held out by England, and had turned a deaf ear to the blandishments of Tone. Their petition had been flung back into their faces. Pitt, if still in their favour, was unwilling or unable to force his wishes on the Parliament. Further pressure was evidently necessary. Their difficulty hitherto had been from the secession of the moderates. The claim of the Committee to represent the Catholics of Ireland had been disallowed; they had been termed in contempt ' shopkeepers and shoplifters,' and Keogh and Byrne, the principal leaders, resolved on a bold stroke. The Volunteer Convention of '83 had failed because it was a body in arms and illegal. The Congress of '84 could not get itself chosen, for the High Sheriffs were afraid to hold the elections. If the Catholic bishops would assist, a Catholic Convention could be elected to which no valid objection could be made, and of the right of which to speak for the general body there could be no uncertainty. There would be difficulty. The Protestant gentry would do their utmost in opposition. The Bishops were timid, accustomed many of them to depend on the Castle, and unwilling to offend the leading Catholic nobility. It was unlikely that they could be brought to act without support from other quarters, and Keogh now boldly called in Wolfe Tone, and with Tone the alliance with the United Lodges. Keogh himself was more or less serious in his religious belief. Tone and his friends were frank in their admissions that they believed nothing. The Catholic Committee were not particular. They desired to show the world that sooner than fail they would fling themselves on the Revolution. Wolfe Tone was appointed their special agent. Richard McCormick, a United Irishman also, became their secretary. The combination and the intentions of the Convention were no sooner formed than they were known at the Castle. Fitzgibbon, who alone was under no illusions, was for taking measures as prompt and decisive as those with which he had crushed the Congress in '84. If an independent representative assembly was allowed to meet and debate, he was confident that it would overset the Parliament. It would be better to act at once, he said, when the Committee were weak, than to wait till they had collected money and had gained the confidence of the people. He proposed to issue a proclamation against unlawful assemblies, and to intimate privately to the principal Catholics that if they took part in elections they would be prosecuted. Neither the Chancellor nor Lord Westmoreland had any doubt of their power to check this new movement, on one condition, that they could be sure of being backed by the Cabinet. Here was the real doubt. From some quarter, perhaps from Beaconsfield, Keogh had learnt that he had nothing to fear in that quarter. The object of the Convention was to petition the King in the name of the Catholics of Ireland ; and the Committee asserted in a manifesto, with the use of the largest capitals, that ' they had the FIRST AUTHORITY for saying that the application would have infinite weight.'

Could it be true that notwithstanding their disclaimer of Richard Burke, the Cabinet were still secretly encouraging Irish agitation unknown to the legitimate authority to whom they had delegated the Government? Major Hobart was in London. The Viceroy directed him to see Pitt and Dundas, and ascertain their real sentiments. Nothing could be more dangerous, nothing more fatal to the respect which, in Ireland, beyond all countries in the world, the executive administration required to maintain, than the belief that some other body was the true representative of the opinion of the advisers of the Crown. 'If,' Westmoreland wrote, ' you can plainly ascertain from them that they will support the existing Establishment, if they will treat with decided coldness any ambassador or address from any other body, no mischief can happen. It is the suspicion of English toleration that causes the present bustle. I am as sensible as they can be that it is good policy that the Catholics should be attached to the English Government, but we must take care that in the flirtation we do not lose our power. If the dislike they manifest to Reform in England extends to Ireland, we may be confident of their support. No English Reform is so dangerous as this Catholic National Assembly. Endeavour to sift what steps Pitt thinks we might venture. If the Assembly is *bonâ fide* elected and subsists, we must decide whether we will oppose or submit.'[1]

Mr. Pitt, like other sanguine statesmen before and since, had discovered that Ireland had been troublesome for want of 'Irish ideas' in the management of her. The Protestant gentry had made themselves a

[1] 'The Earl of Westmoreland to Major Hobart, June 7, 1792.' S. P. O.

bye-word. The Protestant Parliament, in the debates on the Commercial Propositions and on the Regency, had behaved like an assembly of Bedlamites. The Belfast Whig Club was in open sympathy with the Jacobins. In the well-disposed, loyal, and pious Catholics he was hoping to find a Conservative element to cool the revolutionary fever. He would have been less confident of his own judgment could he have seen the party who, under Keogh's auspices, were preparing for a summer campaign to agitate for the Assembly of the Catholic Convention. They appear in Tone's Diary, half-a-dozen of them in all, and each passing by a nickname. Tone himself passed modestly under the soubriquet of Mr. Hutton; Keogh, the moving spirit, was Gog; McCormick, the Committee's secretary, was Magog; Whitley Stokes, the Dean of Trinity, was the Keeper; Napper Tandy was the Tribune; 'the Hypocrite' was Dr. MacDonnell, a distinguished Dissenting leader in Ulster. The first object being to secure the thorough support of the Presbyterians, Belfast was chosen for the opening of the operations, where the ground was already prepared. The Belfast petition for the removal of the Catholic disabilities having been rejected by Parliament, the Republicans had replied by a demonstration. On the 19th of April there had been a United dinner there of Catholics and Protestants, where the toasts had been 'Tom Paine and the Rights of Man,' 'Napper Tandy and the Rights of the Subject,' 'Wolfe Tone and Reform of Parliament,' while the Catholic parish priest had proposed 'Religion without Priestcraft.'[1] On the 14th of July there was to

---

[1] *History of Belfast*, April 10, 1792.

be a second revolutionary celebration, and the occasion was taken for Keogh and his friends to appear on the scene.

Let the reader, then, start from Dublin on the 9th, with Wolfe Tone and Whitley Stokes, and with Tone's journal to tell the story. Keogh was himself in Munster, but was coming up to join them.

'July 9.—Set out with the Keeper. Breakfast at the Man of War. Stokes dull. Proposed picquet. Doubt the Keeper is a black-leg.

'July 10.—Sup with Neilson and the old set. Bed at one o'clock.

'July 11.—Rise with headache.

'July 13.—The Hypocrite made the Keeper drunk last night. Hear the Tribune is arrived, and say Oh! to him. The hair of Dr. Haliday's wig grows grey from fear of the Catholics. Several comets appear in the market-place. Good news from Munster. Gog preaching for three days to six bishops, who are at last converted. Ça ira. The Keeper dines this day in the country with the Hypocrite. Suppose he will make a beast of himself again.

'July 14.—Anniversary of the taking of the Bastile. Procession of Volunteers, seven hundred strong. Meeting at the Linen Hall; like the old German meetings in the woods, the people sitting, the armed warriors in a ring standing round. The effect of the unanimous Aye of the assembly when passing the address.[1] Mr. Hutton[2] so affected that tears stood in his eyes. Sentimental and pretty. More and more satisfied that moderation is stuff and nonsense. Business settled at Belfast. Huzza! Dinner at the Donegal

---

[1] For Catholic Emancipation.   [2] Tone himself.

Arms. Everybody as happy as a king. God bless everybody, Stanislaus Augustus, George Washington. Who would have thought it this morning? Generally drunk. Home, God knows how and when. God bless everybody again generally. Bed, with three times three.

'July 16.—Breakfast at the Grove with Simms.[1] All the Catholics from Dublin there. Council of war in the garden. Gog explains the plan of organizing the Catholic body. If the Dissenting interest were with us, all would be done. Simms says the thinking men are with us; but if Government attacks the Catholic Committee under the new system in two months, the North will not be ready to support them. Dinner. MacTier in the chair. At the head of the table a Dissenter and a Catholic. Delightful. The four flags —America, France, Poland, Ireland, but no England. Bravo! Huzza! Three times three. God bless everybody. Go up stairs with a Catholic.

'July 18.—Leave Belfast. Set off with the Catholics on the way to Dublin. Gog converts a Bishop at Newry, another at Downpatrick. Gog insufferably vain, fishing for compliments, of which Mr. Hutton is sparing. Gog then praises Mr. Hutton, who relents, and lays it on in return pretty thick. Nothing too gross. A great deal of wine. Bed between one and two. Bad! Bad! Bad!

'July 21.[2] Rode out with Gog to Grattan. Entertained all the way with stories of Burke, who is become odious to Gog. Burke scheming with the Catholics here to raise his value in England with the Ministers. A puppy or worse! We arrive at

---

[1] Another Presbyterian leader.   [2] Again at Dublin.

Grattan's. Tell him of the state of the North and South. He approves. Talk of next winter. If the Committee are firm Mr. Grattan thinks the House will submit. Say " Oh ! " to him and depart.

'July 22.—Gog expects Burke at Cork,[1] who pretends to have come over on his own private affairs. Private fiddlesticks! Gog in a rage. Determined to thwart him and put him down with the Catholics. Burke is by far the most impudent, opiniative fellow that I ever knew. Gog wants a round-robin not to invite him to their houses. Does he want another 2,000 guineas? Mad as his father about the French Revolution.

'August 1.—The vintner[2] hangs back. Old cowardly slave ! The Catholic spirit quite broken. *They do not even beat one another!* Sad. Sad. Busy all day folding papers for the Munster Bishops. Damn all Bishops. Gog not quite right on that point. Thinks them a good thing. Nonsense! Dine at home with Neilson and McCracken. Very pleasant. Rights of man. French Revolution. No Bishops, &c.

'August 2.—Gog not equal in steadiness to Magog,[3] and as vain as the devil. Magog not a grain of a papist.

'August 14.—Walk out and see McCracken's new ship the " Hibernia." " Hibernia " has an English crown on her shield. We all roar at him. Dine with Neilson. Generally drunk. Vive la Nation ! Damn

---

[1] 'Dundas took credit with Westmoreland for having received Burke with great coolness on his return to England. He was coming back to Ireland, however, still insisting that he was in the confidence of the Cabinet.—Major Hobart to Evan Nepean, October 4.' S. P. O.

[2] Edward Byrne, the great spirit merchant, and first Catholic in Dublin.

[3] McCormick, secretary to the Catholic Committee.

the Emperor of Russia. Generally very drunk. Bed, God knows how. Huzza! Huz . . . .

'August 15.—Wake drunk.

'August 16. — Damn the Aristocrats! Mug a quantity of mulled wine. Generally drunk. Union of Irishmen, with three times three.

'August 17.—Rise as sick as a dog. Breakfast with Lord Moira, and ask leave to introduce Gog, which he grants with much civility.'[1]

The vividness of Wolfe Tone's portraiture is a guarantee of its fidelity. The effect of his and companions' exertions was, that after some hesitation the election of delegates went forward. The Government threatened the Catholic Bishops. The gentry talked of reviving the Volunteers to counteract the Catholic combinations.[2] The Burkes protested against the alliance with the revolutionists. Edmund Burke wrote affectionate letters to Keogh, and invited his sons to stay with him at Beaconsfield. Richard tried once more the effect of his own presence. But they only made themselves objects of ridicule and coarse suspicion.[3] The Irish prelates cast in their lot with the Committee, either in earnest or as a menace to the

---

[1] Extracts from the Journal of Wolfe Tone, summer and autumn of 1792.

[2] 'Westmoreland to Dundas, August 13.'

[3] 'September 5. Burke is come, Gog says as a spy for Dundas. His impudence is beyond all I have ever known. Edmund Burke has Gog's boys on a visit, and has written him a letter in their praise. He wants to enlist Gog in behalf of his son, but it won't do. Gog sees it clear enough—wants two thousand more guineas for his son, if he can. Edmund is no fool in money matters. Is this "Sublime or Beautiful?" Gog has given Burke his congé. Burke mad as the devil, but cannot help himself.' — *Tone's Journal*, September 1792.

'In the State Paper Office there is a letter on the subject of Burke from Keogh to Doctor Hussey, a prominent Catholic priest, who was in the confidence of the Cabinet. It was to warn Dundas against regarding Burke as in any degree authorised to speak for the Catholics of Ireland, and to complain of the

Government, and Catholic representatives were chosen for every county, to meet in Dublin on the 3rd of the approaching December.

As the prospects of the Protestant revolutionists ten years before turned on the fate of the American war, so now the prospects of their Catholic heirs and successors hinged on the future of France. The Jacobin fury was displaying itself in its terror. The September massacre was filling England and Protestant Ireland with indignation and horror. The Duke of Brunswick was advancing, and if he reached Paris Tone's labour would have been thrown away. All would be over with the Committee and the United Irishmen. Two of the new delegates, one of them a priest, was found in correspondence with Condorcet. The Government intercepted the letters and recommended them to the better thoughts of Dundas.[1] Relieved of fear on the side of France, Pitt would trouble himself little about Irish agitation; and Tone was so well aware of the fighting value of the noisy patriots, who talked sedition with so much fluency, that at one moment he and his companions, after all the hurrahs and toast-drinkings, were again contemplating emigration. If Lord Moira would put himself at the head of a rebellion, which he appeared to think not wholly impossible, there might still be hope.[2] If not, Tone knew a sergeant's guard would keep the peace of Ireland for all the fight that was in the mobs of Dublin and Belfast.[3] But the fates were merciful.

---

confusion which he had caused. This letter being among the Secret Irish Papers, was evidently forwarded by Doctor Hussey to Dundas.'—*Irish MSS.*, October 2, 1792.

[1] 'Major Hobart to Evan Ne-pean, October 20. Secret.' S.P.O.

[2] 'Lord Moira may, if he chooses, be one of the greatest men in Europe.'—*Journal*, September 18.

[3] 'September 11.—Ride with Warren. Wet to the skin. Pro-

In October came the news of Valmy. The Duke of Brunswick was hurled back, the Revolution was triumphant, and aspiring Ireland breathed again.¹ The Bishop of Killala, a little startled at the tone of things, suggested that he and his brother prelates might as well have more influence in the Committee. 'Damned kind,' was Tone's remark. ' Gog revolts like a fury and tells Mr. Hutton he begins to see the Catholic Bishops are all scoundrels.' On the 1st of November the Catholic parts of Dublin were illuminated for Dumourier's victory. ' Singular,' observed Major Hobart, ' that the same event should have produced mourning in Beaconsfield and illumination in Dublin ; but in proportion as Popery declines in France Mr. Burke is determined to make it flourish in Ireland.'² Tone, Hamilton Rowan, McCormick, and the rest of the United leaders had a dinner on the same occasion. The chief talk was of ' tactics of treason.' Tone was surprised to see two glasses before him, and that Hamilton Rowan had four eyes. He was himself, 'like the sun in the centre of the system, perfectly sober when all else were drunk;' but 'when he attempted to walk across the room he was unable to move rectilineally, from his having eaten a sprig of watercresses.'

pose a general emigration to America, if our schemes fail. Whitley Stokes to be principal of a college to be founded. We get drunk, talking of our plans. God bless everybody.

' September 17. The devil to pay in Paris. Mob broke open the prisons, and massacred the prisoners. An Irish mob would have plundered, but shed no blood. Which is best? I lean to the Frenchmen—more manly. Our mob very shabby fellows. Never would have stood as the Parisians did on August 10. A sergeant's guard would drive the mob of Dublin.'—*Journal*, September 1792.

¹ ' October 11.—Dumourier's victory. Huzza! If the French had been beaten it was all over with us. All safe for this campaign.'

² 'Major Hobart to Evan Nepean, November 1, 1792.' S.P.O.

There needed still but a firm word from England for faction to slink into its den, but the word was not spoken, and the impression prevailed, which Dundas's private letter certainly justified, that Pitt intended to leave Irish Protestantism to its fate.[1] A revolution was now openly talked of, and Tone was applied to for protection when the rebellion should break out.[2] The signal was to be the meeting of the Convention, and the patriots prepared for action. Arms were privately imported. Rowan and Tandy, under cover of the lingering respect for the Volunteers, raised two battalions of a National Guard, each a thousand strong, with green uniform, harp buttons, and in the place of the crown a cap of liberty. Mr. Jackson, an ironmonger, gave them the use of his forge to cast cannon.[3] The Whiteboys in the provinces, or Defenders, as they were now generally called, made haste in the winter nights to disarm the Protestants.[4] Donegal was in the hands of a mob of incendiaries. In Meath a bold attempt was made to carry off a battery of field artillery. Under these conditions the Convention was about to assemble.

Major Hobart had brought back strict injunctions from Dundas that the elections were not to be interfered with. The gentry did not mean to part with their property without a struggle, and on their side were

---

[1] 'I am persuaded that a steady and declared intention on the part of the British Ministry to support the Irish Government against violence will prevent mischief here; but, however strange it may appear to say so, it must be declared.—Major Hobart to Evan Nepean, November 1.'

[2] Tone says that Plunket asked him for Carton, when the land should be re-distributed. He replied that Plunket could not have Carton, because the Duke of Leinster was his friend, but that he might have Curraghmore.

[3] 'Westmoreland to Dundas, December 5.' S. P. O.

[4] In Louth alone, in this year, a hundred and eighty houses of Protestants were entered and plundered of arms.

arming also. Three weeks before the meeting Lord Westmoreland made another effort to open Pitt's eyes, or at least to obtain from him some definite directions.

'However opposed to these measures,' he wrote, 'the threats of the democratic leaders have forced the clergy into co-operation and the gentry into acquiescence. The elective franchise is accepted by them all. They mean to press it as a prelude to the abolition of all distinctions. The attainment of the franchise they consider decisive of their future power in the State. They have coalesced with the United Irishmen and with every turbulent spirit in the country. . . . The Committee already exercise the functions of Government, levy contributions, issue orders for the preservation of the peace—a circumstance perhaps more dangerous than if they could direct the breach of it. Their mandates are taken by the lower class of people as laws. Their communications are rapid, and are carried on, not by the post, but by secret channels and agents. The lower Catholics connect the franchise with the non-payment of rents, tithe, and taxes.

'As universal as is the Catholic demand for it so is the determination of the Protestants to resist the claim. There is no risk they will not run rather than submit to it! In Down a thousand Protestants are in arms, but to preserve the peace, and their object is to keep the Catholics down. They are arming in Monaghan on the same principle, and Volunteering will become general if Government will not act. I have consulted the Chancellor and the other confidential friends of Government. All are unanimous not to yield anything at present, and all agree that the British Government must speak out plainly, to quiet the suspicions of the Protestants. I asked if they were prepared for the consequences of their language, and what means they could employ for resistance. On this head I found in no one the smallest apprehension, provided Government spoke with firmness. They apprehend no immediate convulsion, nor any convulsion, if Great Britain is firm.

'If the hour is not come it may not be distant when you must decide whether you will incline to the Protestants or the Catholics; and if such necessity should arise it cannot be doubted for a moment you must take part with the Protestants. If the Protestants, after being forced into submission, should, contrary to their expectations, find themselves secure of their possessions without British protection, they will run into the present State-making mania abroad in the world. You must expect resentment from the Protestants, and gratitude from the Catholics is not to be relied on. Concession of the franchise will make no difference in the conduct of the Catholics, nor will the question come before you in that shape. The question will be, whether England will permit the existing Government to be forced in Ireland. Suppose the Ministry to propose a relaxation of the Popery laws, and be defeated in Parliament. If the Catholics resort to violence the force of the empire must necessarily be exerted in support of Parliament.'[1]

The reply of the Cabinet to this important letter was to inform Westmoreland curtly that 'England required all the force she possessed at home to protect herself from her foreign and domestic enemies.' 'He must therefore act on his own responsibility.' The 'comfortless communication' was unattended with so much as a hint of what the Ministers really desired, or why 'the Viceroy was left so completely independent.' To leave him thus, however, was perhaps better than to have hampered him with ambiguous utterances. Flung on his own resources, Lord Westmoreland turned to the Chancellor, who knew better than Pitt what Dublin sedition was made of. The danger was for the Convention to meet, and to find an armed force at its disposition. The National Guard was rapidly organising; other battalions were expected

---

[1] 'The Earl of Westmoreland to Dundas, November 17, 1792. Secret.' S. P. O.

from Belfast, and notice had been given of a review which was to be held on the 9th of December.[1] Fitzgibbon issued a proclamation against unauthorised bodies assembling in arms. The National Guards would meet at their peril. It was an anxious moment. Rowan, Keogh, and Tandy roared their loudest; hired bands of vagabonds roamed about the streets at night, crying 'Liberty, Equality, and no King!' 'What they are to attempt,' Major Hobart wrote to the ministers on the 5th, 'when the Marseillais arrive from Belfast a short time must develope. You have more at stake in Ireland than you are aware of. You think it is a mere question between Catholic and Protestant. I wish it was. It is of deeper concern to us all, and goes to the complete overturning of the Constitution.'

The result proved how well Fitzgibbon knew his countrymen. When the day came for the force to show itself which was to overthrow the Constitution, there appeared on the parade-ground Napper Tandy, Hamilton Rowan, and Carey, the printer. These three were present in their green uniforms, their buttons, and their cap of liberty, and no more.

The National Guards, like Falstaff, showed their valour in its better part. The Convention, having its teeth drawn, was then allowed to meet without interference. That such an assembly should exist at all was a menace to the peace of the country. The ambiguous language of the Cabinet forbade the Castle to proceed to a direct inhibition of it. The easy

---

[1] Belfast was going fast and far. There, too, there was an illumination for Valmy. One of the transparencies was a gallows, with an inverted crown, and the words, 'May the fate of all tyrants be that of Capet.'

suppression of the National Guards taught the delegates that the time was not come to carry the Constitution by escalade. Thus the Back Lane Parliament, as the new body was called, came together; the first Catholic elective assembly which had existed in Ireland since the Parliament of King James. The occasion was celebrated with the usual high-flown language. Edward Byrne took the chair, 'the spirit of liberty running like an electric fire through every link of the Catholic chain.' The immediate business was to prepare a petition to the Crown, or rather to revise and sanction it, for the petition itself had been already composed by Tone. It was a document like all which came from the same hand, with the same gaudy diction and the same regardlessness of truth. It professed the most burning loyalty. It asked for the franchise on the ground that the Catholics had merited confidence, and that confidence would make their attachment to the throne more secure; while Tone's own admitted object was separation from England, and his central conviction was that every Catholic in his heart hated England.[1]

Such as it was, the Catholic representatives adopted it as their own. It was signed by Dr. Troy the Catholic Archbishop of Dublin, and by Dr. Moylan the Bishop of Cork, on behalf of the Catholic prelates and clergy of Ireland. The delegates signed for themselves and the laity. The Catholic community had now unmistakeably declared their wishes, and the immediate business was concluded. Five of the body were selected to lay the petition before the throne—Edward Byrne himself, Keogh, Christopher Bellew,

---

[1] 'Petition of the Catholic Convention.'—*Plowden*, vol. iv. Appendix 95.

John Devereux, and Sir Thomas French. The thanks of the Convention were given to Tone for his services, and they then separated, with the significant resolution that 'they would meet again when summoned, if it was on the other side of the Atlantic.'

The five gentlemen set off for England, taking Tone along with them. To give *éclat* to their mission, they went by Belfast, where the people took their horses from the carriage and drew them through the streets to the quay where they embarked. In London they were received by Lord Moira, who entertained them in his house, and promised that if the Ministers refused to present them to the King, he would claim his privilege as a peer and introduce them himself. Hobart wrote an ineffectual warning, especially against Keogh, who, he said truly, was connected with the worst men and the worst intentions in the country, but 'so plausible and subtle that there was danger in communicating with him.' The Cabinet had, unfortunately, made up their minds, in the face of proof to the contrary, that Catholics could not be revolutionists; that they were rather the necessary and natural enemies of revolution; and that the delegates therefore ought to be received. Dundas presented them; they delivered their petition, and it was graciously accepted. They informed Dundas afterwards, in a private interview, that the peace of Ireland depended on concession, and Dundas believed them. They assured him that although their actual demand stopped at the franchise, yet that nothing would really satisfy them short of total emancipation. He did not discourage them. He told them that their present claims should be recommended to Parliament from the throne; that he looked to them, in return, to support order and authority; and they left him with the belief that the Cabinet contemplated the entire abolition of all religious distinctions at no distant period.

'Our opinions are not altered,' Lord Westmoreland wrote, when the news of this extraordinary performance reached him. 'The Chancellor, the Speaker, and the Archbishop of Cashel still consider it most unwise. The alarm at concession is aggravated by the principle on which it is made. You expect it will give quiet here. It will not, unless you say emphatically that the Irish Parliament, having made this concession, will then receive the cordial support of the British Government. The recommendation from the throne appears as originating from the petition of the Catholic Convention. At this moment a daring insurrection prevails among the lower Catholics in neighbouring counties for the purpose of disarming the Protestants. This is part of the intimidatory system of the Catholic Committee. How is it to end? If year by year it is to be the same story, gentlemen will prefer the hazard of resistance now to strengthening those with whom they must hereafter contend.'[1]

'Intimidation,' said Hobart, 'is too glaring on the face of the whole proceeding. Instead of satisfying the Catholics, the public tranquillity will be in greater danger from the concessions than if none were made. Every man of talent we have considers himself sacrificed for England's convenience. Be assured, unless England speedily interposes energetically with regard to Ireland, we shall have a commotion of a very serious

[1] 'The Earl of Westmoreland to Dundas, January 9, 1793.' S. P. O.

nature. I see plainly it will not be understood till it is too late. They are now setting up the King against the Government, to undermine the Constitution. It is precisely the French system, and will produce the same consequences. Believe no one that would persuade you that Keogh's party—and it leads the Catholics—are not Republicans.'[1]

Westmoreland and Hobart formed their opinions from knowledge of Ireland. Dundas and Pitt formed theirs from knowledge of human nature generally, which they conceived that they could apply to Ireland; they stood sulkily to their purpose, and intimated plainly that the concession of the franchise was not to be the last. 'We are perfectly ready,' Dundas replied to their letter, ' to declare our determination to support the Protestant Establishment of Ireland, and maintain its form of government; but, unfortunately, we and his Majesty's servants in Ireland differ essentially as to the best mode of securing those objects. We consider the Catholics less likely to concur in disturbing the existing order of things when they participate in the franchise, than if totally excluded from those benefits which must be most dear to men living in a country where the power of an Independent Parliament has been recognised. Had the franchise been granted a year ago it would have been enough; now it will probably not be enough. We recommend to your Excellency and your Irish advisers a candid consideration of the whole subject, and the danger of leaving behind a sore part of the question.'[2]

---

[1] 'Major Hobart to Evan Nepean, January 9 and 19, 1793.'

[2] 'Dundas to the Earl of Westmoreland, January 23, 1793.' Abridged.

BOOK VIII.
1793.
January.

Political disaffection was to be conciliated by concession of power; internal anarchy was to be healed by a homœopathic remedy of a similar kind. Meanwhile the plunder of arms and the attacks of the peasantry on the houses of the Protestants in Meath and King's County had become so systematic and so daring, that the gentry had associated for self-defence. Fifty gentlemen were attacked one night in the beginning of January by six hundred Irish. The Catholic peasantry were not caitiffs like the Dublin mob. They fought desperately; and though beaten off at last, held their ground till six-and-thirty of them were left dead on the field.[1]

The comment of the Cabinet was to insist on the impropriety of continuing an unnecessary and impolitic disqualification. Since the Catholics had such a passion for possessing arms, they considered it would be wiser to place them at once on a level with other citizens.[2]

[1] *MSS. Ireland,* January, 1793. S. P. O.

[2] 'Dundas to the Earl of Westmoreland, January 23, 1793.'

CHAPTER II.

THE FITZWILLIAM CRISIS.

SECTION I.

DUNDAS had alleged the recovered independence of the Irish Parliament as the explanation of the anxiety of the Catholics to obtain admission to it. The veiled sarcasm perhaps explains the motives which were working in the mind of Mr. Pitt. He was told from Dublin Castle that he had only to be firm for order to be restored. But had order in Ireland, as understood by the Protestant gentry, been so very beautiful a thing? Was the power of England to be exerted to maintain rack-rents and absenteeism?—to maintain a Parliament which could be held to its duties only by systematised corruption? England was again on the eve of a desperate war. · The Protestant Parliament of Ireland had taken advantage of her embarrassment, in her last great struggle, to extort the Constitution of '82. Nine years had already passed since a Volunteer Convention, composed exclusively of gentry of the Established Church, and headed by a bishop, had made an armed demonstration of rebellion. Annual motions directly hostile to England had been brought forward by revolutionary patriots, and had been defeated only by lavish bribery. Protestant Belfast had declared itself a disciple of

BOOK VIII.
1793.
January.

Tom Paine, and the National Assembly at Paris was offering muskets and cannon to all oppressed nations who desired to assert their liberties. What security had Pitt that, after some French success, the principles of the United Irishmen would not be adopted by Grattan and the Protestant Parliament ?—that a reform equivalent to a revolution would not be insisted on as the alternative of separation, the Protestant gentry placing themselves at the head of the Irish nation, like the Geraldines in the sixteenth century? The conduct of the Irish Parliament on the Regency question was a recent proof that no dependence could be placed on them. The Cabinet was confronted with an immediate practical problem. The agitation of Reform among the Protestants had encouraged the Catholics to demand the suffrage. To refuse their petition was to throw them at once upon the Revolution, and give to the French three million ardent allies in Ireland; while at any moment, in some wild dream of liberty, the Nationalist leaders might carry Parliament along with them, as they had done before, themselves take up the Catholic cause as against England, and become the champions of Irish independence.

It is unlikely that either Pitt or Dundas contemplated allowing Ireland to fall really under a Catholic Parliamentary majority. Under the present Constitution some years would elapse before even complete emancipation would obtain admission for them in formidable numbers. Already Pitt was looking to a union as the only effectual remedy. To propose a union to a body of men who had received as an insult the suggestion that they should contribute to the Imperial navy, would have been to open the bags of Æolus.

They might be more reasonable if the Catholics were admitted amongst them, and their ascendancy and their estates in danger. The workings of Pitt's mind on the Irish subject, obscure even to Grattan after close and confidential conversation with him, became partly visible in a letter written in December 1792, by Lord Westmoreland to Dundas, before the arrival of the Catholic delegates in London.

After a few words on the desirableness of granting a peerage to Mr. O'Niel, to detach him from the levellers, the Viceroy continues:—

'The situation has very much changed within the last month, but miraculously almost in the last fortnight. The Protestants and people of property, from an idea that England was indifferent about the Catholic question, and therefore about the fate of the Establishment and property, have fallen into a most miserable state of despondency, which has worked a spirit of conciliation to the Catholics, on the principle of attaching the Catholics to the Constitution, to save it from the levellers. I don't yet find either the panic or the conciliatory inclination much gone to the country; and as it certainly is panic and not favourable disposition, upon any appearance of strength the resisting determination will probably return, even in this town. . . . Nor, if we should find it expedient to advocate conciliatory measures, am I prepared to say they could be carried, or that if they were carried against the opinion of the privileged classes, that English Government would not be ruined by the concession; that all the politicians would not either, from resentment or policy, look to popularity in Ireland; and that, by a junction of factions, every unpleasant Irish question of trade, particularly the Indian one, and every popular scheme to fetter English Government, would not be pressed in an inevitable manner? The conduct of the Catholics renders concession dangerous, for if given in the moment of intimidation, who can answer for the limit that may give content? And if Keogh should persuade the Catholics that the concessions were owing to the

Convention, the influence of Keogh and a few other dangerous men will be increased to such a degree, that all the Catholics will follow them.

'Don't suppose from what I say that concession can be carried if it is thought advisable. I only wish to acquaint you with the state of opinion here. The Chancellor, the Speaker, Beresford, and Parnell continue unvaried in the sentiments they have before expressed. The most desirable point is to get rid of the Catholic Republican Government, in the name of the Committee or the Convention, and I am at a loss how to effect it. Concession could only give it additional influence, if concession was supposed to be worked through them. . . . If the Protestants are alienated, the connection between the countries, in my opinion, is at an end. If concession is found advisable, and we can manage the business in a manner not to alienate the Protestants, it will not be so dangerous, though it will certainly be hazardous; and at least every step of conciliating the two descriptions of people that inhabit Ireland *diminishes the probability of that object to be wished—a union with England.* Before the present panic it was a good deal in the thoughts of people as preferable to being overwhelmed by the Catholics, as the Protestants termed concession, or continuing slaves, in the Catholic phrase. That conversation, since the Protestants have been persuaded that England could not or would not help them, has subsided.

'In the meantime the levellers have burst forth with a degree of impertinence and noise most astonishing. They are guided by a sect called the United Irishmen. They have money. I cannot conceive where it comes from. They have appeared in every sort of sedition. The soldiers are attempted in the alehouses. The playhouses and Amphitheatre are every night attacked with Ça ira. They have publicly professed a determination of raising several thousand men in a national battalion, with French mottoes, for the reformation of Parliament. Their end is, destroying English influence in this country. The great Catholic body is not connected with these people, but the leaders of the Dublin Committee are; and Keogh, who is the present mover of the Catholics, is a member of this society, and has been particularly active in endeavouring to form this national battalion.

'The great danger is from the North, where the Volunteering spirit has gained ground from dislike of the Catholics; and if that dislike should be done away, or resentment for concession actuated them, their Republican principles may lead them to any possible mischief. . . . The minds of men are in a great ferment, the mob expecting to be relieved from tithes, rents, and taxes by relief from Catholic laws; the Protestants alarmed and offended, and the levellers elated with the success of France.

'I believe a Big word from England of her determination to support the Protestant Establishment would set everything quiet, but England must convince the Protestants that she thinks the connexion of importance. Every species of mischief is in agitation. They have assassin clubs —marked individuals—in short, the whole systematic Jacobin plan. My great object is to strengthen ourselves as much as possible before the Parliament. . . . If concession should seem to you proper, let me entreat you not to be hasty, but leave it to me. Be assured you shall have early knowledge what can or cannot be done, and do not let out your mind in any way to these delegates.'[1]

The language in which Westmoreland speaks in this letter of the Union seems to show that it was already the object at which the Cabinet was aiming. If the object most to be feared was the drawing together of the Catholics and Protestants, the readiest way for England to prevent it was to force emancipation upon the present Parliament, and to make the Catholics feel that they owed their relief to the English Ministers. The Union might then be accomplished in time to prevent serious mischief. This interpretation renders conduct explicable which

---

[1] 'The Earl of Westmoreland to Dundas, December 12, 1792.'

otherwise might have appeared delirious. The Big word was not spoken. The Cabinet did precisely what Westmoreland begged that they would not do: they explained their intentions to the delegates in the fullest degree, as if the object was to divide the English Government from the Irish with marked emphasis, to teach the Catholics that England was their friend, and to raise, in doing so, deliberately the bitter animosity which the Protestant gentry were certain to feel.

Never did Viceroy encounter Parliament with a more stormy outlook, or under harder conditions as concerned himself, than the Earl of Westmoreland, when on the 10th of January he opened the session of 1793. The speech recommended the situation of the Catholics to the serious attention, the wisdom, and the liberality of the Legislature. The words implied as everyone understood that the Irish Parliament was required to make a concession, to which in the preceding year the House of Commons had declared, by an overpowering majority, that they would never consent. The address was moved by Lord Tyrone. The seconder was the younger son of Lord Mornington, Major Arthur Wesley, who, on this occasion, made his first plunge into public life. His speech was brief but characteristic. He expressed no doubts of the loyalty of the Catholics. He advised the House to approach the subject with moderation and dignity; but he stepped out of his way to applaud Westmoreland for his firmness 'in preventing men calling themselves National Guards from appearing in military array.' Grattan as usual moved an amendment, separating the Castle from the King, and giving the latter the credit of the intended measure. Tom Conolly declared that he approved of every part of the address save of the paragraph which thanked the King for continuing the Earl of Westmoreland in the Government. When the address to the Crown was carried, there followed the address to the Viceroy. It was the signal for the outpouring of patriotic indignation, which was hardly appeased by Dennis Browne, who, though he usually voted with the Patriots, declared now that he had heard of no act of the Viceroy injurious to the liberties of his country, and that a Government deserved support under which public and private credit, trade, and revenue were all thriving.

This address too was passed. Then followed notices of motions. William Ponsonby announced that he intended to introduce a Reform Bill. Grattan moved for a committee to enquire into the abuses of the Constitution. George Ponsonby guessing plainly the aim of England in promoting emancipation, and believing that he could still baffle Pitt if the Irish Constitution could first be popularised, supported Grattan and his brother, insisting that Ireland should no longer be the plaything of English Ministers. The rule of the session was to be conciliation wherever conciliation was possible. Mr. Corry for the Government consented to the appointment of a Committee, to enquire, not into ' the abuses ' which presumed the conclusion, but into ' the state ' of the representation, which might admit alteration. Grattan agreed to the change, though without pledging himself that the subject of abuses should not be revived. Still more significant was the attitude of Government on Mr. Forbes' annual motion to exclude holders of pensions and State appointments from Parliament. The Cabinet no longer objected to the introduction of the Bill, and in consenting to an abrogation of the time-honoured method by which public business had been so long carried on, appeared to admit that the Irish Parliament could not continue on its present footing.

The Government on the other hand called on the Legislature to sanction measures already begun for the repression of anarchy. On the 31st of January the House was invited to thank the Viceroy for having prohibited the parade of the National Guards. George Ponsonby gave a grudging assent. Grattan did not oppose, but warned the Secretary against making the extravagance of the Republicans a plea for touching those sacred guardians of liberty, the Volunteers. One voice only was raised in definite protest. Lord Edward Fitzgerald, whose light nature boiled at a lower temperature than that of ordinary Whigs in the disaffected atmosphere of Leinster House, had been swept into the revolutionary ferment. He had been at Paris with the Anglo-Irish deputation which had congratulated the National Assembly on the events of the 10th of August. The abolition of hereditary distinctions had been drunk as a toast at a republican dinner; and Lord Edward, amidst enthusiastic cheers, had declared that he renounced his title. Citizen Fitzgerald in his place in the House of Commons rose and said:—

'I give my most hearty disapprobation of the address of thanks, for I think that the Lord-Lieutenant and the majority of this House are the worst subjects the King has.'

Cries of 'To the bar!' 'To the bar!' 'Take down his words,' brought an explanation which was rejected as insufficient. The next day the young lord apologised, and, after a debate of two hours and a division, the apology was allowed.

Preliminary movements over, the great questions of the session now approached. In the first week Major Hobart had given notice that he would introduce a Bill for the removal of the Catholic disabilities. Was the removal to be complete or partial? and if partial, was the Catholic body prepared to accept it? On this point the leading members of the Catholic Committee had been at issue with their allies. Wolfe Tone had been for rejecting everything short of total emancipation, desiring to keep the wound open to feed the spirit of disaffection. Dr. Troy and the bishops were willing to meet the Government half way, to take gratefully as much as should be offered, and to wait till opinion had ripened for the full concession of equality. The ' Convention before it separated refused to receive a deputation from the United Irishmen for fear of compromising itself too deeply.'[1] Hamilton Rowan published a fierce address to the Volunteers, inviting them to resume their arms, calling on the Irish soldiers in the army to remember that they were citizens, and that their first duty was to their country, demanding complete and instant emancipation, and inviting another meeting at Dungannon to compel it.[2] Keogh had talked bravely to Tone of his hopes that the Cabinet would refuse to receive their petition in order 'to rouse the people.' Major Hobart's measures, it was now understood, extended only to the franchise. The delegates when they went to London had expected no more. Their reception and Dundas's language to them had raised their aspirations; and as soon as Hobart had given

---

[1] 'Keogh begged Hamilton Rowan not to press this, as now it might create divisions among them.' —Westmoreland to Dundas, December 12. S. P. O.

[2] *Publications of the United Irishmen*, December 14, 1792.

notice of his Bill, and the limitations of it were known, four of the five were deputed by the Catholic Committee to tell him that they had been promised seats in Parliament, and that they must have them. Hobart answered peremptorily that they must take what he was ready to give or they would have nothing. They were cowed and faintly acquiesced.[1] The part of the Committee which was under Tone's influence stood to their guns. They said 'the sneaking spirit of compromise would be fatal.' They drew a petition for complete repeal. When Keogh himself modified it, they made a display of force, and the Goldsmiths' corps of Volunteers re-appeared in arms and paraded in defiance of the proclamation. The Corps were ordered to disperse instantly under threat of having their arms taken from them. They thought of resisting, but they reflected that there were now 2,500 soldiers in Dublin, and obeyed. Dr. Troy and five other bishops published a Pastoral to be read in every chapel in the kingdom. 'Loyalty and obedience to law had ever peculiarly distinguished the Roman Catholics of Ireland.' Those qualities 'should be more than ever conspicuous when the beloved Sovereign, the father of all his people, with unprecedented benevolence and condescension, had recommended their claims to the Legislature.'[2] Wolfe Tone began to perceive that he and the United Irishmen had been used by the Catholic Committee to frighten the Government, and had been flung over

---

[1] Tone comments—'Sad! sad! I am surprised at Sir Thomas French. Merchants, I see, make bad revolutionists. So Gog's puffing has come to this.'—*Journal,* January 21, 1793.

[2] 'Address of the five bishops, January 25, 1793.'— *Plowden,* vol. iv.

when the end was gained. 'Will the Catholics be satisfied?' he wrote. 'I believe they will, and be damned.'[1]

Dundas was scarcely less alarmed for the opposite reason. The Cabinet had consented to the limitation, 'to gratify the prejudices of the Protestants, and from a belief that larger concessions could not be carried in the Irish Parliament.' He was led to fear 'that the British Government had been the dupe of men who were either insincere in their expressions of apprehension, or had got the better of them when it suited their purpose.'[2] The Catholics, he was afraid, would reject the Bill, and the national party in Parliament would outbid the Government, again appeal to national sentiment, and raise the cry of a United Ireland.

Amidst these various alarms and distractions, Major Hobart's own opinion remained unchanged, that to yield to Irish intimidation never had and never would or could come to good. On the 4th of February, however, he fulfilled the task imposed upon him, and explained the details of the intended measure. The Catholics had been for ten years restored to their civil rights. The Act of '92 had opened the bar to them. But on the novel theory that no man was free who was not a consenting party to the laws by which he was governed, they were still slaves. Their shackles were now to be struck off. Their unremitting loyalty for a hundred years, Major Hobart said, showed the continuance of these political disabilities to be no longer necessary. He proposed to admit Catholics to the

[1] *Journal*, February 4, 1793.
[2] 'Dundas to Westmoreland, February 9.' S. P. O.

franchise, to the magistracy, and the grand juries, on the same terms as Protestants. An English Act was about to open the army and navy to them. The Arms Act was to be repealed so far as affected Catholics possessing real estate or moderate personal property, and was to be extended to Protestants who had none.[1]

Sir Hercules Langrishe seconded Hobart with peculiar grace. The Catholics, he said, had come forward on earlier occasions to resist the invasion of a foreign enemy. They were coming forward now to resist the invasion of foreign principles more dangerous than armies, more cruel than the sword. The old dangers from Popery were extinct; new dangers had arisen against which the Catholics would be the truest allies.

If this was true, all would be well; but there followed Langrishe a speaker to whom it appeared not to be true, and who could give a reason for the faith that was in him. There had entered the House in 1790, among other new members, a certain Dr. Duigenan, sprung from the old stock of the O'Dewgenans, born in a mud cabin, Catholic of the Catholics, Irish of the Irish. Educated at a hedge school, and designed for the priesthood, young Duigenan had caught the eye of a Protestant clergyman, who introduced him into a grammar school. Thence having changed his religion and modified his name he found his way to a fellowship at Trinity College, and thence to distinction at the bar and to Parliament. Coarse in manners, rough in tongue, exactly informed of his country's history, and acquainted with his country-

---

[1] *Irish Debates*, February 4: compare *Irish Statutes*, 33 George III., cap. 21.

men's character, he was a vulgar edition of Fitzgibbon, and resembled him as the buzzard resembles the eagle.

This man rose to speak for the first time when Langrishe ended. He held in his hand the Catholic petition which he described as uprooting the policy which had resisted the shock of three general rebellions. He denied the loyalty of the Irish Catholics. He pointed to the Irish brigade in France. He spoke of the Irish regiments in the French service who had fought under La Fayette in America. More justly he pointed to the Whiteboys and Defenders, and to the midnight incendiaries who were plundering Protestant houses of arms—these at least the spontaneous growth of the Irish soil, who in all that they did ' were manifesting immortal hatred to the British name and nation.' 'The Irish Catholics,' he said,[1] ' to a man esteem all Protestants as usurpers of their estates. To this day they settle those estates on the marriage of their sons and daughters. They have accurate maps of them. They have lately published in Dublin a map of this kingdom cantoned out among the old proprietors. They abhor all Protestants and all Englishmen as plunderers and oppressors, exclusive of their detestation of them as heretics. If the Parliament of this kingdom can be so infatuated as to put the Irish Catholics on a better footing than the English Catholics, and if the English nation shall countenance such a frenzy, either this kingdom will be for ever severed from the British Empire, or it must be again conquered by a British army. The Protestants of Ireland are but the British garrison in an enemy's country, and if deserted

[1] And if Ireland was to remain a separate kingdom, his argument was as unanswerable as his facts were authentic.

by the parent State must surrender at discretion. English ministers are simply blind. I tell them they are greatly deceived if they have been induced to believe that an Irish Catholic is, ever was, or ever will be, a loyal subject of a British Protestant King or a Protestant Government.'

Not a man in the House, not Grattan himself, if put on his oath, could have denied that in this last sentence Duigenan was speaking more than the bitter truth; but nothing is so unpalatable as truth when it cannot be acted on. Speaker after speaker rose to deny what it was inconvenient to admit. Sir Henry Cavendish said that not another member in the House agreed in it. One member only, Mr. Ogle, of Wexford, had the courage to say that he did agree.

'The effect of the measure proposed,' Mr. Ogle said, 'must be either a total separation or a union. I have always thought I would rather lay my head on the block than consent to a union. But I declare before the Almighty, I would rather pass an Act of Union than the Bill before the House.'

Duigenan's and Ogle's words, though unsupported in debate, found an echo in too many hearts to fail of their effect. Major Hobart sent word to the Catholic Committee that unless he could tell the House that they were satisfied, unless they would pledge themselves to dissolve, and cease to agitate thenceforward, the Bill would be dropped. The Parliament would prefer to resist where they stood, rather than give their opponents additional strength by yielding.[1]

The Committee received at the same moment a most significant intimation that whatever the Eng-

---

[1] *Tone's Journal*, February 8.

lish Cabinet might say or think, the Irish Executive did not mean to be trifled with. A secret committee of the House of Lords had sat under Fitzgibbon's directions from the first day of the session to enquire into the causes of the general disorder. They had reported against Volunteer Corps and pseudo-representative conventions as incompatible with tranquillity. The day after the introduction of Hobart's Bill the Attorney-General alarmed the House with the information that large quantities of arms were being imported and distributed. A Bill was introduced and rapidly passed forbidding the importation or possession of guns or powder without licence, or the removal of cannon or powder from one part of the country to another, and giving the magistrates power to search either ship, dwelling-house, or store where they had cause to suppose arms were concealed.[1] The Act was a sentence of death to the revived Volunteer Corps, which were instantly disarmed and suppressed. On the 6th of February, Sir John Parnell moved for a new and effective Militia Bill, which would produce a force of 16,000 men, and at the same time he proposed the increase of the regular army to 20,000 men. Grattan enquired for what purpose such a force was needed. Hobart declined to explain. He said merely that the Government had reasons of their own for asking for it, and if the House refused consent, on them would rest the responsibility. There was no difficulty in gaining consent. The House, in their present panic, would have voted martial law if they had been asked. So armed, Major Hobart was able to present his alternative

[1] 33 George III., cap. 2.

to the Catholic Committee, and to make them feel that he intended to adhere to it. They were sore and savage. These loyal subjects, whose deep and tried devotion to their Sovereign was to receive its reward in an extension of confidence, debated long and bitterly on their answer. Very unwilling were they to promise to abandon their trade of agitation, break up their gallant convention, declare themselves contented and satisfied. But the alternative, as Tone perceived, lay plainly before them. Were they ready to fight? Hobart showed no signs of flinching, and they decided that they were in no condition for 'tented fields.' They gave the assurance demanded of them. They said they did but ask the Irish Parliament 'to coincide with the will of the best of kings.'

Hobart was now ready to proceed. The Bill came on for the first reading on the 18th of February, and was the occasion of a remarkable speech from Sir Lawrence Parsons. Parsons was in favour of admitting the Catholics to seats in Parliament, but under conditions of the franchise which would have excluded the mob of Catholic peasants from a voice in the election, and would have restricted the right of voting to men of property and substance. In many points he was an advanced Whig, and the words, therefore, with which he opened the subject, contrasted as they were so remarkably with the opinions expressed by Edmund Burke, have peculiar value.

'The Catholics,' he said, 'have been deposed from power for a century, and I will lift my voice against any man who defames our Protestant ancestors for that deposition. I look to the temper of the times. I look to England and I see the same spirit. I look to France and I see Louis XIV. revoking the Edict of Nantes. What in France and England was persecution, in Ireland was policy.' 'The conditions were now altered. Protestants were no longer agreed in excluding the Catholics from a share in power. England no longer desired it. On the eve of a desperate war it was unsafe to maintain any longer the principles of entire exclusion.' Major Hobart's proposal to extend the franchise generally, however, to the forty-shilling Catholic freeholders Parsons considered could only have risen from ignorance of the condition of the country. The admission of the Catholics to the right of obtaining freeholds had already completely revolutionized the southern and western provinces. The great grazing farms held by Protestants had been broken up. 'Seven or eight Catholics were now holding the ground which one Protestant held formerly.' Poor, ignorant, bigoted, and now four times the number of the Protestants, these new constituents would rapidly obtain an entire control. The present Bill might only concede the franchise, but the exclusion from Parliament would not and could not be maintained. 'Give the Catholics the forty-shilling franchise, they would be a majority of electors. Being a majority of electors they would return the majority of the House of Commons. The majority of the House of Commons would control the supplies, and controlling the supplies would be masters of the country.' Parsons declined to make over the State to the rabble. He would not admit such a multitude, he said, if they were Protestants and had been Protestants for twenty generations. The elections would be a scene of complete riot and bloodshed. He would propose instead to combine the two questions which were agitating the country.

There were three classes of Catholics—the gentry, who aspired to seats in Parliament; a middle class, with freeholds of 20*l.* a year and upwards; and the peasantry. The Government Bill excluded the gentry and included the mob. His own opinion was that the gentry should be admitted to the Legislature, and the franchise be confined to those who had sense enough to use it properly.

If such a restriction could have been maintained, Parsons' proposal was probably the wiser of the two. Unhappily it contradicted the rising political creed, that wisdom lay in the many and the noisy, not in the few and the intelligent. To be without a vote was to be a slave. The condition of a 20*l.* freehold would disfranchise half the Protestant tenants. Freedom, absurdly so called, was the idol before which Europe was learning to bow down, though as yet in fear and with half averted face. It could not be. The amendment was rejected.

On the second reading, a lower limit was attempted at 10*l.*, but was again defeated.

Grattan was for complete repeal of all distinctions, and talked grandly of ideas germinating in the soul like the child in the womb, and destined, whether men would or no, to grow to their designed proportions. George Ponsonby described the Bill as a trick to seduce Catholics into looking to England for favour. He invited Parliament to throw it out, and bring in another of their own more comprehensive.

'There are three parties in the House,' wrote Edward Cooke, 'those who would give nothing, those who are for everything, those who are for Major Hobart's Bill. The first is the largest, and would be decisive were it not for the influence and wishes of

Government. The second is in reality small, but has been rendered considerable by the desperate opposition of those who act with a view to defeat the Bill, or, if they cannot succeed, to revenge themselves on Great Britain by a reform in Parliament and the establishment of an Administration exclusively Irish. These are the Ponsonbies, Leinsters, Conollies, Grattans, &c.'[1] 'The Government will carry their Bill, but it is feared many of those who cannot obtain the limitation of the franchise will, upon defeat, join in resentment those who are for granting everything. The ground now taken by the Opposition is most dangerous. They say they have done enough to strengthen Government. They will grant no more power without redress of grievances, and I fear the effect of inflammatory language in the unsettled state of men's minds. The Catholics will be satisfied with what is proposed, and declare so unanimously. Had Major Hobart proposed more he would have lost all, *for the Ponsonbies have been lying in wait watching the turn of the business, and the measure for doing away all distinctions would have been so revolting that they might have successfully availed themselves of Protestant feeling.*'[2]

The second reading passed with only three dissen-

---

[1] The meaning of George Ponsonby's speech on the second reading was explained by Major Hobart:—

'George Ponsonby's point was to impute the change of sentiment in the Irish Parliament to what he termed English influence, and recommending the adoption of the Catholics into the Constitution as a means of strengthening Ireland and weakening Great Britain. The principle was too true to be without impression. But the force of it was diminished by the conviction that no man in the country was more averse to the Catholics than the gentleman who pressed the House to grant them everything. He will not easily be forgiven by the Protestants, and he will certainly be despised by the Catholics.'—Major Hobart to Evan Nepean. *Private and secret.* February 20, 1793.

[2] 'To Nepean, February 20.' S. P. O.

tients. In Committee, Mr. Knox proposed the admission of the Catholics to Parliament. He was defeated by 163 to 69. Duigenan revived Sir Lawrence Parsons' proposal for the restriction of the franchise. If the Bill passed in its present form there would, he said, be no refuge but a union; and rather than be a slave to the Catholics he would himself propose it. Sir John Parnell, though as a member of the Government he voted as Pitt required, yet expressed his belief that instead of conciliating the Catholics the grant of the franchise would only re-awaken forgotten animosities. He thought the time ill-chosen, the example dangerous, the experiment one of which no person could foresee the results ; but England chose that the measure should pass, and on England the responsibility must rest. The Speaker, John Foster, was no less emphatic in opposition. He was willing to grant the Catholics the fullest civil toleration. He deprecated giving them political power. An abstract right of voting as an inherent condition of liberty he ridiculed as nonsense. The franchise must be followed by seats in Parliament. Official situations would follow. The Catholic clergy would insist on equality with the Protestant clergy. The Crown alone would remain to save the Protestant interest from overthrow ; and there would thus be a direct and constant provocation toward a dissolution of the connection with Great Britain. He did not blame the Irish ministry. The measure began in England, but the raising the question at all had been an act of extreme folly and indiscretion.

All had been said that could be said, and on the inherent merits of the question Pitt perhaps would have agreed with Foster. He could not avow his true motives. He was aiming at a union, and looked to Catholic emancipation as a means of forcing the hand of the Protestant Parliamentary patriots. These gentlemen conjectured his purpose, and were contending to preserve their nationality. Could the profligate Whig aristocracy have retained their old monopoly of power they would have never troubled themselves about the Catholics. In the existing crisis they were unhampered with convictions, and were on the watch merely to take advantage of Pitt's mistakes. Had the Castle offered a full measure of emancipation they would have rallied the country on the Protestant cry against perfidious England. Had the Catholic petition been rejected in London, they were ready to open their arms to their oppressed fellow-citizens, to fall back, as in '82, on Belfast, Dungannon, and the Volunteers, to force a reorganization of Parliament by a threat of rebellion, and so reign themselves, as they fondly believed that they would, over a united Ireland.

In the face of an opposition composed of—shall it be said — political brigands, Pitt had to feel his way. If his road was crooked, his aim was at least honest. The Bill passed the Commons, and no more words need have been spent upon it; but its passage through the Upper House was distinguished by a speech from the one supremely able man whom Ireland possessed, removed now by his high office from the sphere in which, as long as he was present, he had controlled the questionable elements of which all parties there were more or less composed.

The Peers trod generally the same round of arguments which had already been exhausted. The novel feature in the second debate was that Doctor Law,

Lord Ellenborough's brother, a bishop of the Establishment, delivered himself of an oration in a style which since has become too familiar. Fitzgibbon, now Lord Clare, followed.[1] He said :—

'I have always felt peculiar reluctance in discussing the political claims of the Catholics of Ireland, feeling it impossible not to recur to past injuries, which it is my most earnest wish to bury in eternal oblivion. I could wish again to pass them by; but when the epidemical frenzy of the day has reached even that grave and reverend bench, and a learned prelate has thought fit most wantonly to pour forth a torrent of exaggerated misstatements against the government of this country for two centuries, I cannot leave his indiscretion unnoticed and unreprehended. I should be sorry that anything that may fall from me should stop the progress of this Bill. After what has passed in Great Britain and Ireland, it may be essential to the momentary peace of the country that your lordships should agree to it, and I do not desire to be responsible for the consequences of its rejection. Therefore, I hope it will be understood that, much as I disapprove the principles of this Bill, whatever I may say upon the subject is intended to open the eyes of the people to the real state of the country, in the hope, if it be possible, to stop the further progress of innovation.

'I lament that religious distinctions should prevail among us. I well know they have proved the source of bitter calamity to the people of Ireland. Religious bigotry produced Tyrone's rebellion; religious bigotry produced the rebellion of 1641, and the horrid excesses which attended it; religious

---

[1] The speech, which can be given here only in a most abridged form, is recommended to the careful student of Irish history.

bigotry produced the rebellion of 1688, and the tyrannies and proscriptions of James the Second and his Parliament; and I am sorry to say that religious bigotry is at this hour as rank in Ireland as at any period to which I have alluded. A very great majority of the people are as zealously devoted to the Popish faith as the people of Spain or Portugal. I do not state it as a reproach. I wish in this particular the Protestants of the Established Church would take example from their Catholic brethren; but when their political claims are discussed in Parliament the merits of the men must be dismissed from consideration. We must look to the principles of their religion, and to the unerring influence which those principles have had upon the political government of every country in Europe for centuries. From this point of view there is not a single instance in which Protestants and Papists have agreed in exercising the political power of the same State; and as long as the claims of Rome to universal spiritual dominion over the Christian world shall be maintained, it is impossible that any man who admits them can exercise the legislative power of a Protestant State with temper and justice.

'There is not a country in which the Reformed religion has been established where its progress has been so slow and inconsiderable as in Ireland; and it is a strange argument to urge the abhorrence in which the Protestant religion is held by a majority of the people as a reason for admitting them to a full share of power in a Protestant State; yet this is the strong ground on which the advocates for emancipation rest their claims. They tell us the expectation of making Ireland a Protestant country is vain;

that the people are unalterably devoted to the Catholic faith, and that justice forbids their exclusion from the State. That the people of this country are devoted to the Popish faith is too notorious to be disputed. When the other nations in Europe were engaged in religious controversies they were in a state of barbarism and ignorance below the reach of curiosity and speculation. Licentious habits had long engaged them in resistance to the British Government. The example of the English settlers would have alone sufficed to make the Reformation odious to them; but from the first moment that the Act of Supremacy was promulgated in this country the habitual aversion of the natives to the English name and nation became savage and inveterate antipathy.'

Passing in rapid review the Elizabethan wars, the Ulster settlement, the rebellion of 1641 and the confiscations which ensued upon it, the last desperate struggle under James the Second, and the final defeat of the native Catholic party, the Chancellor continued:—

'Far be it from me to revive the memory of these things; but so much upon this subject has been addressed to the passions, and so little to the judgment, of Parliament, that I hold it the duty of every honest man to oppose broad and glaring facts to a loud and impudent clamour. The penal laws enacted in this country were a code forced on the Parliament by hard necessity, and to these old Popery laws, I do not scruple to say, Ireland stands indebted for her internal tranquillity during the last century. Let philosophers who exclaim against this code, as subverting the immutable principles of sentiment and fraternity, condescend to look to the situation of the Protestant settlers at the Revolution. They were an

English colony in the country of an enemy, reduced by the sword to sullen and refractory allegiance. In numbers they were a fourth of the inhabitants. The experience of a century had shown that the natives of the country had contracted an incurable aversion to them. They could not stand their ground except by disarming the enemies who surrounded them of political power.

'These laws in part disabled the native Irish from renewing hostilities against the English settlers or embarrassing the British Government; but there is another cause to which the tranquillity of the past century is to be attributed. From the Revolution to 1782 the aim of the possessors of power and property in this nation was to cement the connection between Great Britain and Ireland, and to cultivate the confidence of the British nation. In 1782 a new scene was opened. Having advanced claims which were acceded to in full by Great Britain, the two Houses plighted the national faith to stand and fall with her; yet, fatally for our country's welfare, from 1782 to this hour the policy of the men who call themselves friends of the people has been to hold up Great Britain to the people as their rival and enemy—to concentrate the force of Irishmen of all religions against the English connection. The avowed object at this day of Irish reformers and Catholic emancipators is separation from Great Britain; and if they succeed, separation or war must be the issue.

'From the moment that this fatal infatuation appeared in the other House of Parliament I stated in that House that it would lead to the event which I have now only to lament. In 1785 and 1789 I warned the nation of the consequences to which the giddy and fantastical speculations which then prevailed must lead. Till the modern Irish patriots had divided the Protestants of Ireland into opposite factions, we never heard of claims for political power advanced by Papists—nothing at all in the shape of a claim of right. What they desired was sued for as a favour; whatever was granted was accepted with gratitude . . .

'I meddle not with the speculative opinions of any Catholic. If he choose to subscribe to articles of faith which my reason and understanding reject, that is his business, not mine; but I object to all communication with the Court of Rome. Those who adhere to the Court of Rome are enemies to the realm of England, and unfit for any trust in a Protestant country. I wish young gentlemen who have urged the expediency of a total repeal of the Popery laws, and have offered to embrace their Catholic brethren for the wise purpose of resisting English influence, would take the trouble to look into the laws of the Roman Catholic Church, where they will find the principles of fraternity on which their Popish fellow-subjects are willing to meet them, and the Constitution under which they will be governed, should this become a Popish country . . .

'There is, as I learn from a modern publication of Doctor Troy, a standing Cabinet of Cardinals at Rome for the government of Ireland—I presume the Cardinal of York is at the head of it—and the mild superintending influence of this Cabinet on the Irish Catholics will have the best effects in cultivating the hereditary attachment to the British nation . . . . I do not scruple to say that, in my opinion, it is an act of insanity in the Parliament of Ireland to open the efficient political power of the State to persons in communion with the Court of Rome. If they do not make use of them to subvert a Protestant Government, they must resist the ruling passions and propensities of the human mind . . . If we go a step further in innovation, if we agree to what is called Reform, this country is lost. I very much fear we have already made a precipitate and indiscreet experiment. The right reverend prelate says that the Catholics demand emancipation, that the people of Great Britain demand it for them, and that Great Britain will no longer assist the Protestants of Ireland in a system of oppression. The crooked folly of man could not have suggested a more mischievous observation. Great Britain must maintain her connection with Ireland, and she can only maintain it by maintaining the descendants of the English settlers, who, with few exceptions, form the Protestant interest there; and they in turn, however foolishly some of them may have acted in the last ten years, must know they can maintain their own position only by adhering to Great Britain.

'The descendants of the old Irish who constitute the Catholic interest feel that they can never recover the situation which their ancestors held in Ireland but by separation from Great Britain; and therefore if any man in Great Britain or Ireland is so wild as to hope that by communicating political power to the Catholics of Ireland they can be conciliated to British interests, he will find himself bitterly mistaken. Great Britain can never conciliate the descendants of the old Irish to her interests upon any other terms than by restoring to them the possessions and the religion of their ancestors in full splendour and dominion.'

BOOK VIII.
1793.
March.

Having thus relieved his mind, and having spoken what, however English statesmen might please to quarrel with it, was, is, and will be the exact truth upon the subject, the Chancellor concluded with saying that he would not divide the House against the Bill; and it was allowed to pass.

No immediately serious consequences were to be apprehended till the passing of a Reform Bill, and against a Reform Bill the Cabinet was firm. The Dungannon Convention met on the 15th of February, and decided that they must have it. Grattan brought the question before the House without waiting for the report of the committee. He electrified his hearers with the brilliancy of his oratory, but he failed to convince them that the Reform and Emancipation combined did not mean revolution. They admired the rhetoric; they acted by common sense.

'We have risks,' said Dennis Brown, 'like other countries, but risks peculiar to ourselves. Timidity is not the way of safety. If we are to be directed by every breath of discontent, there is an end of us; property, life, and liberty will be buried in anarchy and confusion.'

The Reform Bill had been called in the debate 'an olive-branch of peace.' 'The olive,' said Bushe, 'is like other trees, and will not take root if planted in a storm. If you must touch the foundation of the building which has sheltered yourselves and your ancestors, let it be when the winds are at peace. You are choosing the Equinox, when Government and Anarchy are contending like day and night.' Grattan himself would probably not have demanded Reform at such a moment, had he not known that success was impossible. The House understood that after the concessions to the Catholics their hope of safety lay in strengthening the Executive Government, and they threw out the Reform Bill by a majority which for the present quenched the agitation.

The strength of Government was concentrated in resisting Reform, because Reform, among its other effects, would have been fatal to the Union; on all else the rule was to give way. After resisting for sixty years, the Cabinet consented to a limitation of the Pension List, which was reduced to 80,000*l.* a year; the Hereditary Revenue was surrendered and exchanged for a Civil List;[1] while a further Act for securing the independence of Parliament closed a scandalous chapter in the constitutional history of Ireland; and persons holding pensions during pleasure, or any salaried office under the Crown, were declared ineligible to any future Legislature.[2] The present House had still four years to run. In parting with the power which hitherto had alone enabled the Viceroys to carry on the Government, Pitt, it is likely, had already determined that the days of an independent Irish Legislature were numbered.

[1] 33 George III., cap. 34. [2] 33 George III., cap. 41.

SECTION II.

BOOK VIII.
1793.
April.

Had the gains and losses in the game of intrigue been confined to the players, their strokes and counter-strokes might have been observed with contemptuous interest. Behind Ministers and delegates lay unhappily the Irish people, who were being driven mad by visionary hopes, and through a thousand channels were taught to look for the day when Ireland would be once more their own, and the tyranny of centuries would be over. They were told that they were emancipated. To them emancipation meant that they were to pay no more rents and tithes. They heard of religious equality. If religious equality was to be worth having, it implied equality of property, land at ten shillings an acre or no shillings, and the sacred soil of Ireland no longer trampled by the hoof of the invader.[1]

The determination of Pitt to force on the Catholic question had passed like a stream of oxygen over the half-smothered and smouldering ashes. Savage at the submission of the Catholic Committee to Major Hobart's terms, the agitators told the peasantry that they were betrayed. The Defenders became every hour more numerous and more audacious. The United Irishmen of Dublin published a furious attack on the Secret Committee of the Lords which was almost an invitation to violence. The Government had little fear of open rebellion. They had great and well-grounded fears for the lives of the Protestant fami-

---

[1] Miscellaneous reports from the South and West of Ireland, April and May, 1793. S. P. O.

THE FITZWILLIAM CRISIS.

lies who were scattered over the country by secret assassination.

To chain up the incendiary spirit before the fire spread further they summoned Simon Butler and Oliver Bond[1] to the Bar of the Upper House, sent them for six months to Newgate for breach of privilege, and fined each of them 500*l*. The increase of the army made possible at last more vigorous measures against the Defenders. Throughout the midland counties the peasants were now armed, either out of the Volunteer stores surreptitiously dispersed among them, or by the plunder of the houses of Protestants. They were not afraid to meet the troops in the field: 'in Louth fifty of them were killed in a single fight in February; above a hundred were lodged in gaol; yet the Government felt that they were not yet at the bottom of the plot.'[2]

Undeterred by the suppression of 'the National Guard' in Dublin, the Northern Republicans paraded in green uniforms at Belfast. General Whyte was sent down in March to enforce submission. The Liberal journals published blazing stories of dragoons dashing through the streets with drawn sabres, insulting Patriot tradesmen and behaving like infuriated savages, till the heroic Volunteers drew out and drove them from the town.[3] General Whyte tells what really occurred. He had sent four troops of the 17th Dragoons to disarm the 'Guard.' On the evening of the 9th of March a corporal and a private, off duty, strolled out of the barracks into the city, where they met a crowd of people round a fiddler, who was

1793.
April.

---

[1] The Chairman and Secretary of the Dublin lodge.
[2] 'Ed. Cooke to Nepean, Feb. 26, 1793.'
[3] See Tone's *Memoirs*, March, 1793.

playing *Ça ira*. They told the fiddler to play 'God Save the King.' The mob damned the King, with all his dirty slaves, and threw a shower of stones at them. The two dragoons, joined by a dozen of their comrades, drew their sabres and 'drove the town before them.' Patriot Belfast had decorated its shops with sign-boards representing Republican notables. The soldiers demolished Dumourier, demolished Mirabeau, demolished 'the venerable Franklin.'[1] The Patriots, so brave in debate, so eloquent in banquet, ran before a dozen Englishmen. A hundred and fifty Volunteers came out, but retreated into the Exchange and barricaded themselves. The officers of the 17th came up before any one had been seriously hurt, and recalled the men to their quarters. In the morning General Whyte came in from Carrickfergus, went to the Volunteer committee room, and said that unless the gentlemen in the Exchange came out and instantly dispersed, he would order the regiment under arms. They obeyed without a word. 'Never,' said Whyte, 'was any guard relieved with more satisfaction to themselves.'[2] The dragoons received a reprimand, but not too severe, as the General felt that they had done more good than harm. On the 11th the Sovereign of Belfast was informed that the meeting of unauthorised armed associations was now forbidden by law; the Volunteers must cease to exist, and if they again assembled they would be apprehended and punished. The order was obeyed. 'The citizen defenders of Ireland's liberties,' said the 'Northern Star,' the organ of the United Irishmen, 'considered it more

---

[1] McCabe, the owner of one of these shops, hung up his own portrait afterwards in the place of the destroyed friend of liberty, with the words 'McCabe, an Irish slave.'

[2] Report of General Whyte, enclosed in a letter of March 19 from Westmoreland to Dundas.

magnanimous' to bow for the present to tyranny. 'The time would come, and come shortly, when Ireland might see the saviours of the country once more in formidable array.'

To this had sunk the famous Volunteers of Ireland —the wonder of the world. The time for their reappearance did not come, and here was their final end. Their glory was to have won an independence which when brought to the test of fact was found 'a thing of sound and fury, signifying nothing.' Independence which was to be more than a name had first to be fought for; and the Volunteers being formed of materials too worthless even for rebellion, were at last extinguished with ignominy.

The peasantry, unhappily for themselves, were made of sterner stuff. They boasted less. They passed no resolutions about the inalienable rights of man; but they had in them the ancient inbred hatred of the Saxon conquerors. Coercion had awed them into submission, but with the first signs of weakness in the ruling powers the hereditary animosity revived. The landlords had sown the wind and were to reap the whirlwind. The Irish nation, as it is passionate and revengeful, so beyond most others it is malleable by just authority. The Celtic 'earth-tiller' will repay his liege lord for kindness and generosity with romantic fidelity. Two centuries had been allowed to the Saxon intruders to win the affection of the native race. The Irish peasants remained in rags like their ancestors; lodged under one roof with their pigs and cows, paying rent to masters who had no care for their bodies; paying tithes to clergy who cared as little for their souls; maintaining gallantly, in the midst of their wretchedness, their own hedge-schools and their own priests; crooning their own songs and airs, and nursing their melancholy history; every rock and glen peopled with traditions of some battle with the Saxons, some daring exploit of hunted rapparees. So it had gone on till they were told that their chain was broken. They looked into the justice which was said to have been done at last, and they found that it meant no more than the privilege of helping to send one of their Protestant masters to Parliament. They heard that if they wanted more they must arm, as the Volunteers had armed. They must make the Government afraid of them, and the Government would then give them their way.

So long as the Catholic Committee was sitting in Dublin the outbreaks of violence had been local, and under the influence of the priests the advanced Catholic patriots had abstained from organised conspiracy. In that body there was no longer hope. A general meeting of the Committee was called on the 16th of April, to review the conduct of Keogh and the delegates. They had accepted Hobart's terms, and had promised that the Committee should be dissolved. Half the members of it believed that the cause had been betrayed. The Secretary ought to have been told to take back his Bill. The delegates ought to have insisted on the fulfilment of Dundas's promises. The country would then have been roused, and complete Emancipation and Parliamentary Reform would have been carried together. Keogh defended himself, but little to the satisfaction of his revolutionary friends. He was suspected of looking coldly on France, and of doubting whether the Catholic interests would be promoted by an alliance with the Jacobins. For a week it hung uncertain whether the Committee would consent to disappear, or whether it would continue as a 'National Congress, pledged to the most violent measures.'[1]

1793.
April.

The moderate party carried the day at last. The members promised to work individually for Reform. As a representative body they decided to cease to exist. They passed a vote of thanks to the Viceroy in the name of the Roman Catholics of Ireland. The acceptance of it gratified their pride.[2] Not to quarrel with their revolutionary supporters, they voted 1,500*l.* to Wolfe Tone for his services, and as much to Simon Butler and Todd Jones; and the Catholic Committee and the Catholic Association, which had now merged into one, then suspended their further sessions. But they parted in discontent. The moderate Catholics, though successful for the moment, lost their influence in the country. The United Irishmen became now the recognised leaders of all who desired the regeneration of their country, and the Catholic Defenders, passing rapidly under their orders, became the recognised army of liberty.

With the avowed purpose of preventing the enrolment of the militia, the peasantry rose simultaneously in Sligo, Mayo, Roscommon, Leitrim, Limerick, Clare, and Kerry. The regular army was still far short of its numbers, and was entirely unequal to the task of controlling so large a tract of country. Mr. Tennison's house at Coalville was burnt, and three soldiers were killed. Marcray Castle, in Sligo, the house of Mr.

---

[1] 'Mr. Hamilton to Major Hobart, April 22.' S. P. O. Compare Tone's *Journal*, April 16.

[2] 'It was represented to the Viceroy that the designation implied that the Committee was a representative body, and that he ought not to receive it. Had he refused he would have thrown them into the arms of the United Irishmen. The pail of milk would have been kicked down, and all the confusion renewed.'— Mr. Hamilton to Major Hobart, April 22.

Cowper, a staunch Protestant member of Parliament, was sacked, the arms carried off, and the cellars emptied. Mr. Wilson's house at Castlecomer was destroyed, and Mr. Wilson murdered. The town of Carrick was attacked. Some dragoons in the barracks there charged the mob, shot down thirty or forty, and took many more. The prisoners were sullen and savage; they were heard to mutter that 'in a month not a Protestant would be alive in Ireland.'[1] The spirit of 1641 was awake again. The insurgents' oath in Mayo was to pay neither tithe nor tax, quit-rent or landlord's rent.[2] A Defender, mortally wounded in a fight, declared 'that when the Protestants and Presbyterians were disarmed they were all to be murdered in one night.' Copies of Paine's 'Rights of Man' were sown broadcast by the agents of the United Lodges. As summer approached Queen's County, Carlow, Wexford, Kilkenny, caught fire also. The cry rose that the French were coming to set Ireland free. A mob attacked the barracks at Dingle, meaning when they had destroyed the soldiers to dispose afterwards of the gentry. They were disappointed. The soldiers received them with a volley; fourteen fell dead; the rest fled, and were pursued and bayoneted. Thirty-six miserable wretches were killed at a fight in Erris. There was another sanguinary engagement at Enniscorthy, in Wexford. The village of Bruff, in Limerick, was occupied in force, the streets were barricaded, the houses loopholed, and the Defenders were only driven out of it at last by cannon.

'The country,' wrote a correspondent of Mr. Burke

---

[1] 'Reports from the West, May 20, 1793.' S. P. O.

[2] 'Westmoreland to Dundas, June 8.'

from Limerick, in July, 'is in a state of complete insurrection. We hear of nothing but outrages committed by armed mobs; and the country people, notwithstanding the numbers of them that have been already killed in these engagements with the army, seem to increase in ferocity and resolution in proportion to their losses. A few days ago there was an engagement at Kilfinnan, in which the greatest part of the town was destroyed; and the next day at Bruff, in which many of the poor wretches were killed. They have no fixed object, but a spirit has been excited of general discontent and opposition. Parties of armed people go about administering oaths, in some places against the militia, in others to pay no taxes, in others to pay no tithes. The consequence is, a furious spirit of opposition to the ruling powers in the lower classes of the people.'[1]

Supported by this bloody outbreak of disaffection, the United Irelanders opened their agitation for Parliamentary Reform, as the only measure which it was supposed would now quiet the disturbance. They published an address to the Catholics, inviting them

[1] This letter was forwarded by Richard Burke to Dundas, with characteristic comments of his own. 'I know,' he said, 'that an anonymous letter will have more weight with you than the most deliberate opinion which I or my father can give. Such is the effect of the service which he has rendered your Government. I also have been of service to you. If any part of the empire, or the whole of it, should be lost by the incurable alienation and distrust of the present Government towards us both, it will be a great fatality, but one which is within the bounds of possibility. I have done my best to prevent it—if that were the way to prevent it—by bearing without complaint or discouragement the worst possible treatment. What you are to do with Ireland in the condition to which those who have the honour to govern that country, under your auspices, have reduced it I am sure I know not: it begins to be above me. I shall endeavour, however, to exculpate myself from the effects of their misgovernment.' — R. Burke to Mr. Dundas, from Beaconsfield, July 30, 1793.

BOOK VIII.
1793.
June.

to join in demanding a measure without which they would find the franchise useless to them.¹ They informed 'the people of Ireland' that in declaring war against the Revolution, England was declaring war against liberty. They bade them 'Assemble, assemble, and with the voice of injured millions demand their rights;' and having felt the strength which agitation gathered from having at its head a representative Assembly, they invited Ireland to choose another, this time a true national association, which traitors should have no power to mislead; and they chose for the place of meeting, not Dublin, where Fitzgibbon might have them in his grasp, but Athlone, far away in the country, in the heart of the faithful Catholic population.

Parliament was still in session, busy with its Responsibility Bill and its new Civil List. The Catholic Committee had not been dissolved that its place might be taken by another and more dangerous Assembly of a similar kind. The Athlone Parliament would be composed of the most violent agitators in Ireland, and if allowed to meet would provide the anarchists with an organised Directory. On July 8 Fitzgibbon introduced a Bill into the House of Lords declaring the assemblage of bodies of men calling themselves representatives under any pretence whatsoever to be thenceforth illegal.² The glamour of '82 had not yet entirely vanished. Patriotic sensibility was wounded by a measure which reflected on the great Dungannon meeting. The Duke of Leinster and Lord Charlemont fought against it in one House. Grattan, in the other, spoke of it as the boldest step yet made to introduce military government.

¹ *Proceedings of the United Irishmen*, June 7, 1793.
² 33 George III., cap. 29.

Patriotic oratory, though it could still enchant, could no longer wholly make men blind. Tom Conolly, who was drunk when he rose to speak, said that although he must vote with his friends, he heartily approved of the resolution which the Castle was showing. The Bill was carried, the teller for the Government in the Commons being Arthur Wellesley; and the meeting of a fresh Convention, which in the distracted state of the country 'would have been an engine of mischief almost irresistible,' was thus prevented.[1]

With the Convention Bill the session which had restored the Catholics to the Constitution came to an end. The concession of the franchise, in itself so momentous, was accompanied by the surrender of those irregular methods by which England had hitherto controlled the independence of Parliament. The millions to whose 'unfailing loyalty' these gracious measures were designed as a reward had received them in a manner which anyone who knew Ireland could have foretold with certainty. The Irish peasant, like some half-tamed animal, docile under restraint, and obedient and uncomplaining when governed with firmness and justice, if let loose and told to be his own governor flies with a blind instinct at the hand which has unlocked his chains. Pitt and Dundas, partly misled by Burke, deceived partly by their own theories, partly feeling their way by a tortuous road towards a Union, had taken a step which made the Union a certainty, but no less certainly made inevitable, as preliminary to it, a desperate and bloody insurrection.[2]

[1] 'Major Hobart to Evan Nepean, July 20.'

[2] Major Hobart left Ireland at the close of this session, to be

SECTION III.

THE air was charged with revolution. Each week brought news from France which set the patriots' pulses bounding. Lord Moira, who was now the hope of the Irish incendiaries, allowed himself to play with their expectations. They gave him a dinner in

created Lord Hobart, and to be sent as Governor to Madras.

Richard Burke was so indignant at an appointment which he regarded as a sign of the Cabinet's approval of Hobart's conduct in Ireland, that he actually remonstrated with Dundas, and sent Hobart a copy of what he had said, with a very curious letter:—

'Brighton, October 28.

'My Lord,—On the entrance to a political and criminatory discussion, to disclaim motives of personal animosity is a proceeding that may be liable to inconvenience. It may appear like mean affectation, or an ungenerous desire to extenuate the hostility which necessarily belongs to adverse discussions. On the other hand, not to disclaim those motives is to forego the satisfaction warranted by the most vulgar example of doing my part at least to divest the contests we engage in from every mixture of private asperity. The former inconvenience seems to me to be the least. I do not, therefore, hesitate to assure your lordship that I act on the present occasion solely upon public grounds, and without any resentful recollection of any occurrence in Ireland less pleasant which might be attributed to your lordship. I allude particularly to the treatment I received in the House of Commons on the day of Sir Hercules Langrishe's proposition. And if there is anything in my letter to Mr. Dundas which may appear peculiarly invidious and offensive to you, it does not proceed from personal ill will, but is, as I conceive, necessitated by the circumstances which do not allow me to remit anything of the strength of my case.

'In the next place, I have to assure your lordship that the sole objection I have to your appointment to the Government of Madras is that it operates as a sanction and ratification to those measures which I feel myself under an indispensable obligation to criminate, as the only means to obviate the ill effects upon the peace and welfare of Ireland, upon his Majesty's Government there, and upon the unity and strength of the empire.

'Mr. Dundas will inform your lordship that I have never ceased to represent the measures of your Government in the same point of view that I do now, which, if he has not informed you of, it is not my fault; and if your lordship will recollect the conversation I had the honour of having with you at your

Dublin, and an ardent orator spoke allusively of the great work which might lie before him. Moira, not disclaiming the possibility, replied, 'that when he appeared it would be as a rainbow to notify to distant countries that the tempest was over.'[1] But for the present the Convention Bill, backed by the militia, drove in the disaffection. The United Irishmen confessed themselves baffled, but 'vowed revenge.' Hamilton Rowan was reported as having grown 'morose, sullen, and determined.'[2] Thomas Muir, who was tried afterwards at Edinburgh for treason, had paid the society a visit in Dublin. The society in return voted an address to their Scotch brethren, and Rowan was sent over in charge of it. A prosecution was already hanging over him for a treasonable address. The Chancellor, finding forbearance thrown away, sent a warrant after him to Scotland. He was

house in the Phœnix Park, you will not be surprised that I arraign your conduct criminally, and particularly in the capacity of a servant of the Crown. Many other measures have since occurred which I have the misfortune of considering in a still more serious point of view. Your late appointment is no further the occasion of the step I am now taking than that it hastens the execution of a first intention to render these affairs the subject of public discussion in this kingdom; and as, by the marked recognition of the measures of the Irish Government implied by that appointment, it induces me to lodge a series of criminal charges against that Government in the person of your lordship.

'After what I have said at the beginning it is almost unnecessary for me to express that I do not decline any sort of public or private responsibility which may attach to the course which I have taken, or may hereafter take. The charges I shall pursue by such methods as shall appear to me most advisable to give them solemnity and effect.

'I have the honour to be, &c.,
'RICHARD BURKE.
'Rt. Honble. Lord Hobart.'

Hobart, enclosing the letter to Nepean, says:—'Every circumstance induces me to agree with you in thinking him entirely mad, and I only regret that the discovery was not made some time ago.'—*MSS. Ireland.* S. P. O. October 1793.

[1] 'Major Hobart to Evan Nepean, August 27, 1793.' S. P. O.
[2] Note, unsigned, from an informer. 1793. S. P. O.

arrested, brought back, tried, and sentenced to two years' imprisonment, and to pay a fine of 500*l*.

There was now an interval of calm. The conspirators were frightened. The session of 1794 was a blank. The Opposition in Parliament was disheartened and divided, all but the most reckless patriots having been sobered by the bloodshed of the past summer. William Ponsonby tried a Reform Bill again. It was extinguished by a decisive division of 142 to 44. The revolutionary peace party was equally unsuccessful. Grattan had promised Parnell that if the Place and Pension Bills were conceded, he would make no further 'vexatious opposition.'[1] He redeemed his word by speaking in favour of the war and by repeating what he had said in 1782, that in a foreign contest Ireland was bound to stand or fall with Great Britain. The authority of Grattan was decisive with all who were not consciously disloyal.[2] The supplies were voted. All necessary business was hurried over, and in the general desire to leave the Executive untrammelled, Parliament was prorogued on March 25.

The Executive had need to be free. Driven from the open field, the United Irishmen were now preparing for rebellion. The eye of the Castle was on them. From the very first, traitors among themselves carried their most secret whispers to the Secretary. Every step on which they ventured was known, but so known only that it could be watched, not interfered with. Informers' evidence was not producible in a court of justice. Occasionally the conspirators were

---

[1] 'E. Cooke to Evan Nepean, February 7, 1794.' S. P. O.

[2] 'I never saw greater marks of chagrin painted on countenances than on those of Geo. Ponsonby, Curran, Egan, and the lawyers in opposition, when Grattan declared his resolution to support the war.'—*Ibid.*

startled at their work by some public proclamation which proved that they were betrayed. The informers in such cases were removed from Ireland, and settled with a pension in another country.¹ Sometimes the information came from England. A week after Parliament rose the Viceroy was warned to be on the lookout for a dangerous visitor. The French Directory were anxious to discover the resources of the advocates of liberty in England and Ireland. They had employed a Protestant clergyman named Jackson, a friend of the famous Duchess of Kingston, and an ardent disciple of the new doctrines, to feel the pulse of the two countries and ascertain what kind of reception might be expected by an invading force. Jackson came from Paris to London in February, and there renewed his acquaintance with the Duchess of Kingston's attorney, a man named Cockayne. He was indiscreet enough to reveal the nature of his mission. Cockayne carried the information to Pitt, and at Pitt's suggestion he volunteered to accompany Jackson to Ireland, and communicate his movements to the Castle.

The pair arrived in Dublin on the 1st of April. Jackson called at once on a second old acquaintance, MacNally, a popular barrister. MacNally invited him and Cockayne to dinner, where they met Simon Butler, Ed. Lewines, another United Irishman, and several more. The conversation was free and

---

¹ Mr. Collins, a silk mercer, of Dublin, was one of the first of these useful betrayers of the secrets of the United Irishmen. He was a member of the Dublin lodge; and, from the day of his election, was in communication with Lord Westmoreland. After Rowan's imprisonment, his further residence in Ireland was unsafe. 200*l.* a year was settled upon him, and he was recommended for a situation in the West Indies.—' Cooke to Nepean. Secret. May 26, 1794.

treasonable. Jackson asked to be introduced to Hamilton Rowan, who was then in Newgate. The prison rules were construed lightly in favour of gentlemen of fortune. Rowan was allowed to entertain his friends in his private room, and having learnt Jackson's object in coming to Ireland, received him and Cockayne at breakfast, Wolfe Tone making a fourth, as a fit person to negotiate with France. Tone had already sketched a paper to be laid before the Directory, describing the state of Irish parties, the numerical weakness of the gentry, the hatred felt for them by Catholics and Dissenters, and the certainty that if France would assist, the Government could be easily overthrown.[1] It was suggested that Tone himself should go to France and concert measures with the chiefs of the Revolution. Tone hesitated, remembered that he had a wife and children, and for the first time in his life showed prudence. Rowan copied out the paper, and gave the copy to Jackson, who folded and sealed it, addressed it to a correspondent at Hamburgh, and gave it to Cockayne to put in the post. Cockayne, who had already set the police on the alert, allowed himself to be taken with the paper on his person. Jackson was arrested. A friend warned Rowan of his danger; and he knowing that if his handwriting could be proved he would be hanged, persuaded the gaoler to let him go that night to his own house to see his wife. The gaoler went with him, to ensure his safe return to Newgate, but not to intrude upon his prisoner's privacy, waited during the interview in the passage. Rowan slipped through a back window, mounted a horse, and escaped

---

[1] This paper is printed in the *Life of Wolfe Tone*, vol. i. p. 277.

to a friend's house at Howth, where he lay concealed till a smuggler could be found who would convey a gentleman in difficulties to France. A couple of adventurous men were ready with their services. A day's delay was necessary to prepare their vessel, and meanwhile a proclamation was out with an offer of a reward of 2,000*l.* for Rowan's apprehension. The smugglers guessed who their charge must be; but in such circumstances a genuine Irishman would rather be torn by horses than betray a life trusted to him. They swore to land Rowan safe, and three days after he was in Brittany.[1]

Rowan was beyond the reach of the Government, but Tone remained; and there was Dr. Drennan, also an energetic incendiary, with whom Jackson had communicated, who had long been an object of anxiety. Dundas, to whom the Viceroy wrote for advice, recommended that Jackson should be admitted as an approver. With Jackson and Cockayne for witnesses, Tone and Drennan could be tried and hanged. The Viceroy was obliged to answer that no Irish jury would convict on such evidence. The attempt would end in disgrace.[2] Jackson himself could be convicted; but about this, too, there was difficulty, for Cockayne had disappeared. Knowing that his life would not be safe in Dublin for an hour, he had stolen away on the instant that the mine was exploded, and was again in London. He was found

---

[1] Hamilton Rowan here disappears from the story. He went to America, and was condemned in his absence for treason. Fitzgibbon, however, interfered to save his large estates for his family, and in 1799, when the rebellion was over, promised to procure his pardon. Fitzgibbon died before the promise could be redeemed, but he left it in charge to Castlereagh's care. In 1805 the pardon was made out, and Rowan returned to Ireland, where he lived quietly the rest of his life.

[2] 'Westmoreland to Dundas, May 12.'

and carried back to Holyhead, where he fell ill with terror, and could not be moved. At length, but not till after a year's delay, he was carried over and kept under guard, and in April 1795 Jackson was brought to the bar. His trial was the first of the list in which Curran was to earn immortality as the advocate of misguided patriots. Curran, George Ponsonby, MacNally, T. Emmett, Guinness, all the strength which Irish Liberalism could command, was enlisted in the prisoner's service. Curran's skill in torturing informers was as striking as his eloquence. He stretched Cockayne as painfully as ever the rackmaster of the Tower stretched a Jesuit. He made him confess that he had been employed by Pitt. He showed that if Jackson was a traitor to the State, Cockayne was a far blacker traitor to the friend who trusted him. Lord Clonmel, who presided, explained to the jury that if they disbelieved Cockayne the case must fall. But Jackson's guilt was too patent to leave excuse for doubt. The trial lasted till four in the morning, but the jury required but half-an-hour to consider their verdict. A remand was ordered for four days, at the end of which the prisoner was to be brought again to the bar to receive sentence. Irish history is full of melodrama, but never was stranger scene witnessed in a court of justice than when Jackson appeared again. It was April 30, 1795. On his passage through the streets in a carriage he was observed to be deadly pale; once he hung his head out of the window and was sick. The crowd thought he was afraid. At the bar he could scarcely stand; and Lord Clonmel seeing his wretched state, would have hurried through his melancholy office. The prisoner was told to raise his hand. He lifted it feebly and let it fall. He was called on to say why sentence should not be passed against him. He could not speak. Clonmel was proceeding, when first Curran and then Ponsonby interposed with points of form. As Ponsonby was speaking Jackson fell forward over the bar. The windows were thrown open. It was thought that he had fainted. The attendants caught him, and he sank back into a chair insensible.

'If the prisoner cannot hear me,' Clonmel said, 'I cannot pass judgment. He must be taken away. The Court must adjourn.' 'My Lord,' said the Sheriff, 'the prisoner is dead.' To escape the disgrace of execution he had taken arsenic in his tea at his breakfast, and chose to leave the world in this theatric fashion.

In a note which he had left in his room he had bequeathed his family to the French Directory, but philosophy had not entirely stifled the sad voice of the creed of his earlier age. In his pocket was found a paper, on which was written in his own hand: 'Turn thou unto me and have mercy upon me, for I am desolate and in misery. The troubles of my heart are enlarged. Oh bring thou me out of my affliction. Look on my affliction and my pain and forgive me all my sins.'

SECTION IV.

BOOK VIII.
1794.

BEFORE the appearance of Jackson in Ireland a French invasion had been contemplated as a too likely possibility.[1] There was no longer a doubt that a campaign in Ireland was deliberately contemplated, and if attempted would cause immediate insurrection. A powerful party, of whom Burke was the principal, were for ever clamouring to Pitt that the renewed disturbances were only due to the imperfect confidence which had been placed in the Catholics, and to the exasperation created by the repressive measures of Lord Westmoreland. The Cabinet was modified in the summer of 1794 by the accession of the moderate Whigs. Portland, Spenser, and Fitzwilliam became members of Pitt's Administration. Portland, who had had experience of Ireland, was less sanguine than his friends on the good effects to be expected from conciliation. Spenser and Fitzwilliam were as confident as Dundas that if the Catholic gentry and prelates could be introduced into the Government, the body of the people would immediately return to their duty. In August leading Irishmen of different shades of opinion were invited to London. The two Ponsonbies, Grattan, Sir John Parnell, and others

---

[1] 'The French will not act with the desperate ability which they have manifested on other occasions if they do not make some attempt on Ireland. If once established here, in however small numbers, they might raise a convulsion that would require the whole exertions of England to repress. The people of property are well-disposed, but the lower orders would rejoice in every opportunity of plundering them, and revenging what they would call the cause of their ancestors.'—'Westmoreland to Dundas, January 14.'

saw Pitt collectively and separately. They found him
cold and reserved, rather looking for their views than
offering his own. They spoke of drawing together
the Protestant and Catholic gentry. 'But whose,' he
asked sharply, remembering the Commercial Propositions, 'whose will they be when they are reconciled?'
'What did Ireland want?' he said to Grattan. Her
taxes, in proportion to her wealth, were lighter than
the English; the East Indian monopoly had been
relaxed in her favour. Not a single commercial
privilege which England possessed was withheld from
her. What more would she have? Grattan said she
required the admission of the Catholics to Parliament,
and Pitt let him go away with the impression that
although it would not be made a Government measure
it would not be opposed.

To give political power to men already in a state
of incipient rebellion as a bribe to quiet them has
never, except in Ireland, been considered a hopeful
policy, nor in Ireland has it been found to succeed
better than elsewhere. Pitt was thinking of a
Union; and could he have been sure that the Union
could be secured, the venture, though a hazardous
one, might still have been risked without extreme
imprudence: but the companion measure of Emancipation would be almost necessarily Reform; and
Pitt's ignorance of the country must have been extraordinary, even in an English Prime Minister, if he
could dream that Catholic Ireland, in constitutional
possession of the power which the majority of numbers
would confer on the Catholic party, would then be
persuaded to part with her ascendancy. No one
now can tell what Pitt precisely thought. Certain
only it is that he resolved at last, and that he

brought the King to consent, to recall Lord Westmoreland, and to appoint in his place Grattan's intimate friend, and a most ardent supporter of Catholic Emancipation, Lord Fitzwilliam. It is certain also that the appointment of Lord Fitzwilliam was to imply a change of measures, an attempt of some kind to conciliate, and the admission into the Council of the leading members of the Irish Opposition. There had been hesitation and more than one change of purpose. In August Fitzwilliam told Grattan that all was settled, that he was going over, as the Duke of Portland had gone in '82, with power to act as circumstances might require.[1] Two months passed. Pitt was still undecided, and Grattan had learnt that if Fitzwilliam went at all it would be with precise instructions, which he would not be at liberty to set aside.[2]

The difficulty may have arisen with the King. George the Third knew his own mind about Ireland, and could he have been listened to, would have made crooked things straight there thirty years before without Catholic Emancipation. The resolution, however, was taken at last. Fitzwilliam was to go, and took the oaths in the King's presence on December 10, Grattan being present at the ceremony. It was to be presumed from the selection of a person whose opinions were so well known that in some degree he was to be allowed to act on them. But in detail his hands were tied. He had desired to dismiss the whole body of the Irish advisers of Lord Westmoreland as personally hateful to the people. He was forbidden to dismiss any of them

---

[1] 'Fitzwilliam to Grattan, August 23.'—*Grattan's Life*, vol. iv.

[2] 'Grattan to McCan, October 27.'—*Ibid.*

without special permission from England. With regard to the Catholic question, 'Lord Fitzwilliam was to endeavour to prevent it from being agitated at all. If he failed, he was to use his diligence in collecting the opinions and sentiments of all descriptions of persons and transmit them for the information of his Majesty.'[1]

The limitation was unsatisfactory to Grattan, whose dream was to force Emancipation, and by Emancipation realise at last his passionately hoped-for Irish nationality. It should not fail, at all events, for want of agitation. Instantly, on the completion of the ceremony, he hurried back to Ireland. With less than his usual truthfulness, he made free use of Fitzwilliam's name. He told the Catholics that they had only to ask loud enough for all their demands to be conceded, and a committee was organised, on which were the names of Dr. Macneven and Richard McCormick,[2] to address Fitzwilliam on his arrival in the name of the Catholic body.

Fitzwilliam had misconceived his directions, or imagined that he had, after all, discretionary power. Fitzgibbon was too high game to be struck at without preparation; but the first act of the Viceroy on arriving at the Castle, notwithstanding positive commands to the contrary, was to shake off such servants of the Crown as had been especially in Lord Westmoreland's confidence. John Beresford, the Chief

---

[1] 'This is the account which was given by the Cabinet in the following March to Lord Camden.'—*MSS. Ireland. Secret.* March 20, 1795. S. P. O. . . . It may be taken as conclusive on this much-disputed point.

[2] McCormick was Tone's friend Magog, whose religious opinions the reader will remember. Macneven, when examined afterwards before the secret committee of the House of Lords, acknowledged that Catholic Emancipation was never more than a pretence to help forward a revolution.

BOOK VIII.
1795.
January.

Commissioner of the Customs, received his dismissal; Edward Cooke received his dismissal. The Attorney and Solicitor Generalship were required for George Ponsonby and Curran; and Wolfe and Toler received an intimation that as soon as formal consent could be obtained from England their services would no longer be required.[1] Personally convinced of the necessity of giving way on the Catholic question, Fitzwilliam naturally found the agitation irresistible which Grattan had excited. Society was disorganised, respect for law destroyed, life and property totally without protection. The country would be uninhabitable without the instant enrolment of a constabulary and a yeomanry cavalry; but then a local force must necessarily be composed of Catholics, and Fitzwilliam had discovered that they could not be trusted with arms till the last of their political disabilities had been removed.

The first argument for admitting the Catholics to the Constitution had been their approved loyalty. Now the argument was their disloyalty, which no other remedy would remove. Yet so satisfied was Fitzwilliam with the force of his reasons, that he forgot or set aside his instructions. Instead of collecting opinions from persons of different views, and forwarding them for consideration of the Cabinet, he informed Portland, within a few days of his arrival, that delay was impossible, and that unless he was positively forbidden he should act on his own judgment.

'I distinctly for myself say,' he wrote, 'that not to grant cheerfully on the part of Government all

---

[1] 'Wolfe was to be pacified by the grant of a peerage to his wife.' —'Fitzwilliam to the Duke of Portland, January 8.' S. P. O.

the Catholics wish, will not only be exceedingly impolitic, but perhaps dangerous. The disaffection among the lower orders is universal. Though the violences now committing are not from political causes, but the outrages of banditti, they are fostered by that cause. The higher orders are firmly to be relied on ; the wealthy of the second class hardly less so, because they are fearful for their property; yet the latter at least have shown no forwardness to check these outrages, and this can only arise from there being something left which rankles in their bosoms . . . Don't delay to speak with Pitt on the subject. If I receive no peremptory directions to the contrary, I shall acquiesce with a good grace, to avoid the appearance of hesitation. Even the appearance will produce incalculable mischief—the loss of confidence of the Catholics, and the giving rise to a Protestant cabal . . . We know it must come sooner or later. Delay will only make the Catholics useless in the interval, if not dangerous.'[1]

Fitzwilliam had landed on the 4th of January. Ten days had sufficed to work so strong a conviction, that even the Cabinet was not to be allowed time for reflection. The Catholics were to be admitted into an Irish Parliament under conditions which must almost immediately give them an enormous preponderance, because they would no longer be loyal subjects of the Crown under other conditions. To such an attitude had concession brought the three million loyal hearts and hands who in the American war, when the penal laws were at their height, had laid themselves at the feet of the best of kings.

---

[1] 'Fitzwilliam to Portland, January 8 and 15.' Abridged.

Parliament opened on the 22nd. Fitzwilliam did not venture to fly so directly in the face of his orders as to recommend the Catholic claims from the throne. The speech was long, pompous, and flatulent, but was silent on the great subject. Grattan, however, in the quasi position of a minister of the Crown, loaded the table with petitions industriously procured by his agents, and announced that on an early occasion he would himself introduce a bill for the complete abolition of all religious distinctions. Fitzwilliam informed the Chancellor that 'now that the question was in agitation, he should give Grattan his full support.' Fitzgibbon replied 'fully and earnestly, stating his alarms and the grounds of them;' but he concluded that the Viceroy must be acting by instructions, and that Pitt had decided finally in carrying out the policy which he knew to have been for several years in contemplation; he said that if England chose to have it so, the Irish Parliament could, no doubt, be forced into acquiescence.

Fitzwilliam implied as little uncertainty in his report to the Cabinet that he would meet with the fullest approbation of Pitt. He informed Portland on the 28th that everything would run smoothly

'Ireland,' he said—writing, of course, what Grattan told him—'will go even beyond my wishes. We propose to have forty thousand men in arms, raising the militia to twenty thousand, and the regulars to as many. We will send men to England; you must send others here, and I earnestly beg that we may have them . . . Besides these I look to a yeomanry cavalry; *but it must not, as I said, precede the Roman Catholic business. It will be prudent not to hurry the yeomanry question; for should the Catholic question fail*

THE FITZWILLIAM CRISIS.

we must think twice before we put arms into the hands of men newly irritated.' [1]

The misgiving implied in the last words referred evidently to the Irish Parliament, and not to any anticipated difficulty on the part of England. Meanwhile the Cabinet remained silent. One significant indication Pitt did give that he was not satisfied. He intimated his disapproval of the changes at the Castle. Beresford, who had gone to England to see him, returned to resume his place at the Revenue Board. He brought back with him an intimation that the resignations of Wolfe and Toler would not be accepted. But on the Catholic question the Viceroy received no directions at all. He had concealed nothing. He had spoken as plainly as possible of his own intention to support Grattan, yet week passed after week, and he heard nothing. Without fuller knowledge of what had passed privately between himself and Pitt before he left England, he cannot be acquitted of culpable precipitancy. As little is it possible to acquit the Cabinet of extraordinary negligence in allowing Fitzwilliam to commit himself so deeply if they were themselves still undecided; still less can they be acquitted for having kept in complete ignorance of the contents of Fitzwilliam's despatches a person whose consent was indispensable to any intended change.

Grattan's motion was fixed for the 12th of February. Perplexed rather than alarmed at finding his letters unanswered, Fitzwilliam begged him to postpone it, and again appealed to Portland.

'I trust,' he said, 'you and your colleagues will recom-

[1] 'Fitzwilliam to Portland, January 28, 1795.' S. P. O.

mend his majesty to permit the matter to be brought to a point. Equality is already granted in the Act of '93. It remains to be considered whether the symbol of it shall be granted or withheld. The peace, tranquillity, and harmony of the country may now be sealed and secured for ever. We cannot depend on the affection and attachment of the lower orders. The whole united strength of the higher may be necessary to control the lower in allegiance. In the face of what is going on abroad we must unite all the higher orders in a common cause. . . . Mr. Grattan's plan is a short and simple one. First, a general repeal of all restrictive and qualifying laws; that done, to alter the oaths, that the people may be made one Christian people, binding themselves by one civil oath in a common cause. You will ask do I mean to carry the principle to the full extent of a general capacity for every office? I certainly do, for all not regal or ecclesiastical. These I reserve, and these only. I would not reserve the highest office in the State—not the Seals nor the Bench. To make a reservation would be to leave a splinter in the wound. Should an enemy land, the safety of the kingdom depends on the unanimity of the higher orders, and that only—such is the insubordination of the lower, such their disaffection. These are my sentiments. Lay them before his majesty, and impress his majesty with the extent of the mischief that may probably arise by any attempt on my part, so acting in his Government, to oppose or circumscribe the measure of favour to the Catholics.'[1]

The worship of a formula by modern politicians is the exact equivalent of ancient idolatry, and is equally proof against the plainest evidence of sense. A Reform Bill would be the necessary consequence of emancipation. The peasantry already enfranchised would then be in possession of the entire power of the State, and their inveterate insubordination and disaffection was alleged as the reason for bestowing it upon them. Unfortunately, it was not only the alleged reason—it

---

[1] 'Fitzwilliam to the Duke of Portland, February 10. Secret and confidential.' S. P. O. Abridged.

was the real reason. The Viceroy, and to a large extent at least the Cabinet behind him, was possessed with the 'Irish idea' that fire could be extinguished by pouring oil upon it; and Grattan, who understood the situation, took care that the agitation should not slacken. Instead of emancipation, he moved on the 11th of February, as a means of restoring order, for the repeal of Fitzgibbon's Police Bill. On the 12th, unexpectedly, since it was understood that he was to apply for a postponement, he brought in his Catholic Bill, and Fitzwilliam on the 14th wrote once more with the most earnest emphasis to Pitt to tell him that the country was on the edge of rebellion, and that nothing but the Relief Bill could save it.

There are times in the highest affairs of State, as well as in matters of ordinary personal conduct, when the weak things of this world are chosen to confound the wise—when instinct is blind, and simplicity and honesty have their eyes open. If political ability consists in pursuing honourable aims, and in choosing means by which those aims can be effectually obtained, the ablest directions for the conduct of Ireland had been those which were drawn by George the Third in the year after his accession. Now at this critical moment, when the advisers of the Crown were walking in a dream, and would if left to themselves have doubtless gone where Grattan pleased to lead them, the King, whose advice had been neglected before, chose this time to be obeyed.

Up to the 5th of February, when the Cabinet had been themselves for three weeks at least aware of what Fitzwilliam was doing, the King had been kept in ignorance that any immediate step in favour of the Catholics was in contemplation. On that day he was informed, 'to his greatest astonishment,' that the Lord Lieutenant of Ireland had proposed a total and immediate change in the principles of government there, and that on the very next day the question was gravely to be laid before the Cabinet. With a simplicity equivalent to the keenest satire he informed Pitt that he could not reconcile himself in such hasty fashion to reversing the entire policy of the past century. To be told that former indulgences availed nothing without consenting further to a revolution, ' was the strongest justification of the old servants of the Crown in Ireland' who had objected to those indulgences. The course now entered upon must tend sooner or later to a separation of the kingdoms. It was contrary to the principles on which the House of Hanover was invited to the crown. In fact, and in short, he would not permit the Cabinet to encourage the Lord Lieutenant to go further 'until the leading men of every order in the State' had been consulted.[1]

Ten days followed of pain, uncertainty, and, it is to be hoped, humiliation; for under any and every hypothesis the conduct of the Cabinet had been inexcusable. Private notice, probably, was sent to Grattan, and led him to the precipitate introduction of his Bill. It was not, however, till the 16th that the result of the deliberations was made known formally to Fitzwilliam. On that day two despatches were addressed to him by the Duke of Portland. The first, which was intended to be shown to the Irish Council, was a repetition of the instructions which Fitzwilliam had carried with him to collect

[1] 'Letter from the King to Pitt, February 6, 1795.'—*Life of Pitt*, vol. ii. Appendix, p. 23.

opinions on the probable effects of concession, and to send them over. From the tone of this letter no decisive inference could be drawn. The second and private letter was totally different. The Duke indicated a disagreement from Fitzwilliam on his own part so total, that the misunderstanding is explicable only on the supposition that Portland, who knew Ireland, had been overruled all along by Pitt and Dundas, who knew nothing of it.

To yield to the clamours of the Irish Catholics, he said, was the way to make them irresistible and ungovernable; must change the constitution of the House of Commons, and with it overthrow the Church Establishment. The House of Commons was composed largely of members for small boroughs erected purposely to maintain the Protestant ascendancy. Common sense and human nature forbade that these boroughs could survive the change now intended. A Reform Bill would follow, and all the declarations and assurances which might now be given could not prevent a consequent revolution in Church and State.[1]

Fitzwilliam did not yet realise that the Cabinet had come to an unfavourable conclusion. He continued to argue as if the question was still open.

'You are thinking,' he replied, 'of a union between the two kingdoms, as a good to be expected from deferring the concession. Depend on the hope of that, and it will be the union of Ireland, not with Great Britain, but with France. You calculate on confusion arising from which the union will be welcomed as an escape. Church and State are safe as

[1] 'Two letters from the Duke of Portland to Lord Fitzwilliam, February 16.' Abridged. S. P. O.

long as the laws stand. Conciliate the higher Catholics by concessions, and if the laws are threatened and a union is necessary to save property, they will cry for it as loudly as the Protestants.'[1]

The uncertainty might have been protracted through further correspondence had not Grattan ended it by the introduction of his Bill. He, and perhaps Fitzwilliam with him, believed that the Cabinet would be not ill-pleased to find themselves committed by an irretrievable step. They had heard probably from other quarters that the King had interposed, and they wished to make retreat impossible. They had miscalculated the King's resolution. The step which they had ventured was unknown when Portland wrote on the 16th; on the 17th the news arrived in London that the Irish Government had openly committed itself, and that 'the outlines of the intended Bill had been laid before the House with the consent of the Viceroy, before an opportunity had been allowed to the Cabinet of expressing an opinion upon it.' The Duke wrote at once, kindly indeed but emphatically, to tell Fitzwilliam that there was not a difference of opinion in the Cabinet on the extreme impropriety of his conduct. He 'could not repress his astonishment' that Grattan should have been allowed to introduce his Bill. He directed Fitzwilliam ' in the plainest and most direct terms to take the most effectual means in his power to prevent any further proceedings with it until his majesty's further pleasure should be signified to him.'[2]

Five days later he wrote again, ' by the King's command,' that as circumstances might arise to satisfy Lord Fitzwilliam of the undesirableness of his

---

[1] 'To the Duke of Portland, February 21.' Abridged. S. P. O.

[2] 'Portland to Fitzwilliam, February 18.' S. P. O.

remaining in the Administration, he was 'authorised to resign'—'the manner was left to his discretion.' Fitzgibbon and the Speaker, the two most vigorous opponents of Emancipation, were named with the Primate 'Lords Justices.'[1]

All was now confusion. The most confident expectations had been excited. The political patriots and the priests had each regarded Ireland as their own. The United Irishmen had counted the one step gained to which the next was to be separation from England. The peasantry believed that they had paid their last sheaf of tithes and their last shilling of rent. At once the cup was dashed from their lips. Many a mad exploit had been achieved in Ireland by the negligence or folly of Ministers, but this last was above and beyond them all The Catholic Committee reassembled in haste in Dublin. They again reviewed their forces and found themselves unequal for the present to an unassisted insurrection. They determined to organise. They debated the propriety of applying for help to France.[2] Meanwhile Keogh and Byrne and McCormick were sent to London with a petition to the King that the Viceroy might remain with them. The Committee itself passed a vote of thanks to the Belfast Republicans for their early and steady support of Emancipation. To Grattan they

---

[1] 'Portland to Fitzwilliam. Most secret and confidential. February 23.' S. P. O.

[2] 'I am informed, through a channel which has been much relied on in former administrations, that the Catholic Committee are forming a select and secret committee of a few, who in future are to be trusted with larger powers. They are to take an oath of secrecy and perseverance. It is said that, on a close investigation of their strength and influence on the recall of Lord Fitzwilliam, they despair of anything effectual without the assistance of the French, and it is seriously in contemplation to send an embassy to Paris, if the Catholic question should be lost in the Irish Parliament.'—'Pelham to the Duke of Portland, March 30.' S. P. O.

voted an address, in which they declared that 'Protestants and Catholics were united to resist the outrage which had been offered to Irish pride,' and that if Fitzwilliam was taken from them, his successor should be received by the hisses of a betrayed and irritated nation. Grattan answered that Emancipation would still pass. It might be the death of one Viceroy, but it would be the peace offering of another. He declared that he would himself proceed with his own Bill, and carry it he would, immediately or hereafter. In recalling Fitzwilliam, Britain had planted a dagger in Ireland's heart.[1]

Parliament, which had supposed itself deliberately abandoned, was at first at a loss to conceive what had happened. The Duke of Leinster carried a resolution in the Lords that Fitzwilliam deserved their confidence. Sir Lawrence Parsons carried an address to him in the Commons not to abandon the country. Gradually it began to be understood that there had been some extraordinary mistake, but where or how was unexplained. 'If,' said Parsons, on the 2nd of March, 'the Irish Administration has encouraged the Catholics in their expectations without the countenance of the British Cabinet, they have much to answer for. If the British Cabinet has assented and afterwards retracted, the demon of darkness could not have done more mischief had he come from hell to throw a firebrand among the people. Let the ministry persevere, and the army must be increased to myriads, and five or six dragoons must be quartered in every home in the kingdom.'

[1] 'Address of the Catholics to Grattan, with Grattan's answer, Feb. 27, 1795.'—*Plowden*, vol. iv.

The opponents of Emancipation made their advantage of the confusion. 'May no one, then,' enquired Sir John Blaquiere, 'have an opinion of his own on the Catholic question, without a guard of soldiers to protect him?'

'Are we to listen to such words as these?' said Ogle, 'and are the Roman Catholics to gain credit for loyalty?'

The temper of men was so excited on all sides, that the transfer of authority to the Lords Justices was held too dangerous to be ventured, and the Chancellor and the Speaker themselves begged the Viceroy to remain till a successor arrived. Fitzwilliam was careful to explain that he continued in Dublin only in consequence of their request. 'Apprised as he was of the sentiments of H.M.'s confidential servants that nothing short of the annihilation of H.M.'s Government was impending by his remaining in office,' he yielded 'reluctantly to the entreaties of the respectable persons whom H.M. had pointed out for Lords Justices,' and undertook not to abandon the Government before the end of the month.[1]

On all grounds the interval of uncertainty was made as brief as possible. To replace Fitzwilliam the choice of the Government fell on Lord Camden, the son of the Chancellor, who was already favourably known in Ireland, and whose sister was the mother of Lord Castlereagh. Mr. Pelham, who had been already for a short time Secretary under Lord Northington, was prevailed on to resume duties which had already made him acquainted with the leaders of the Irish Parliament. The line to be followed by the

[1] 'Fitzwilliam to the Duke of Portland, March 7.' S. P. O.

new Government was indicated in the following instructions:—

'The circumstances are so peculiar,' the Duke of Portland wrote to Camden, 'that I must inform you of the reasons why Lord Fitzwilliam was appointed, and why you are to succeed him. As to the Catholic question, it was understood that Lord Fitzwilliam was to prevent it being agitated at all. If he failed he was to use his diligence in collecting the opinions and sentiments of all descriptions of persons, and transmit them for the information of his majesty. Things are no longer in the same state, but our general directions to you are the same. You cannot prevent the discussion, nor should I advise you, even if you have the power, to negative the first reading of Mr. Grattan's Bill. The most desirable means by which it can be stopped are those which will be most likely to convince the better and more reasonable part of the inhabitants of Ireland that in the present state of the country the measure only gives them the choice of evils. Either the proposed concession will create in the Catholics a power and influence which will place them above control, or if, as the friends of the measure contend, it will prove incapable of affecting the civil and ecclesiastical establishments, it will leave the Catholics in the state which makes the groundwork of their present complaints.

'You will find great firmness necessary to rally the friends of the Protestant interest, and give them courage to meet the question fairly. The divisions among themselves, the opinions which cannot but have prevailed too generally of the favourable disposition of Government to the Catholic pretensions, must all have tended to dispirit and enervate the Protestants in general. You must, therefore, hold a firm and decided language from the first moment of your landing in Ireland, and take upon yourself to give the tone in which this business shall be talked of by the supporters of Government. Unless it shall be made evident by your Lordship that there is no difference whatever between you and the King's servants on this occasion, and that it is your joint and deliberate opinion that a stand should be made if possible against the further claims of the Catholics, it will be in vain for us to look for any exertion, or even for a fair, unbiassed, and impartial opinion from any individual Protestant. . . . When you have distinctly explained to such gentlemen as you may send to for that purpose the designs and wishes of the Government, you may then require their sentiments on the subject of resistance, and you may state to them *that the further steps to be taken must depend upon them;* that resistance will be ineffectual unless carried on by the hearty co-operation of the Protestants; that it is for their interests you are contending; that provided the great body of the Protestants will exert themselves in the contest, you are authorised to give them the most decided and unreserved support, and make every exertion they can desire to prevent the admission of the Catholics to seats in the Legislature.

'At the same time you will satisfy the Catholics of the liberal and conciliatory disposition entertained towards them, to give them the benefit of the concessions of '93, so far as their conduct shall render it practicable. You will do this in the best way you can. Of measures likely to improve the condition and satisfy the minds of the Catholics, without endangering the Protestant Establishment, I submit the following, *which were the subjects of conversation with Lord Fitzwilliam before he went to Ireland:*—The establishment of seminaries for the education of Catholic priests; the making some provision for the Catholic parochial clergy. If any mode should occur to you for facilitating the education of the lower ranks of Catholics, to put them on a par with Protestants, you may be sure of the countenance and support of the English Government. . . . I recommend these measures. . . . Should, however, your endeavours prove unsuccessful, and should you become convinced that resistance would be dangerous or ineffectual, even in that case you will not suffer the measure to proceed till you have represented to us the state of the country and the disposition of men's minds, and till you receive further instructions from home.

'As Lord Fitzwilliam's retirement may be attributed in

part to the distribution of official situations, I must not pass over that subject in silence. We wished to unite all parties in support of Lord Fitzwilliam; we wish to do the same in support of yourself. But I mean to be understood. The supporters of Government must do what they profess, and not be suffered to avail themselves of their supposed connection with Government to bring forward measures which have not the avowed sanction of your Lordship.

'One caution more. You will need all your prudence. Those who fancied they were about to be sacrificed will assume airs of exultation and triumph little suited to conciliate those who have been stopped in the career which they had just entered; and the disappointment of the latter may be productive of great ill-humour and some violence. Moderate, soothe, conciliate these jarring spirits. We have great confidence in your judgment, firmness, and discretion.'[1]

[1] 'Instructions to Lord Camden, March 10, 1705.' S. P. O.

SECTION V.

PELHAM was despatched first to prepare the way for Camden. At Holyhead he met Lord Milton, who refused to see him. From gentlemen who had crossed in the same packet he learnt that Fitzwilliam 'was unwell and much agitated,' and that public opinion in Dublin, though not in favour of the Catholics, was 'against the Beresfords.' In the objection to the replacement of John Beresford at the head of the Board of Revenue, Pelham himself sympathised.[1]

On landing in Dublin he sent a polite note to Fitzwilliam, who declined, however, all communication with him, and sailed the next day. The people drew the carriage of the departing Viceroy through the streets to the water-side. The shops were closed. The houses were hung with mourning. Before his departure Fitzwilliam published his own defence in the shape of two letters to Lord Carlisle, in which he described himself as a sacrifice to a change of policy

---

[1] He explained his reasons in a note written from Holyhead to the Duke of Portland:—
'If it should take that turn, and sacrifices are necessary, Pitt must submit to Beresford's removal. I am sorry to say it, but I must, on such a critical occasion, express my feeling that Pitt seems more animated about men on this occasion than he ought to be. I was by no means satisfied with his conduct about Beresford when I met him at his house with Lord Camden. I cannot boldly defend a job, even in Ireland. The peace of Ireland is too great a stake to set against the interest of any *clique*. If once the notion of a trick is entertained, our task will be a difficult one, for nothing so excites discontent, and so soon drives the common people into acts of violence and despair, as the notion of having been imposed upon.'—'Pelham to the Duke of Portland, March 22, 1795.' S. P. O.

in the Cabinet, whom he accused of manœuvring for a Union, and quoted as proof a passage from a secret despatch of the Duke of Portland.[1]

Fitzgibbon asked Pelham plainly if he was to understand that the suspicion was well-founded. Pelham for himself denied it. He had the strongest objection to a Union, he said, on account of the effect which the Irish members might produce on the British Parliament. If that was so, Fitzgibbon said, Lord Camden would do well to remove public anxiety by an explicit declaration on meeting Parliament.

Pelham had, of course, much to hear. He learnt how artificially the Emancipation question had been forced forward by Grattan's agitation. The Catholics, 'if they had not been invited to come forward, were very willing to have remained quiet.' He was shown an inflammatory letter from Burke declaring that the Catholics must have Emancipation, that Parliament would be disgraced by postponing it, and that England some day would gain popularity at the Protestants' expense by promoting it.

'The evil of all this,' said Pelham, 'is the general mistrust of English Government, and the advantage given to the disaffected, who represent the connection with Great Britain as the source of all the evils that attend the country . . . The people have been

---

[1] 'The letters were distributed among Lord Fitzwilliam's friends, and are now in general circulation. One passage is much talked of here. It is a quotation from a confidential despatch from your Grace, in which you say that deferring this question would be the means of doing a greater service to the British empire than it has been capable of receiving since the Revolution. The construction put on these words by many people (though falsely, in my opinion) is that the intention of ministers was to keep the Catholic question alive, and in suspense, till a peace, and then employ it as a means of forming a union between the two countries.'—'Pelham to the Duke of Portland, March 30. Secret.' S. P. O.

brought forward so often as the instrument of intimidation, and the Government has yielded so readily, that they naturally think that they have an adverse interest, and that they have the means of carrying anything.'[1]

Lord Camden followed in a week. He landed at Blackrock on the 31st of March. The streets were quiet as he entered Dublin. At the Castle he was sworn in as usual by the Lords Justices. His arrival became known during the ceremony, and as the Lords Justices drove away when it was over they were received at the gates by a dense and angry crowd. Stones were thrown at the Primate's carriage. Fitzgibbon, who was an object of far more serious hatred, was attacked by a knot of well-dressed, dangerous-looking men, who evidently meant mischief. The coachman lashed his horses and broke through them. They made for his house in Ely Place by a short cut, and were there before him. As he drove up heavy paving-stones were flung through the carriage window, one of which struck the Chancellor on the forehead. Passers-by, or the police, whom Grattan had not yet extinguished, gathered round and protected him from further mischief. The mob surged off and attacked the Speaker's house and the Custom House. They were at last fired on by the troops. Two were killed, and the rest sullenly dispersed. It was an ominous reception. The revolutionary politicians, disappointed in their hope of obtaining their object through the imbecility of the English Government, evidently intended to show that if not conceded they meant to take it.

[1] 'Pelham to the Duke of Portland, April 6.' S. P. O.

BOOK VIII.
1795.
April.

Keogh and Byrne returned from London to report that they had gone on a bootless errand. Keogh, finding that plausibility and smooth speeches would serve his turn no longer, rose to the height which Wolfe Tone desired, and declared in the Catholic Committee that Ireland must now be roused to assert her rights. The Protestant peers and country gentlemen, on the other hand, gave Camden the assurance which Portland instructed him to demand of them, and promised their cordial co-operation in resisting further encroachments.

The ground being thus cleared, and the first effects of the shock having passed off, the suspended session recommenced. Lord Camden was not allowed to give the assurance which Fitzgibbon desired. The Union, in fact, was and long had been Pitt's object; the Cabinet agreed with him; and Camden, if not Pelham, was in the secret.[1]

Grattan, as the father of the independence of the Irish Parliament, came again to the front. The victory had been snatched from him at the moment when he believed it won. He saw his country again about to relapse under a regimen like Lord Westmoreland's. He rose on the 21st of April to move for a committee to enquire into the state of the nation, and to deprecate the return of 'the pernicious and profligate

[1] 'The arguments in Mr. Pelham's letter,' Portland wrote to the Viceroy, 'biassed the opinions of the Cabinet against his making any speech at all.' The Duke said he was prepared for the construction which would be placed upon his words. The Secretary must neither avow nor disavow it. The private correspondence between men in public employment ought to be kept religiously secret, and Mr. Pelham was not to allow himself to be betrayed into explanations. He was rather 'to enter his solemn protest, once for all, against any reference to information of so delicate and sacred a nature.'—'Portland to Camden, April 13. Private and secret.' S. P. O.

system' which had made Ireland a disgrace before the world. He had been reproached with the violence of his language in replying to the address of the Catholic Committee. He protested that he had said nothing ' so blasted as the horrid declaration, worthy of the corrupt lips of a herald of profligacy, that certain parliamentary provisions were defensible or expedient to purchase the members of the House.' He reasserted that the recall of Fitzwilliam was a dagger planted in the Irish heart. He stood in his place to meet inquiry and confront his enemies.

The mob in the galleries shouted applause, but the House, relieved from fear of Pitt, had regained its courage. Mervyn Archdall said calmly that Lord Westmoreland had done more for Ireland than all the Viceroys from Strafford to Fitzwilliam. With robust sense he denounced the word Emancipation as applicable to the Catholics. 'Emancipation meant that a slave was set free. The Catholics were not slaves. Nothing more absurd had ever been said since language had been abused for the delusion of mankind.'

Forcing a division, Mr. Grattan found himself in a minority of more than a hundred. On the 24th Pelham introduced a proposal for the establishment of a Catholic college. It was opposed by the Patriots, partly because it might allay the sense of disappointment which they desired to exasperate—partly as tending to divide the Catholics and Protestants, whom they wished to combine in the interest of a common nationality.[1] The Government carried

---

[1] 'Grattan presented a petition in opposition "from his majesty's Roman Catholic subjects of Ireland." He set forth "the inexpediency of establishing an educational institution from which Protestants should

their point without difficulty, and an Act was passed for the foundation and endowment of a Catholic academy, which has since become known as Maynooth.[1]

The battle had still to be fought over the Emancipation Bill. Grattan had announced that he should persist with it. It had been read a first time on the 24th of April without opposition, as the Cabinet had directed. On the 4th of May it came on a second time. The debate lasted through a long May day, through the night, and till ten o'clock the following morning. The arguments of the advocates and the opponents, with the light on them of eighty years' experience, can still be read without fatigue.

'History,' said the Solicitor-General (Toler), in rising to move the rejection of the Bill, 'shows that we cannot allow an *imperium in imperio* or that rival and sovereign authority which the Roman Catholic

---

be excluded, inasmuch as it tended to perpetuate the line of religious separation."

Strongly advocating mixed education, the petitioners said, that "when the youth of both religions were instructed together in the branches of education which were common to all, their peculiar tenets would afterwards be no hindrance to a friendly intercourse in life." The Catholics, having been already admitted to Trinity College, "saw with deep concern the principles of separation and exclusion revived and re-enacted." '—*Parliamentary Debates*, April 29, 1795.

This petition has been sometimes referred to as an evidence of the presence of large-minded and liberal sentiment in a part of the Catholics of Ireland at the end of the last century. The Catholic spirit is no doubt more modest and tolerant when held in subjection, and becomes arrogant and encroaching when indulged. But this petition, and Grattan's connection with it, had nothing to do with liberal sentiment.

The hope of the party of revolution was the union of Catholics and Protestants. The aim of England was to prevent the union from being accomplished. The motion for the establishment of the college, on one side, and for the opposition to it, on the other, were both exclusively political.

[1] 35 George III., cap. 21. The original design was for the education of lay students as well as priests.

Church claims, and wherever it has power will assert. It has cost us dear to shake off that power. I will not open the door for its return. The better sort of Catholics have not lent themselves to this agitation. Others, not they, have raised an outcry which has produced outrage in the remotest corners of Ireland; and has inflamed the peasantry, who have been taught to think that Emancipation means the lowering of the price of land. The United Irishmen are the managers of the Catholic cause. Their publications are bound up with those of the Catholic Committee. They appeared armed with the insignia of rebellion, parading the streets of Dublin. Nothing less than rebellion was hatching, and their plan has ended in the fate of that man who was buried yesterday[1] with all the honours of high treason, attended by the leaders of that society. I trust the gentlemen of Ireland will prove that they are not affected by lies and clamour, and that when the Constitution is attacked they will say with the bold Barons, " *Nolumus leges Angliæ mutari.*" '

Mr. Grattan had spoken brilliantly as usual, but with more than usual gesticulation and violence, foretelling the ruin of all things if the Bill was rejected. Dr. Duigenan, in replying, drew a valuable picture of Grattan's person and manner in debate.

'When,' he said, 'I see a gentleman equal as an actor to Garrick, Barry, or Sheridan get up in this House, horror and dismay in his countenance, his hair standing on end, and hear him conjuring up all the hideous spirits of battle, murder, and sudden death as the consequences of rejection—in solemn tones, from

---

[1] Mr. Jackson was kept in prison for a year, and had but just been tried.

the lowest key of his voice, as if he was enclosed in a hogshead and was speaking through the bung-hole— though I admire his ability in acting, yet am I in no way terrified by the unsubstantial goblins he has conjured up.'

'Admit the Catholics,' said Pelham, 'and you cannot stop. For myself, I am free to say if Parliament becomes Catholic, the Church Establishment ought to be of the same persuasion. The Bill, if carried, must weaken the connection between England and this country; and if it have that tendency—I am not speaking for Protestants, but for mankind—to whom is Europe to look for liberty at the present crisis but to the protection and power of Great Britain?'

Mr. Cuffe enquired what benefit had been derived from the concessions made already. The Bill of '92 was followed by the alliance of the Catholics and Republicans. Those who formerly came to them as suppliants came now as swaggering bullies.

Sir Edward Newenham said, like Sir Robert Peel after him, that 'religious equality in Ireland was impossible. There must be either a Popish ascendency or a Protestant ascendency. As little could the Ethiopian be washed white as the Church of Rome taught to endure an equal in power.'

Sir Hercules Langrishe, on the other hand, maintained, in modern style, 'that the days of restraint were passed.' 'Reason, persuasion, benevolence, extinction of prejudices, were the weapons which should now be relied on. The Pope was an inoffensive, unaspiring prince, defending himself feebly against French infidelity. That the British connection would be endangered by the admission of the Catholics to the Constitution was a dream.'

'Adopt the measure,' argued Sir George Knox,

'and we shall liberalise the Catholic gentry. They will see that their property, their liberty, their lives, depend on the connection with Great Britain. The Catholic gentleman is not so silly or so light as to sacrifice the Constitution to a few ignorant priests. Rather taking in view the spirit of the times, the Catholic gentlemen, already more than half Protestants, will bring up their children to a conformity which opens to them the profits of the Church.'

'Where is the Papal power?' asked Mr. Osborne? 'Does a shadow of it exist to give hope to the greatest bigot of the Popish persuasion, or alarm to the greatest bigot of ours?'

George Ponsonby accused the Protestant speakers of charging the Catholics with opinions which no man in his senses could entertain. The Catholics did not think Protestants would be damned for not belonging to the Church. Dr. Troy[1] didn't think so. Dr. Troy knew well he would as soon be damned for riding on horseback. 'The Pope! Were they afraid of the Pope? The Pope was the only man in Europe of whom no one was afraid, and who was afraid of everybody.'

Narrow-minded Protestant prejudice was keener-sighted than modern enlightenment. Grattan, too, was as far astray as Ponsonby; not, indeed, blinded, like his friend, by the flatulent conceit of liberalism, but by the instinctive and indelible longing of an Irish patriot for the humiliation of Great Britain.

'The English Ministers,' he said scornfully, 'oppose this Bill.' 'Will they, after losing Holland, losing Brabant, losing a great part of Germany, losing the terrors of the British name—will they reject the

---

[1] The Catholic Archbishop of Dublin.

Catholics of Ireland? Will they, after losing America, with an increase of debt of two hundred millions, with a new Republican empire rising upon them— dreadful from its principles, its power, and its victories — will they reject the Catholics of Ireland? Have they left themselves room for internal proscription, for eternal persecution, for tyranny under the mask of religion? Have they left enough of territories to proscribe three-fourths of this island, and a fourth of their empire? To what allies have the Ministry resorted, that they would exclude the Irish Catholics? Are not their armies mostly Catholic? Is not your militia mostly Catholic? Is not a good portion of their seamen Catholic? Are not the confederate princes Catholic?'

The debate excited little interest out of doors. The agitators knew that the Bill would be lost, and with a spirit which revealed the value of their protests of loyalty, were already busy with other and darker methods.[1] The usual crowd was absent from the galleries. No angry mob thronged the doors of the Parliament House. Still speaker followed speaker, as if every member desired to relieve himself of the burden of his emotions. Curran rose at six in the morning, with the May sun shining through the windows on the weary assembly. Sir John Blaquiere spoke at ten. The Attorney-General wound up the discussion with a few vigorous words, and the question of Catholic Emancipation was dismissed from the Irish Parliament, to be raised again as opportunity offered for purposes of faction, but never more with serious prospect of acceptance, as long as Ireland had a separate constitution.

[1] 'Camden to Portland, May 5.'

SECTION VI.

REBELLION was now a question of time, and under one condition might become seriously formidable. The Northern Presbyterians had not revenged themselves on extortionate landlords and insolent churchmen by house burning and midnight murder. They had none the less resented the distrust which had deprived them of their civil rights, and the rapacity which had stolen the profits of their industry. They had been American in the war of Independence. They had made the strength of the Volunteers, and at the outset the same instinct had led them to sympathise with the French Revolution. Could Wolfe Tone make his alliance a reality, could the artisans and farmers of Antrim, and Down, and Londonderry be induced as a body to combine in earnest with the disaffected Catholics, the tenure of the administration at the Castle might be precarious indeed. At one time the union appeared to have been completed, but the phenomena of 1641 were repeating themselves. The Ulster Puritans had then combined with the Papal Irish against Strafford and the Bishops. In 1792 they were inclining to protect themselves by a similar alliance against Lord Donegal and his imitators. From the first, however, there had been a counter movement, which gained strength as the Catholics became more violent. Protestant Ireland had not yet forgotten the scenes in which the agitation of 1641 concluded. The Scotch-Irish of Ulster traced their blood to the defenders of Derry. Bitter as they might be against landlord oppression, they had a more immediate quarrel with the Catholic tenants who had been intruded into the Antrim farms over the heads of so many of themselves. The spread of Defenderism and the fierce eagerness of the Catholics to obtain arms aggravated their suspicions, and the devilish outbreak of ferocity in the mutilators of the Barclay family had already determined the best of them to shut their ears to the United Irishmen, and refuse to help forward an insurrection which was too likely to turn, like its predecessors, into universal massacre. The effects of the recall of Fitzwilliam in the Catholic provinces were still more alarming. The Defenders, who were all Catholics, fell back into an attitude of open defiance. Defender lodges were formed in every county in the island, and the Catholic peasantry were universally sworn in. The blacksmiths went to work to hammer pikes. Private houses were again entered in search of guns and muskets. Two thousand stand of arms were taken in Roscommon alone. In Longford in eight months there were one hundred and fifty-seven robberies and murders. Stray parties of militia were set upon and plundered. A revenue officer and nine men were waylaid and killed, and the bodies were horribly mutilated.[1] A deadly and determined spirit was silently spreading, to which even the well-affected did not dare to refuse obedience. Servants left their places with tears in their eyes, telling their employers they were afraid to remain with them.

These symptoms were frightfully suggestive. The

---

[1] 'Pelham to the Duke of Portland, April 27.' 'Account of the insurrection in Roscommon, forwarded by Lord Camden, May 1795.' S. P. O.

massacre of 1641 had not yet been resolved into a legend by steady lying and sentimental credulity. It remained in the memory of every Irish Protestant a definite and dreadful fact, which might recur if opportunity served; in Armagh and Antrim especially the small Protestant farmers combined, in fear and exasperation, to disarm in time the Catholics settled among themselves; and at last, when nothing else would serve, to expel them out of Ulster and force them to return into the South. The friends of liberty made the air ring with eloquent shrieks. Protestant girls might be ravished. Protestant farmers and gentry might be murdered. No matter. It was but punishment overtaking tyranny. When a Catholic was injured by a Protestant, the very heart of humanity was invited to bleed. To such persons it did not occur to enquire why the Catholics, who were forbidden to possess arms, were in such haste to obtain them. But the question occurred very strongly to the Protestants, in the midst of whom these persons were living. When they found and felt that they were in the midst of a conspiracy which was enveloping the island, they resolved naturally that they would not be caught sleeping a second time. If they were rough, violent, and unscrupulous, the blame lay most with those who had brought Ireland into incipient insurrection.

Such a temper was a formidable obstacle to Wolfe Tone and his friends. They could carry with them the city mob at Belfast, but Jacobin clerks and shopboys were poor creatures beside the rugged and determined countrymen. Many an effort had been made to compose the feud between the two wings of the intended army of insurrection. After two years of exertion, Tone believed that he had accomplished his object. On the 18th of September a peace was formally signed at Portadown between the Peep-of-day Boys and the Defenders, and the hatchet was apparently buried. But the incongruous elements were drawn together only for a more violent recoil. The very same day, Mr. Atkinson, one of the Protestant subscribers, was shot at. The day following a party of Protestants were waylaid and beaten. On the 21st both parties collected in force, and at a village in Tyrone, from which the event took the name by which it is known, was fought the battle of the Diamond. The Protestants won the day, though far outnumbered. Eight-and-forty Defenders were left dead on the field, and the same evening was established the first lodge of an institution which was to gather into it in succeeding years all that was best and noblest in Ireland. The name of Orangemen had long existed. It had been used by loyal Protestants to designate those of themselves who adhered most faithfully to the principles of 1688. Threatened now with a general Catholic insurrection, with the Executive authority powerless, and determined, at all events, not to offer the throats of themselves and their families to the Catholic knife, they organized themselves into a volunteer police to prevent murder, to see the law put in force which forbade the Catholics to be armed, and to awe into submission the roving bands of assassins who were scaring sleep from the bedside of every Protestant household. They became the abhorrence of traitors, whose designs they thwarted. The Government looked askance at a body of men who interfered with the time-honoured policy of overcoming sedition by tenderness and softness of speech.[1] But the lodges grew and multiplied. Honest men of all ranks sought admission to them as into spontaneous vigilance committees to supply the place of the constabulary which ought to have been, but was not, established; and if they did their work with some roughness and irregularity, the work nevertheless was done. By the spring of 1797, they could place twenty thousand men at the disposition of the authorities. In 1798 they filled the ranks of the yeomanry, and beyond all other influences the Orange organization counteracted and thwarted the progress of the United Irishmen in Ulster, and when the moment of danger arrived had broken the right arm of insurrection.

---

[1] Lord Camden took the most unfavourable view of the Orangemen:—

'A spirit of another kind,' he said, 'has manifested itself in Armagh. The Protestants in that county, finding themselves the most numerous, have been induced to commit acts of the greatest outrage and barbarity against their Catholic neighbours; and, notwithstanding the exertions of Government, the disturbances neither have ceased nor diminished. This has been owing to the magistrates in that county having imbibed the prejudices which belong to it. I have sent Colonel Cradock there, for the suppression of outrage and disorder, from whatever quarter it may arise.—To Portland, January 22, 1796.' S. P. O.

BOOK IX.

CHAPTER I.

THE FRENCH AT BANTRY.

SECTION I.

There are persons who believe that if the King had not interfered with Lord Fitzwilliam, the Irish Catholics would have accepted gratefully the religious equality which he was prepared to offer them, and would have remained thenceforward for all time contented citizens of the British Empire. There are those also who say that if Fitzwilliam had not been sent to give them encouragement, they would not have entertained the hopes the disappointment of which drove them into rebellion. To the careful student of Irish history these positions are alike incredible. The Catholic cannot be content with equality when he can command ascendency. The Irish patriot sets his heart on separation from England, and values political concessions only as advancing his parallels nearer to the citadel which he means to storm; and though Fitzwilliam may have precipitated the crisis, a convulsion became inevitable from the moment that England allowed the Catholics of Ireland to see that she was afraid of them. Humble and even abject so long as she dared assert her strength, they pressed on her, when they saw that she was flinching, with menace and intimidation; and as no English statesman could allow himself to contemplate an Ireland really independent as a possibility, the alternative was either to postpone the collision by successive retreats, till the Catholics held the powers of the State, with a Parliament of their own to represent them in the final struggle, or to resist at once while the authority was still in Protestant hands, and the Protestant party in the country remained unbroken. The Cabinet, with a European war upon their hands, and themselves embarrassed with the new theories of constitutional liberty, preferred the first. The King, governed by what are called prejudices, adhered to conclusions formed by intelligent statesmen of past generations, and based on the experience of centuries, too late to prevent a rebellion, not too late, however, to prevent it from assuming the dimensions of 1641 or 1690.

Had the Catholic Committee been wise in their generation, they would have concealed the hollowness of those professions of loyalty on which they had demanded admission to the constitution. They made haste, as if on purpose, to show how correctly George the Third had estimated their character. The Catholic bishops and peers retired from the front, affecting to deprecate consequences which they could no longer avert. The revolutionary part of the Committee gave their hands finally to Wolfe Tone and his Jacobin confederates; the two armies, the Catholic Defenders and 'the National Guards' of Belfast and Dublin, were amalgamated into a common force, and the cause of Catholic Ireland became the cause of France and liberty.

The Catholic Committee met for the last time to hear the report of its delegates from England. In the speeches on that occasion, which were published in the Catholic newspapers,[1] the war of England against France was described as an impious conspiracy against freedom, and the Irish soldiers and sailors in the Crown service were invited to desert their colours. The victories of England were described as public calamities at which Irishmen should rather weep than rejoice. Keogh informed the committee that it would meet no more as a separate body. The Catholics were identified thenceforward with the Protestants of Belfast, and their common action would be guided by a common directory.

The first essential was to inform France that Ireland was at her service. Jackson, the French emissary, was buried with public honours. Wolfe Tone, the genius of Irish revolution, came again out of obscurity to the front. After the apparent satisfaction with which the Catholics had accepted the concessions of '93, Wolfe Tone had despaired of them and despaired of his country. He had been cautious of committing himself with Jackson, whom he suspected to be an emissary of Pitt. On Rowan's flight he went to Beresford, told him what he knew, and declared with ingenious plausibility, that though as an Irishman he considered that he had a right to desire the emancipation of his country, he regarded Englishmen who took their part as traitors, and would have nothing to do with them. Talk of this kind would not have served his purpose could the Government have made a case to prosecute him. But they found

---

[1] See the speech of Dr. Duigenan, May 4, 1795.—*Irish Debates.*

that even if they admitted Jackson as an approver, they could not make sure of convicting Tone. The Attorney-General, Wolfe, who was perhaps his kinsman, befriended him; and as he had confessedly taken up with rebellion out of resentment for personal neglect, there was a thought at one time 'of giving him some employment in the East Indies out of reach of European politics.' Like all Irish patriots, he would have accepted greedily any tolerable appointment from the Government which he had been execrating. But they changed their minds. They allowed him, as he said, 'to withdraw his head, like the crane in the fable, from the jaws of the wolf.' They spared him prosecution, and they accepted an easy promise from him to go to America at his early convenience. He lingered on to see the issue of Jackson's trial. Had Fitzwilliam remained in office, his connection with Jackson would have been forgotten, and he would perhaps have been taken into employment at home.[1] On Fitzwilliam's fall, prudence called on him to depart, and as events were turning out, his journey could be made supremely opportune. He had bound himself to go to America. He had not undertaken to remain there. He proposed to his friends, Keogh and McCormick, that from America he should return at once to Paris, and invite the Directory to send a force for their deliverance.

'I received, as I expected,' he said, 'the most cor-

---

[1] He says that overtures were made to him, but that he declined to connect himself with a party whom he mistrusted. 'The Whigs,' he adds, 'were angry at his refusal, and might have been inclined to win credit for their moderation by making a victim of a Republican leader.' George Ponsonby, who expected to succeed Wolfe, said, 'Perhaps Mr. Tone will not find the next Attorney-General so accommodating as the last.'

dial approbation. They both laid the most positive injunctions upon me to leave nothing unattempted on my part to force my way to France and lay our situation before the Government, observing that if I succeeded there was nothing in the power of my country to bestow to which I might not fairly pretend.'[1]

Empowered to speak as he conceived in the name of Catholics, Dissenters, and Defenders, he undertook his memorable mission. Before his departure he spent a month with his United friends at Belfast—Russell, Neilson, the two Simms's, and other enthusiasts now radiant with hope. Each day in the bright May weather they had some fête or banquet in anticipation of approaching deliverance. Finally, at MacArts Fort, on Cave Hill, the whole party swore an oath together never to desist from their efforts till they had subverted the authority of England, and had made their country independent.

[1] *Memoirs of Wolfe Tone, by Himself.*

SECTION II.

MEANWHILE the word had gone out among the Defenders to resume work and secure the arms of the Protestant gentry. First in Connaught, and then gradually in all parts of Ireland, bodies of men, who seemed to have started out of the earth, were out at night on the prowl like wild beasts. Houses were burnt, cattle houghed with the peculiar ferocity which characterises the Irish peasants when roused to violence; the udders of the cows belonging to Protestants were sliced off. When arms were demanded and were not delivered death was the punishment. Barracks were surprised in the darkness. Parties of militia were attacked even in open day with desperate courage. And by whom these deeds were done remained for the most part a mystery. In every cabin the grown men were sworn to secrecy, and to be true to their country and to France, and instant and dreadful justice overtook any miserable wretch suspected of having broken his oath.

Notwithstanding this precaution the veil was in places lifted. General Luttrell, now Lord Carhampton, went down and took command in Connaught. Informers offered their services, provided their presence was not required in the witness-box. A priest named Phillips 'caused himself to be made a Defender with a view of giving information.'[1] Others came 'whose names the Viceroy dared not place on

---

[1] 'Camden to Portland, July 20, 1795.'

paper.' With the help of these men Carhampton was able to arrest many of the Connaught leaders; and legal trials being from the nature of the case impossible, he trusted to Parliament for an Act of Indemnity, and sent them by scores to serve in the fleet. Thus, amidst the shrieks of patriots and threats of prosecution, he succeeded in restoring some outward show of order.[1]

The spirit, however, was repressed in one district only to break out in others under the auspices of the new organisation in which Defenders and United Irishmen were now combining. The Committee of Public Welfare, which had undertaken the direction of Irish disaffection, consisted of five members continually changing, whose names were known only to themselves, and to those through whom their orders were immediately transmitted. They had no fixed place of meeting. They assembled once a month, sometimes at Belfast, sometimes at Dublin, to hear reports, draw resolutions, and issue commands. Below the General Committee were the County Committees. Below the County Committees were Baronial Committees. Below the Baronial Committees were the Elementary Societies,

---

[1] 'Among the secret informations are several curious accounts of the organisation of the Defenders. Their central lodge was at Armagh, with lodges affiliated through the four provinces. They were all Catholics, yet all Jacobins or Fifth Monarchy men, believing that "all men were equal, and that there was no King but the Almighty." The immediate object was a union between Ireland and France. The "Cavan Catechism" ran:—

'"The French Defenders will uphold the cause; The Irish Defenders will pull down the British laws."

'Another catechism was found on a man who was hanged at Carrick:—"Are you concerned?—I am. To what?—To the National Convention. What do you design by that cause?—To quell all nations, dethrone all kings, and plant the true religion that was lost at the Reformation. Who sent you? —Simon Peter, the Head of the Church."' — *Irish MSS.* 1795. S. P. O.

each containing eighteen members and no more, one or more of whom were to be found in every town in Ireland, and at last in every village. Each eighteen had its four officers, changed every fortnight, and elected by lot. Each single member contributed a shilling a month or more according to his means. They appeared under the most innocent disguises, as book clubs, parochial charity clubs, or trading societies; and so rapidly the infection spread through the poisoned atmosphere, that before the end of the summer of 1795 Lord Camden was informed that more than a million members were already sworn.[1] The militia were now everywhere enrolled to overawe them; but the militia being themselves chiefly Catholics, were objects of assiduous and generally successful seduction. The weavers and tradesmen of Dublin 'were indefatigable' in their attempts on the loyalty of the Irish in the regiments of the line ; and so energetic was the propagandism, that in August the more sanguine leaders believed that they were ready for revolt, and a plot was laid which resembled singularly the precedent of 1641. The day selected was the ominous 24th of August. Dublin Castle was to be surprised. The two regiments on duty there, the 104th and 111th, were gained over. The signal was to be an attack on the guard on Essex Bridge and the seizure of the colours. Camden was to be killed by the first means that came to hand. Fitzgibbon was to be hanged in state in St. Stephen's Green ; the Protestants, according to the ambitious instincts of

[1] This must have been an enormous exaggeration. The population of Ireland at this time was estimated at 4,100,000, of whom three millions were Catholics. The number, however, did at last reach half a million, and included almost every able-bodied Catholic in Ireland.

the Catholics, who were already outrunning the guidance of the Union leaders, were to be driven out of the island or destroyed. The purpose was betrayed by secret informers, who were never wanting in Ireland. Half-a-dozen of the conspirators were arrested, one of them a private in the Guards. The incriminated regiments mutinied. The most guilty deserted, disappeared in the city lanes, and were heard of no more. Similar disaffection showed itself in a regiment at Cork, but was promptly quelled. In September Lord Camden made a progress in force through the South, to overawe the rising rebellion by a display of power and justice.

One of the O'Connors had been convicted of administering the United oath to a soldier in the garrison at Naas. O'Connor was hanged while Camden was in the town; and to produce an effect his head was struck off and set up on a pole over the door of the gaol.[1]

It availed nothing. Insurrection did not gather to a head, but the elements of it were everywhere. Magistrates were waylaid, witnesses were murdered, constables who had been too busy beaten, piked, or brained. The militia could not be trusted. The regular army was scarcely in a better condition; and though its numbers were increased on paper, was so feeble as to tempt rebellion. The best troops had been sent abroad. Their places had been supplied by invalids and Fencible regiments, and even of these, instead of the 20,000 voted by Parliament, there were but 10,000 in all Ireland. The country gentlemen, so forward ten years back in volunteering to over-

---

[1] 'Camden to the Duke of Portland, September 9, 1795.'

awe the English, were hanging back and 'hedging' against the day of evil. 'Since the Roman Catholics were allowed to vote,' Camden bitterly said, 'the gentry canvass for their support at the expense of the tranquillity of the kingdom.' 'Feudal notions were passing away. The rights of man were growing up instead of them ; and the people having seen England more than once yield to intimidation, were encouraged to persevere in agitation by experience of its success.' [1]

At the end of September there was a second alarm. The Castle was warned that an order had gone out for every Defender and United Irishman to rise on a specified night under pain of instant death. Often, doubtless, such stories were invented to mislead and harass. The present informer was telling nothing but the truth. Tone's friend, Russell, excited, perhaps, by the oath at MacArt's fort, had urged a universal insurrection immediately after harvest. He had been hardly restrained by his more prudent companions,[2] and Keogh wrote to America to Tone to hasten his movements.[3]

The Cabinet, when post after post brought in these gloomy reports, regretted, it is likely, the King's obstinacy, which had brought the trouble in their day, which but for him they might have passed on to their successors. Portland confessed inability to suggest a method by which the spirit which had been let loose could be re-chained.

'Were the country gentlemen,' he wrote, 'or rather

---

[1] 'Camden to Portland, September 25, 1795.' S. P. O.
[2] '—— to Wolfe Tone, September 21, 1795.' — Printed in Tone's *Memoirs*.
[3] 'Keogh to Wolfe Tone, September 3.'—*Ibid.*

were the great landed proprietors—an event impossible to take place—to reside on their estates, were the parochial clergy more numerous or more generally resident, were the gentlemen more active, the provincial magistracy better filled, the duties of it discharged with impartiality, and the police establishment made general through Ireland; were the wages of the labourers better regulated and paid in specie; were the lands so occupied as to give the landlord an influence over the farmer, and the farmer an interest in the goodwill of the proprietor of the estate, then much might be done for the improvement of the kingdom and the happiness of its inhabitants.'[1]

Admirable Duke of Portland, sitting in his chair with his hands folded and mourning over what he called impossibilities, never remembering, even in his dreams, that it was the business of him and the other Ministers of the Crown to make these 'impossibilities' into facts, that the secret of all Ireland's disorders was the shameful and scandalous forgetfulness of duty on the part of every person in the empire connected with the management of it, from the sovereigns who had quartered their mistresses on the Irish revenue to the lowest customs' officer, who contrived to be sick in his bed when the Kerry smuggler landed his cargo.

[1] 'Portland to Camden, October 13.' S. P. O.

SECTION III.

Times were changed since the Viceroys looked with dread to the meeting of Parliament, uneasily counted their resources and compared them with the expectant pack whose voracity they must satisfy or look for a Short Supply Bill. Tamed out of their patriotism by the unpleasant outcome of it, which now threatened their estates and even their lives, the Irish Members assembled at the beginning of 1796 with but one desire, to strengthen the hands of the Executive. Lord Camden, in opening the session, dwelt naturally on the treasonable organisation which was overspreading the island. Grattan attempted, as usual, an amendment on the Address, but he was listened to with impatience, and voted down with emphasis. The House was eager to learn how Government proposed to deal with the United Irishmen.

The Attorney-General announced that he should ask for a Bill of Indemnity for Carhampton and the Connaught magistrates, to stop impending prosecutions.[1] Further, he intended to introduce a Bill to repress conspiracy to murder. 'Assassination,' he said, 'had become as familiar as fowling.'

---

[1] 'Whereas, in the year 1795 several parts of the kingdom were disturbed by treasonable insurrection, and the lives and properties of many peaceable and faithful subjects destroyed. And whereas, to preserve the public peace, magistrates and other officers have apprehended and sent suspected persons out of the kingdom, have seized arms and entered houses, and done divers acts not justifiable according to law, all suits for things done to preserve the public peace since January 1, 1795, shall be void,' &c.—36 George III. cap. 6.

Magistrates were murdered. Police were murdered. Witnesses were murdered to prevent their appearance in court, or were murdered after they had appeared, to deter others from doing the same. He proposed to give the magistrates summary power to deal with vagrants. He should invite Parliament to make the administering treasonable oaths a capital offence; and, a more considerable and most important innovation, to make the written deposition of a witness who might be murdered after he had given it, evidence to lay before a jury. As a preliminary the Attorney-General proposed a resolution that the present power of magistrates was inadequate to the emergency. To this one voice only was raised in opposition. Lord Edward Fitzgerald, with his French wife,[1] were rapidly verging towards treason. As yet within the limits of the Constitution and in his place in Parliament, Lord Edward protested against coercion, and insisted that if grievances were removed the people would return to their allegiance.

More prudent, more plausible than Fitzgerald, Mr. Grattan made a counter-attack upon the Orangemen. 'Much,' he exclaimed, 'had been said of the Defenders, nothing of the new version of the Lord George Gordon riots, of the bigotry of the Protestant banditti, who, being of the religion of the State, had with the greater audacity committed the most horrid murders, massacreing in the name of God, exercising despotic powers in the name of liberty.' Curran followed, with the patriot phalanx in his rear, clamouring that 1,400 Catholic families had been forcibly expelled from their homes in Armagh.

[1] Pamela, daughter of Madame de Genlis and, as was supposed, the Duke of Orleans.

The Government was silent. The Orangemen, however, were not undefended.

Mr. Verner, a gentleman of the incriminated county, rose to say that half the stories to which he had listened were monstrous fictions. 'The Orangemen were members of the Established Church, loyal to the King, and well-affected to the Constitution. If they had come in collision with the Catholics in Armagh, the Catholics were themselves the cause. They had been robbing Protestants of their arms; they had been assembling, in their own language, "to destroy man, woman, and child of them." Under a pretence of making peace they had fallen on the Protestants without notice. They had been beaten, and had been beaten ever since, as often as they had tried the experiment. Of those who had left the country many had been concerned in outrages, and were afraid of arrest. Others had sold their interest in their farms and had emigrated to get cheap land in Connaught. The Orangemen had been accused of many crimes. They had not threatened the lives of magistrates, or destroyed cattle, or burnt the houses of those who attempted to enforce the laws. In some instances they had acted improperly, but not till they had been goaded beyond the forbearance of human nature.'[1]

In a country on the edge of a dangerous rebellion a society which had formed itself spontaneously in defence of the existing Constitution might naturally have expected encouragement. The Orangemen had shown no antipathy to the Catholics till the Catholics had begun to arm themselves in the face of the law. Experience had taught the Protestants too well the

[1] *Irish Debates*, 1796.

probable meaning of the universal eagerness for muskets and powder among those who were forbidden to possess such things. If they had taken on themselves to enforce the law it was because the Government was apathetic or incapable, and the Government had but to adopt the strength of the Orange Lodges lying at its feet to convert it into the most powerful instrument for the repression of disorder of all kinds. The militia were corrupt, the army feeble. Of these the United Irishmen had no fear. The Orangemen they made no secret of their fearing most deeply. Samuel Neilson, the most determined and dangerous of the United leaders, told a supposed confederate, who was a spy of the Castle, that 'he was in far greater dread of the Orangemen than of the soldiers.' 'They were very powerful and very desperate.'[1] Had Camden bravely made the Orangemen his allies, treason would have crept back into its den and been heard of no more. Unhappily, under constitutional governments spontaneous loyalty is the last virtue which obtains recognition. The friend who is a friend on principle can be relied on as a forlorn hope, however coldly looked upon. The supposed business of constitutional governments is not to encourage the good, but to conciliate the bad if necessary by the sacrifice of the deserving. Lord Camden, yielding to the cant of Liberalism, affected deeper indignation at the disorders of the Orangemen than the outrages of the Catholic assassins. He admitted to Portland that if France interfered he believed Ireland to be lost. He had 19,000 militia, but he could not trust them. He knew that rebellion was in-

---

[1] 'Secret Information, July 30, 1706.' S. P. O.—*Irish MSS.*

tended. He knew the leaders, yet he could not act upon his evidence. He doubted whether any force which he could raise in the kingdom could be depended on, yet in the very same despatch he took credit to himself for the zeal with which he was acting 'against the party of Dissenters named Orangemen.' 'Though not aimed against the Government,' he regarded the Orange combination ' as more dangerous than direct conspiracy.' They 'justly irritated the Catholics,' he said, ' and gave a pretence to the disaffected.'[1]

The Orange disturbances were pleaded skilfully as one reason, among others, for the powers which the Attorney-General demanded. The Indemnity Bill was then passed without difficulty, the Assassination Bill,[2] and a third Act of still graver consequence for the better suppression of insurrections,[3] which, if an Act of Parliament was all that was needed, would have sufficed to restore peace. But, as Mr. Brown, of the College, observed, the thing needed was not so

---

[1] 'To Portland, August 6, 1796.' S. P. O. The nervous anxiety of Camden to avoid offending the Catholics was shown curiously in another instance during the session. Lord Athlone, the descendant and representative of Ginkel, had fallen into penury in Holland. George III. recommended him for a pension on the Irish Establishment, and Camden displeased the King by declining to propose Lord Athlone's name. He thus defends himself to Portland:—

'I will not conceal from your Grace that political considerations influenced my opinion. The very nature of the grant, and the reason for it, are so connected with the Protestant cause in this kingdom, that, although I personally wished to show, not only every attention, but every liberality, towards those who supported it then, as much as I do every encouragement to those who support it now, I yet thought that in a session where so much useful unanimity has been shown, when the Catholic question appeared to be asleep, it was not wise to bring forward a measure which might have the appearance of a degree of triumph on the subject.' —'To Portland, March 8, 1796.' S. P. O.

[2] 36 George III. 27.

[3] *Ibid.*, cap. 20.

much new statutes as the enforcement of the laws already existing.

The Act itself was not, indeed, more severe than others which have since been found equally necessary to preserve peace in Ireland. The most singular circumstance connected with it was the surprise of the Cabinet that such a measure should be required, and the ignorance which they thus unconsciously displayed of the condition into which their weak and wavering policy had brought the unhappy country.[1] Pelham replied, with not unjust irritation, 'that the need of the measure could be doubted by no one who had read the accounts of the machinations of the United Irishmen, the Catholic Committee, and the other disturbers of the peace, which had been transmitted by the Viceroy.' 'It is the universal opinion in Ireland,' he said, 'that if this Bill does not restore peace and give the laws and the Constitution the necessary strength, we must have recourse to the sword.'[2]

The Act shared the fate of most other Acts in Ireland, and remained 'an absolute dead letter.'[3] The magistrates had received ample authority, but they had not received, for the most part, either the courage or the will to make use of it. The Parliament separated when it had done its work in passing the statute. The effect of the session was only to define more clearly the position of parties and individuals, and to show everyone that to the sword the appeal must be

---

[1] 'Of your Insurrection Act I will only say, that although the necessity of such a measure is but too well established by the facility of its passage through Parliament, my astonishment at the existence of such a necessity in a country enjoying the same form of government as this is not abated by the event.'—'Portland to Camden, March 24.' S. P. O.

[2] 'Pelham to Portland, March 31.' S. P. O.

[3] Report of the secret committee of the House of Commons, 1798.

made. The executive council of the United Irishmen retorted with a published defiance. Since Parliament had been pleased to threaten with death those who combined for 'the virtuous and honourable purpose of liberating their country,' they held themselves absolved from their allegiance. The revolutionists of 1688 had called in the aid of a foreign Republic to liberate them from their oppressors. 'A more mighty republic had now arisen, to be the universal friend of struggling and suffering nations, and to this they would appeal.'[1] Lord Edward Fitzgerald and Arthur O'Connor took the United Irishmen's oath, passed at once to the front rank of the society, and independent of Tone, of whose mission they knew nothing, they assumed for themselves the office of ambassadors, and undertook to open an immediate negociation with the Directory. O'Connor had been Sheriff of Cork in 1791. He was nephew and heir-expectant of Lord Longueville, and had been personally intimate with Erskine, Grey, Sheridan, the Duke of Norfolk, Lord John Russell, and Fox. The brother of the Duke of Leinster, and the friend of the great English Whigs, were persons to whom credence would be given, and who might be assumed to speak with authority. Lord Edward had a house at Hamburgh, where Pamela usually resided. Through Pamela he corresponded with the many friends which he possessed in Paris. There was nothing to excite suspicion in his going over to join his wife, or in his taking his friend with him. From Hamburgh they went privately to Switzerland, where Hoche met them by appointment; and the negociation being already

---

[1] 'Resolution of the executive council of United Irishmen. Summer of 1796.'—*Plowden*, vol. iv.

in train, as will be presently seen, through Wolfe Tone, Hoche held out hopes to them that France would take up Ireland's cause—that, in fact, he would himself at no distant time attempt a landing there.[1]

This secret was well kept. Serious ground as they had for suspecting both Lord Edward and O'Connor, the visit to Switzerland was unknown till the autumn of the ensuing year. The Government, however, knew more than enough to show them the problem with which they were confronted, while they were utterly at a loss how to deal with it. They had an army of informers, whose universal stipulation was that their names should be concealed, and that they should not be called on to give open evidence. One of these especially, whose name is still a mystery, was in the closest confidence of the Belfast leaders. He had been among the most enthusiastic of the original members of Tone's society, but he had fallen into debt to others of the confederates and had been expelled. In revenge he sold himself to the Government, satisfied his creditors with money which he received from Pelham, and was at once taken back into confidence.[2] Among others he became an intimate associate of William Orr, a Belfast tradesman, afterwards executed for treason, who at this time was a member of the Head Northern Committee. Orr told him that everything was ready. Dublin, Cork, and Limerick were waiting only for orders to rise; and when the word was given the movement was to be universal and simultaneous. They had 200,000 men already

---

[1] Report of the secret committee of the House of Lords, 1798.

[2] 'Strange infatuation!' he wrote to his employer; 'when I would have laid down my life to have saved theirs they treated me with insolence and contempt. Now they hail me as their friend. The money wrought miracles in my favour.'— '——to Pelham, 1796.' S.P.O. MSS.

officered in regiments, they had pikes and muskets for 150,000, and more were on the way. The militia were almost to a man United Irishmen; and in fact, according to Orr, they would have risen in the preceding autumn but for some differences among themselves.

For himself, the informer thought that nothing would be attempted till the arrival of the French. The Belfast men, Neilson, Orr, the two Simms's, the party who had taken the oath with Wolfe Tone on Cave Hill, he described 'as wealthy, wily, avaricious, tenacious of their property, distrustful of one another, and if afraid of nothing else, *desperately afraid of the Orangemen, who were five times stronger than people in general believed.*' They had authentic news that Hoche might be expected in the fall of the year, and then undoubtedly an effort would be made. If Hoche came, they were perfectly confident that Ireland would be a republic before Christmas. The instant that the signal was given the whole Orange party were to be assassinated; and the hope and belief of the Central Committee was that nothing could save the Government but treachery among themselves, or twenty or thirty thousand Scotch, English, or German soldiers.[1]

'It is my fixed opinion,' said the informer, sum-

---

[1] The informer, in his letter to Pelham, mentioned a curious story. 'To show you,' he says, 'that they tell me their secrets, here is the account told me of the death of Mr. McMurdoch, of Lurgan. Don't name it. If it get out, they will know whence it came, and my life will be the certain forfeit. McMurdoch was an Orangeman. On July 12 he and others were parading the street, and he quarrelled with a soldier of the 26th Militia. They fought. McMurdoch had the best of the battle. The soldier shouted for help. McMurdoch, seeing some people coming, fled. Delaney, another soldier, came up, and seeing his comrade down, whispered a word, changed coats, pursued McMurdoch, murdered him, and escaped on the trial from a confusion in the evidence.'

ming up his general conclusion, 'that unless Government disarms the militia or lands a large army of foreigners, the Royal authority will be overthrown. Were the militia done away with and the Orange party embodied, they, with their friends, might avert the blow. As it is now, the Government would be as safe with a republican army of Frenchmen in the island as they are with the militia. I asked Simms what they would do for specie when they had made their revolution. Send to the Jew brokers in Spain, said he, and mortgage the estates of the aristocrats, whose property would devolve to those from whom it was wrested. Be assured that what I have told you is true. The original agitators have been kept concealed even from the knowledge of the common people. The medium of dissemination has been the priests, and they have concealed from their congregations, on whom they have so effectively wrought, the names of those who have set them on, merely saying that there were men of influence, fortune, and power ready to come forward. The motive of the original agitators—and I mean by them the members of the Catholic Committee that sat in Dublin and many of the Convention that were not on the Committee—was to carry the Catholic Bill through Parliament by the influence of terrorism. I do not believe that they intended what was certainly an object of the Defenders—plunder and massacre—yet I am well convinced that at this day, in consequence of the rejection of the Bill, there are many who would risk the consequence of an invasion; and to a man their grand object is separation from Great Britain. On this there is no difference of sentiment.'[1]

[1] 'Secret information enclosed by Lord Camden to the Duke of Portland, August 6, 1796.'

That this and similar information which came in to them from a hundred quarters contained the exact truth the Irish Council were painfully aware. They were in the extraordinary position of an executive administration in possession of the inmost secrets of an intended and already organised insurrection. They had the names in their hands of most, if not all, of the leaders. They had evidence which, if they could have produced it, would have enabled them at once, and almost without effort, to have trampled out the danger; yet they could not publish what they knew, and appeal for permission to suspend the Constitution, for the Whigs in England would have clamoured that they were seeking excuses for introducing arbitrary power. Every witness that they possessed would have forsworn himself if dragged forward into a court, and thus they were condemned to sit still, as if enchanted, to watch the approach of a convulsion which, had they been free to act, they could have checked with the touch of a finger; and to bear the reproach in later times of having wickedly encouraged the rebellion, that they might ask afterwards for a renewal of the lease of tyranny.

To Lord Camden the prospect became daily more gloomy. A tree of liberty was planted in Antrim; passengers on the road were made to stop and touch their hats to it, and shout for France and freedom. The militia camp at Limerick 'was so infected with disloyalty' that General Dalrymple recommended the dispersion of the division stationed there. A soldier suspected of giving information to his officers was murdered. A sergeant of a Fencible regiment was shot at and mortally wounded for the same reason. Lord Carhampton had secreted two informers in his own park at Luttrell's Town. It did not save them. They were tracked out and found dead. So profound and so well-founded was the distrust of the militia that the country gentlemen applied for permission to raise companies of Yeomanry out of persons on whom they knew that they could depend. It was the Volunteer movement once more, but entered on by men who were now 'clothed and in their right minds.' The Government was reluctant. Lord Camden shivered at the thought that 'he would be charged with arming Protestants against Papists.' But 'in a moment of danger there was no remedy.'[1] Permission was given. Loyal Protestant Ireland drew its breath at last, and flew to arms in town and country.

The Orangemen, disowned in their special corporate existence, entered by hundreds into the Ulster regiments. The Corporation of Dublin raised four regiments of infantry, and four troops of horse. The Dublin Bar raised a corps. Lord Ormond brought into the field two troops of light cavalry at his own expense.[2] The national press screamed its loudest. Keogh and his friends applied for leave to raise Catholic corps beside the Protestant. Pelham congratulated them on their anxiety to defend their country, and told them that 'their services would be most welcome if they pleased to enter the regiments of their Protestant fellow-subjects; the Crown knew no differences of religion.' The Catholics turned off in pretended resentment. The movement went forward the more earnestly. In a few weeks more than 30,000 men were enrolled, and with the help of the

---

[1] 'Camden to Portland, August 24, 28, September 3. Portland to Camden, August 29.' S. P. O.

[2] 'Camden to Portland, September.' S. P. O.

Government stores most of them were armed. The militia were no longer masters of the situation; and with renewed confidence at the spirit which had shown itself Camden ventured a blow at the insurgent leaders. Napper Tandy, scenting danger, had fled, but Keogh was arrested in Dublin; and on the sam day Downshire and Castlereagh stooped down on Belfast with a regiment of dependable troops, seized Neilson, Orr, Russell, the two Simms's, and five other gentlemen, and brought them as prisoners to the Castle. Struck thus on the brain at a critical moment, and overawed by the rapidly-forming Yeomanry, the rebel organisation was embarrassed by its own completeness, and for many months—months, it will be seen, in which Ireland's fortunes were hanging in the balance—they were unable to rally from the blow. The Viceroy called Parliament together to legalise the Yeomanry and to justify these prompt measures by suspending the Habeas Corpus Act.

The autumn session was made as brief as possible, for the country gentlemen were needed at their homes. But though brief it was stormy. The Opposition, who had counted on the agitation to terrify the Government into conceding the Catholic claims, were furious at the success of measures which threatened the reassertion of Protestant ascendency. They professed to abhor rebellion: that the country should be kept upon the brink of it was vital to their hopes, and within the limits of the Constitution they played upon Irish passion with as much zeal as the Belfast Committee.[1]

[1] 'The Opposition are endeavouring to inflame the minds of the people; and as the channel of the House of Commons is the most legal, so it is the most dangerous mode of infusing that poison.'— 'Camden to Portland, October 13.'

An amendment to the Address was moved again by Grattan, who inveighed, as in the spring, on the impunity of the Orange outrages. He insisted that England should capitulate, as he called it, recall Fitzwilliam, and restore peace by abolishing distinctions of religion. To everyone who desired that Ireland should remain connected with Great Britain it was by this time certain that distinctions of religion could not be abolished there so long as a separate Parliament sat in Dublin. To propose the admission of the Catholics under a menace of invasion and insurrection was to presume on the presence in the House of a degree of folly and cowardice which even Grattan could not believe to exist there. His aim was not to convince the House, but to inflame the people out of doors. Pelham told him calmly that his speech might have come more fitly from a member of the French Convention, and that the exclusion of the Catholics from Parliament was necessary for the maintenance of the empire.

'Will the Catholics,' shrieked Grattan in reply, 'will the Irishmen suffer a stranger to tell us on what proud terms the English Government will consent to rule in Ireland?—to dictate the incapacity of the nation as the term of their dominion, and the base condition of our connection and allegiance?'

To this question, in a house of a hundred and sixty-one members, a hundred and forty-nine were found to answer yes, for twelve only followed Grattan to a division.

Undaunted by his friend's defeat, George Ponsonby opposed the suspension of the Habeas Corpus Act. 'The Irish Ministers,' he said, 'were men of vindictive spirit, and he would not sacrifice the liberty of the subject to the lovers of vengeance.'

The times were too serious for folly. Ponsonby was defeated more heavily than Grattan, by a hundred and thirty-seven to seven.

But the object was the publication of the speeches in the Dublin journals. Again Grattan brought up Emancipation, and let loose upon it the torrent of his eloquence. His motion was that the admission of the Catholics to Parliament was consistent with the security of the empire; his argument, the so-called Liberal assertion that the demands of the majority of a nation ought to be and must be conceded.

'It has come to this,' said Mervyn Archdall; 'in 1793 the Catholics were to be eternally grateful for admission to the franchise; they say now, Admit us to Parliament, and we will not thank you—refuse, and we will rebel.'

'Mr. Grattan tells us,' said Dr. Duigenan, 'that if his motion is not complied with, three million Catholics will rise in rebellion and join the Gallic murderers in an invasion. The agitators in Dublin are to a man republicans and democrats. The enemy which we have to confront is hatred to England and to the principles of the Revolution of 1688. Mr. Grattan speaks of the people of Ireland as if there were none but Catholics. Are we nothing, then! we Protestants? I said that the admission of the Catholics to Parliament had been the cause of all the trouble in Ireland from the time of Elizabeth to the Revolution, and I was called a prejudiced fool. Then were Burghley, Walsingham, Hampden, Russell, Somers, Hardwicke, all prejudiced fools, for the reason which influenced them in England exists at this moment in Ireland in all its forms?'

Grattan was of course defeated almost by as large a majority as before. Even among those who agreed with him in principle the sense was that his motion was ill-timed. 'The effect of the debates,' wrote Camden, ' was that the question had lost its weight. The few supporters felt the subject languid. The Government was on stronger ground than before. The small minority was to the full as advantageous as unanimity.'[1]

[1] 'Camden to Portland, October 18, 1796.' S. P. O.

SECTION IV.

ALTHOUGH the Government had collected sufficient courage to allow the Protestants to arm, they were still nervously anxious to avoid appearing to distrust the Catholics as such. Whatever their inward thought, they chose to appear to believe that the conspiracy was unconnected with religion, and that the agitation, although the Catholics had been tempted to join in it, was essentially revolutionary. Keogh was the only prominent Catholic who had been arrested. The gentlemen taken at Belfast were Jacobins or atheists. Lord Camden's amiable hope was that he might still detach the great body of the people, or if not the people, the militia and the soldiers of the line, from their dangerous leaders, and he became nervously anxious to re-establish 'private communications with the principal Catholic clergy and laity.' There was, in fact, but one condition under which the Catholic clergy and laity would ever really be useful to a British Government. As soon as they had been made thoroughly to understand that they were subjects of the British Crown, that England was strong enough to compel them to remain in their allegiance, and that she would exert that strength to the very utmost if they chose to play with rebellion, then there would be no longer reason to distrust them. No sincere Irish Catholic could ever, as Lord Clare said, be voluntarily loyal to a Protestant sovereign; but he would understand the duty of submission, and the duty of enforcing submission upon his countrymen, when he was made to see without disguise or circumlocution the nature of the alternative. Neither Pitt nor Camden could recognise so unpalatable a truth. The educated Catholic clergy came about them, soft and smooth-spoken, deprecating distrust, deploring the prejudices on both sides which embittered every question, and made a mutual understanding so difficult. An experience too uniform had shown that at critical moments these gentlemen had never practically succeeded in controlling the violence of their people; it was uncertain whether they had tried to control it. Yet the Government still listened to them, and still clung to the belief that they might be persuaded into lending genuine assistance in reestablishing order.

Lord Camden was looking earnestly among the Catholic priests for some one to assist him. He believed that he had found the person that he wanted in a certain Dr. Hussey, the friend and correspondent of Burke, and titular Bishop of Waterford. Dr. Hussey, in the eyes of Liberal politicians, was the model Catholic of his time—an enlightened ecclesiastic, who rose superior to the bigotry of his creed, and combined the spirit of genuine Christianity with the cultivated intelligence of a man of the world. He had been for some time in communication with the Cabinet on the condition of the Irish militia. He had affected to deplore the spread of disaffection in the ranks. He was in England during the autumn session, impressing upon Portland and Pitt his conviction that if the Catholic clergy were trusted they could restore a better spirit among them. He had offered his own services. So great, indeed, was his zeal and his anxiety, that he sued for and obtained some commission from the Pope in connexion with the Catholic soldiers; and in a conversation with Portland he intimated that his influence would be more beneficial if it could be combined with a recognition from the British Government, and 'a commission as Chaplain-General.'[1] Portland enquired what his Papal commission consisted in. Dr. Hussey said it was a power to confer on the Catholic chaplains of the Irish regiments the faculties necessary for their functions; and on this understanding Portland gave him his commission from the Crown. Thus armed the ingenious gentleman passed over to Ireland. He announced that the Pope had appointed him 'Vicar Apostolic over all the Catholic military in Ireland.'[2] His English commission saved him from risk of interference from the Castle, and suggested the impression which the revolutionary party especially desired to create, in order to weaken the Executive Government, that England was on the Catholic side, and disapproved of the coercive policy. His first official act was to throw an unjust and false stigma on the Castle authorities, and create a grievance which had no existence. He pretended to have discovered[3] that the Catholic soldiers in the militia were taken to Protestant churches, and were forbidden to attend services of

---

[1] 'The anxiety he expressed to obtain the appointment of Chaplain-General was stated by him to rise out of the necessity or advantage of his being placed in such a position by the Government as would qualify him to dispense or distribute the powers he had received from Rome to those for whom they were destined; meaning, as I understood, the chaplains. Had I the least suspicion that he would have made an improper use of these powers he never would have been entrusted with either.'—'Portland to Pelham, November 1, 1796.' S. P. O.

[2] 'Pelham to the Duke of Portland, October 26.' S. P. O.

[3] 'On enquiry it proved to be false. He was totally mistaken.'— 'Pelham to Portland, October 26.' S. P. O.

their own. Had Dr. Hussey really desired to quiet the mutinous spirit which he came over, as he said, to combat, he would have remembered, even if the charge had been true, that in Spain, as in the Papal dominions, a soldier who had refused to accompany his regiment to mass under plea of being a Protestant, would have been instantly shot for mutiny; and he would have remonstrated quietly and privately with the Viceroy or the Commander-in-Chief. But the supreme object of Irish incendiaries, from highest to lowest, was at that moment to stimulate disaffection in the army, and hatred against the Irish Administration. This enlightened and virtuous prelate, representing himself as speaking with the combined authority of the Pope and the English Cabinet, first invented an untrue charge, and then by letter instructed a priest in the camp outside Dublin ' to warn the artillerymen against the sin of attending the Protestant service, and directing them to resist by force.'[1] 'He then,' Pelham informed Portland, ' wrote a long exhortation to the Catholic soldiers in Ireland generally.[2] It is the most inflammatory and dangerous production that bigotry could suggest. He addresses the soldiers in a character which he says your Grace obtained for him from the Pope. He says he received his authority from the Pope, and that the Duke of Portland applied for it.'

Finally, in his character of peace-maker, Dr. Hussey published a pastoral to the clergy of his diocese, bidding them refuse the sacraments to parents who

---

[1] Pelham's secretary saw this letter.

[2] 'As it was certainly written with ability, his vanity got the better of his prudence, and that letter I have in my possession.'— 'Pelham to Portland, October 20.'

allowed their children to attend the Charter Schools; re-asserting that Catholic soldiers had been forced to attend Protestant places of worship, and bidding the priests instruct them that under such circumstances they were bound to disobey their officers.[1]

Lord Camden had brought into Ireland, as he supposed, a serpent of healing. Dr. Hussey had proved a reptile of a more common type, and had turned on him and stung him. Under any circumstances the eve of a rebellion was not the moment to invite soldiers to mutiny. His official recognition by the Cabinet was an additional obligation to forbearance. With ingenious wickedness Dr. Hussey took advantage of the opportunity which the Government had allowed him to aggravate to the very utmost the danger which he had undertaken to counteract, and exhibited in a remarkable instance the value of the support which the English Cabinet was so eager to conciliate.

In the Yeomanry the Castle possessed a force unassailable by the arts of priests. Coarser methods were therefore adopted to embarrass and weaken it. Countrymen who dared to enlist received warnings to withdraw, and refusing to obey, were assassinated. On the 1st of November the Government arsenal at Belfast was broken into and plundered. Informers stated that an organised system of murder was set on foot to terrify the Protestant clergy and magistrates into inactivity;[2] and whatever may have been their defects when contending in the open field, Irish

[1] 'Pastoral Letter by R.R. Dr. Hussey.'—*Plowden*, vol. iv. Appendix, 109.

[2] 'The principle of the United Irishmen is to *cure*, by which is meant to assassinate all persons and magistrates who actively oppose them.'—'Information forwarded by Lord Camden to the Duke of Portland, November 13.' S. P. O.

conspirators have always been signally successful with the midnight pike and pistol. The state of Ulster became so alarming, owing to the compelled inaction of the Orangemen, that Carhampton went to Antrim, in November, to apply the methods which had been successful in Connaught.[1] But the Cabinet were nervous and frightened; Portland expressed a hope that he would restore order without being driven to acts of severity.[2] Lord Camden said that the Cabinet's wishes, coupled with their remarks on the Insurrection Act, made him most unwilling to resort to its powers; but how without severity he was to deal with murders, threats of murder, plundering and sacking houses, waylaying and wounding soldiers, he was for his part at a loss to comprehend.[3]

In spite of cruisers and coastguard officers muskets and powder continued to pour in. In December an American brig was seized on the coast of Antrim with 20,000 stand of arms on board, and a train of artillery. In significant defiance the confederate peasants assembled in thousands to dig the potatoes and cut and carry the corn of the arrested leaders, and gave their field-work the ostentatious appearance of military display.[4]

---

[1] 'Camden to Portland, November 1.'

[2] 'Portland to Camden, November 5.'

[3] 'Camden to Portland, November 14.' S. P. O.

[4] Sir George Hill describes one of these singular scenes, in a letter to Secretary Cooke. Having notice of an intended assembly for potato-digging, he took sixty soldiers with him and repaired to the spot, with the Sheriff and Lord Henry Murray. 'About eleven,' he writes, 'we saw an immense crowd coming along the hills, from the mountains which separate the Maghera side from the Newtown side of the county of Derry. About a thousand came to the river which was between us. Five hundred forded it immediately; and as they came directly up to us, we imagined it might turn out a troublesome affair to them. We left the military at a distance, rode up, and ordered

Throughout the island, or the greater part of the island, the people were ready with arms concealed to rise and fall into the ranks assigned to them under local leaders already chosen. Happily for the peace of Ireland, they had been deprived at that particular moment of the central authority on which they relied for general direction of the men through whom was passing the correspondence with France, by the arrest of those on whom devolved the duty of giving the signal when the invaders were to be looked for.

them not to proceed. The Sheriff read the proclamation. I spoke to them. They remonstrated with all imaginable cunning professions of peace and humility. Would we impede them in the charitable work of digging a forlorn woman's potatoes, whose husband was in gaol? If we persisted to order it they would disperse; at the same time begged to be informed if they were at liberty to dig their own potatoes on their respective farms. I answered, and they dispersed. We withdrew a quarter of a mile with the soldiers. Then they galloped up again, their numbers being by this time trebled. We brought up the soldiers a second time, and gave them ten minutes to disperse, which they did. There was no shouting, no imprecations, no seditious language, uttered by any of them. About half had spades. What alarmed me most was to observe the calmness observed by people assembled in such multitudes, and yet acting with one system, evidently under the control of invisible guidance, no leader or heads appearing. Every man held his spade like a musket, and seemed, notwithstanding the humble cant, to show you, by the manner he balanced it, and his erect gait, that he could manage the other as well.'
'Sir G. Hill to Mr. Cooke, November 14.' S. P. O.

SECTION V.

BOOK IX.
1796.

THE story returns to Wolfe Tone, who was left embarking at Belfast for America, after devoting himself anew to the cause of his country at MacArt's fort. His companions on that remarkable occasion were now at Dublin, in Newgate. He himself, after a successful voyage across the Atlantic, arrived with his family at Philadelphia at the end of the summer of 1795. Here he found his friends Rowan and Napper Tandy. Here, too, he made acquaintance with M. Adet, the Minister of the French Republic; and whether it was from the aspect of a new country, the advice of Rowan, who had forsworn Irish politics, or the coolness of Adet, when he communicated to him his hopes and purposes, certain it was that Tone began to think that life might have better objects than making revolutions, and was making up his mind to a quiet residence in America. He bought a farm at Princeton, in New Jersey, where he settled his wife and children. He was accustoming his hand to axe and plough, and was sinking into useful industry, when he was roused by letters from Keogh and Neilson, which told him how fast Ireland was ripening, and pressed to lose not a moment in bringing France to their help. Tone's nature was easily set on fire. The Simms's sent him money. Taking his letters to Adet, and receiving in return introductions in cypher to M. de la Croix, the Minister for Foreign Affairs at Paris, he once more committed himself to the ocean, sailed for Havre, and landed there on the 2nd of February,

1796. Thence, in high spirits, lively, and jaunty as ever, he proceeded to Paris.

Of all the United Irishmen, of all Irish rebels of whom the history of that country retains a record, Wolfe Tone is the least offensive. He tells no lies about himself. He never deals in inflated sentiment, unless when he confesses to have been drunk, or when drawing a programme for his society, at which perhaps he laughed in his sleeve. He hated England because he considered that England had slighted him, but he never conceals that he would have accepted gladly the most common-place employment if Pitt would have condescended to bestow it upon him. His frankness disarms indignation, for he paints himself as he really was, light, rollicking, ignorant, unread in everything except in Shakespeare, with a talent for ornamental writing, which he valued at no more than its worth, hating humbug and pretence, and plunging along the career of revolution with a careless impetuosity, more as if he was riding with the Kilkenny foxhounds than concerned in any serious purpose.

On the 12th of February he was in Paris, the paradise of republican imagination. Fresh from the expenses of Philadelphia, he found himself in luxury which cost him next to nothing. He breakfasts and dines in the Maison Égalité, claret and Burgundy flowing like water; and the enjoyments once the privilege of the few, now, under the blessed auspices of the Revolution, being within reach of the humblest. He saunters in the Champs Élysées, and his eyes glisten in sympathy with the laughing crowds. At the theatre the band plays the 'Marseillaise.' The entire audience is on its feet to join in the Litany of Freedom. At the words 'Aux armes, Citoyens!' the

National Guards deploy upon the stage. The spectacle transforms itself into a superb revolutionary pageant; every heart beats, and with sublime emotion every youth pants for an opportunity of pouring out his lifeblood for his country. No wonder that Tone, to whom France had for five years been a land of promise, was delighted with what he saw, and none the less, when the papers began to fill with accounts of the doings in Italy of the young Napoleon. Who could say but Napoleon might be liberator of Ireland, or if not Napoleon then Hoche, the hero of Quiberon? He waited on de la Croix, and presented Adet's letter. The Foreign Minister was civil. The Directory had long known that Ireland was England's vulnerable side. Their difficulty had been to understand so singular a people, who in faith were ardent Catholics, yet in politics were said to be eager for insurrection. Tone was ready with abundant explanation. None could speak with more authority than he. He could say with truth that he had been agent of the Catholic Committee, that he was the founder of the United Irishmen, and was in the confidence of the chiefs of the Defenders. With less truth, but not without foundation, he assured the Directory that the whole of Ireland was ripe for revolt, except the lords and gentlemen and clergy of the Established Church. Nor was Ireland all; for more than half the seamen in the British fleet were Irish; half the British army were Irish—the Yeomanry not being yet enrolled. England, he could say correctly, had but a handful of troops in the island on which she could rely, for the militia was heart and soul with the nation; and on the first sight of the green flag every Irish soldier and sailor in the service would turn upon his officers.

The Directory, when so flattering a report was brought to them, enquired naturally why, if this was the true account of the situation, Ireland was doing nothing for herself? The brighter the colouring of Tone's picture the more inexplicable the apathy.

The true answer would have been, not that Tone had given an inaccurate account of the disposition of his countrymen, but that while no people talked more passionately of their nationality, no people also had so few of the virtues on which national life depends. The Irish had no coherence, no fortitude, no power of self-sacrifice. The patriotism of which they boasted was from the lips outwards. Even Tone himself would at that moment have become a faithful subject of King George if Pitt had offered him a writership in India.

To the French Government he could but insist that the fact was as he described it. If France would send help, the Irish would rise effectually. If left to themselves, their local and partial insurrections would be easily and savagely repressed. The chain would only be drawn tighter, and the common enemy of Ireland and France would be stronger than ever.

De la Croix enquired if it would not be sufficient to supply arms. Tone said it would not. Would two thousand men be sufficient? Tone told him he might as well send twenty. Two thousand men would be overwhelmed before the people could join them, and there would be a second Quiberon. This, too, seemed strange, if the twenty thousand militia were prepared to mutiny. The negociation hung fire. It had been conducted so far through subordinates. Tone consulted Monroe, the American Minister. Monroe advised him to go straight to head-quarters, and demand an audience with Carnot. He tells the story of the interview with characteristic *naïveté*.

'Feb. 24, 1796.—To the Luxembourg. I am a pretty fellow to go to the Directoire Exécutif! In a fright—conning speeches in execrable French all the way. What shall I say to Carnot? Whatsoever the Lord putteth in my mouth that surely shall I utter. Pluck up my spirits. Mount the stairs like a lion. Request to see Carnot. Clerk stares, but sends me up. Admitted. Carnot in white satin with crimson robe. In horrid French I said I was an Irishman, secretary and agent to three million Catholics in that country, representative also of nine hundred thousand Dissenters of that kingdom, all eager to throw off the yoke of England. He doubted my numbers. I reasserted them. The population of Ireland was near about four millions and a half. Of these three million nine hundred thousand were for France and against England. He asked what we wanted. An armed force, I answered, as a *point d'appui* to begin with, with arms and a little money. He put many questions which showed that he had been thinking the subject over. I am to see him again. Perhaps my abhorrence and detestation of the name of England makes me too sanguine. What will Fitzgibbon say now? He used to call me a viper in the bosom of Ireland. He lies. I am a better Irishman than he and his whole gang of rascals. I am as vain as the Devil. Allons, Enfans de la patrie.'[1]

M. de la Croix now sent for Tone again. The British navy, he said, was France's difficulty. But

[1] *Memoirs of Wolfe Tone*, by himself. February 1796. First interview with Carnot. Abridged.

for the British navy sixty thousand men could be landed in Kent, march on London, and settle England and Ireland together. Could not the Irish seamen, if they were as numerous as Tone said, bring about a convenient mutiny?

There was much to be done in that way, as was found two years later at Portsmouth and at the Nore, but Tone did not respond. He did not like circuitous methods. Let Home Rule be first established in Dublin, and every Irishman in the British Empire would then have a centre of allegiance there. He was impatient to be on the way. Moments were precious. In a few weeks the Channel fleet would be at sea. He heard that military camps were forming in Ireland. A German contingent might be sent. The British army might be reinforced. A thousand things might happen if France was long in making up its mind. He consoled himself by his old methods.

'I finish my choice bottle of Burgundy every day. Too much. I resolve every morning to drink but half, and every day break my resolution. I wish I had P. P. here,[1] and then perhaps I should live more soberly. Oh, Lord! Soberly! Yes, we should be a sober pair of patriots. It is squires' custom every afternoon as soon as he is drunk. Huzza! I hope to see a battle yet before I die. The French have an abominable custom of adulterating their Burgundy with water.'

By-and-bye Carnot bade him draw up some plan, that he might judge of it. He offered two. The first, which he thought certain to succeed, would be

[1] His friend Russell.

to land twenty thousand men close to Dublin. The capital must fall, and the Catholic Committee and the United Irish leaders would be on the spot to form a new Government. If twenty thousand men could not be spared, five thousand might be thrown on shore somewhere near Belfast. They could seize the line of the Few mountains, and the country would have time to organise before they could be dislodged.

Carnot, with all Europe on his hands, had no leisure to discuss details. He turned Tone over to General Clarke, an Irishman of the 'Old Brigade.' Clarke, who was a gentleman, and had inherited old-fashioned traditions, had no objection to an orderly conquest, but doubted the propriety of letting loose the ferocious Irish Catholic peasantry. Infinite horrors he thought would follow unless the mob could be held in order.

Tone admitted that many shocking things were likely and even certain to happen, but a massacre on the most extensive scale would be no more than retributive justice. No men on earth had been more oppressive and tyrannical than the gentry of Ireland, and they and their families would be the principal sufferers.

Wretched gentry of Ireland! It was for this, then, that they had armed the Volunteers of '82, and demanded a Constitution at the bayonet's point, with Grattan at their head. Like the companions of Ulysses they had let loose the winds with their own foolish hands, and were now likely to perish in the tempest.

To the apostle of the new creed General Clarke appeared 'thirty years behind his age;' unequal altogether to the era of the Guillotine and the Rights of Man.

Amidst these discussions the project of invasion was mistily taking shape. Bonaparte's campaign in Italy made the Directory sanguine. In April they began to contemplate seriously sending a fleet to the Irish coast, and landing arms and cannon. But while the grass grew the steed was starving. News came of Gunpowder Acts and Insurrection Acts, and sharp measures in Connaught, and then of the arrest of Keogh,[1] the penitent Gog, just when he had abjured his errors and was on the right track.

'That infernal Government of Ireland!' was Tone's comment; 'if I cannot prevent his fall I will revenge it. The Irish aristocracy shall take the consequences. They show no mercy, and they deserve none. If ever I have the power I will most heartily concur in making them a dreadful example. Oh, France! France! what do you not deserve if you suffer this crisis to escape you?'

There was no lack of will in France; but the 'Organiser of victory' had not conquered Holland and Italy, and driven the Germans over the Rhine, by blindly rushing on in the dark. Ireland, with its priests and its patriots, its blazing promises and ineffectual performances, was a questionable problem, to be well scanned before it was meddled with. Again Tone sought Carnot. Carnot told him that they wanted more information.

Three more entries in the journal record his dreams and his impatience.

'May 2.—The Luxembourg. They will send a

---

[1] Keogh was arrested in the spring of 1796.

trusted agent to Ireland, and will be guided by his report. Nothing definite. I begin to fear it will be the backwoods of America again. Delay! delay!

'June 20.—My birthday. Thirty-three years old. At that age Alexander had conquered the world, and Wolfe had expired in the arms of Victory. The British fleet is in the Channel, so nothing will be done before the winter.

'June 28.—Oh, if the British were once chased from Ireland, as the Austrians from Milan! Who knows? But this fleet torments me. Damn them! Sink them! with God knows how many admirals!'

No foreign power had ever meddled with Ireland without repenting it. Twice the Popes had sent help to their afflicted children. Gregory the Thirteenth had sent a legate and a few hundred Italians. The legate perished in a bog; the bodies of the Italians were buried in the sands at Smerwick. When the massacre of 1641 restored Ireland for a brief interval to the native race, Innocent the Tenth despatched the Cardinal Rinuccini to restore and reinvigorate the Church. The Irish themselves made the country intolerable to him. He struggled in vain to coerce them with spiritual thunder, and abandoned his task as impossible. Philip the Second sent an army to assist in completing the destruction of the British power there, which was described to him as all but annihilated. The British power proved strong enough to defeat the Irish, to take the Spaniards prisoners, and send them home wiser than they had come. Louis the Fourteenth had taken up the cause with the fairest prospects of all, yet Louis had prospered no better, and wearied of his allies after a brief taste of their quality. The Directory, it is likely, after carefully considering matters, would have decided unfavourably but for the unexpected support which the cause suddenly received in communications from Lord Edward Fitzgerald and Arthur O'Connor. General Hoche, who had been already consulted on Tone's schemes, was deputed to meet them, and substantially, as far as concerned the prospects of an Irish rising, they confirmed what Tone had said. Here was something substantial. The brother of the Duke of Leinster, and the heir of an Irish peerage, carried an authority even among republicans which could not be allowed to an adventurer like Tone. Their adherence, at any rate, seemed a security that the intended rebellion would not be a simple rising of a savage peasantry against the wealthy and the educated, but a respectable revolt against a foreign oppressor.

The interview was a profound secret, but Hoche returned from it with his mind made up. One day in the middle of July, when Tone was sitting despondent in his room, he was summoned to the Luxembourg. He found himself in the presence of a distinguished-looking officer, who told him that he was General Hoche, and proceeded to question him on a number of points—how an army could be fed in Ireland, what was the disposition of the priests, the humour of the militia, the condition and numbers of the British force. He then alluded, as if incidentally, to Arthur O'Connor, and asked if he was not in Parliament. 'There is a lord too in your country who is a patriot, the son of a duke, is there not?' he added. Tone spoke applaudingly of both Lord Edward and his friend, without guessing the motive of the question. He praised the Duke of Leinster, who, he said, would be neutral if not favourable. The rest of the aristocracy he apprehended would be massacred through the just indignation of the people, whom they had so cruelly oppressed.

The reply to this was a sharp and unexpected expression of disgust. Hoche, however, said little, and the ambitious genius of the Young Irelander was somewhat overawed. 'Hoche,' writes Tone, with creditable candour, 'told Clarke he had got me by heart. Was that a compliment? I fear he does spy into the bottom of this Justice Shallow. Never mind. If the business is done, it matters little whether I have any talents or not.' Hoche, indeed, saw through Tone, but still on the whole liked him. He determined to take him with him, as likely to be useful in landing; and, that he might have a chance, if taken, of escaping the gallows, he gave him a commission in the French army.

All was now running smoothly. The expedition was to sail, and sail as soon as transports could be got ready. Tone mentioned the English fleet. Hoche laid his hand on his arm:

'Ne craignez rien,' he said; 'nous irons, vous pouvez y compter,' but again intimated, like de la Croix, that a mutiny of the Irish seamen would be highly convenient. He was equally positive as to the point on which the invasion was to be directed, and he would have acted more wisely if he had listened to Tone's opinion. The most dangerous and the best organised of the United Irishmen were the Ulster Republicans. Tone advised that the expedition should sail from some port in Holland, and be directed upon the North of Ireland or on Dublin. Hoche decided to sail from Brest, and to land in Munster. The essential thing, however, was to land somewhere, and about this no question was longer entertained. The plans were arranged. Hoche was to take with him 'the very élite of the Army of the Ocean,' and as large a number as Tone himself had asked for. They went together to Brest in October to hurry forward the preparations. At Brest they heard that the Irish Government had taken the alarm, and had arrested the members of the Belfast Committee. At the moment Wolfe Tone was unable to realise how serious a blow had been struck. In a society at once secretly and severely organised an injury to the brain is temporary paralysis. He had been kept in ignorance of the accession of Lord Edward and O'Connor to the cause, and outside his own circle there was no one known to him to whom information could be sent of the intended expedition, that the separate lodges might be prepared. To deceive the English, the armament assembling at Brest was represented in the papers as designed against Portugal. The Irish County Committees were at the mercy of rumours. The French were actually coming, and there were no means of letting the Irish insurgents know it, that they might prepare to receive them.

For his reception in Ireland Hoche relied wholly upon Tone. In his own share of the matter he meant, as he said, to leave nothing to chance. An English squadron lay between Brest and Ushant. There would perhaps be a fight, but he intended to be in overwhelming force. An American officer, Colonel Tate, was despatched as a diversion with eleven hundred ruffians of the Légion Noire to surprise and burn Bristol.[1] Admiral Joyeuse was busy day

[1] This party landed at Milford, and were almost immediately taken prisoners.

and night in harbour and dockyard with the equipments of the fleet. Hoche, to Tone's disgust, amused himself in the interval with a pretty Breton aristocrat, risking a bullet which might ruin all. Tone himself plunged daily up and down on the ramparts, watching the sea and ships, and cursing the lagging hours.

On the 1st of December Joyeuse announced that he was ready, and orders were issued to embark. The expedition was on a scale which, if it reached Ireland, could not fail to effect something considerable. The fleet consisted of seventeen ships of the line and eleven frigates and corvettes. In addition there were fifteen transports, large and small. The army was composed of fifteen thousand of the very best troops which France possessed, with heavy trains of field artillery, and sufficient spare muskets and powder to arm half the peasants in Ireland. The reputation of General Hoche was second only to that of Napoleon. The officer next in command was Grouchy. The point of attack was to be either Cork, Waterford, or Limerick, as circumstances might determine. The weather was unusually fine. The wind had hung in the east throughout November, and remained in the same quarter, blowing straight for the Irish coast, with the water as smooth as at midsummer.

The inveterate negligence which characterised English policy whenever the interests of Ireland were at stake had left Brest for a moment unwatched. The blockading squadron, so inattentive while at its post that a French admiral had passed in without a shot being fired, bringing five large ships to Joyeuse, had drawn off afterwards, leaving the sea entirely open. Independent of the Yeomanry, Lord Camden had not ten thousand men on whom he could rely, and to bring them into the field he must strip of its garrison every town in the country. Could Joyeuse carry his fleet into some safe Irish harbour, and could Hoche throw his army on the shore, nothing short of a miracle could save the English power in Ireland from temporary destruction or the unhappy country from an insurrection which would reproduce on a yet more extended scale the crimes and miseries of 1641.

The troops embarked as they were ordered. Day passed after day and the east wind blew fair; yet still one obstruction after another delayed their departure for a fortnight. On the evening of the 15th of December the signal was made at last to prepare to weigh. The morning following the entire fleet, forty-three sail in all, cleared out of the harbour and were on the way to the Irish coast. The weather was still so fine that they ventured the passage of the Raz, a narrow sound, peculiarly dangerous from the violence of the tide which sweeps through it. Night came on them before they had reached the open water. The 'Séduisant,' with five hundred men on board, struck on a rock and was lost with all hands. Her misfortune was unknown to her consorts. From bad seamanship, or some other cause, the ships were scattered. When day broke eighteen sail only were visible from the deck of the 'Indomptable,' an 84-gun line-of-battle ship, on board which were Tone and the regiment to which he was attached. The 'Fraternité,' a frigate, which carried Hoche and his staff, was nowhere to be seen. The rendezvous, in the event of separation, was Mizen Head. The orders to each vessel which might have strayed was to cruise off Mizen Head for five days, then to proceed to the mouth of the Shannon and wait there for three days; if by that time the rest of the fleet had not appeared, she was to return to Brest. On the 18th there was a dense fog, which partially lifted towards evening. The same eighteen ships were in sight. The 'Immortalité,' with Grouchy, was made out to be one of them. At dawn, on the 19th, twelve other vessels were showing, but there were still no signs of the 'Fraternité.' The fog was followed by a dead calm, which continued all day, a sure precursor in those seas at that time of year of a shift of wind or change of weather. Three more stragglers drifted up in the afternoon. Thirty-three out of the forty-three were now collected. The wind on the 20th chopped round to the westward, bringing mist and haze, but it remained light, and at night there was again a calm. On the 21st Cape Clear was in sight, twelve miles distant. Thirty-five sail were then counted, and only two frigates missing; of the two, however, one was still the 'Fraternité,' with her precious freight. As the wind stood they could then with ease have either made Kinsale, where there were but two English men-of-war to oppose them, or they could have forced their way through the weak defences of Cork Harbour, or have run up to Waterford. Bantry Bay was open before evening. At any time during that day or the next, had Grouchy ventured to act on his own responsibility, he might have chosen his own point of landing, and Cork must inevitably have fallen. It had no land defences, and on the side of the sea no batteries which a couple of line-of-battle ships could not have silenced. General Dalrymple, who was in command there, had four thousand men only. Had Grouchy known Dalrymple's weakness, and had he known also that at that moment there were in

Cork two years' provision stores for the British navy, valued at nearly two millions, he would probably have risked the displeasure, or rather have earned the gratitude, of his senior officer by stooping at once on so splendid a prize.

Then, as twenty years later, on another occasion no less critical, Grouchy was the good genius of the British Empire. He continued to cruise as he was directed, standing off and on upon that uncertain coast. On the evening of the 22nd the wind whirled back into the east, and surged down the rifts between the hills with fitful menacing gusts that foretold a storm. Beating in the face of it with extreme difficulty, sixteen of the best sailors, the 'Immortalité' among them, recovered Bantry Bay and beat their way into it to Bere Island, where they anchored. The rest were blown to sea, to stay there till the wind should abate.

On the morning of the 23rd it was blowing a gale, and blowing with the peculiar fury to be met with only in long narrow bays enclosed within mountain ranges. Snow was falling fast, hiding the land and hiding the ships from one another. During that day they were unable to communicate. On the 24th there was a lull. A council of war was held in the cabin of the 'Immortalité.' The division in the bay was found to contain between six and seven thousand soldiers, with the largest proportion of the small arms and cannon. Tone advised that they should proceed immediately as they were, and work the ships to the head of the estuary, to the sheltered roadstead behind Whiddy Island. There a landing would be easy, and they could push their way instantly to Cork. The officers were eager and in high spirits. Grouchy agreed, the anchors were lifted, and the fleet began to struggle towards Bantry. Unhappily for them, the wind rose again and blew dead in their teeth. After eight hours of desperate effort they had not gained a yard. At dark they anchored again at their old places.

Wilder yet broke Christmas Day, the bay brown with dirty foam, the hills deep in snow, the tempest shrieking over the water. What was to be done? Every moment was precious. Their arrival had been a surprise, but their presence on the coast must have been by this time signalled over the island, and whatever troops the English had must be on the march to the threatened point. Tone had calculated, and perhaps rightly, that could they have landed on the 24th they would have taken Cork without firing a shot. Now, at least, they would have to fight a battle, and visions began to float before him of capture and a possible gallows. He was fertile in expedients. The troops in Limerick would be on the way to Cork. As the wind stood it would be easier to reach the mouth of the Shannon than Bantry. To take Limerick might be even better than to take Cork. But Tone could give no commands, and the 'Immortalité' was anchored on the other side of the bay, and the sea was too wild to allow a boat to live. Another day went by, spent in curses upon weather which refused to mend. At night a frigate swept by the 'Indomptable.' Some one on her deck shouted through the screaming of the storm to cut cable and make for sea. The officers of the 'Indomptable' knew not what the frigate was or who had hailed them. They waited for day, and day brought a fog so thick that they could not see the length of their own ship.

Six days now in Bantry Bay, the Irish shore almost

within speaking distance, the wind fair from England, and the English fleet still neglecting to come in search of them. Yet with so fair an opportunity they were prevented from using it by an accident which might not occur in a bay like Bantry once in a dozen years.

On the 27th the tempest was so furious that they dragged their anchors. One by one they cut their cables and were swept, under bare poles, to sea. By midday eight vessels only remained. But these were the best in the fleet. They had still four thousand men, afraid of nothing, and equal to any work which soldiers could do. The chance of Cork was lost, but they might try some other point on the West coast. They were ashamed to go back having attempted nothing. The eight ships weighed and sailed, intending to keep together and attempt a descent on Clare.

But it was the story of the Armada over again, and in the same sea where the mightiest of the Spanish galleons had gone down the revolutionary invaders were encountered by the same enemies. As they ran out clear of the Durseys the hurricane backed towards the west. The sea, which, as long as the wind was off shore, had been moderately smooth, now rose with a fury with which French seamanship could not dare to contend. A huge wave struck the 'Indomptable,' stove in the quarter-gallery, and swamped the cabins. At a signal from the commodore the remnant of the magnificent squadron wore round and retraced its course towards Brest, where, after having met with no human opposition, having never seen an English flag, and having been baffled only by an extraordinary combination of accidents, all the ships but four eventually reappeared. The 'Séduisant' and one other vessel were lost; two, being crippled by the storm, were picked up by English cruisers. The 'Fraternité,' which had parted from the fleet on the night after they had sailed, had never reached Ireland at all. She had strayed from her course in the fog; and being afterwards caught in the gale, had crept into Rochelle.

SECTION VI.

Such is the story of the French invasion of Ireland in 1796, so far as it was known to Wolfe Tone on the deck of the 'Indomptable.' The inner or Irish side of it is equally curious and instructive.

On the 23rd of December, Mrs. White, the wife of Mr. White, of Seafield, near Bantry, rushed breathless into Cork barracks to tell General Dalrymple that twenty-five French men-of-war were beating into Bantry Bay. An O'Sullivan from Berehaven came immediately after, saying that he had himself counted eighteen large ships, and that ten more were reported to have been seen in the offing. A third messenger from Dunmanus[1] came with further news that a boat had landed there, the crew of which declared that the whole number of the fleet was thirty-eight, and that on board they had fifty thousand men. It was clear to Dalrymple, at all events, that a large French force of some kind had arrived. An express was sent off to Dublin and an express-boat to England. Dalrymple set what force he had in motion without a moment's delay, and pushed forward to Dunmanway, where fresh information was waiting for him. Mr. White himself, knowing the importance of time, was doing his best to obstruct, if he could not prevent, the expected landing. The people, having received no orders from the Revolutionary Committee, were

---

[1] The south-east side of Bantry Bay, opposite Berehaven.

falling into their natural places. White reported that all ranks were supporting him, and every hour was bringing him fresh volunteers. For the moment the weather made landing impossible. Should the storm abate he undertook to do his very best,[1] and he received unexpected and valuable help in a naval officer, Lieutenant Pulling, who came up from Berehaven. Admiral Kingsmill, having heard at Kinsale that a large fleet was on the coast, had despatched his Flag Lieutenant, Mr. Pulling, in a revenue cutter to reconnoitre. Pulling had followed the French fleet into the bay, had slipped in behind Bere Island into Castletown, and after attempting in vain to examine the ships more closely, had ridden off to Bantry, to Mr. White's house. Had the weather moderated they could have offered but little resistance, but at any rate there was as yet no disposition visible in the peasantry to join the invaders.

Dalrymple's experience was not less favourable. On the road between Cork and Dunmanway he described the people as 'behaving charmingly,'[2] and on the people everything depended. If there was a general rising, troops could not be spared to reinforce him from other parts of the island.

If the same spirit which prevailed in Cork prevailed elsewhere, and if he was allowed but a week before Hoche attacked him, he counted that by that time he would have of regular Yeomanry and militia perhaps fourteen thousand men, and with them, though all too few, he hoped to make a stand. He calculated with certainty that before many days the Portsmouth fleet would be in the bay. If due ex-

---

[1] 'Richard White to General Coote, December 24.' S. P. O.

[2] 'Dalrymple to Pelham, December 24.'

pedition was made, it might come in time to find[1] the French army still on board, and take or destroy them.

He might look long before he would see the Portsmouth fleet. While Dalrymple was straining every nerve at Dunmanway, the Duke of Portland was calmly writing to Lord Camden that there was no harbour in France except Brest where a hostile expedition could be equipped, and Brest had been so closely watched that it was impossible such a force could have come out as the news from Ireland reported.[2] Camden too, when the Cork express reached him, 'confessed himself not to entertain any strong expectation that the fleet would prove to be that of an enemy.'[3] Camden, however, did not rest in his incredulity. Acting as if the worst was true, he sent from Dublin every man that he had, 'the Yeomanry corps displaying the most splendid spirit,' and taking charge of the city while the garrison was wanted in the field. Limerick and Galway 'vied with each other in demonstrations of loyalty.' From all parts of the southern provinces regiments of the line and of the militia were streaming by forced marches towards Dunmanway. The militia betrayed no signs of backwardness. Snow fell and lay deep. The peasantry 'showed the troops the utmost hospitality.' They lodged them at night in their cabins; they shared their potatoes with them when they rested in the villages at midday. Though sworn probably to a

[1] 'If the wind fly to the west, which it probably will, and if it snows, which we expect, they cannot leave Bantry Bay, and must fall a sacrifice to that which, I suppose, must arrive, unless the probable never happens.'—'Dalrymple to Pelham, December 26. From Dunmanway.' S. P. O.
[2] 'Portland to Camden, December 26.'
[3] 'Camden to Portland, December 24.' S. P. O.

man to join the French when they arrived, they turned out with their spades to clear the snow from the roads for the baggage-waggons.

It was now a question of time. Could reinforcements reach Dalrymple before Hoche could land and destroy him and make himself master of Cork? Most nervously he watched the sky. Another French boat had come on shore. The officer was made prisoner, brought to Dalrymple's head-quarters and questioned. He told the exact truth, and the truth was not reassuring.

' Unless our fleet arrives,' he wrote again on the 26th, ' the first fair day the French will assemble in the bay and the troops land. They will find difficulties; but composed as they are of the chosen part of the army, I am inclined to think they will find the way. I cannot say what we shall do. The troops suffer extremely from the inclemency of the weather.[1] The greatest alertness appears in the Yeomanry and the people in the towns. I would fain hope the attachment will not change in case of misfortune. Time will prove.'

The next morning Dalrymple was at Bantry, breathing somewhat more freely.

' December 27.—The tempest continues. No debarkation has been effected, and we have had more time to prepare than we expected. The arrival of the troops from Limerick will enable us to cover Cork. The French fleet must soon go to sea, but they will probably land the soldiers, and not unlikely occupy Bere Island, which may easily be defended.

---

[1] It was the usual story. The call for service was sudden, and there were neither tents, blankets, spare clothes, nor any one other requisite for a winter campaign at hand.

The season has been uncommonly severe. The troops were little prepared for war, and have suffered.

'December 28.—Blew a hurricane last night. Report says they are driven to sea. If forced by superior strength, we mean to fall back towards Cork; at all events, to endeavour to secure Cork, which we shall not abandon unless forced by imperious circumstances.'[1]

A few hours later Mr. White briefly announced—'They are all gone to the devil.' He was premature. After the first detachment had disappeared, stray ships dropped in with the mending of the weather from the rest of the scattered fleet, and the expedition was thought to be returning. On the 31st four line-of battle-ships, a frigate, and two sloops were in the mouth of the bay, and four others were in the offing. On the 3rd of January six large ships were at the Berehaven anchorage, two frigates at Whiddy Island, and four other frigates in the bay. They formed a part of the fleet which had been in the mouth of the Shannon, and were returning in search of their consorts.[2] But no consorts appeared, and at length they gave up expecting them. On the 7th they were reported to have finally disappeared. The suspense was over, and a danger so great that only when it was over men were able to understand what they had escaped, passed away as suddenly as it had appeared.

Two points, before uncertain, had been established by the attempt—

First, that Ireland could never more rely on the

---

[1] 'Letter from General Dalrymple to Pelham, December 1796.' S. P. O.

[2] 'Dalrymple to Pelham, January 3, 1797.'

BOOK IX.
1797.
January.

protection of the British fleet. A French expedition had been able to leave Brest, to approach the Irish shore, to lie in and about its bays for a fortnight, and return to France without being met and fought with. Admiral Kingsmill had at Cork and Kinsale the 'Monarch,' an eighty-gun ship; two frigates, the 'Magnanimous' and the 'Diana;' and the guardship. On the first alarm the 'Powerful,' a seventy-four, was sent over, and half-a-dozen frigates. Two of the latter came into Cork so shattered by the storm that they were described as wrecks. As soon as Portland could be brought to believe that the expedition was a real fact, Lord Bridport was ordered over from Portsmouth; but instead of hurrying to Bantry, where he might still have been in time to catch the last division which left it, he lingered in the mouth of the Channel, and took at last one ship and one frigate, and that was all.

When the worst was over the Cabinet made light of the peril. Portland affected to regret that the landing had not been attempted, 'so confident was he of the loyalty and bravery of the troops.' As soon as Bridport had sailed he promised Camden 'that he should hear no more of the Armada but its disasters and distresses.' 'The French fleet should be again in Bantry Bay, but brought there as an example of their rashness, and trophies for the loyal and brave people of Ireland to contemplate.'[1] Bombast was a bad substitute for energy. 'The loyal and brave people of Ireland' had received but poor encouragement at a moment when England was needing their services to the full as much as they needed the help of England; and the proved facility by which a

[1] 'Portland to Camden, January 17, 1707.'

French invasion could be accomplished on the largest scale was an obvious temptation to the Irish rebels to expect, and to the French to venture, a second experiment.

'We have had an escape,' Lord Camden wrote, on the 10th of January, 'which, on account of the impression which it has made, I wish had not been owing so entirely to the winds. I should not deserve the confidence with which I am honoured if I did not apprise you that a universal discontent prevails here that a hostile fleet should have presumed to have insulted our coast for three weeks. They argue that a descent was to have been expected. They feel their situation much less tranquil if the French may think their fleet has been here so long unmolested by that of Great Britain. Great dissatisfaction is expressed at the conduct of the absentees, who have neither contributed in person nor by subscription to the defence of their country.'[1]

The second point on which the attempt at invasion had appeared to throw light was the disposition of the country. It had been represented as universally disaffected. Lord Camden wrote, on the 10th of January, that on the whole, 'reviewing what had passed, the best disposition had been shown. The regular troops had behaved excellently. The militia, so much dreaded, had not been backward. The Antrim regiments, which there was cause to suspect, had been specially forward. The Downshire men said they had seen their folly, and would fall in with their officers. Noblemen and gentlemen of large fortune had been employed in escorting baggage and

---

[1] 'Camden to Portland, January 10, 1797. Secret.' S. P. O.

carrying expresses. Mr. John La Touche, the banker, a private in his son's corps, rode twenty-five miles in one of the severest nights with a message. The merchants of Dublin, many of the first eminence, marched sixteen Irish miles with a convoy of arms to the North. A useful impression had been made on the minds of the lower Catholics by Dr. Moylan, Bishop of Cork. The Viceroy anticipated 'the best effects on the disaffected at home and the enemy abroad from the spirit which had been shown.'[1]

So far Lord Camden had spoken only of those who might naturally have been expected to exert themselves in the interest of order. But of the great revolutionary organisation said to pervade the island no signs had been outwardly visible. The people had shown a good will towards the troops. No advantage had been taken of the opportunity for local riots. Dalrymple, indeed, had confessed a fear that in the event of a reverse a different disposition might manifest itself. But it seemed impossible that the description which Wolfe Tone, Arthur O'Connor, and Lord Edward had given to the French Government of the reception on which they might calculate in Ireland, could have resembled the fact. The British Cabinet especially, and English opinion generally, came to a conclusion that the Irish Government had been needlessly alarmed; that the discontent of which they had heard so much, so far as it was real, had been created by the bigoted prejudices of the Castle Administration, and had been designedly exaggerated for the purposes of Protestant faction. They were misled, as the event proved, into a mischievous and even fatal delusion.

[1] 'Camden to Portland, January 10, 1797.'

The revolutionary leaders in their subsequent confessions referred the conduct of the peasantry simply to the want of orders from head-quarters. The organisation had been deranged by the Belfast arrests. The appearance of the French was a surprise. The impression among the local committees was that the expedition had been postponed, or was not to be looked for till the spring. The insurrection was intended to be sudden; local independence of action had been strictly forbidden; and the French fleet had departed before it had been thoroughly understood to have arrived.

The explanation was correct as far as it went, but it was not the whole truth. It had been shown also that the mass of the people, if left to themselves, were not spontaneously disaffected to the British connection. As an agrarian conspirator the Irish peasant is effectively dangerous. He clings to his home and his land. He has a keen consciousness of injustice; and when the law has been his enemy he has not scrupled to avenge his own wrongs, often with the ferocity of a savage. Politically he allows himself to be worked upon by scoundrels, who flatter his hopes and play upon his grievances. He talks, he shouts, he affects to conspire for a cause in which, nevertheless, in his heart he has little belief, and for which, so long as he is left unplundered, in his heart he cares not at all. Political disaffection in Ireland has been the work, on the one hand, of the representatives of the old disinherited families—the Kernes and Gallowglasses of one age, the Rapparees of the next, the houghers and ravishers of a third; on the other, of the restless aspirations of the Catholic clergy, who refuse to live on even terms with other religious communities, who have compelled the so-called heretics to pare their claws and draw their teeth, and have thus maddened themselves in secret by brooding over their imagined wrongs. On the back of these, and bred out of misgovernment, have come the political adventurers—the Lucases, the Floods, the Grattans, the Wolfe Tones, the O'Connells—who have used the discontent and oppression of their countrymen as instruments of a wild ambition after an impossible national independence; and working in a country where neglect and tyranny had gone hand-in-hand, where laws were so unjust that Nature herself rejected them, and where the people were singularly susceptible of rhetorical appeals to their emotions, these elements might and did create a state of things which appeared on the surface like universal national hostility.

The appearance was not the reality.

The peasant in the British army fights by the side of his Scotch and his English companions, and the enemy knows no difference between them, save that where the fray is hottest the Irishman is first to the front. Enlisted in the police corps, he is the most loyal servant of order, and faces undismayed the fiercest frenzy of men of his own blood and creed. In the militia, in the approaching rebellion, the instinct of the soldier was stronger than the seductions to which he seemed to have yielded. For the most part he was found true to his colours, if false to his nationalist oath. Physically brave, he is morally a coward. In his own cabin at home he sinks before the terrorism of the secret societies. He consents to be sworn, because he is marked for vengeance if he refuses. He will give no evidence in court, because he knows that the English Government cannot, or will not, protect him; while the power that will punish him is at his door. He clings to his creed and to his farm. The appeals of demagogues to his superstition, or their denunciations of his oppressors, make him drunk for the moment like whisky, and he becomes capable of the most horrible atrocities. But this is not his real nature. He is too shrewd to believe in the illusions with which he allows himself to play. So long as disloyalty can gain its ends by the help of the assassin or the incendiary, there is a vile minority in Ireland who will shrink from no atrocity; and so long as he is himself treated with injustice, the peasant will look on with indifference or with secret sympathy. But he will fight in the field only in the ranks of a legitimate force, under orders from the officers of a lawful government. When left to his own impulses he allows himself to be guided by his natural chief, the owner of the soil on which he lives. Let the law and the landlord become his friends indeed, and the instinct will then turn to active loyalty, and the field of Irish agitation will cease to yield a harvest.

CHAP. I.

1797. January.

CHAPTER II.

THE SECESSION OF THE OPPOSITION.

SECTION I.

BOOK IX.
1797.
January.

A PARLIAMENTARY Opposition is the most finished product of modern political genius. The functions of it are to teach the people that they are ruled by men who are unfit for the position which they occupy, and are pursuing measures impolitic and mischievous. The Opposition is assumed by the theory to consist of persons who are the intellectual and moral equals of those whom they denounce, and are prepared to take their places, if they can persuade a majority in Parliament to agree with them. Men of ability and character will not advocate a cause which has not elements of justice and wisdom in it ; and the result is, that either the two parties in the State must divide between them the principles of political administration, each when in power consciously regarding but half the truth—doing what it ought not to do, or leaving undone what it ought to do, to avoid trespassing upon its rival's province—or else each must of deliberate purpose blind one of its eyes, lay aside its better knowledge, consent to be a representative of passion, prejudice, and ignorance.

Each party also when in Opposition must assist in bringing Government itself into contempt by holding up those who hold the reins to public ridicule or detestation. Under the Plantagenets and Tudors differences of opinion between leading statesmen were confined to the Committee of Privy Council, which was composed of men of rank and intelligence, irrespective of the complexion of their views. The Cabinets of Henry the Eighth and Elizabeth contained Conservatives and Radicals, Anglicans and Puritans, Catholics and Protestants. Difficult questions were argued in private like the plan of a campaign in a council of war, and the passions and conceits of the multitude were not blown into a flame by hearing the measures taken by the Administration publicly reprobated by persons of accredited consideration. To the world outside the Government appeared undivided, and thus commanded the respect and submission which the rank and file of an army pay to their officers.

The public, no doubt, experience a general satisfaction when the debates of their rulers are submitted to their own judgment. They can test the abilities of their representatives; they can pass their own criticisms on the questions submitted for discussion; and at times, when deeper passions are asleep, when the motives at work are the common forces of selfishness, and dangers are to be anticipated rather from the intrigues of individuals or of classes, than from a false choice of policy, the advantages of the modern system may for a time outweigh its evils.

As certainly in times of excitement, when reason is unseated by passion, and large masses of men become possessed with illusions under which, like sheep, they bleat but one senseless note, and can be driven in multitudes where any barking demagogue desires to misdirect them, a constitutional Opposition must be composed of materials different from any of which we have yet had experience, if it is not the most effective of the instruments of anarchy. It embarrasses the executive Government when it most requires discretionary liberty of action, and brings discredit upon it by unscrupulous abuse when its difficulties require most candid consideration. It encourages the hopes of fanatics and enthusiasts, provides madness with argument, and tells the incendiary and revolutionist that his objects are good, and are resisted only by selfishness and wickedness.

In no country and at no time could an Opposition in Parliament have worked more mischievously than in Ireland at the existing crisis. Grattan had sown the seeds of disorder by feeding the nation with hopes of an independence to which no political short-cut was possible. If Ireland was to be independent, the road towards it lay through order and industry, and practical energy and union. The liberties which she desired were for ever impossible so long as the passions were alive which he had stimulated by his fervid declamation. He had persuaded his Irish clients that a millennium was only waiting for them till they had thrown off the authority and influence of England. They had gained step after step, yet the millennium was no nearer. As the direct power of England declined, English influence had become more all-pervading than ever. Their obvious conclusion was that they had not liberty enough; they must strike at the point where that influence was seated. They must have Parliamentary Reform; they must have Catholic Emancipation; they must place the power of the country where England would be unable to reach it; and independence would then be a reality.

Mr. Grattan insisted, and perhaps he believed, that Ireland in complete possession of self-government would become a loyal member of the empire; but he had led the country to expect that with self-government her material misfortunes would give place to plenty and prosperity; and when this hope was disappointed, when, instead of prosperity and internal union, they found only internal quarrels and consequent increase of misery, was it not inevitable, had it not been the unvarying experience in the history of every revolutionary movement recorded, that when the millennium proved still an *ignis fatuüs*, that when the hoped-for prosperity still hovered unobtained beyond the people's grasp, they would have carried Grattan's arguments to their natural conclusion, and have insisted on complete separation? The rule of England, Mr. Grattan told them, had been the source of all their woes. The rule was gone, but an English Viceroy was still at the Castle; there was still the baneful connection under the Imperial Crown. The reins would have been snatched by bolder hands, or Grattan himself would have been swept away in the torrent. The demand would have risen that Ireland should be as free as America; and England must have either yielded to her own destruction or drawn the sword at last at a worse disadvantage than in 1690, when the control of the army and the police, and the internal functions of the executive authority of the State, had been allowed to pass out of her hands.

The United Irishmen had avowed from the beginning that Emancipation and Reform were but means with them towards a further end. The leading

Catholics professed to be loyal; but every one who knew the genius of the Catholic Church knew also that when the power was in its hands it would be content with nothing short of complete ascendency, and the ascendency of a Catholic majority meant a return to the measures of King James's Parliament. The feeble and half-affected moderation of a few bishops and noblemen would have been but a bulwark of straw against the will of three million Celts clamouring for a restoration of the lands, and under these conditions the continuance of a shadowy connection between the islands could have been purchased only by acquiescence in a confiscation to which England could never consent without dishonour and degradation.

These consequences of the political measures which Grattan demanded were so obvious on the surface, and were so undisguisedly confessed as their real objects by the conspirators out of doors, that the Parliamentary Opposition, the Duke of Leinster and Lord Moira, the two Ponsonbies and Grattan, must be credited with weaker intellects than they possessed could they have been really blind to them. They probably considered that the war with France would fail, that democracy was to be in the ascendant over Europe, that Ireland was to achieve separation, and that it would be better arrived at constitutionally than through open rebellion. Grattan may have calculated that his services to the patriot cause would secure him the first place in the new Commonwealth which was to be added to the Sovereign States of Europe. Moira and Leinster may have hoped to secure their estates amidst the general wreck of the Protestant proprietary. Their more hot-headed and younger confederates were less able to wait for the slow process of a Parliamentary campaign, or perhaps the rule of proceeding continued as before. The Constitutional leaders were to persevere in pressing their demands through the legitimate channels, while agitators out of doors were to enforce their arguments by terrorism.

Arthur O'Connor had been one of the few persons who on the appearance of the French had passively if not actively opposed the enrolment of the Yeomanry. His loyalty had been reflected upon in a publication which he attributed to the Castle; and as he had himself by his own subsequent confession personally invited the invasion, and was at that moment a member of the Executive Committee of United Irishmen, it must be admitted that he was not accused without reason. He could not afford at the moment to show his true colours. He had steady friends and supporters in the English Whigs, with whom it was necessary to keep on terms. The English Cabinet was known to be wavering in its Irish policy. He used the opportunity, therefore, to publish an open and insolent defiance of the Government at the Castle. He delivered himself, through a newspaper at Belfast, of an address to his fellow-citizens. 'In the conscious integrity of his heart' he repudiated the charge of disaffection. He represented himself as a martyr to the cause of the Catholics. He had been disinherited, he said, for his devotion to their interests by his uncle, Lord Longueville. Interpreting the future by his hopes, he described Great Britain as an ancient tyrant, now reeling to her ruin; and in a cataract of that fatal eloquence which hides truth from Irishmen, as coloured fireworks hide the stars, he thus addressed Lord Camden and Fitzgibbon and the other members of the Irish Executive:—

'Abandoned Administration, who have trampled on the liberties of my country, do you presume to accuse me of dissuading my countrymen from arming to oppose an invasion which your and your accomplices' crimes have provoked? Is it that the inalienable rights of free-born men to make their laws by delegates of their choice should be bartered and sold by usurpers and traitors that I should persuade them to arm? Is it that our markets, our manufactures, our commerce, should be sold to that nation which appoints our Government and distributes our patronage, that I should persuade them to arm? Is it to support the Gunpowder Bill, which deprives them of arms, or the Convention Bill, that I should persuade them to arm? Is it to support the suspension of the Habeas Corpus Bill? Is it to rivet the bolts or guard the dungeons of their fellow-citizens, who, torn from their homes and families, vainly demand that trial by jury which, by proving their innocence, must establish its guilt, that I should persuade them to arm? Is it that a vile pander of national honour and legislative duty should be invested with uncontrolled power over the opinions and persons of an injured, gallant, and generous people, that I should persuade them to arm? Go, impotents, to the Catholics, whose elevated hopes of all glorious freedom you have been appointed to blast! Hence, contemptible Administration, from those you have insulted and levelled to those you have raised! Go to the monopolists of the representation of Ireland and ask them to arm. Go to the swarms of petty tyrants, perjured grand jury robbers, army-contractors, tithe-proctors, and land-sharks, and tell them how necessary it is for them to be armed. The Volunteers have been discouraged because they threw off the open and avowed dominion of Great Britain. These yeomen corps have been raised to support the concealed deadly influence she has gained by corruption and treason.'[1]

The Administration might be impotent to arrest the progress of secret conspiracy, but it had spirit and power to resent the open insolence of Mr. O'Connor. It could not furnish him with the halter which was his due. He was not even suspected of having ventured into actual crime. But a public defiance, re-issued as it was in loose sheets, spread broadcast over the country, and showered from the galleries of the theatres, was not to be passed over, and the passionate patriot was provided with a lodging in the Birmingham Tower, at Dublin Castle.

Sir Francis Burdett, who was O'Connor's relative, made his arrest an occasion of a philippic in the British Parliament, characteristic both in its presumption and its ignorance of the tone of English Liberal politicians in speaking of Irish subjects.

'One person,' he said, in a savage invective against the Viceroy and the Chancellor, 'now immured within the walls of a dungeon in Dublin Castle, I have the honour of being connected with, whom I know to be as incapable of treason towards his country (good God! that treason to Ireland and the name of O'Connor should be preposterously coupled together) as he is capable of everything that is generous and noble for his country's good; a man whose private virtues equal, they cannot surpass, the integrity of

[1] See *Plowden*, vol. iv., Appendix 10, where there are ten pages of this rhodomontade.

his public conduct. When such men become objects of fear and hatred to Government, it is not difficult to ascertain the nature of that Government.'

The reproaches which have been showered by historians on Lord Camden's government of Ireland are based on the same ignorance of fact which so grossly dictated the laudations bestowed by Sir Francis Burdett on the most worthless of Irish traitors. The ignorance has no longer an excuse, but the prejudice continues. The florid rhetoric of patriotic incendiaries has been so agreeable to the palate of modern Liberal philosophers, that the crimes and follies of the United Irishmen are forgotten in the spurious beauty of political sentimentalism. Public opinion upon Ireland has been formed by men

> Whose virtue is
> To make him worthy whose offence subdues him,
> And curse that justice did it.

SECTION II.

THE Constitutional friends of liberty were choosing their ground with more judgment, and using arguments more likely to receive attention. Arthur O'Connor had all but invited the Irish, in an open address, to ally themselves with France. Lord Moira used their apparent orderliness at the time of the invasion as a plea for a conciliatory policy. The Prince of Wales was induced to offer his services as Viceroy. Moira, supposing the time come for the rainbow to show itself, was prepared to attend him as Commander-in-Chief. The Prince submitted to Pitt an outline of the healing measures which his Irish advisers recommended; while Grattan and Ponsonby were denouncing, in the Irish House of Commons, the negligence which had exposed the country to a danger from which only accident had saved her, and were finding willing listeners.

The attack was made in various forms. It was urged plausibly that the ease with which the attempt had been made encouraged a repetition of it. Rumour said the armament was being refitted, and the chances of a second expedition were on every one's lips. It was alleged also, and with perfect truth, that the least confident of the Irish were encouraged by the fact that the French had actually come, and were venturing boldly and enthusiastically into the conspiracy.[1] The Government had affected to compliment

[1] 'Evidence of Dr. MacNeven.'—'Report of the Secret Committee of the House of Lords, 1798.'

the peasantry on their loyalty, as if they had depended on it beforehand, and had been justified in their confidence.

BOOK IX.
1797.
February.

The Irish gentry, who knew better how the truth stood, were indignant at such idle folly. They were perfectly aware that if Hoche had landed with his entire force, Dalrymple must have been overwhelmed, Cork would have been taken, the whole of Ireland would have been in arms. Where, it was angrily asked, had been the vaunted British fleet? and the answers did not tend to allay uneasiness. Admiral Colpoys ought to have been outside Brest with fifteen sail of the line. For some unknown cause he had been off his post when Hoche slipped out; and when he found Hoche was gone, instead of following him, he had gone up Channel to Portsmouth. It was reported at the Admiralty on the 20th of December that the French expedition had sailed. Lord Bridport was at Spithead with the Channel fleet. He might have joined Colpoys and gone in pursuit, and the east wind would have carried him to Bantry in forty hours. But as late as the 26th the Cabinet was incredulous. On the 27th the wind had gone round, a westerly gale was blowing, and he could not leave his anchorage.

This was small consolation to Ireland. The sheet-anchor of her safety had failed at the hour of need. To secure protection for the future, either, it was argued, there must be concession to the Catholics, and the pretext for disaffection must be removed, or the military force must be increased. Parliament must vote additional taxes. Private gentlemen must strain their embarrassed fortunes in raising Yeomanry. Especial bitterness was felt against the noble lords and gentlemen who, drawing their incomes from Ireland, were spending them in London, and contributing nothing, either in purse or person, to the public defence. If new taxes were to be laid on, what more proper than an absentee tax? Such a tax was certain to be proposed should Government ask for more money, and Camden wrote to Portland for instructions how to act towards a measure 'which would be very unpleasant to the feelings of the absentees.'[1]

Lord Shannon, Lord Ely, Lord Waterford vehemently pressed it. The best men in the country, the most active friends of Government, as Camden admitted, were in its favour. 'The impolitic backwardness of the absentees in not stepping forward with decision and liberality in the late alarm had added a feeling of resentment to the sense of public injury.'

Mr. Vandeleur at length brought the subject forward formally, and proposed a tax of two shillings in the pound on the net produce of the absentee rents. As a speaker he was unequal to what was called 'influencing the debate,' but no one ever spoke more truth in the Irish Parliament. 'All the disturbances which had taken place there, which had disgraced its character and checked its growth,' he accurately declared to 'have been found to commence on the lands of absentees.' Had they been resident, as they ought to have been, their authority as landlords would have prevented disorder, and acts of kindness would have removed the temptation to it. 'A tax,' Mr. Vandeleur said, 'which would compel the landowners to return to their duties would do more to tranquillise Ireland than all the repressive laws which Parliament could devise.'

[1] 'Camden to Portland, February 20, 1797.'

Sir John Macartney considered a tax of two shillings in the pound to be too small. The injury done by the absentees to Ireland he regarded as greater than any contribution which could be laid upon them would equal, and he proposed to raise the two shillings to four.

Some friend of the absentees argued that a man had a natural right to choose the place where he would live. Mr. Smith replied that society of its very nature was a restriction of natural rights. The poor man had as much natural right to eat his salt untaxed as the rich landowner to spend his rents in luxuries at a distance from his estates.

Here once more the deepest of the real wounds of Ireland was opened. The Ponsonbies staid away from the debate. Grattan supported the tax, but feebly and without spirit, being 'tied,' as Lord Camden said, 'to Lord Fitzwilliam, Lord Bessborough, and the Duke of Devonshire.' These noble advocates of the cause of the people were themselves the greatest criminals against the people; and the patriotic orators, whose business was with imaginary wrongs, were languid and apathetic when genuine evils were taken in hand.[1] Their coolness and indifference would not have obstructed the Bill. The better mind of Ireland had declared itself, and the Viceroy himself confessed that the non-residence of landowners was the true cause of all that was amiss. 'The absentees,' he admitted, were bound to visit the estates, 'to expose themselves to the duty by which they held their property and their situation in the country:'[2] but his orders from England were to prevent the passing of a measure which would

---

[1] 'Camden to Portland, March 1.' S. P. O.
[2] 'Camden to Portland, March 9.'

have irritated powerful interests in both Houses of the British Parliament. Ireland was sacrificed that Pitt's majority might not be weakened, and the supporters of the Castle with bitterness at heart were required to vote against their consciences and against what they knew to be right.

The United Irish agitation was carried on with renewed energy. 'The appearance of the French had given the conspirators fresh courage.'[1] Several of the arrested leaders were released for want of producible evidence to detain them. The places of others were filled up. There was to be no second failure, as, indeed, if the French had landed, there would probably have been no failure at all. Connaught and Munster were vigorously organised. So dangerous in January was the state of Ulster, that the greater part of it was placed under the Insurrection Act and proclaimed. 'A system of terror had been established' to paralyze the law; and the Viceroy found himself obliged, as he said, notwithstanding the outcry that was certain to be raised, 'to show the loyal and well-disposed that the Government was the stronger party.' The Orangemen had been severely checked in deference to Grattan's clamours. The disaffected peasants and artisans had gathered courage from the suppression of the only body whom they really feared, and assassination became the law of the province. Murder had followed murder. In the middle of the winter Mr. Comyn, an active magistrate at New Town Ards, was shot. In February a Donegal farmer was shot, as a lesson to others for enlisting in the Yeomanry. The sacrifice of the next victim, from his character and position, attracted keener

[1] 'Camden to Portland, January 30.'

attention. Dr. Hamilton, a Fellow of Trinity and rector of a living near Lough Swilly, had given offence by exerting himself in detecting crime. He had been shot at once unsuccessfully. One night at the end of the same month he was dining at the house of a Mr. Waller, when a party of ruffians who had marked him down burst into the room. Hamilton, hearing them coming, had escaped for the moment through a side-door. Mr. Waller being a cripple and unable to move, his brave wife threw herself in front of him ; three shots were fired at her, and she fell dead. The men then swore they would burn the house and kill everyone that was in it if Dr. Hamilton was not produced. The servants betrayed his hiding-place. He was seized and forced out of the house. He clutched at the staple of the hall-door. One of the villains held a candle to his hand to make him loose his hold. He was then dragged upon the lawn, thrown upon his knees, and piked.

'It is the system of the United Irishmen,' wrote Camden, in telling this story, 'to prevent the magistrates from acting. The unanimous opinion of the country is that mild measures cannot eradicate the evil, and that if the French land it cannot be in a worse state than it is at present. I have therefore ordered General Lake to disarm the districts where such excesses have been committed, to establish patrols, take up those who assemble at night, prevent assemblies, and not suffer the cause of justice to be frustrated by the delicacy which might possibly have actuated the magistracy.' 'If,' Camden continued, 'I thought the United Irishmen's measure of reform in Parliament was really the remedy, and if reform could be made without shaking the connection between the kingdoms, it might be wiser in the King's Ministers to consider whether the attempt should be made. But reform is only a popular question under which to shelter the treason which they are plotting and executing, and it would be weakness to be deceived by the pretended cause of their discontent. If Reform is resisted, the kindred subject of Catholic Emancipation must be resisted also. The success of either of these questions would shake to the foundation the English interest, and as long as the present system of governing Ireland is adopted they ought not to be entertained. If a better can be devised—and there are many grievances to which the peculiar situation of this island is subject—it will be to be considered how those grievances should be remedied; but while the war lasts, great and alarming discontent will appear, and must be assuaged by the vigour of the Government and the attention of the gentry.'[1]

General Lake, who was entrusted with the duty of taking away the arms from the mutinous and murderous conspirators of Ulster, became afterwards Lord Lake of Delhi and the conqueror of the Mahrattas. He had already distinguished himself in the American war and in Holland. He was an officer of singular moderation and humanity, and a better selection could not have been made for the discharge of a delicate duty, in which mistake or excessive severity would be visited instantly by the most factious animadversion. On the 13th of March he sent out a proclamation from Belfast that daring outrages were being perpetrated in many parts of the province with. the deliberate purpose of superseding the laws by terror. The civil power was defied. Loyal subjects who had enrolled

[1] 'Camden to Portland, March 9.' S. P. O.

themselves as Yeomanry under the King's commission were murdered; the interposition of the army had become necessary for the protection of the well-disposed; and Lake, therefore, gave notice that he had received authority to act as the public safety might require. He enjoined all persons, peace officers and soldiers excepted, to bring in their arms and surrender them. He expressed a hope that immediate compliance would render the use of force unnecessary. He entreated the disaffected to consider the misery which they were provoking. He invited the loyal to act with energy and spirit, and assured them of protection. He promised informers reward and inviolable secrecy if they would indicate where arms and ammunition were concealed.[1]

Grattan declared in Parliament that such a proclamation was a subversion of the Constitution. He did not care to enquire whether the powers of the Constitution could be abused to protect a deliberate and avowed conspiracy to overthrow it by force. In a country where a second secret authority had been established superior to law, and enforced its orders by assassinating the officers of the legitimate Government, the executive servants of the Crown, who had hesitated to use the powers committed to them to put down so audacious a usurpation, would have deserved to be stigmatised as poltroons, and punished as traitors themselves. Mr. Grattan was hard to please. The Lords Justices of 1641 were accused of having permitted the rebellion to break out when they foresaw it coming, as an excuse for spoliation and confiscation. Lord Camden was accused of provoking the rebellion of 1798 by using force to disarm

---

[1] Proclamation of General Lake, March 13, 1797.

a population who were preparing, without concealment, for open insurrection.

Irish conspirators have never wanted traitors among them. Unennobled by true or generous purpose, without heart for the open field of courage and honour, and pursuing their ends with the assassin's dagger and the incendiary's torch, they cannot impart a temper which they do not possess; and therefore, in their committees and lodges, there were always men who were ready to sell a dangerous secret, when the Government was willing to purchase it and would undertake to protect them from publicity. General Lake found ample assistance of this infamous kind. He was able rapidly to make a second arrest of two of the leading committees of Belfast, and to seize papers which revealed the correspondence with France, the extent of the revolutionary armament, and the measures taken for the seduction of the army and militia. The papers were sent to Dublin, and were laid immediately before a secret committee of the House of Commons. The prisoners were indicted at the Spring Assizes at Armagh, and were acquitted either for want of evidence or through the cowardice of the juries. Lake, however, went on with his work in the search for arms, and seized in all fifty thousand muskets, twenty-two cannon, and seventy thousand pikes, Lord Moira's estate being one of the principal arsenals. The seizures were not effected without severity. Men who had provided themselves with arms with a serious purpose did not part with them in answer to a mere request. Where pikes and muskets were known to be concealed their existence was fiercely denied. Entire villages combined in determined resistance. Individuals of whose guilty complicity secret information left no shadow of doubt were compelled to reveal the hiding-places by the whip and the picket. Houses were burnt, and entire families were exposed to serious suffering. Particular officers, it is likely, exceeded their orders. The officers of the Yeomanry were taken from the local gentry, whom the murder system had not disposed to feel tenderly towards the accomplices of assassins. In some very few instances the innocent may have been confounded with the criminal. When society is disorganised, and peace can only be preserved by the strong hand, such misfortunes occur inevitably, and the responsibility for them rests with those who have rendered the use of force indispensable. But the result was that in the part of Ireland where the populace was most dangerous, and the insurgent organisation most complete, the teeth of the rebellion were drawn.

SECTION III.

THE disarming of Ulster furnished a ready occasion for Parliamentary declamation. The offer of the Prince of Wales had been declined. Lord Moira had not achieved his desired position of Commander-in-Chief. But as a private peer he could still do his friends a service in his place in the British House of Lords. Calling attention to General Lake's proceedings, he moved an address to the King to interpose his paternal authority in behalf of his afflicted children. He described them as being exasperated into rebellion by gratuitous and barbarous tortures.

The objects of the United Irishmen were no secret to him, for many of them were his special friends; yet he dared to say that the Irish Government were victims of an illusion. Their fears were chimerical; the people were utterly innocent of evil design. 'Kindness,' he declared, 'was all that was needed to call forth that fond affection of the inhabitants of Ireland to England, which circumstances could cloud, but could not extinguish.'

Moira had the support of the whole Opposition. The Duke of Bedford insisted that Fitzwilliam should be replaced. Fox, in the House of Commons, rang the changes on the same note, demanding the staple measures of 'conciliation'—Reform and Emancipation.

Pitt answered, with effective satire, that under the Constitution of '82 the British Parliament had no longer a right to interfere in the internal government of Ireland; and that to remodel the Irish Constitution in the existing state of the world would be an experiment too rash to be ventured.

In England Pitt was supported by the common-sense of both Houses. In Ireland, where the blood was hotter, the battle was fiercer. At Grattan's instance a meeting of the Dublin freeholders was held in the Exchange, to petition the King for Lord Camden's removal. The resolution was carried, with the help of the mob, who were introduced into the building, and was presented to the Viceroy himself for transmission. In the Irish House of Commons Mr. Grattan, in one of the most passionate of his speeches, denounced Lake and all that he was doing, and accused Camden of violating the laws. A debate followed, or series of debates, in which the forces of the two parties were arrayed in fiery antagonism.

Grattan thundered his loudest. De Blaquiere rebuked him for misusing his great abilities in encouraging anarchy. The Government were embarrassed by the nature of their information, and could not produce a tithe of the evidence which they possessed; but when magistrates were being assassinated, and peaceful and loyal citizens were robbed unjustly of their arms, the Attorney-General turned to scorn the pretence that the conspiracy was unreal. 'Was the Government to sit by and suffer such things?' he asked. 'Were they to wait till the fire was lighted, and the whole country had burst into flame?'

The Prime-Sergeant, Fitzgerald, said desperate cases must be met with desperate remedies. If the French invaded the South again, and the army was forced to collect to encounter them, was Ulster to be left in a condition to rise in their rear?

The sensitive vanity of Irish patriotism showed itself especially in abuse of England. Ponsonby complained of the contempt felt by England for the Irish. Lord Sheffield, it seems, had consulted Gibbon on some Irish question. Gibbon had answered, 'While I am engaged in writing the History of the Decline and Fall of a great Empire I have neither leisure nor inclination to attend to the affairs of a remote petty province.' 'Remote!' exclaimed Ponsonby, 'and sixty miles distant. Petty! The whole kingdom of Ireland! It is useful to cure this habit in the people of England.'

Ireland ought to learn that she will be respected when she deserves respect, and that till then respect for her is impossible. The debate degenerated into personalities. Egan, once a patriot of the patriots and a supporter of Fitzwilliam, but now in the service of the Crown, told the Opposition that if they would not work at the pumps they ought not to increase the leak; and, with an evident allusion to Grattan, said that 'a man who overlooked the dangers of his country, and thought only of his own diminished influence, deserved the guillotine.'

Egan, after his manner, had spoken coarsely and roughly. Grattan rose, and after taunting him with deserting his party, said, 'The honourable gentleman spoke of cutting off my head, and that in a manner so peculiarly his own, in the fury and whirlwind of his passion, that though I did not see the guillotine, methought I saw the executioner.'

'I will have no allusions made to me with impunity,' roared Egan. 'No little duodecimo volume shall discharge its contents at my character and person without meeting the treatment it deserves. I would have the honourable gentleman know that no part of the support I gave Lord Fitzwilliam was directed to him. When he was in the zenith of his power, and strutted in pigmy consequence about the Castle, I avoided his intimacy. I once admired his talents; but when I reflect on the acrimony and inflammation which he has since poured on the popular mind, when I reflect on the mischief his doctrines have created, I see that he has done away his services, and betrayed his country, to his own disappointment.'

Again Grattan rose, the wild Irishman showing as in a dissolving view through the Parliamentary decorum.

'The honourable gentleman's swaggering,' he said, 'is no indication either of talent or spirit. I have read somewhere—

> An angry fool's a very harmless thing.

The folly of his paroxysms and the blockheadism of his fury are too ridiculous to excite serious notice. I smile at them. The honourable gentleman in his contortions represented to my mind the idea of a black soul writhing in torments, and his language is like that of a certain description of the fair sex, whom in manner and language he seems desirous to imitate.'[1]

Neither eloquence nor invective could hold together Grattan's Parliamentary following... In a House of 143, sixteen members only supported him on a division against the Castle measures.

Four days later George Ponsonby renewed the attack, and moved the repeal of the Insurrection

---

[1] *Irish Debates*, March 1797.

Act. His object was no longer to persuade the Parliament, but to inflame the people out of doors. He described England as struggling hopelessly with the French giant. He pictured the attitude of Ireland as a magnificent spectacle of determination to submit no longer to tyranny. The Irish, he said, demanded liberty, and liberty they would have, if not at the hand of England, then from France.[1]

There was a second display of oratorical fireworks; Grattan brilliant, as he always was, Curran sparkling with wit; the fine speaking all on one side, truth and good sense upon the other. The same majority which defeated Grattan defeated Ponsonby.[2]

Parliament was firm, both in England and Ireland. In the Cabinet, however, the same influence was still at work which had led to the appointment of Fitzwilliam. The Government refused to let the

---

[1] *Irish Debates*, March 24.
[2] 'The inability of the Patriots to understand the real sores of Ireland was as conspicuous as their fury with the imaginary ones. In an interval of this debate Sir John Blaquiere recalled attention to the Foundling Hospital, the condition of which he had exposed some years before. A committee of enquiry had reported that out of 2,200 children annually received into the Hospital, 1,000 disappeared unaccounted for. Blaquiere had twice attempted to introduce a measure for a change of management. The first time he was opposed by Grattan. The second time "his bill was lost by the unaccountable apathy of gentlemen who could not be brought to give it support." Having been unsuccessful in his efforts, he had hoped that the publicity of their misdeeds would have shamed the governing body into attention. He had lately, however, he said, been again invited to take up the subject in the interests of humanity; and, on enquiry, he had found that the same mortality continued. Out of 540 children received into the house between December 1795 and March 1796, 473 were murdered by negligence. The loss of life had been concealed in the formal returns. On the books three deaths alone had been entered, and the truth was only brought out on a strict examination. Blaquiere said he had personally inspected the hospital, and in one instance had found fourteen children thrust away into a garret to die.'—*Irish Debates*, April 12, 1797.

Opposition dictate to them, but were themselves still wavering, and Camden could obtain no help in the form of additional troops, and no definite encouragement. At the secret prompting of their English friends, Lord Kenmare, Lord Fingal, and other Catholics whose loyalty was unquestionable, presented a petition for Emancipation. The Viceroy in transmitting the petition showed that he was aware of, and that he acutely felt, the uncertain position in which he was placed. The quiet and good behaviour of the peasantry at the invasion had affected Portland and affected Pitt. Camden said that his own opinion remained unchanged. If the Cabinet disagreed with him, however, he entreated that no consideration for him should be allowed to embarrass them. He was heartily willing to retire.[1]

The severities of the North had been much descanted on, he wrote a few days later, on receiving a copy of Lord Moira's speech; his own doubt was whether, if the policy of severity was right, the measures adopted had been severe enough. The alternative was to grant a boon to disaffected people, the want of which they pretended was the cause of their discontent, but no moderate concession would satisfy either the Northern Reformers or the Catholics. There were objections to the present Constitution, but as long as the two countries were connected Ireland must be governed by an English party. The Catholics could not be admitted without a change in all the establishments in the country, and to make such a change in the existing humour of men seemed to him impossible. Conciliation, therefore, by those methods was not in his opinion to be thought of, and

---

[1] 'Camden to Portland, March 23.' S. P. O.

THE SECESSION OF THE OPPOSITION.

meanwhile murder and terrorism could not be permitted.[1] He could encourage no hope that the conspiracy would be suppressed without bloodshed, but he insisted that the responsibility was with the United Irishmen; that in his measures of coercion he was not attacking opinion, but a deliberate design of revolution; and in proof of his words he enclosed a statement which had been secretly made to him by a member of the Military Committee of the society, that the cry of Reform was a mere blind; 'that a total separation from England and the establishment of a Republic was the sole object of the conspirators; that they had a plan to surprise the army in one night all over the kingdom.'[2]

The Duke of Leinster now took upon himself to add to Lord Camden's difficulties, with the object, perhaps, of forcing him to resign. On the 25th of April he informed the Viceroy that he could no longer be a passive spectator of his country's sufferings. He did not hold himself responsible either to Lord Camden or to any one in the kingdom, but he thought proper to inform him that he intended to invite the county of Kildare to join him in a petition to the King to change the Government.'

The Dublin mob had set an example which the Duke of Leinster did not think it unbecoming to follow. Camden, embarrassed as he was, could not venture to resent the Duke's insolence, but begged

---

[1] 'Camden to Portland, April 3.' Abridged. S. P. O.

[2] 'Camden to Portland, April 15.'—The informer in this instance was a miniature-painter, named Nevile. This man added one remark in his deposition which is extremely characteristic: 'In Down they are pretty well disciplined. Not so in Belfast. The idea of the United Irishmen was that discipline was not necessary. They needed only to give one fire and rush on with the bayonet, like the French.'

humbly for a few minutes' conversation. The Duke 'desired leave to decline the honour, for his mind was made up.'[1]

Two murders followed in April of a clergyman and a magistrate in Meath. At the beginning of May the secret committee of the House of Commons, which was still sitting and collecting evidence, received information which, if true, made the situation appear almost desperate.

'It is with the utmost alarm,' Camden wrote on the 6th of May, 'that the Committee have heard that on Sunday se'nnight Mr. Edward Byrne[2] and Doctor Troy[3] appear to have been sworn of the Society of United Irishmen, as well as about sixty priests. The person who gave the information had seen several of the Kilkenny and Kildare Militia sworn. When the intelligence is confirmed by accounts from the other parts of Ireland, it is impossible to deny that confidence to a testimony of the kind which its extraordinary tendency would otherwise induce me to pause upon. The Committee urge my impressing the necessity of a force being sent to this kingdom more to be relied upon than its own soldiers. It is really my opinion that an insurrection may take place any day, and the dreadful effect of its success if it could be attained must fill the minds of his Majesty's servants with infinite uneasiness and alarm.'[4]

On the back of these communications from Ireland came the mutiny of the British fleet. First at Portsmouth, and then at the Nore, the seamen, exasperated

---

[1] 'Correspondence with the Duke of Leinster. Enclosed by Camden to Portland, April 28.' S. P. O.
[2] Late Chairman of the Catholic Committee.
[3] Catholic Archbishop of Dublin.
[4] 'Camden to Portland, May 6.' S. P. O.

at official inattention to their complaints, deposed their officers and seized the ships, and for six weeks such a storm appeared to have overtaken England as had never before touched her in the darkest hour of her fortunes. No Irish element was visible in the demands of the mutineers. Yet it was singular that to corrupt the fleet with the help of the Irish seamen had been a favourite idea of M. de la Croix. Though Tone at first listened coldly, he afterwards caught the notion with enthusiasm. Half the sailors and petty officers in the service were Catholics, and in fact it was discovered, when the causes of the mutiny were enquired into, that the United Irishmen had been busy instruments in inflaming discontent. Lee, who was one of the leaders, had been sworn to the society in Dublin and had enlisted but a few months previously, ' probably with a view to create the mutiny for which he was condemned.'[1] Wolfe Tone, in a published address, had invited his fellow-countrymen to use an opportunity to make themselves masters of the ships, and he promised them as a bribe the plunder of English commerce. The Secret Committee of the British House of Commons discovered that the crews had been largely sworn to be true to Ireland, to erect a Catholic Government there, and ' to be faithful to their brethren who were fighting their cause against tyrants and oppressors.' There had been plans among them to carry different ships into Irish harbours, to kill the officers if they hindered them, and to hoist the green flag, with the harp in the place of the British ensign, and afterwards kill and destroy the Protestants.[2]

[1] 'E. Cooke to Mr. Greville, July 4, 1797.' S. P. O.
[2] Report of the Secret Committee of Commons. England. 1799.

The mutiny gave the French the opportunity for which they had looked so earnestly. The sea was open; the fleets at Brest and in the ports of Holland had six weeks in which they could have gone where they pleased without danger of being fought with. The seamen at the Nore had not returned to their duty till the 15th of June, and those in England best able to form an opinion were expecting daily to hear that Hoche was again on the coast of Ireland.[1] Under these circumstances the resolution of the Cabinet gave way. Pitt and Dundas recurred to the hopes with which they had played, and Portland wrote to tell Lord Camden that he must 'weigh and consider whether means could not be devised to reconcile the Catholics, bring their support to the Establishment, and dissolve the unnatural coalition between them and the Dissenters.'[2]

The Secret Committee of the Irish House of Commons had at that moment completed their report, and Camden, for answer, sent it over for the Cabinet's perusal. The designs of the United Irishmen had been unravelled from their origin. The political reforms which they had demanded had been pursued avowedly as a means of disuniting Ireland from England and establishing a Republic, and by the side of the political agitation the leaders had made preparations for rebellion to take advantage of the confusion and excitement which must, under any circumstances, accompany a change in the Constitution. They had a hundred thousand men secretly organised and officered. Notwithstanding Lake's exertions they

---

[1] 'Unless the business of the fleet can be speedily adjusted, a few days must place a French army in Ireland.— Cornwallis to General Ross, May 9, 1797.'— *Cornwallis Correspondence*, vol. ii. p. 326.

[2] 'Portland to Camden, May 13, 1797.' S. P. O.

had still large quantities of arms. They had a revenue, the last quarter of which had been collected before the usual time, in anticipation of a French landing. The magistrates were held in terror by a secret tribunal of assassination, and efforts were made in all parts of the island to seduce and corrupt the soldiers.

'You ask,' said Camden, 'whether his Majesty should be advised to accede to a concession which is made the excuse of rebellion. Rebellion must first be overcome. It will afterwards be to be considered how the country is to be governed. As to what you say of disuniting Catholics and Dissenters, it appears to me to be merely an expedient to divert a present danger, and that the country must either be governed according to its present system, or a change more extensive must be adopted. I cannot conceal how melancholy a presage I consider the system to which we appear to have been forced, of yielding to the demands of persons who have arms in their hands.'[1]

[1] 'Camden to Portland, May 18.' Abridged. S. P. O.

SECTION IV.

BOOK IX.
1797. May.

THE Secret Committee spoke of attempts to seduce the troops. Those attempts had been so successful that four of the Monaghan and two of the Wexford Militia were tried and shot as an example to the rest. They spoke of the existence of an assassination tribunal. While they were preparing their report, sentence of death had gone out against Lord Carhampton, the Commander-in-Chief, who next to the Chancellor was the best-hated man in Ireland. So long as Luttrell was at the head of the army the rebel leaders knew that their game would be dangerous. Luttrell, therefore, was to be taken away. The interesting gentlemen who were dreaming of making themselves masters of Ireland were not growing more true to each other as the melodrama developed itself. A member of the Assassination Committee, James Ferris, was in Carhampton's pay, and gave him notice that his death had been determined on. A meeting had been held to talk the subject over. A blacksmith named Dunn had volunteered his services; and being one of Carhampton's tenants, born on his estate, living at his gate, in constant employment about his house, and so thoroughly trusted that he had access to the grounds at Luttrell's Town at all hours, he was welcomed as well fitted for his work. Already he had given proof of his qualifications. He had himself been the murderer, as he confessed afterwards, of two obnoxious persons to whom Carhampton had given shelter, and who had been found dead in the park.

The day fixed for the death of the Commander-in-Chief was Sunday, the 14th of May. Luttrell was in the habit of driving out from Dublin to his house on Sunday mornings. He carried pistols, and was known to be a cool and certain shot. The assassin proposed to follow the carriage on horseback, with three or four companions armed with blunderbusses, fire a volley of slugs into the windows at Luttrell and his aide-de-camp, and then shoot the postillion and the servants. If the plan failed, a bold villain, named Farrell, said that he would kill Carhampton in the street single-handed.

Ferris consenting, contrary to general experience, to give evidence in court, there was no occasion to wait till the assassin could be caught in the act. Dunn and several others were arrested; and Carhampton, knowing the man so intimately, visited him in his cell, and enquired the meaning of such a return for his past kindness. Carhampton, with all his experience, confessed himself astonished at the coolness of the answer. The man, who had been in his own service from his childhood, told him he considered it would be a meritorious act to kill him, and acknowledged frankly that he had meant to do it with his own hand. A second time Carhampton went to see him, accompanied by Lord Enniskillen. Dunn was on his knees praying when they entered. He repeated his confession without a sign of contrition. As it was not impossible that the man might spring on him, Carhampton on these occasions had his pistols with him. The third time on which he saw him he had nearly reason to regret that he had omitted the same precaution. The prisoner was then unfettered, walking in the yard. His demeanour was changed. He denied all that he had confessed, swore he was falsely accused, and swaggered up so close and so menacingly to his visitor that Luttrell bade him sharply to keep off, struck him across the face with a switch, and laid his face open. He was tried; and though Curran as his advocate did his best to discredit the approver's testimony, was convicted and hanged.[1]

The blindest enthusiast for Irish liberty must now have been aware of the spirit with which the Government had to reckon. The occasion of the conspiracy to kill Carhampton was appropriately selected by the Ponsonbies and Grattan for their last effort in Parliament. They knew that their friends in England were working upon the Cabinet, and they knew that the Cabinet was undecided. The mutiny in the fleet was at its height. Any hour might bring news that a French squadron was in the Shannon or in Lough Swilly. On the 15th of May George Ponsonby brought forward a series of resolutions in the House of Commons—that all religious disabilities must be abolished; that it was the indispensable right of the people of Ireland to be fully and freely represented in Parliament; that the Constitution must be remodelled, the country must be divided into electoral districts of six thousand houses each, and every district must return two members.

Lord Camden had to act on his own responsibility, without the support from England which at such a moment the Cabinet was bound to have extended to him. By their own intolerable folly in 1782 and in 1789 the Protestant Parliament of Ireland had set the agitation rolling of which they were now discovering

---

[1] 'Trial of James Dunn.'—*State Trials*, vol. xxvi.

the meaning. They had taught English statesmen to know that they were not to be depended on; and though the Cabinet declined to force them to strike their colours, they left them to gather the bitter harvest of their infatuation, and deal as they could with the wild spirit which they had let loose. They had insisted on the exclusive right to manage their own affairs. Pitt was taking them at their word, forgetting that he and Dundas had contributed their own share to the present danger in forcing on the concessions of '93.

At this moment Fitzgibbon was the sustaining genius of the Irish Administration. He had himself from the first foreseen the issue to which the fine talk of independence was tending. Lord Camden, undirected from home, consented to be guided by the one man whose advice had never been neglected without penalties, or followed without being justified in the result.

Ponsonby's motion was felt to be a final effort. The debate lasted through the night and long after the risen sun was shining through the windows. Pelham declared for the Government that, with the report of the Committee in his hands, he would not consent to launch Ireland on a career of revolution. As the argument proceeded it appeared more and more clearly that the neutrality of England would not affect the result, and that the resolutions would be rejected by an enormous majority.

Grattan spoke last, the stream which the world calls eloquence flowing like a mountain torrent, metaphor and simile flashing like prismatic colours in the spray. Towards the end he fell into a tone of prophetic solemnity. He affected a conviction that the Government policy must fail, the resolutions must triumph, and that for himself and his friends nothing remained but to wash their hands, like Pilate. 'You argue,' he said, 'that you can neither emancipate the Catholics nor reform the Constitution till the insurrection is put down. You cannot put it down. Coercion has failed; the war against democracy has failed. The evil has only been made worse. Agitation, once insignificant, has been able to influence every county in the kingdom, to levy an army, to provide arms and ammunition. As coercion has advanced the United Irishmen have advanced. The measures taken to disarm have armed them, to make them weak and odious have made them powerful and popular. What remains, then, but to try our plan and reform the Parliament? You say you must subdue before you reform. Alas! you think so. But you forget that you subdue by reforming. It is the best conquest you can obtain over your own people. Suppose you succeed, what is your success?—a military Government. And what may be the consequence of such a victory?—a separation. Suppose the war continues, and your conquest interrupted by a French invasion, what will be your situation then?'

Was Grattan sincere in pretending to believe that the United Irishmen would be subdued by reform? Did Grattan suppose that the war with the Revolution would fail? that France would triumph? that England this time was going finally upon the rock, and had no second rally before her as she had rallied after losing America? Who can tell? This only he found indisputably, that his power over the House of Commons of Ireland was gone; and having made the discovery, he concluded with shaking himself free of further connection with a body to which he had once considered it his proudest achievement to have committed the destinies of his country.

'We have offered you our measure,' he said. 'You will reject it. We deprecate yours. You will persevere. Having no hope left to persuade or dissuade, and having discharged our duty, we shall trouble you no more, and from this day we shall not attend the House of Commons.'[1]

As the echo of the words died away the House divided. Of two hundred members present a hundred and seventy supported Lord Camden. Mr. Grattan and his followers seceded, and the Parliamentary Opposition of Ireland died by its own hand.

The peril of the situation was scarcely increased. The Constitutional channel for the discharge of incendiary rhetoric was closed at least on one side of the Channel, and the Government was left free to deal with the problem out of doors. Lord Camden had to encounter enemies as unscrupulous as they were cowardly and cruel. Enthusiasts for popular rights, if unwise, are usually honourable, and in the absence of other virtues are rarely without courage and truthfulness. The United Irishmen pursued their object through secret murder and open lying. General Lake had been doing his work in the North with as much tenderness as was compatible with his duty. The Revolutionary Committee of Belfast published a manifesto against him on the 14th of April, in which they invited the universe to be a witness of their wrongs.

Their fellow-citizens, they said, 'were confined in Bastiles; their wives and daughters were made the

[1] *Irish Debates*, May 15, 16, 1797.

daily victims of a licentious foreign soldiery.'[1] The Government accused them of horrid crimes. The Government, in reality, was endeavouring to goad them into rebellion by premeditated cruelty. For the sake of their country they had endured hitherto their unparalleled sufferings, but a time was approaching when forbearance might be a crime. Should they ever be roused, the armies of United Ireland would trample their oppressors into dust. They appealed to the 'national armed force,' the Militia. They appealed to the Yeomanry. They appealed to the British nation. They appealed to the great Father of Mankind to look upon their wrongs and redress them.

To this language Lord Camden replied on the day after Grattan's secession, giving the Committee an opportunity to make good their words:—

'Whereas there exists in this kingdom a traitorous conspiracy by persons calling themselves United Irishmen to subvert the authority of his Majesty and Parliament, and to destroy the Constitution. And whereas, for the execution of those wicked designs they have planned open violence, and formed secret arrangements for raising, arming, and paying a disciplined force, plundered houses of arms, cut down trees for pike-handles, have attempted to disarm the Yeomanry, and fired on his Majesty's troops. It is now necessary to use the utmost powers with which Government is by law entrusted for the suppression of such traitorous attempts. And whereas the exertion of the civil power has proved ineffectual, We, the Lord-Lieutenant and Council, determined to suppress such attempts, and desirous to prevent the evil-disposed or misled from falling into dangers to which ignorance may expose them, do forewarn all men from entering into the said societies. We

---

[1] These charges were examined into in the following year by a committee of the House of Commons, and it was found 'that the search for arms had been conducted with all possible mildness.'

charge all persons having knowledge of those meetings to give information of them; and as it has become necessary to employ military force, we have ordered all officers to oppose such as should resist them in the execution of their duty with the exertion of the utmost force. We command our officers, civil and military, and all other subjects, to use their utmost endeavours to discover pikes, guns, swords, weapons, and ammunition of all kinds concealed. We charge all persons having such arms in their hands to deliver them at their peril. Believing that many of his Majesty's subjects may have joined these societies without knowing their nature, or from intimidation, and may be willing to return to their allegiance, we promise full pardon to all persons so seduced who, before the 24th of June, will surrender to any magistrate of the county where they reside, take the oath of allegiance, and give recognisances for their good behaviour.'

A copy of this proclamation was sent to every magistrate and to every officer in command of a detachment. Precise directions accompanied it to disarm the people everywhere, to send parties of troops to search where arms were supposed to be concealed, and to treat every person as a rebel who resisted them in the discharge of their duty.

The gauntlet was thus thrown down. The Government had given a clear intimation that they would yield no further, and now was the time for the United Irishmen to show of what metal they were made. The French negotiation was hanging fire. The precious interval of the mutiny was passing away. On the appearance of the proclamation a secret meeting of Delegates, from all parts of Ireland, was held at Dublin to decide what they should do. The Ulster men were for an instant rising. The Militia they believed to be disaffected to a man. They asserted, with or without ground, that they had friends in the Castle garrison who would assist in a surprise. There were depôts of arms and ammunition at Athlone and Mullingar which they were confident of being able to secure. If they had Athlone in their hands, the country was expected to rise between that place and Drogheda. Communication with the North would thus be cut off, and Lake could be overpowered. Arthur O'Connor was for immediate action also, and undertook to raise twenty thousand men in the South.

At that time, and while the disarmament had been only commenced, they might doubtless have effected something considerable. But the Dublin Committee, magnificent on platform or in leading articles, were in action arrant cowards. They insisted that the French must be waited for. High words rose. The hard republican Northerners, when they went into a conspiracy, meant business by it, not blatant timidity. When the Dublin men refused to go with them, they thought at one time of attempting the Castle alone. There were seventy or eighty of them who could depend on one another. They trusted that the mob would join when a beginning had been made; and only an accidental change of the guard made them relinquish their purpose after all. They returned to Belfast, meaning to rise alone against Lake, but they were embarrassed and alarmed by the frequent arrests of their leaders. Treachery of some kind was evidently at work. A coolness arose between them and the Southern Catholics. They distrusted their allies; they doubted whether, in company with cowards, they could make the revolution the glorious thing which they had anticipated. They began to think it was time to take care of themselves—some went abroad, others stayed at home, and meddled no more in politics, and from that moment the interest of Ulster in the rebellion began to decline.[1]

Wolfe Tone, in France, bewailed bitterly his Dublin friends' poltroonery. Keogh he had long known to be a poor creature, but he confessed himself astonished that Emmett had not shown more energy. The labour of years was crumbling away. One after another his comrades joined him with the same pitiful story, that the United Lodges throughout the Northern counties were disheartened and dissolving. The people waited till the last day mentioned in the proclamation, and then, seeing their leaders passive and no help reaching them from abroad, 'submitted almost entirely,' gave up their arms, and took the oath of allegiance.[2] Tone consoled himself with the hope that when the French landed the oath would be forgotten, or, as he expressed it, 'that their present submission would not prevent the people from doing what was right.' But the loss of Ulster was, in fact, the loss of the right arm of the insurrection. The Presbyterians fell away, and gradually re-united themselves to their own Orange kindred. The conspiracy declined rapidly into the form which rebellions in that country inevitably assume, and became a strictly nationalist movement of the Catholic Irish, with a few foolish enthusiasts of no religion at all in the Committee by which it was nominally ruled.

The supreme direction passed now to the Dublin executive. Wolfe Tone was not completely in their confidence. An attorney named Lewines, who had

[1] 'See a most curious account of the Dublin meeting, and the consequences of it, given by one of the Ulster Delegates to Lord Downshire in London, October 8, 1797.' S. P. O.

[2] *Wolfe Tone's Journal,* August 5, 1797.

been bred as a Jesuit, was sent to Paris as their resident agent with the Directory. A memorial was drawn up, indicating the points of the coast where an invading force could most easily be landed, and where it would be most certain of receiving support from the people. Doctor MacNeven, the ablest member of the association that remained, undertook the delivery of it, and followed Lewines[1] to France. Difficulties had arisen with the French Government as to the scale on which assistance was to be rendered. The Directory, if it meddled with Ireland, preferred to invade with a force which would make France master of the country after the English had been expelled. The Irish Committee desired to limit their dangerous auxiliaries to numbers which would be insufficient to enable them to make Ireland a second Italy. Suspicions, which had arisen on both sides, were now dispelled. MacNeven's memoir was received, and favourably considered. The Irish agents pressed for immediate assistance. The Directory promised to use the very first opportunity, and undertook meanwhile to make no peace with England of which the independence of Ireland was not a condition.

Thus on all sides the situation was clearing. The memoir said that the Irish priests were no longer alarmed at French irreligion, and were now well-affected to the cause.[2] The English Cabinet ceased

---

[1] 'Doctor MacNeven is a physician, very eloquent and very clever; a member of the Catholic Committee, and calculated by his talents to take a lead in the treason entrusted to him. He has been in close habits of intimacy with Lord Edward Fitzgerald. I did not know this person was so much employed as he appears to be. He must be strictly watched, both here and in England; and an exact description of his person, which is a very remarkable one, shall be transmitted.'—'Camden to Portland, August 30.' S. P. O.

[2] It is remarkable that although MacNeven himself carried the me-

to worry Lord Camden with suggestions of a change of policy. Their hearts had failed them after Grattan's secession. The hatred of Carhampton had led them to think of superseding him by a more popular Commander-in-Chief. Lord Cornwallis had been spoken of, and Carhampton and Camden, who had no love for their ungrateful office, were but too willing to pass over to him the responsibility both of the command of the troops and of the Viceroyalty itself, if he would accept it.[1] Cornwallis's solid qualities were unequal to the understanding of the Irish problem. He believed, perhaps under the influence of his friend Lord Moira, in the common platitudes of the Liberal party. In a conversation with Pitt and Dundas he declared it impossible for him 'to engage in the business . . . unless means were taken immediately to separate the Catholics and Dissenters.' He considered that 'very great concessions, little, if at all, short of what was called Catholic Emancipation, were necessary, and ought not to be withheld.' When pressed to undertake the command he replied that, 'if Ireland was invaded, or was in immediate danger of invasion, he would go there;' but that otherwise he was convinced that no force that England could employ would reduce the country to obedience, and 'that he could not honestly undertake a task which he believed could not be accomplished.'[2]

moir to Paris, and no suspicion has been suggested of MacNeven's treachery, the original document, not a copy, but the memoir itself, was in a few days in the hands of the English Cabinet, and was by them forwarded to Lord Camden.

[1] 'Camden to Lord Cornwallis, May 23, 1797.'—*Cornwallis Letters*, vol. ii. p. 327.

[2] 'Portland to Camden, June 10. Most private.' S. P. O.

SECTION V.

BOOK IX.
1797.
August.

Wolfe Tone meanwhile, inspired by steady hate of England, and refusing to be dispirited by his disappointment at Bantry, had unweariedly kept the cause of his country before General Hoche, who had taken Ireland for his peculiar province. The spring passed without fresh efforts; but with the summer came Lewines and MacNeven, and on the 21st of June Hoche told Tone that a second expedition had been resolved upon, but on a scale so large that two months must pass before the preparations for it would be completed. The opportunity of the Mutiny of the Nore had been allowed to pass unused. It was now over, and the men had returned to their duties; but the impression prevailed in France that the fleet was still unfit for active duty. Both Tone and Lewines besought instant action. If a landing could be effected in Ireland at once, they undertook that the Irish seamen would again make themselve masters of the Channel squadron, and that 5,000 men at that moment would be worth more than 25,000 in the autumn or winter. Hoche listened; the Directory listened. There was a Dutch fleet prepared for sea in the Texel, and a Dutch army of 15,000 men eager to distinguish itself. General Dandaels offered to go as commander of the land forces. Admiral de Winter said his ships could be ready in a fortnight. To the Dutch the Irish campaign was made over; and Tone, who was in despair at parting from Hoche, was consoled by hearing from him that French jealousy would be piqued, and that he would himself be despatched immediately after with a second expedition from Brest.

De Winter had not overstated his forwardness. In the first week in July the army was on board. Tone, who was to accompany the admiral, was delighted with the appearance of the ships—sixteen sail of the line and ten frigates, all in excellent fighting order, with seven-and-twenty transports. Here once more was hope. Admiral Duncan lay outside with the blockading squadron. Twelve and sometimes fourteen sail could be counted from the shore, but in Tone's eager eyes they were filled with his injured countrymen, whose hearts were beating time with his own. There was no fear of Duncan, either in him or in the Dutch commander, who was looking forward to an engagement outside the harbour with enthusiasm and confidence. The difficulty was to sail out and meet him. In Bantry Bay a gale from the east had divided the French fleet and prevented a landing. In the Texel a steady wind from the west confined the Dutch to their anchorage. Day followed day, week followed week, and still the west wind blew, while, warned by MacNeven's memoir, the Admiralty sent Duncan reinforcements, and the twelve ships increased to twenty.

Once more we observe the scene through Tone's impatient jottings.

'July 16.—A spy sent out. Returns last night with news that the English fleet is twenty-four sail of the line. I believe it is a lie. Duncan has fifteen or sixteen at most. We sail instantly that the wind will let us. July 17.—A wind foul as the devil. July 18.—Foul as possible this morning. Cannot be worse.

BOOK IX.
1797.
August.

'Hell! hell! hell! July 19.—There never was and never will be such an expedition as ours, if it succeeds. It will change the destiny of Europe, open the sea to the commerce of the world, and subvert a tyranny of six hundred years. Gun exercise every day. They fire incomparably well. July 28.—Fair wind yesterday at last, but so late and feeble we could not weigh anchor. July 29.—Wind fair, but so light we cannot stir. The admiral counted to-day the English fleet at anchor. Twenty-five three-masters, fifteen or sixteen liners, the rest frigates. Wind excellent to-night. We are off to-morrow.'[1]

At daybreak the signal was flying to weigh. The sails were dropping from the yards, the rigging of sixty vessels all black with busy figures clinging to the ropes. If the wind held, they would be engaged before noon.

The perverse wind which had mocked their hopes edged to the south and thence to the south-west, with a gale and a thunderstorm.

'There is a fate in this business,' was the entry of the 2nd of August. 'We have been twenty-five days on board when twenty-five hours are of moment. For five or six weeks the sea was open through the mutiny. We could have gone where we pleased. Nothing was ready, and the chance was lost. Had we been in Ireland at the moment of the insurrection at the Nore, we should, beyond a doubt, have had that fleet at least.'

'August 8.—Wind foul. They talk now of the lateness of the season. England is a second time saved by the wind. I begin to grow desperate.'

The delay was exhausting the provisions. There

[1] *Wolfe Tone's Journal*, July 1797.

were no longer stores to enable De Winter to risk a voyage round Scotland, with the chance of detention at sea. A council of war was held, at which two of the Belfast Committee, Lowry and Tennant, were present, and De Winter suggested sending off a small squadron and three thousand men. The Irish leaders said that before Lake had disarmed Ulster five hundred would have been sufficient. The conditions were now changed, but the organisation was not yet completely broken up. They thought that with three thousand men the venture might be made. Now, however, Dandaels made a difficulty. Dandaels refused to go with less than four thousand, and De Winter said he could not provide for so many. Finally, the Dutch Government decided that the original design must be adhered to. The troops must be landed for the present, the transports re-victualled, and De Winter meanwhile must go out when an opportunity offered and destroy Duncan.

CHAP. II.

1797. October.

Readers of English naval history know what followed. On the 11th of October De Winter sailed out of the Texel, not to destroy Duncan, but, after a desperate engagement, to be utterly ruined by him. This time the Irish gentry had no reason to complain that the English fleet neglected their defence, and the brief absurd dream that Catholic Ireland was to find a champion in Calvinist Holland was ended at Camperdown.

A second blow to Tone's hopes almost more severe was the death of General Hoche by rapid consumption. In Hoche he lost the only Frenchman in whom he had been able to kindle a genuine interest in his country. The direction of the foreign military policy of France passed to Napoleon, and in Napoleon he found cold civility and nothing more. Ireland was not to be thrown over so long as chronic disturbance served to divert and embarrass England, but to loud talk of a re-established Irish nationality Napoleon closed his ears. He refused to believe that the native Irish were more than two millions, and he wounded patriot vanity by the contempt with which he spoke of them.

The invasion was thus again indefinitely postponed, and the number of Irish refugees in Paris became considerable. Having brought Ireland to the edge of a conflagration, they preferred to remain out of danger on the Continent till the French were ready to place them at the head of their admiring countrymen. Some were traitors in Pitt's pay. The rest chilled still further the cooling interest of France in their cause by their petty jealousies and childish vanity. Each insisted that he and his own knot of friends were the true representatives of Irish opinion. Among others there appeared again on the scene Napper Tandy, from America, giving out that he was some great one. Wolfe Tone and Lewines were civilians; Napper, who had commanded the Dublin Volunteer Artillery, presented himself as an experienced officer. He had money. His sons still carried on business in Dublin. He declared that when he set foot in Ireland it would be the re-appearance of Achilles; thirty thousand soldiers would spring to his side.

These foolish beings were the scum and froth which the rebellion was working off and throwing from it. The serious part remained at home. Lord Camden had hoped that the break-up in Ulster might dissolve the conspiracy. He found to his sorrow that the Committees in Dublin and elsewhere were at work as vigorously as ever. He might arrest individuals, but the system baffled him.[1] The Duke of Leinster had seceded from the Parliament with Grattan and Ponsonby. The attitude of the Opposition was interpreted by the people as a constitutional sanction to rebellion and an open encouragement to them to transfer their allegiance to France.[2] The preparations in the Texel were on everybody's lips, and kept alive the excitement and irritation through the summer and into the autumn. At the end of September the Dutch were still eagerly looked for;[3] and confident in their new allies, and forgetful or careless now that Dutch theology was not precisely their own, the Catholics refused any terms of reconciliation with the Government short of the establishment of their religion.[4]

Undisturbed by clamour, and with a courage deserving higher commendation than the Cabinet dared to bestow upon it, Lord Camden, with the invasion hanging over him, stood to his work of disarming Ulster. It was Ulster which he chiefly dreaded.

---

[1] 'Camden to Portland, June 17.' S. P. O.

[2] 'The line of conduct pursued by the Opposition has tended more to alienate the people of this country, and dispose them to connect themselves with France, than any other circumstance.'—'Pelham to Portland, September 20.' S. P. O.

[3] On the 20th Mr. Cooke sent a note to Mr. Greville, which he said he had received from a person 'high in confidence among the United Irishmen, who had never deceived him.' The note was this:—

'From undoubted authority I assure you that an invasion is now considered inevitable. Assurances are received from France that the Government is determined, and that Ireland shall have complete independence. Tandy, Tone, and Lewines are the chief agents. The time fixed is the first fair wind after the equinoctial gales are over. Tandy will have a commission, and Tone comes as secretary to the commander of the land forces. All mouths are at work whispering the intelligence through the country. In a few days it will be known through every village in the kingdom.' — *MSS.* S. P. O. September 20.

[4] 'Nothing short of the establishment of the Catholic religion will satisfy those of that persuasion; and as the property of the country is in the hands of Protestants, such an event can never take place without civil war.'—'Pelham to Portland, September 29.' S. P. O.

If Ulster could be either pacified or handcuffed, he believed himself capable of encountering the disaffection of the Southern Provinces. Severe measures were used, and the severity may at times have been excessive. Camden did not deny that he meant 'to strike terror.' 'Terrorism had been the policy of the rebels.' 'They had brought the North of Ireland into such a state that a tenant did not dare acknowledge his landlord, and the assassinations of informers were without number.' Such a system could be confronted only by proof that the Government had the harder hand. The 'Northern Star,' the patriot organ at Belfast, had distinguished itself by inviting the militia to perjury. The infected Monaghan regiment, four privates out of which had been shot, was quartered there, and the loyal comrades of the men who had been executed, 'knowing that the "Star" had been the means of seduction,' attacked the office, destroyed the press, and wrecked the printer's house. Cottages, and even villages, had been burnt, where large quantities of arms had been found concealed. Orders had been given, and were strictly enforced, that lights should be extinguished at an early hour of the night; and persons found abroad after dark were made to give a sharp account of themselves. A shot was fired at the house of a tenant of Lord Moira, by which a woman was frightened, though not hurt. Incendiarism and murder, when committed by the rebels, were the venial effervescence of a too zealous patriotism. Severity, inflicted in the interest of order, was the only form of outrage which in the opinion of Irish patriots was held to merit reprobation. The Liberal newspapers in both islands were filled with accounts of the barbarity of General Lake's soldiers. The outcries rose to a scream when the Government seized a member of the Executive Northern Committee whom they had long known to be one of the worst and most dangerous of them, and against whom, by the help of an informer, they had at last obtained legal evidence. William Orr was tried at Carrickfergus, in October, for high treason. The most passionate efforts were made to save him, but the proofs were too clear. He was convicted and duly hanged. His body was carried off, his veins were opened, and calf's blood was injected, in the hope of restoring the circulation. When all failed he had a public funeral, which was attended by thousands. His cap was cut in shreds, distributed in relics, and worn in rings and bracelets by the patriotic daughters of Ireland. 'Remember Orr' was thenceforth added to the secret bywords of vengeance which were taking possession of the Irish ear and driving the people to madness.

General Lake's measures were felt to be successful, and the rage was proportionately extravagant. There now appeared at intervals a paper called the 'Union Star.' It was printed on one side of a sheet, so that it could be pasted upon the walls. The avowed object was 'to denounce by name the partners and creatures of Pitt and his sanguinary journeyman, Luttrell,' and offer them one by one to what was called 'public justice.' A Government proclamation having spoken of the 'Star' with the indignation which it deserved, the 'Star' replied with the following passage:—

'We have seen a paper with the name of Camden prefixed attempting to hurt the "Union Star" by naming it a vehicle for inviting assassination. The "Union Star" in the opinion of honest Irishmen will not be less valuable. We are not advocates for assassination, but we know on the authority of history that assassination preserved the liberties and rescued many of the ancient republics from aspiring villains. . . We certainly do not advise, but we do not decry assassination, as we conceive it is the only mode at present within the reach of Irishmen to bring to justice the royal agents who are constantly exercising rapes, murders, and burnings through our devoted country. We appeal to thy noble and venerated name, oh! Brutus. Prince of patriotic assassins, thy noble and virtuous spirit should pervade our land.'[1]

The 'Star' preached tyrannicide. The Dublin Committee employed agents like the blacksmith Dunn to practise it. Simultaneously the patriots of higher grade had abandoned the field in the Irish Parliament only to transfer their efforts to the sister country, where they could count better on popular ignorance, and where they knew that they could appeal with effect to the national abhorrence of oppression. The Duke of Leinster drew up a formal indictment against the proceedings of General Lake. The London press took it up, and the misgovernment of Camden and Clare was represented as the only cause of the disquiet of Ireland. Lord Moira threatened a second attack in the House of Lords, and the Prime Minister wrote to Pelham and Camden for an explanation of particular acts of cruelty with which Lake was popularly charged. Pitt himself did not affect to believe them, but to special accusations he desired to be able to give a special reply.

The answer was painfully easy. The policeman who has stunned a man with his staff may appear a

---

[1] Report of the Secret Committee of the Commons. Appendix, 27.

gratuitous savage till it has been shown that the man whom he struck was beating his wife to death. Camden had but to send authentic proof of the conduct and temper of the people with whom he had to deal.

The Irish complaint reduced to plain language was simply this:—You English, they said in effect, have conquered this island, and we wish to have it for ourselves. We will not fight for it, but we require you to let us alter our Constitution so that we shall be free in spite of you. If you refuse, we will conspire with your enemies, we will murder your friends, we will make it impossible for you to govern us; your magistrates, your constables, your witnesses shall die if they put your laws in force against us; and if in return you dare to punish us by shorter methods, we will proclaim to the world that what you call our crimes are the fruits of your own tyranny.

For eighteen years the air had been filled with the windy declamations of Grattan, and the fierce and sullen spirit which lies at the bottom of the Irish nature like the sleeping fire of a volcano was now awakening in its dreadful reality.

Camden and Pelham wrote at length in painful detail.[1] Each morning's post brought with it some fresh tale of horror. Before the Viceroy had closed his letter news came from the South that one magistrate had been murdered, another wounded; a constable had been found dead with his limbs hacked in pieces, and a label left in his hand threatening the same treatment to anyone who should bury him. At Two Mile Bridge, near Youghal, a farmer, his

[1] 'Pelham to Pitt, November 2. Lord Camden to the Duke of Portland, November 3. Private and secret.' S. P. O.

wife, his servant, his pigs, his dogs, even his poultry, had all been slaughtered. The bowels of the man had been torn out, and on him too a label was lying, that such was the reward of an informer.

Were these things to go on? were the tears of the friends of liberty to flow in streams for the sullen scoundrel who was flogged till he confessed to the store of secret arms which he had laid up for deeds of devilry; and was there to be no pity for the victims who were nightly sacrificed because they had dared to exert themselves for his detection and punishment?[1]

[1] Let the reader who desires to understand Lord Camden's position study the following letter from Mr. Rolleston, of Green Park, Youghal, dated October 20, 1797. Mr. Rolleston had already reported the mutilation of some horses and cows, almost within view of his windows:—

'On the night of the 23rd,' he wrote again,[1] 'a day remarkable in history,' a murder of the most atrocious kind was committed on three persons, at a village named Two Mile Bridge . . The surgeons and physicians who went to view the bodies came away sickened. The deceased were a man, his wife, and a servant-maid. The head was a respectable, wealthy farmer, who first provoked the miscreants by not selling his milk at their reduced prices. For that they houghed his cows. He gave information to Mr. Swayne, a magistrate here, and two men were taken up and sent to Waterford Gaol. The night but one following, this murder was committed, and the people of the village pretend to say they heard nothing of it, so determined are they on secrecy. The terror system is universal. We hear of fresh murders every day. Mr. Power had a tenant, whose bowels were torn out. . . The clerk of Temple Michael parish has been murdered. . . Forty pounds are publicly offered for Mr. Swayne's head; but, in fact, all yeomen are proscribed. This day I got a hint not to join in out parties; that my father, my uncle, and myself were loved and respected, and that I should not wantonly deprive my children of their father. I answered, I preferred an honourable death to a dishonourable life. I would always endeavour to bring a murderer to justice, and defend my property. We were ready to hear any real grievances, but could not allow our properties to be torn from us. . . We have little composed sleep. I cannot place entire confidence in any servants I have; they are either under the influence of terror, or their minds are vitiated. . . A little time will show what our tenants mean to do. Tithes are not their real object—they have a much

[1] The anniversary of the outbreak in 1641.

To drive the peasantry to madness forged Orange oaths were hung on the doors of the chapels, threatening Catholics with extermination. When the battle of Camperdown had destroyed their hopes of invasion, they were told that the Irish seamen in the fleet had won the day; that at the 'moment when the blood and brains of generous Papists had adorned the last victory of the wooden walls of England, but not of Ireland, the bloody dastardly hand of tyranny was pointing the dagger at their hearts.' They were reminded 'that while the honest United Irishmen were grasped with the iron hand of ferocity and cruelty, the infamous Orangemen, who thirsted after blood and murder, were caressed and encouraged by the heavenly Government.' They were informed— and the sham oath was referred to as a proof—'that the Orangemen had sworn to be true to the King and Government, and to destroy the Catholics of Ireland.' They were invited to believe that an Orangeman had invented a toast, 'That the skins of the Papists should be drumheads for the Yeomanry,' and that the framer of that toast had been appointed secretary at the Castle.[1] A list was posted against a chapel door at Nenagh, of certain Protestants in the neighbourhood, whom the people were desired by no means to injure, but were advised to remember their names.[2]

In the condition of the public mind these stories were accepted as truth, reported in the papers, and

wider view. They want fairly to overturn us. If my house is attacked, we shall all go together, for the bloody ruffians did not leave a dog or a cat alive in the last massacre. I am well assured the Defenders' oath goes to a general massacre of all Protestants.'—' Extracts of a letter from Mr. Rolleston, October 20, 1797.' S. P. O.

[1] 'Letter posted on the door of the Catholic chapel at Nenagh, November 1.—Enclosed by Camden to the Duke of Portland.' S. P. O.

[2] *Ibid.*

gained credit even in England. Pelham thought at one time of going over and dragging before the English Parliament the situation in which the Castle was placed. He was deterred by the fear of exasperating further the bitterness between the two countries.[1] Camden said that only dreary familiarity with details of outrage and cruelty prevented every one of his despatches from being filled with accounts 'of murders of magistrates, assassinations of informers and yeomen, and conspiracies against persons of rank.'[2]

Pelham, perhaps, would have been wiser if he had been less cautious. Lord Moira took advantage of the silence of the Irish Government in the midst of the clamour with which it was assailed to come forward a second time as the advocate of the miscreants, whom he represented as victims of Lord Camden's barbarity. He had been in Ireland in the autumn. If he visited his own estates he must have seen that they were the arsenal of the Northern rebels. As the advocate of Irish ideas he conceived, perhaps, that assassins could be best disarmed by caresses.

'He had seen in Ireland,' Lord Moira said in the English House of Lords, on the 22nd of November, 'the most disgusting tyranny that any nation ever groaned under, a tyranny creating universal discontent and hatred of the English name.' The long nights were the murderers' opportunity; but to Lord Moira it appeared a monstrous thing that General Lake should have ordered the people to stay at home after dark, or that where lights were seen in cabin

---

[1] 'Pelham to Pitt, November 2.' S. P. O.

[2] 'Camden to Portland, November 15.' S. P. O.

windows the patrol should call and order the extinction of them. He appealed to British sentiment, and complained of the revival of the curfew, the badge of ancient slavery. He knew the superstitious horror felt by England for the name of the Inquisition. The Inquisition, he told the Lords, and through the Lords the English world, was in force in Ireland in all its horrors. Persons against whom no crime had been proved were torn from their families, flogged, racked, picketed, and threatened with the gallows. He did not tell the Lords that in no instance were severities resorted to except where the guilt of the parties was accurately known, or that by these means tens of thousands of pikes and muskets had been discovered. General Lake had required the people to surrender their arms. Lord Moira ignored the Insurrection Act, and insisted that the possession of arms was a constitutional right. The people, he said, felt a just indignation when their arms were taken from them, and to punish them for natural resistance was cruel and intolerable. Great Britain was justly jealous of the liberty of the press. Lord Moira forgot to say that the press of Ireland was inviting soldiers to break their military oaths, and was preaching the virtues of tyrannicide. He denounced the brutal soldiery which burst into offices of the journals that exposed their tyranny, and destroyed the printing presses, to prevent the truth from being published. 'If the press was interfered with,' he said, ' the last spark of freedom was extinguished.' If Lord Camden's Government continued, ' Ireland would not remain five years longer connected with England.'

It was easy for Lord Grenville, it was easy for Lord Loughborough, to dispose at the moment of

Lord Moira's fable. They had but to relate a few stories out of the daily returns of atrocities committed by his interesting clients; they had but to read a few specimens of the publications of the virtuous and injured Irish press for the House of Lords to dismiss with contempt the extravagant caricature which had been presented to them. Lord Moira was to receive in another place the full measure of chastisement which his disloyalty or his folly had provoked. By what irony of fate have the speeches of Lord Moira been allowed to govern the opinions of later generations of Englishmen?

SECTION VI.

When patriotism is genuine it confers on the most misguided enthusiast a certain nobility of temperament. It may blind his conscience. It may tempt him to look without dismay, and even with applause, on actions which a cooler judgment must for ever reprobate as crimes; but in the enthusiast himself it creates a disregard of self, a fulness of devotion, a readiness to forego private advantage, to sacrifice fortune, life, even reputation itself, to the cause which he has embraced.

The character of political combinations may be fairly tested by the quality of the men concerned in them, and by the disposition which they are able to inspire. The conspiracy of the United Irishmen produced, perhaps, a larger number of deliberate villains than have ever been found arrayed in a movement which has called itself national. From the first moment of its institution the most trusted members of the society were traitors to it. As the design proceeded, and information became more valuable, men deepest in the secret and seemingly most ardent, were selling their knowledge to the Castle, stipulating only for concealment from the execration and revenge of their confederates. An instance has now to be related, remarkable for the ingenious perfidy with which it was attended, for the mystery which still attaches to the principal performer, and for his connection with the fortunes and fate of Lord Edward Fitzgerald.

Lord Edward's movements had for some time been observed with anxiety, as much from general uneasiness as from regret that a brother of the Duke of Leinster should be connecting himself with conspiracy and treason. His proceedings in Paris in '92 had cost him his commission in the army. In the Irish Parliament he had been undistinguished by talent, but conspicuous for the violence of his language. His meeting with Hoche on the Swiss frontier was a secret known only to a very few persons; Hoche himself had not revealed it even to Tone; but Lord Edward was known to be intimate with Mac-Neven. He had been watched in London, and had been traced to the lodgings of a suspected agent of the French Directory;[1] and among other papers which had been forwarded by spies to the Government there was one in French, containing an allusion to some female friend of Lady Edward, through whom a correspondence was maintained between Ireland and Paris. Lady Edward's house at Hamburgh was notoriously the resort of Irish refugees. Lord Edward himself was frequently there, and the Government suspected, though they were unable to prove, that he was seriously committed with the United Irishmen. One night early in October 1797 a person came to the house of Lord Downshire, in London, and desired to see him immediately. Lord Downshire went into the hall, and found a man muffled in a cloak, with a hat slouched over his face, who requested a private interview. The Duke took him into his library, and when he threw off his disguise recognised in his visitor the son of a gentleman of good fortune in the

---

[1] 'Camden to Portland, August 30, 1797.' S. P. O.

North of Ireland, with whom he was slightly acquainted. Lord Downshire's 'friend' (the title under which he was always subsequently described) had been a member of the Ulster Revolutionary Committee. From his acquaintance with the details of what had taken place it may be inferred that he had accompanied the Northern delegacy to Dublin, and had been present at the discussion of the propriety of an immediate insurrection. The cowardice or prudence of the Dublin faction had disgusted him. He considered now that the conspiracy was likely to fail, or that, if it succeeded, it would take a form which he disapproved; and he had come over to sell his services and his information to Pitt. In telling his story to Lord Downshire he painted his own conduct in colours least discreditable to himself. Like many of his friends, he had at first, he said, wished only for a reform in Parliament and a change in the Constitution. He had since taken many desperate steps and connected himself with desperate men. 'He had discovered that the object of the Papists was the ruin and destruction of the country, and the establishment of a tyranny worse than that which was complained of by the reformers; that proscriptions, seizures of property, murders, and assassinations were the certain consequences to be apprehended from their machinations;' that he had determined to separate himself from the conspiracy. He was in England to make every discovery in his power, and if Lord Downshire had not been in London he had meant to address himself to Portland or Pitt. He stipulated only, as usual, 'that he should never be called on to appear in a court of justice to prosecute anyone who might be taken up in consequence of his discoveries.'

Lord Downshire agreed to his conditions; but, as it was then late, desired him to return and complete his story in the morning. He said that his life was in danger even in London. He could not venture a second time to Lord Downshire, or run the risk of being observed by his servants. Downshire appointed the empty residence of a friend in the neighbourhood. Thither he went the next day in a hackney-coach. The door was left unlocked, and he entered unseen by anyone. Lord Downshire then took down from his lips a list of the principal members of the Executive Committee, by whom the whole movement was at that time directed.[1] He next related at considerable length the proceedings of the United Irishmen during the two past years, the division of opinion, the narrow chance by which a rising had been escaped in Dublin in the spring, and his own subsequent adventures. He had fled with others from Belfast in the general dispersion of the leaders. Lady Edward Fitzgerald had given him shelter at Hamburgh, and had sent him on to Paris with a letter to her brother-in-law, General Valence. By General Valence he had been intro-

---

[1] ' Jackson and his son; Oliver Bond; John Chambers, a bookseller; James Dixon, a tanner; Casey, a red-faced Dublin priest; Thomas Addys Emmett; Doctor MacNeven, a physician, who had great weight with the Papists; Braughall; John Keogh; and R. McCormick, who belonged to the Committee, though they did not attend; Samuel Turner; Lord Edward Fitzgerald; Arthur O'Connor; Alexander Stewart; two Orrs, one an attorney, and a dangerous person, the other of Derry, described as a clever, sensible, strong-minded man; Barclay Teeling; Tennant, of Belfast; Agnew, of Larne; Lawless (Lord Cloncurry's eldest son); Hamill, of Domenick Street; Inishry, a priest, a canting, designing, dangerous man, who swore-in Lord Edward Fitzgerald and Lawless.'— ' List and description given to Lord Downshire, October 9, 1797.' S. P. O.

duced to Hoche and de la Croix. He had seen Talleyrand, and had talked at length with him on the
condition of Ireland. He had been naturally intimate
with the other Irish refugees. Napper Tandy was
considered mad, strolling about the streets in uniform, and calling himself a major. Hamilton Rowan
had been pressed to return, but preferred safety in
America, and professed himself sick of politics. After
this, 'the person,' as Lord Downshire called his
visitor, keeping even the Cabinet in ignorance of
his name, came to the immediate object of his visit
to England. He had discovered that all important
negotiations between the Revolutionary Committee
in Dublin and their Paris agents passed through Lady
Edward's hands. The Paris letters were transmitted first to her at Hamburgh. By her they were forwarded to Lady Lucy Fitzgerald, in London. From
London, Lady Lucy was able to send them on unsuspected. Being himself implicitly trusted both by
Lady Edward and by Lady Lucy, he believed he could
give the Government information which would enable
them to detect and examine these letters in their
transit through the post.

Pitt was out of town. He returned, however, in a
few days. Downshire immediately saw him, and Pitt
consented that 'the person's' services should be accepted. There was some little delay. 'The person'
took alarm, disappeared, and they supposed that they
had lost him. Three weeks later, however, he wrote
to Downshire from Hamburgh, saying that he had
returned to his old quarters, for fear he might
be falling into a trap. It was fortunate, he added,
that he had done so, for a letter was on the point of
going over from Barclay Teeling to Arthur O'Connor,

and he gave Downshire directions which would enable him to intercept, read, and send it on.

Such an evidence of 'the person's' power and will to be useful made Pitt extremely anxious to secure his permanent help. An arrangement was concluded. He continued at Hamburgh as Lady Edward's guest and most trusted friend, saw everyone who came to her house, kept watch over her letter-bag, was admitted to close and secret conversations upon the prospect of French interference in Ireland with Rheinart, the Minister of the Directory there, and he regularly kept Lord Downshire informed of everything which would enable Pitt to watch the conspiracy.

One of his letters, dated November 19, is preserved:

'A. Lowry writes from Paris, October 11, in great despondency on account of Hoche's death, and says that all hopes of invading Ireland were given over. I then saw Rheinart, the French Minister, who begged me to stay here, as the only mode in which I could serve my country and the Republic. I instantly acquiesced, and told him I had arranged matters with Lord Edward Fitzgerald in London for that purpose. I showed him Lowry's letter. He said that things were changed. Bonaparte would not listen to the idea of peace, and had some plan, which I do not know.

'I told him the spirit of republicanism was losing ground in Ireland, for the Catholics and Protestants could not be brought to unite. I mentioned then what Fitzgerald told me in London, viz. that after I left Ireland they had thought of bringing matters to a crisis without the French. Arthur O'Connor was to have had a command in the North, he himself in Leinster, Robert Simms at Belfast; that the Catholics got jealous of this, and Richard McCormick, of Dublin, went among the societies of United men and denounced the three as traitors to the cause and dangerous on account of their ambition.

'All letters to or from Lady Lucy Fitzgerald ought to be inspected. She, Mrs. Matthieson, of this place,[1] and Pamela carry on a correspondence. Lewines, Teeling, Tennant, Lowry, Orr, and Colonel Tandy are at Paris. Tone expects to stay the winter there, which does not look like invasion. Oliver Bond is treasurer. He pays Lewines and MacNeven in London.

'Now for myself. In order to carry into effect the scheme which you and Mr. Pitt had planned, it was requisite for me to see my countrymen. I called on Maitland, where I found A. J. Stuart of Acton, both of them heartily sick of politics. Edward Fitzgerald had been enquiring of them for me. I went to Harley Street, where Fitz told me of the conduct of the Catholics to him and his friends. He said he would prevail on O'Connor or some such to go to Paris. If not, he would go himself in order to have Lewines removed. Mrs. Matthieson has just heard from Lady Lucy that O'Connor is to come. I supped last night with Valence, who mentioned his having introduced Lord Edward and O'Connor to the Minister here in the summer, before the French attempted to invade Ireland. They both went to Switzerland, whence O'Connor passed into France, had an interview with Hoche, and everything was planned.

'I feared lest Government might not choose to ratify

[1] A relative of Lady Edward.

our contract; and being in their power would give me my choice either to come forward as an evidence, or suffer martyrdom myself. Having no taste for an exit of this sort, I set out and arrived here safe, and now beg you'll let me know if anything was wrong in my statements, or if I have given offence. If you approve my present mode of life and encourage me so to do, with all deference I think Mr. Pitt may let me have a cool five hundred, which shall last me for six months to come. To get the information here has cost me three times the sum; and to keep up the acquaintance and connections I have here, so as to get information, I cannot live on less.'[1]

[1] 'Letter of November 19, 1797, from Hamburgh, to Lord Downshire.'—*Irish MSS.* S. P. O.

CHAPTER III.

THE EVE OF '98.

SECTION I.

No statesmen were ever more painfully situated in the presence of conspiracy than those who were responsible for the safety of Ireland on the eve of the rebellion of 1798. The country was preparing for an insurrection which, by the confession of the best-informed of its promoters, was likely if successful to be attended by scenes like those which had disgraced the rising of Sir Phelim O'Neil. The temper of the people was the same, the object was the same. The Government was exactly informed of all that was going forward. The names of the leaders, their purposes, their methods of proceeding were known. The first droppings of the coming storm were apparent daily in the paralysis of the civil authority and an organised system of terror. But the witnesses who in private were ready to betray their comrades or their cause were unavailable for purposes of public order and justice. The villager who with his own eyes had seen a family massacred, and in private, under an oath of secrecy, told his story with trembling lips, found his memory fail him when produced in court to repeat his evidence in public. The magistrate who might have dared the immediate menace of the secret tribunals, remembered that, though the present danger might be overcome, his family and himself must remain in the midst of the people whose undying hatred he might incur by energetic exertion. He had learnt by centuries of experience that those who in times of trouble were most loyal to the British Crown, could count on no support when coercion was succeeded by the fatal desire to conciliate. If he rose superior to his distrust, and grappled successfully with the rebellious agencies, he was proscribed by name in the patriotic press. Proscription was followed by death, and the security with which the sentence was inflicted, from the determination of the people to shield the executioners from punishment, operated as a frightful and too effective warning that, if he valued his own or his children's lives, he must fold his hands and close his eyes.

The machinery of law was out of joint. Two alternatives lay before the authorities at the Castle, each equally dangerous. Either they, too, must sit by till the mine exploded, to be reproached, like the Lords Justices in 1641, for having permitted a rebellion which they might have prevented, as an excuse for further oppression, or they must expose themselves to the moral indignation of the friends of liberty and humanity in both countries by acts of seeming illegality of which they would be unable to avow the reasons, and be accused, when rebellion came, of having provoked it by tyranny.

Those who look back from the secure position of later times have forgotten to allow for a feeling which was never absent, night or day, from the minds of the conspirators, from the minds of the Executive at the Castle, from the minds of the gentry and clergy of

Ireland, whose lives and fortunes were at stake; they have forgotten the real probability that the rebellion might succeed. It had the open support of the strongest military power in the world. The Bantry Bay expedition had proved how easily a French power might be landed. The sailing of the Texel fleet, at a time when Duncan was too weak to stop it, had been prevented only by the weather. If the experiment was not renewed, Bonaparte's victories had already inclined, and might at any time compel, England to come to terms with him, and the Directory had publicly promised that the independence of Ireland was to be a condition of peace.

Already the chances of the game were affecting families of consequence, who were trimming their sails in expectation of that contingency. The Duke of Leinster was doing his utmost within the Constitution to bring the Government into public hatred. Lord Edward was not the only member of his house who was engaged in actual treason. The heir of Lord Cloncurry was a sworn member of the Revolutionary Committee, and was traced on a mission to England to meet a French emissary there.[1] He was accompanied, unknown to himself, by an officer whose business was to watch his motions and report him to the Home Office. Other information reached Camden, the nature of which, for the sake of the parties concerned, was never trusted to paper; but so important was it, that Pelham himself hurried to London to

---

[1] 'Mr. Lawless, Lord Cloncurry's eldest son, is going to England this night, charged with an answer to a message lately received from France. I have sent Captain d'Auvergne in the packet with Mr. Lawless, with directions to find out where he means to go in London, and to give you immediate information.' — 'Pelham to John King, Esq., November 7, 1797.' S. P. O.

communicate personally with the astonished Cabinet.[1]
Inflamed alternately with hope and rage, the newspapers became daily more daring. Arthur O'Connor, after spending a few months in the Castle, had been released on bail, Thomas Addys Emmett and Lord Edward Fitzgerald being his securities. 'The person' who had come to Lord Downshire had revealed the secret of the visit to Switzerland; but without betraying his authority, Camden could not again order O'Connor's arrest. He immediately instituted a publication named 'The Press,' which left far behind the comparatively tame ferocities of the 'Union Star.'

A letter appeared in its columns, addressed to Carhampton, on the failure of the attempt to assassinate him, signed 'Satanides,' and written probably by O'Connor himself. Carhampton was informed that he had escaped Dunn to be reserved for a more public doom. 'It was to be lamented,' the writer said to him, 'that you should perish by the stroke of private justice, and defraud the executioner of his right and the public of its example. Were you at this moment surrounded by the justly enraged populace, were their arms raised to inflict the desired doom, I would throw myself among their poinards. I would say, Suffer him to pollute the air a little longer. The day comes when justice shall prevail, when Ireland shall raise her head from the dust and perform a solemn sacrifice to the Constitution. On that awful day of rejoicing to the good,

---

[1] 'I have had the pleasure of passing the whole morning with Mr. Pelham, from whom I have learnt some circumstances which have astonished and grieved me beyond the utmost extent of my information.'—'Portland to Camden, December 16.' Lord Camden answers: 'I do not wonder at the surprise and indignation which your Grace expresses at some of the information which Mr. Pelham has given you, and which I thought it better should be so communicated than by letter.'

and terror to the wicked, a few victims may be required, and this wretch may be included in the number and meet the doom of a traitor.'

These words were perhaps penned when the French were immediately looked for. At times the mood varied. Public justice seemed far off, and the mind of Satanides reverted to Harmodius and Aristogiton.

'You, my fellow students,' he said in another letter addressed to the patriots of Trinity College, 'you have explored the page of history where the insect courtier is forgotten, the despot is blasted in infamy, and the glorious tyrannicide is immortalised. Can you remember one instance of a people naturally brave, and wanting but the will to be illustrious, succumbing to the domination of their own minions, and passively agonizing under the extremities of oppression? No! Ireland is singular in suffering and in cowardice. She could crush her tormentors, and yet they embowel her. She could be free, yet she is a slave.[1]

'The unheard-of boldness of these publications,' wrote Camden, 'has been produced by the very decided offer of assistance from France. The intelligence with which we are furnished would, if certain persons could be brought forward, be sufficient to bring the conspiracy to light, defeat its ill consequences, and make a salutary impression on the minds of the people.'[2]

Unfortunately 'certain persons' declined to be brought forward. Pelham, when in London, made

---

[1] 'Extracts from "the Press."'—
'Report of the Secret Committee, 1798. Ireland. Appendix, 27.'

[2] 'Camden to Portland, December 2, December 7.' S. P. O.

large offers to Lord Downshire's friend, but without effect. Evidence came in through the Foreign Office, but again 'of a nature which could not be produced.'[1] Camden has been blamed as well for inexertion as for exertion. His most earnest desire was to meet Parliament with a clear statement of all that he knew, to arrest the leaders, and bring them at once to trial. He had proof of the correspondence with France. He had lists of the Assassination Committee and the Committee of Revolution. He knew that in the main they consisted of the same persons; and that by their public conviction the mind of England would be set at rest. The Opposition would be silenced, and the conspiracy, deprived of the sympathy by which it was encouraged, might be even yet extinguished before it assumed a fatal form. But the witnesses, indispensable to success, were not to be moved; and 'those persons who best know the country,' Lord Camden sadly said, 'agree with Mr. Pelham and myself (and I understand it to be the opinion of H.M.'s Ministers), that unless those who are at the head could be prosecuted with success no advantage would accrue by apprehending them.'[2]

When the time came for Parliament to open, therefore, the Speech from the Throne contained no more than a general statement that the country was dangerously disturbed, that the Government was determined to put a stop to treason and murder, and that the King relied upon the loyalty of the Irish gentry. In the House of Commons the field was abandoned to the Government. The remarkable feature of the

---

[1] 'Camden to Portland, January 8, 1708.'

[2] 'Camden to Portland, January 22, 1708.'

beginning of the Session was the appearance of Lord Moira, to repeat in his place as a Peer of Ireland the indictment which he had brought against Lord Camden's administration at Westminster.

It was audacious, for a crisis was evidently near. The day before Lord Moira spoke, the news had come in of the murder, under the most horrible circumstances, of two of the most active magistrates in Cork, Colonel St. George and Mr. Uniacke. But he had been taunted apparently with having delivered his attack where it could be imperfectly met, and the vain and feeble enthusiasm of his character was impregnable to evidence.

He rose, he said, to reassert the charges which he had alleged in the Parliament of Great Britain against the treatment of Ulster by General Lake. Houses had been burnt, innocent individuals had been seized, imprisoned, flogged, and picketed. He did not blame the troops. He blamed the Government for having set them upon a duty so barbarous and so detestable—for having called in the strength of England to coerce and tyrannise over Ireland. If the Lords and Commons of Ireland assisted in depriving their country of its liberties, he warned them that they would themselves soon feel in shame the weight of the chain; they would soon, he said, dropping into weak sentimentalism, 'hear the plaintive genius of Ireland reproaching them for their cruelty.' The people were said to be irreconcilable. From his own experience he insisted that they were misunderstood and maligned. He had held a meeting in his own neighbourhood. He had described the confusion and misery which were created by democratic Republics. He had expounded the blessings of

BOOK IX.
1798.
February 19.

Constitutional Monarchy, and had expatiated on the virtue and benevolence of the Sovereign who filled the throne. 'When he spoke of the generous magnanimity of him who was the future hope of the realm, and of the regard with which he returned the affection manifested to him by Ireland on a melancholy occasion, there was not an eye which did not beam with the honest pride of meriting by heartfelt self-devotion the favourable opinion of such a prince.'[1]

'Appeal,' he exclaimed, 'to the hearts of the people; while you appeal to their fears you will never succeed. You must grant Catholic Emancipation. I give the opinion with the more confidence after the zeal and ardour manifested by the Catholics of the South when a French fleet was in one of your ports. You must grant Parliamentary Reform. The greatest evil to be feared from it sinks to nothing compared to the mischief which is raging at present. The expression of a conciliatory desire on your part would suspend immediately the agitation of the public mind.'[2]

It was not easy for the members of Council, to whom the state of Ireland was better known than to Lord Moira, if he really believed his words, to sit patient under his flatulent declamation. At that moment the Council were weighing intelligence from the friend at Hamburgh, so serious that they had all but resolved on an immediate arrest of the entire

[1] This was too much for the stomach of Wolfe Tone, who said Moira ought to have known better than to pretend that Ireland would be satisfied with constitutional reform. 'I can hardly be suspected,' he said, 'of partiality for the Chancellor, but I declare I have more respect for his conduct on this occasion than for Lord Moira's. He is, at least, an open and avowed enemy.'—*Memoirs*, March, 1798.

[2] Speech of Lord Moira, February 18, 1798.

Revolutionary Committee. The English Cabinet was still in favour of delay, hoping for evidence which would ensure their conviction upon trial. The Irish advisers of the Crown, who had before been of the same opinion, had changed their minds, and were in favour of immediate action. Further hesitation might bring the French in earnest. The arrest of the leaders might precipitate the insurrection, but would deprive it of its directing head; and if the rebels were forced into the field without their allies, they could be encountered with less extremity of peril. Anxious letters had passed and repassed during the first fortnight of February between Camden and the Duke of Portland,[1] which ended in the Duke leaving the Viceroy to act at his own discretion. It was from the discussion of this vital and most critical question that the Chancellor and the other ministers had been called away to listen to Lord Moira.

Lord Glentworth[2] was the first to reply. He contented himself with giving an outline of the United Irishmen's proceedings, so far as they were generally notorious. He read extracts from the patriot newspapers. He gave a list of the most atrocious of the late murders,[3] and detailed the particulars of the last. Colonel St. George dined at Mr. Uniacke's house on the 9th of February. As Mr. Uniacke and his wife were lighting him at night to his bedroom, fourteen

---

[1] '*Irish Correspondence*, February, 1798.' S. P. O.

[2] Sexton Pery, so long Speaker of the House of Commons.

[3] One of the stories which Lord Glentworth mentioned is curiously illustrative of the time. A soldier of the Limerick Militia had informed an officer of his regiment that attempts had been made to seduce him from his allegiance. The wife of one of the confederates was sent to pretend love to him. He was tempted a mile from his quarters, and while she had her arms round him, the hatchet of an accomplice split his skull.

men with blackened faces appeared on the landing-place from the back stairs, while others showed themselves below. Mrs. Uniacke threw herself before her husband. They flung her over the staircase on the pavement of the hall. They stabbed Uniacke through and through, and then hurled him down beside her. They attacked Colonel St. George next, killed him, slashed and hacked at him till they were tired, and then pitching his body on the bodies of his friends, they left them together in their blood.

The facts were not to be denied. A prelate of the Establishment, Dr. Dickson, Bishop of Down, was of Lord Moira's opinion, that such crimes could be best prevented by loving the perpetrators, who were misled by zeal for their country's cause.

Then rose Fitzgibbon. He had long waited for an opportunity to tell the truth about that country in terms which Europe should hear. The occasion had been created for him, and he used it. Lord Moira and his friends had been the fiercest advocates of the independence of the Irish Parliament. Fitzgibbon commenced with observing sarcastically on the impropriety of appeals to the British Legislature by a peer of Ireland against the Government established in Dublin. Then he passed rapidly to the substance of the accusations:—

'The noble lord has told the British peers that the Executive Government of Ireland has taught the soldiery to treat the natives of this country indiscriminately as rebels, and to goad them with unexampled insult and barbarity; that the obsolete badge of servitude, the curfew, has been revived in its vigour and enforced with cruelty and insult; that the detestable principles and proceedings of the Inquisition had been introduced into Ireland; that the natives were tortured to extort from them a confession of their own guilt or that of others. These insolent and distorted exaggerations have passed into general circulation through every seditious and disaffected print in Great Britain and Ireland under the proffered solemnity of the noble lord's oath.[1] It remains for me publicly and distinctly to refute the foul and injurious charges of tyranny and injustice which have been advanced against the Government and Parliament of Ireland.'

'It has long been the fashion of this country to drown the voice of truth by loud and confident assertion. Since the separation of America from the British empire, when the noble lord knows some British politicians successfully played a game of embarrassment against Lord North's Administration, they have been pleased to turn their attention to Ireland as a theatre of political warfare, and to lend their countenance to every faction which has reared its head in this country to disturb the public peace. When the noble lord recommends conciliation as a remedy for the state of this country, I conclude his information flows from this polluted source. If conciliation be the pledge of tranquillity, there is not a nation in Europe in which it has had so fair a trial as in Ireland. For twenty years there has been a liberal and unvaried system of conciliation and concession. Concession and conciliation have produced only a fresh stock of grievances, and the discontent of Ireland has kept pace with her prosperity.'

Running rapidly over the history of those twenty

---

[1] Moira had offered to swear to the truth of his charges.

years, Fitzgibbon showed how the opening of the trade in 1779 had been followed in 1782 by the demands for political change; how a new Constitution had then been formed by Mr. Grattan and his friends; how the Commons had assured the King that thenceforward no question could arise to disturb the harmony of the two countries; yet how brief that harmony had been. Mr. Flood had discovered that the repeal of a law was not a renunciation of a principle; that the Constitution was a bubble, and that the noblemen and gentlemen who pretended to have emancipated Ireland were the accomplices of England's treachery. He then continued:—

'A Bill was introduced by Lord Grenville which passed into law without opposition, renouncing unequivocally all legislation or judicial authority in Ireland. The people of Ireland might now have taken breath and suspended their constitutional labours. But a new grievance was discovered—Parliament must be reformed. After due deliberation it was determined to elect a military convention to meet in the metropolis as the surest, most efficacious, and most constitutional organ through which to convey the sense of the nation. The Convention assembled with military pomp and parade, and assumed the form of a House of Parliament. A Bill for the reform of the representation of the people was regularly presented, read a first time, a second time, committed, reported, and agreed to, and being engrossed was sent at the point of the bayonet by two members of the Convention, who were also members of the House of Commons, to be registered by that assembly. The House of Commons treated this insult with the contempt which it merited. The Convention dispersed, and we had a short respite. But soon a new topic of discontent was started. It was discovered that the manufactures of Great Britain were imported into this country upon terms which gave them a preference in the Irish market, a preference which superior excellence alone can give them, and the remedy proposed was that we should commence a war of prohibitory duties, although it was notorious that the balance of trade was considerably in our favour; and if Parliament had been so infatuated as to yield to popular clamour, we had not the means of manufacturing woollen cloths sufficient for our wants. Hence came the memorable treaty of 1785 for a final adjustment of commercial intercourse. A fair and liberal offer was made by Great Britain to open her markets and share her capital with this country. The offer was wisely rejected by the Irish House of Commons under a silly deception. The people were taught to believe that it was an insidious artifice to revive the legislative authority of the British Parliament. In 1789 came the Regency question, when the intemperate, illegal, and precipitate conduct of the Irish Parliament shook our boasted constitution to its foundations, and contributed to bring our country to its present alarming condition. A political schism followed. The author of it[1] founded a political club for the reformation of public abuses. It was announced to the world with a manifesto in which the British Government was charged with a deliberate and systematic conspiracy to subvert the liberties of Ireland. The measures proposed were a Place Bill, a Pension Bill, a Responsibility Bill. The debate on these subjects in the House of Commons was

[1] Grattan.

carried on in a series of disgusting invectives suited to the meridian of Billingsgate. The people were told that the British Government intended to subvert the liberties of the Irish nation, and their aim became thenceforward to subvert the Monarchy and separate the country from Great Britain. Clubs were formed of United Irishmen. Appeals were addressed to the Volunteers, beseeching them to resume their arms; a general outcry was raised of commiseration and love for the Catholics of Ireland, in which for the first time since the Reformation a great body of the Protestant Dissenters joined, and Catholic Emancipation and Reform went forth as the watchwords of innovation and treason. The object of these Jacobin institutions was to detach the Catholics from the Catholic Committee, composed of the chief noblemen and gentlemen of their communion, and place them under a Jacobin Directory. The Catholics were stimulated to associate under the title of Defenders to disarm the Protestants, so finally to be relieved from tithes, taxes, and rent. A close correspondence existed between the Catholic Directory and the Irish Union. Orders were issued by the Jacobin clubs to levy regiments of National Guards all over the kingdom. .... The noble lord who imputes Irish disaffection to a system of coercion will please to recollect that the system of midnight robbery and avowed rebellion was completely established before any one coercive statute was enacted here. In 1792 and 1793 the project of levying a revolutionary army had been formed. Soldiers were forthcoming in abundance. I will tell the noble lord the conspiracy has been disclosed by evidence the most clear and satisfactory, by the testimony of gentlemen of rank and character, some of them at this moment high in military command in the King's service. The Parliament of Ireland did their duty in framing new laws to repress these outrages. If there be ground of censure on Parliament it is this, that the vigour was not proportioned to the magnitude and extent of the evil. Every man accused by the brotherhood of loyalty was stripped of his arms. If he presumed to defend himself he was murdered. The few magistrates who ventured to execute the law were marked for assassination, and many of them were murdered. In 1796 the Insurrection Act was passed. Magistrates in a proclaimed district were authorised to order all persons to remain in their houses and put out the lights after a certain hour of the night, and this the noble lord represents as a revival of the feudal badge of servitude, the curfew.[1] The United Irish combination is a complete revolutionary government organised against the law. Has the noble lord heard of the murders perpetrated by order of the Irish Union for the crime of putting the laws in execution? Has he heard of the murder of Mr. Butler, a clergyman and a magistrate? of Mr. Knipe, a clergyman and a magistrate? of Mr. Hamilton, a clergyman and

---

[1] In this part of the speech Fitzgibbon remarked sharply on the state of Lord Moira's own estate, which he described as 'a main citadel of treason.' Lord Moira had fiercely denounced the picketing of a certain blacksmith. Fitzgibbon reminded him of what he had been pleased to omit, 'that the man did immediately discover the names of several persons for whom he had manufactured pikeheads, in consequence of which discovery near two hundred pikes were seized.' 'He requested the noble lord to reflect on the number of probable murders which were prevented by that act of military severity; to consider whether the injury done to society by picketing that blacksmith was to be compared to the injury which must have risen from leaving two hundred pikes in the hands of rebels and assassins.'

a magistrate? of Mr. Cummins, whose crime was that he had enrolled in a Yeomanry Corps? of Colonel St. George and his host, Mr. Uniacke ? of the two dragoons who discovered to their officers an attempt to seduce them ? In a word, has he heard of the numberless and atrocious deeds of massacre and assassination which form part of the system of the Irish brotherhood, and are encouraged by the privileged order of innovators ? I hold the dark and bloody catalogue, but I will not proclaim to the civilised world the state of cannibal barbarism to which my unhappy country has been brought back by these pestilent and cowardly traitors. These are the men of sentiment whom the noble lord is anxious to conciliate. These are the injured innocents whose cause he has so pathetically pleaded—innocents who deal in robbery, conflagration, and murder, and scatter terror and desolation over the face of this devoted country. The noble lord may contemplate this scene of horrors with coolness from another kingdom, but he will not be surprised that the gentlemen of Ireland whose existence is at stake do not view it with the same indifference. What alternative has been left to the Executive Government but to surrender at discretion to a horde of traitorous barbarians, or to use the force entrusted to it for self-defence and self-preservation? What would have been the folly and debility of a Government which would have hesitated to assist itself at such a crisis? Lord Camden issued an order to disarm the rebels in the Northern districts. If he had not issued that order he would have betrayed his trust. General Lake has executed this service with the moderation, ability, and discretion which have marked his character as an officer and a gentleman.'

Such in outline, abridged and mutilated for purposes of necessary compression, was the once celebrated oration in which the great Earl of Clare replied to the sentimental advocates of Irish murderers. True as his words were to the last fibre of them, and the more inevitably because they were true, they were received with a yell of fury by those from off whose crimes and follies he stripped the gilding of spurious patriotism; and the echoes of their execrations have rung on to the present age, as if an Irishman and one of themselves had sinned against Irish nationality by holding a mirror before it in which to behold its real image.

England, too, has behaved to Clare like herself. When the danger was passed she fell back into her old dream of conciliating the irreconcilable. She selected for political advancement the incendiaries of the Irish Parliament who had fostered the rebellion, the dangers of which they shrunk from sharing. She gave the Great Seal to Ponsonby, and she made Curran Master of the Rolls. She elevated Grattan by adulation into the most honoured place among the heroes of his country. She sent Moira as Governor-General to India. As in earlier times, she left the gentlemen who stood by her in her hour of trouble to the vengeance of the patriots, caring no more for them when they had served her turn, so when Clare died, the best friend she ever had, she gave a sigh of relief at being rid of his oppressive presence. She permitted the scum of Dublin to dishonour his open grave, and she has left his memory to be trampled on lest she should offend the prejudice of later generations of patriots by confessing the merits of the greatest statesman whom Ireland ever produced.

On one person in Europe, whose opinion at that time happened to be of consequence in these Irish matters, the speech, perhaps, was not without effect. Copies of it were circulated in France, and Wolfe Tone, who could not refuse his admiration of Clare's courage, brought it under the eye of Napoleon, in the hope that he might be encouraged to head the army of invasion in person by the confirmation which it contained of Tone's own representations of the humour of the Irish people.

Napoleon never said what he thought of it, but from that time he listened coldly to the advice of the Directory to make Ireland a principal scene of his duel with England. The chosen friends of the Irish in Paris were the Jacobins, whose principles they adopted, and whose affectations they caricatured. Napoleon did not admire Jacobins, either native or foreign. He had no desire to assist a half-insane nation to an independence which would be a scandal to Europe. The Directory adhered to their views, and acted on them to their misfortune and discredit. Napoleon, says Wolfe Tone's son, in a memoir of his father, disliked the Irish leaders, refused to appreciate Ireland's importance to him, and when Ireland was waiting to receive him carried his arms to Egypt.

SECTION II.

Intelligence more and more alarming continued to be received at the Castle. The intimate knowledge of their proceedings displayed by Fitzgibbon quickened the movements of the conspirators. On the 26th of February a member of the Revolutionary Committee in the pay of Pelham wrote to tell him 'that the military organisation was almost complete.' 'Gentlemen of considerable property were daily uniting.' 'The number of fighting men was increasing with astonishing celerity.' 'The public officers, those in the law departments especially, were furnishing recruits.' 'The Yeomanry were shaking.' 'The clerks in the bankers', merchants', and traders' houses were reckoned upon almost to a man.' Dublin Castle itself was not pure from infection, and 'there was scarcely a house where there were three male servants which could not boast of a domiciliary Committee.' 'The number of men in all Ireland who had returned their names on that day as prepared to take arms was 279,896. Carlow, Meath, Wicklow, Kerry, even Down and Antrim, notwithstanding Lake's exertions, had reported themselves ready to begin. Connaught, however, was still behindhand. The Committee had passed a resolution that the counties which had completed their organisation had deserved well of their country, but had requested them to bear their tyranny a little longer, till the whole country should be in a condition to move simultaneously.[1]

Lord Camden sent the communication to Portland on the day that it was received. A few hours later another informer presented himself at the Castle, of more consequence, who ultimately consented to give public evidence.

Thomas Reynolds, a Dublin silk merchant, had purchased an estate in Kildare. The coming of the French fleet to Bantry had led him to expect another attempt which might be successful. The landing of a French army, he had assured himself, would be followed by a revolution, and he had therefore been sworn in as a United Irishman. In his new county he had become acquainted with the Fitzgeralds. Lord Edward had given him a colonel's commission in the insurgent army. He was treasurer besides, and a member of the Committee. A chance conversation at a dinner talk had first alarmed him as to the prudence of his conduct. He had been further agitated by Lord Edward telling him on the 19th of February, perhaps after Clare's speech, that he was afraid of arrest, and was going to Paris to see Talleyrand and hasten the French expedition. Arrest was a word of ominous sound. Reynolds put himself in communication with Pelham. He told him when and at what hours the Revolutionary Committee met. He pointed out how they might be all captured, together with their incriminating papers.

It happened that at this particular time Lord Downshire's friend was in London, and Pelham knew it. If the friend could be brought over, and could be

---

[1] 'Enclosure in a letter from Lord Camden to Portland, February 26, 1798.' S. P. O.

induced to give evidence, a case could then be established against all the United Irish leaders. They could be prosecuted with certainty of conviction, and the secrets of the plot could be revealed so fully that the reality of it could no longer be doubted.

Most earnestly Camden begged Portland to impress on 'the friend' the necessity of compliance. 'Patriotism might induce him to overcome his natural prejudice.' If patriotism was insufficient, 'there was no reward which he ought not to receive.'[1]

Portland's answer was not encouraging:—

'The friend,' he said, 'shall be detained. As to his coming over to you, I have reason to believe that there is not any consideration upon earth which would tempt him to undertake it. He is convinced that he would go to utter destruction. Better he should stay here and open a correspondence with some of the principal conspirators, by which means you may be apprised of their intentions. If I could be satisfied, or if you would give it as your positive opinion, that this person's testimony or presence would crush the conspiracy, or bring any principal traitor to justice, I should not, and Lord Downshire would not, hesitate in using any influence to prevail on his friend to run any risk for such an object. But if he should fail, and escape with his life, he could render no further service. Weigh well, therefore, the consequence of such a sacrifice.'[2]

Every day's delay made the situation more dangerous, and Camden's position more embarrassing. Evidently neither Pitt nor Portland had yet realised the urgency of the peril, yet each morning continued to

[1] 'Camden to Portland, March 1.' S. P. O.
[2] 'Portland to Camden, March 7.' S. P. O.

bring its tale of murders. In the first week in March two magistrates were killed in open day in Kildare. In the body of one of them was found the bayonet of a Militiaman. A group of labourers were looking on while the work was done, and the perpetrators walked coolly away. The Orange lodges offered their services, and organised for their own defence. The English mind had been so poisoned against the name of Orangemen by stupid and lying declamation that the Viceroy dared not employ them, but felt himself compelled 'to repress their demonstrations;' while the insurgent leaders, though each one of them was known, were allowed to pursue their machinations unharmed. The House of Commons was indignant at what it called the timidity of the Government, and clamoured for the reimposition of the Penal Laws. Those best affected to Government were loudest in demanding measures of most extreme severity. In the country the magistrates were prostrated with fear. 'It was equally difficult,' the Viceroy said, 'to repress the zealous and to give courage to the timid.'[1]

At this moment his difficulties were needlessly aggravated. An officer of experience was required at the head of the Irish army; and Cornwallis having declined, the choice of the Government fell on Sir Ralph Abercrombie, who had just distinguished himself in the West Indies. The English line regiments had been almost entirely recalled from Ireland for service abroad. The troops in the island consisted of a handful of Germans, a very few regiments of British Fencibles, the rest, and by far the largest proportion, being the Irish Yeomanry and the distrusted

---

[1] 'See two extremely interesting letters from Lord Camden to Portland, March 6 and March 10.' S. P. O.

and uncertain Irish Militia. The Yeomanry, though thoroughly loyal,[1] had received no military training. They had volunteered their services to grapple with the unseen enemy who for years had been the terror of their families, had compelled every Protestant house to convert itself into a fortress, and had filled the domestic life of Protestant Ireland with the most painful anxiety. Yeomen and farmers had left their ploughs at the invitation of their landlords; men of business had forsaken their desks; gentlemen had joined with their Protestant servants to encounter and subdue this horrible nightmare. They were scattered in small detachments over the country doing police work, and therefore as soldiers were necessarily disorganised.

The Militia regiments had been assailed secretly with perpetual invitations to mutiny. They, too, had never been regularly disciplined. Their officers in many instances were the worst of the worst class in Ireland, the pretenders to the name of gentlemen. Abercrombie, entirely ignorant of Ireland, prepossessed by the prejudices against the Castle Government, and perhaps under the influence of Lord Moira, was outraged at the condition in which he found the army which he was sent to command. Instead of looking into its real quality—instead of endeavouring to understand its motley elements, and fashion them into shape, he assumed that the disorder was but an illustration of universal mismanagement. Without saying a word to anyone, without paying the Viceroy so much as the compliment of consulting him, he issued an order immediately on his arrival which was

February 26.

---

[1] Catholics afterwards joined the Yeomanry, with a deliberate purpose of treachery.

a censure on the Executive Government. He told the troops that they were in a state of licentiousness which rendered them formidable to everyone but the enemy. On his own responsibility he superseded Lord Camden's orders, and forbade the soldiers to act anywhere under any circumstances in suppressing riots, arresting criminals, or in any other function, without the presence and authority of a magistrate.

The hopelessness of exertion on the part of the magistrates, whom as residents in the country it was unfair to expose to the vengeance of the people, had compelled Lord Camden to pass their duties over to military officers. In issuing an order in direct contradiction of the Lord-Lieutenant, Sir Ralph Abercrombie was himself setting a most signal example of the insubordination which he condemned; and had he been as right essentially as he was utterly wrong and headstrong, his manner of proceeding would have been without excuse.

Lord Camden was unwilling to create a disturbance. He quietly sent round a circular to each officer who held a separate command renewing his own instructions. Abercrombie, he trusted, would see the reason for them when he had larger experience. To Abercrombie himself he said nothing. In his letter to the Cabinet he passed the matter over in silence. His own desire was that it should pass unnoticed.[1] It was in England that attention was first drawn to the ill-omened order, and Camden was blamed by the Cabinet under the impression that he had sanctioned it.

---

[1] Yet Lord Camden has been universally accused by Irish writers of having procured Abercrombie's dismissal, as too just and too humane to execute the cruelties which he intended.

'An extraordinary sensation has been created,' Portland wrote, on the 11th of March, 'by Sir Ralph Abercrombie's general order. Can it be genuine? And if genuine, for what purpose was it issued, and how was it allowed? Our friends here cannot repress their regret at the triumph which they conceive Lord Moira and his adherents, and indeed all the disaffected, will claim over the Chancellor and the heads of your Government. The Irish whom I have seen, and whose conversation has been reported to me, conceive that there must be some division in the Government; that you must have been deluded or intimidated; that protection is to be withdrawn from them; that they will be sacrificed, or forced to join the insurgents. I assure your Excellency I must request a full and immediate explanation, which will enable me to give that satisfaction to our friends and to the public in general which has hitherto uniformly attended every measure of your Excellency's Administration.'[1]

It was, of course, easy for Camden to reply, by telling the literal truth. 'To have noticed the order in the manner which his feelings dictated,' he had feared, 'might have had an injurious effect on the King's service.' 'Sir Ralph might have resigned, or have been recalled, and the Council were all agreed that his leaving the country on such a ground, immediately after his arrival, would have a bad effect in the country.' 'He had therefore passed it over, and explained it away, and in Ireland it was already forgotten.'

The attention called to the matter in England

---

[1] 'Portland to Camden, March 11, 1798.'

obliged Camden to communicate to Abercrombie the contents of Portland's letter. He discharged his task 'as delicately as possible,' with the strongest expressions of personal respect. The spirit in which Abercrombie received the reproof throws a painful light on the motives with which the order was issued, and shows how far in that unhappy time the sense of duty in the soldier was obscured by the passions of the politician. He refused to see Lord Camden; he wrote a letter to him, in which, although his knowledge of Ireland was but a few weeks old, he repeated Lord Moira's accusations, and declared the policy of the Castle to be the cause of the disquiet of the country. Lord Camden had pressed him earnestly to retain the command, as his retirement at such a moment could not fail to weaken further the shaken authority of the Government. Abercrombie closed a petulant defence of his conduct with an abrupt resignation.[1]

In this instance Lord Camden had not to complain of half-hearted support from home. Both the King and the Cabinet expressed their strongest satisfaction with Camden's forbearance and discretion. They felt as he felt, that the resignation, if persisted in, would be taken as a censure on the Viceroy, and a direct encouragement to the rebellion. Entirely unacquainted as Abercrombie necessarily was with the secret information on which Lord Camden was acting, they were willing to pass over his mistake; but they entreated him not to add to their difficulties by persevering in it.

But either Abercrombie had come to Ireland

---

[1] 'Camden to Portland, March 13.' S. P. O.

primed by Lord Moira, and predetermined to thwart the Government (and if this was the explanation his acceptance of the command without informing the Cabinet, of his views was entirely indefensible), or on imperfect knowledge he had taken a rash and ill-considered step, the effects of which he was bound to repair. But his vanity had been wounded by what he construed into a public affront. 'He admitted that he had been misinformed,' 'but it made no difference.' 'He refused to make any concession to the wounded feelings of the country, or remedy the effects of his indiscretion.'[1] 'We must, therefore,' said Camden, 'accept the resignation; and I transmit his request, though with sensations the most painful. The awful situation of this kingdom cannot be too early or too attentively the subject of the deliberation of his Majesty's Ministers. Sir Ralph Abercrombie has withdrawn himself from the command in a manner calculated, I venture to say, more to shake his Majesty's interests in Ireland than any other event could have produced. The army will suppose that they have gained a victory over Sir Ralph Abercrombie, and all that was amiss will grow worse.'[2]

[1] 'Camden to Portland, March 26.' S. P. O.

[2] 'Camden to Portland, March 26.'

SECTION III.

If Sir Ralph Abercrombie had been on the watch for a moment when, by leaving the army without a head, he could best forward the interests of the insurrection, he could not have selected a more appropriate occasion. Fitzgibbon's language in the House of Lords, and whispers of treachery among themselves, had given the Executive Committee of the rebellion reason to suspect that their persons were known to the Government, and that further delay would be unsafe. Lawless had gone to London to see the French agent. Fitzgerald had spoken of the probability of his arrest, and of his intention of going to Paris, to quicken Talleyrand. Fitzgerald, perhaps, felt that he could not be spared, and Arthur O'Connor was despatched instead of him. Among the Irish at Paris, Wolfe Tone mentions a priest named O'Coigly, abbreviated into Quigley, as having been there in the summer of 1797, attached to the faction of Napper Tandy. This Quigley, a ready, busy, cunning person, was skilful in disguises, and had learnt the art of passing to and fro without detection. He had returned to Dublin in the winter following. He had been with Lord Edward at Leinster House. He was now going back to Paris, and Arthur O'Connor determined to go in his company. O'Connor had been released from prison on his recognizances. His movements were suspected; he was called on to appear and take his trial, but he was already gone. It was represented that he had been summoned to England on private affairs, and the excuse was accepted.

On the 27th of February three strange gentlemen appeared at the 'King's Head,' at Margate. They had come from Whitstable, and had brought with them a cart full of luggage. They called themselves officers, and gave the names of Captain Jones, Colonel Morris, and Mr. Williams. They said that they were on their way to Deal, and that they wanted a conveyance for their boxes. They remained for the night at the 'King's Head;' and the servants of the hotel, with the usual curiosity of such persons, questioned the driver of the Whitstable cart as to whence they came, and who they were. The driver's impression was that they were concerned in some smuggling transaction. They had applied to the boatmen at Whitstable to take them across to Flushing. The Whitstable men had set their terms too high, and the driver thought that they meant to try elsewhere. Further enquiry brought out that they had spoken on the same subject to some fishermen at Margate. Strangers in those times of jealous loyalty, seeking a secret passage to the Continent, were persons to be watched. A hint was given to the police, and the next morning, when the party were at breakfast, two officers entered the room, and asked them for an account of themselves. Their story was not ready. They pretended to be unknown to each other, and to have met accidentally at Margate. It was immediately proved that Captain Jones and Colonel Morris had slept in the same room at Whitstable. They denied the luggage to be theirs. It was proved that they had engaged the cart in which it was brought, and that they had spoken of taking it with them to Deal.

The situation became serious. They were searched. In a great-coat, which was hanging in the room, was found a pocket-book, and in the pocket-book was a letter addressed to the Executive Directory of France. The letter when opened was found so absurd as almost to disarm suspicion. To solid Englishmen, inexperienced in Irish political compositions, it seemed like the production of a lunatic. 'With the tyranny of England the tyranny of Europe was to fall.' The great nation was invited 'to pour out its gigantic force.' 'Its triumphs had been watched with rapture. The friends of liberty in England, Ireland, and Scotland had united to forward the common and glorious cause. The sacred flame of freedom was kindled. The United Islands were longing to break their chains, and were waiting with impatience to see the hero of Italy and his brave veterans on their shores.'

Dangerous conspirators did not usually carry compromising documents in coat pockets, nor expose themselves to danger for the sake of communicating to a foreign power such grotesque nonsense. Except for the lies which they had told, and for their appearance which showed them to be gentlemen, the party might have escaped with a few hours in the parish stocks. But there was an evident mystery about them. They and their boxes were sent under a guard to London, when Captain Jones was found to be the Priest O'Coigly, Colonel Morris to be Arthur O'Connor, and Williams to be an English revolutionist named Binns. O'Connor wrote a hurried note to Lord Edward, telling him not to be alarmed, nothing having been taken upon them which compromised any individual. The messenger to whom the note was entrusted was unfortunate or treacherous, for it fell into the hands of the Government.[1]

Had O'Connor known the connection between the Government and Lord Downshire's friend, he would have felt less confident. There was evidence, if it could only be produced, which would send both Lord Edward and himself to the scaffold. As matters stood, he had been caught red-handed in his mission of treason. The Government was in the absurd position of being driven to prove, by imperfect and inferential testimony, what they knew to be beyond the shadow of doubt, and to risk the chance of defeat when defeat would be a victory to rebellion. But there was now no alternative. The three prisoners were committed for high treason, and a special commission was appointed to try them.

The arrest of O'Connor and his companions rendered necessary immediate action in Dublin. The Committee would take alarm, and either give the signal for the rising, or disperse and assemble elsewhere. Camden had been left to act at his discretion. Papers might be seized which would of themselves be sufficient for the conviction of the most guilty, or would supply links which might be missing at Maidstone. At any rate, this knot of dangerous men could no longer be suffered to remain at liberty. Reynolds gave notice that a full meeting was to be held on the 12th of March, at No. 12, Bridge Street—the house of one of them, a merchant, Oliver Bond. The Committee was in two bodies—the General Committee and the Executive Council of the Committee, which was weekly changed. Both these bodies would be found

---

[1] 'Camden to Portland, March 6.' S. P. O.

sitting. The Executive Council on the 12th of March would consist of Mr. Jackson, MacCormick,[1] MacCann, Barclay Teeling, and Lord Edward Fitzgerald. On the 11th Lord Camden informed the Cabinet of the resolution which had been taken to seize them all, and 'having drawn the sword,' to arrest every other person who was known to be implicated.

'The universal opinion of his majesty's servants,' Camden wrote, 'the temper of the friends of Government, and the inconceivable mischief produced by the machinations of this Committee, have induced Mr. Pelham and myself to think the measure one of policy. The longer it is delayed the better the country will be organised. The timid are joining, the zealous are becoming lukewarm. Murders are every day committed, and gentlemen are driven from the country. The assizes approach, and neither grand nor petty juries will be found. It must be shown that the Government is not afraid to act, and the capture of the heads of the conspiracy must be followed by the march of troops into the parts of the country most disturbed. If we delay longer we shall be driven by Parliament into more rigorous measures. There is not a second opinion as to the necessity of the arrest.'[2]

The seizure was effected easily, though unhappily with incomplete success. Major Swan, an officer of the police, repaired at the time indicated by Reynolds to the house in Bridge Street, with twelve policemen in plain clothes. They burst in the door, and surprised the General Committee in full session. Eighteen were secured—secured had they known it

---

[1] Wolfe Tone's Magog, the secretary of the Catholic Committee.

[2] 'Camden to Portland, March 11, 1798.' S. P. O.

from the consequences of their own treason. Mac-Neven, Addys Emmett, Sweetman, two Jacksons, Oliver Bond himself, and twelve others were made prisoners. An attempt was made to throw the papers in the fire, which Major Swan promptly stopped by drawing a pistol; but there was no resistance. The Executive Committee sat in an inner room. Of them Jackson was taken. Lord Edward, MacCann, MacCormick, and Teeling had either escaped or had not arrived. Warrants were sent out instantly for their apprehension. Their houses were searched and all their papers carried off. In Lord Edward's room, at Leinster House, were found many letters, some in cypher, some in ordinary hand. Of the cyphers a key was discovered in O'Connor's dressing-case which was taken with his luggage at Maidstone. The letters read by the help of it referred to his journey to France. Quigley had denied that he had come from Dublin. A note from him proved that he had been at Leinster House on business of importance.[1]

The capture by the police of so many conspicuous patriots created, of course, the most vehement excitement. The people gathered in knots, talking eagerly and full of curiosity, but there were no open signs of anger, and quiet citizens drew their breath with a sigh of relief. Lord Edward seemed to have disappeared. Rumours said that he had gone north to his brother at Ardglass, and from thence would

---

[1] The note was like the address found in the coat pocket, and is a curious illustration of the stilted temper of the period:—

'Dublin, January 14, 1708.

'Citizen,—You will please to remain at home to-morrow, as I intend to call on you precisely at seven in the evening, and talk over that business of the letter, and other affairs of that business likewise.

'JAMES COIGLY.

'To Citizen Fitzgerald,
'commonly called
'Lord Edward Fitzgerald.'

escape out of the country. Orders were sent to every port to be on the watch for him, and a strict and silent search was maintained in Dublin and the neighbourhood.

Leaving Lord Edward for the moment, the story reverts to the Margate prisoners. Their trial was no sooner determined on than they became objects of the most powerful interest. The Opposition, for reasons known to themselves, erected O'Connor into a political hero. They affected to see in him an intended victim of the savage and barbarous Government which was driving Ireland into rebellion, and forcing into exile the noblest of her sons. He was the proprietor of the 'Press' newspaper, and the 'Press' was the advocate of assassination. No matter. Round O'Connor were centered for the time the energy, the intellect, and the passion of the great Whig party of England.

The preparations for the trial were elaborately careful. Three judges—Sir Francis Buller, Sir Soulden Lawrence, and Sir John Heath—were placed on the commission. Lord Romney presided, as Lord-Lieutenant of Kent. Scott, Mitford, and Abbott conducted the case for the Crown. Plumer, Dallas, Gurney, and Fergusson appeared for the prisoners. The evidence against Quigley was that he was carrying a treasonable letter to the Directory; for the coat in which it was found was proved, in spite of his denials, to belong to him. He could offer no explanation of it, and the account which he gave of himself was found to be a tissue of falsehoods. Against O'Connor the direct evidence being still unproducible, the Crown alleged his companionship with Quigley, the letters found in Leinster House, to which the cypher which he was carrying was the key, referring to an invasion which he was going to France to procure, and the numberless contradictions in which he had involved himself, and which proved that he had something to conceal. Quigley's defence was desperate from the first. O'Connor's would have been desperate but for the weight of evidence to character which was brought to his rescue. Plumer pleaded for him that he was a gentleman of rank and fortune, Lord Longueville's nephew, the intimate associate and friend of the most distinguished statesmen of the day. To suppose that such a person would implicate himself in treason was absurd. He had the misfortune to differ in principle from the existing administration of Ireland. He had been already unjustly imprisoned, and he was going abroad to escape further ill-usage. The cyphered letter was allowed to be a mystery. It certainly seemed to refer to the introduction of a French force; but if Mr. O'Connor had really contemplated such a thing he could not be found guilty on the indictment, for he was charged with compassing the invasion of England, and if the allusion in the letter was to an invasion at all, it was the invasion of Ireland. These shifts would not of themselves have availed to save him. So evidently was he on some dangerous errand when he was taken, that he was found to have conveyed his property to his kinsman, Sir Francis Burdett, before he started upon it. In his favour, however—and considering that not only the evidence already in possession of the Ministers, but his own subsequent confession, proved that of all the Irish traitors he was the falsest and wickedest; considering that already he had published sentiments in his newspaper, under the signature of 'A Child of Satan,' in the fullest keeping with the assumed fatherhood of their author, such an appearance in a court of justice on that errand betrays a temper which explains the long exclusion of the Whigs from the service of their Sovereign—the most distinguished members of the Opposition in both Houses of the British Parliament presented themselves to give evidence to O'Connor's disposition.

Lord Moira came to declare his admiration of him, though he must have been acquainted with the wild and traitorous address which had been the occasion of his first imprisonment.

Erskine claimed O'Connor as a personal friend, protested that O'Connor's sentiments were his own, and declared him incapable of a dishonourable action. O'Connor, he said, was going abroad. He had seen him in London on his way from Ireland, and had himself advised him to go, though the friend whom he was thus counselling was avowedly at large on his recognizances.

Charles James Fox was the next witness. He had known O'Connor for four years, and professed to regard him as well affected, enlightened, and attached to the Constitution and the Crown.

One after another these great persons deposed to the same story, at the cost either of their conscience or their understanding. Sheridan had talked often with O'Connor on Irish politics. They agreed in their detestation of the present Administration; but in the face of the address to the people of Ireland, he said O'Connor had always repudiated the thought of applying to France for assistance.

Grattan, who had come to England for the trial, declared that he admired and honoured O'Connor, and dared to say, though on his oath, that he was certain that he could not approve of a French invasion. The Duke of Norfolk considered that there was no difference of opinion between Mr. O'Connor and himself. So did Lord John Russell, so did Lord Oxford, so did Lord Thanet, so did Samuel Whitbread. Grey and Lauderdale were in attendance, and willing to be sworn, but were not called upon.

Either these distinguished persons believed what they were saying—and if they believed it, distempered party spirit had made their judgment blind—or they so detested the Irish Administration and all belonging to it, that they considered treason itself as the excess of a spirit which was generally virtuous, and rather merited applause than censure. Buller summed up fatally against Quigley. Of O'Connor, on the ground of the uncertainty of the evidence and the array of testimony to his general excellence, Buller almost directed the acquittal.

The jury obeyed the Judge's instructions. The meaner villain was found guilty. Arthur O'Connor, another Phelim O'Neil, with the polish of cultivation externally, and with the inner nature of a savage, heard a verdict recorded in his favour. He was leaving the court in triumph, but the Government knew their man too well to let him go so easily. He was at once re-arrested on another charge, and was restored to his quarters in Dublin Castle.

Efforts too were made to save Quigley from the last penalty of the law. When they proved in vain, and he was brought out to die, he inflicted such revenge as was still within his reach on the oppressors of his country, by protesting from the scaffold that his life had been sworn away by perjury, that the papers in his pocket had been placed there by other hands, and that he died a murdered man.

In Maidstone Gaol he composed a sketch of his life. His blood, he said, was from the old Irish tribes. Not one of the plundering settlers did he count among his ancestors. His family had been stripped of the best of their lands by James the First. The remnant of them had fought against Cromwell, and had again suffered under the Act of Settlement. They must have been restored again, for he said that one of them sat for Tyrone in the Parliament of James the Second. His great-grandfather on the mother's side was killed, with seven of his brothers, at the Boyne. Another great-grandfather had constructed the famous boom at Derry, and with three of his brothers was killed at Aghrim. The Orangemen had attacked his father's house, had wounded his father, and had murdered his mother. They had destroyed his own library, his carefully-collected materials for a history of Ireland, and had driven him out as a wanderer over the face of the earth. The bravado with which he took leave of life deprives the story of its claim to credibility. The truth, if truth it contained, cannot be separated from the falsehood, and his obvious design was to represent himself as a member of a family which had devoted itself for the liberties of Ireland. The journal of Wolfe Tone places his connection with the intrigues with the Directory beyond the shadow of a doubt, yet to the last he declared his innocence upon oath. A priest was sent to prepare him for death. The threat of the refusal of the Sacraments failed to wring from him a word of confession. He wrote to Portland, saying that he was one of his lordship's messengers-extraordinary to the other world charged with tidings of his merciful Administration.

A day or two before his death he composed an address to the people of Ireland, to whose cause he was falling a sacrifice. He secured the preservation of an exact account of his closing behaviour. He would not have his death thrown away by the manner of it being belied, and from the platform below the gallows on Pennington Heath, where he suffered, he repeated 'firmly and distinctly,' 'without passion and without extravagance,' that he was an innocent man.

So, with a certain courage—for according to his professed creed he was risking his soul for his revenge—this miserable being, thus raised by accident into momentary and tragic visibility, was swung off and died.

Dying declarations of innocence always throw a certain doubt on the justice of an execution. By his persistence he dealt a blow not wholly ineffective at the Government which he abhorred, and raised himself in the estimation of the patriots, who were as well assured of his guilt as of their own.

'Quigley,' recorded Wolfe Tone in his journal, 'has behaved admirably well, which is more than I expected. He has behaved like a hero.'[1]

---

[1] 'Trials of Arthur O'Connor and James Quigley, at Maidstone, May 1798.' — *State Trials*, vols. xxvi., xxvii. *Journal of Wolfe Tone*, June 12 and June 18, 1798.

SECTION IV.

THE seizure of the Committee restored confidence in Dublin. The House of Commons demanded their immediate prosecution and punishment. But the evidence was still inadequate. Reynolds, the informer, hung back as yet from appearing publicly. The papers taken, though amply justifying the arrest, and proving that the Committee generally were engaged in organising and directing an intended insurrection, were insufficient, in the Attorney-General's opinion, to sustain an indictment for high treason against any individual. The prisoners were therefore left for the present in Newgate. The Cabinet congratulated Camden on his success, and encouraged him warmly to persevere, after so happy a commencement, in the same direction.[1] He was left to his unfettered judgment, the Duke of Portland, however, offering a few suggestions.

'Now, when the Viceroy was displaying his power,' the Duke thought there was a favourable opportunity for making a provision for the Catholic clergy. It would be a timely encouragement to loyalty. It would disarm misrepresentation. It would convince moderate Catholics that they were interested in supporting the Government. It might tend also to separate the Catholics from the Presbyterians—'an object considered always so desirable and of so much importance,' that the Duke 'could not avoid bringing it again under Lord Camden's consideration.'[2]

---

[1] 'Portland to Camden, March 17.'
[2] 'Portland to Camden, March 20.'

With these notions Portland combined others not usually thought compatible with them. He desired the priests to be conciliated, but he wished also to encourage everywhere the friends of order. Camden had been reproached with favouring the Orangemen. He had, in fact, been cold and hostile to them. Portland considered that the assistance of a body of which alone the United Irishmen confessed themselves afraid was not to be lightly thrown away. 'I heard yesterday,' he wrote, 'that the Orange Association in Ulster has been joined by all the principal gentry and well-affected persons of property in that province, for the purpose of protecting themselves against the United Irishmen, and that they have bound themselves by an oath to defend the King and the Constitution. Associations of any sort unless authorised by Government are not generally to be countenanced; but, considering the circumstances of these times, and the necessity of counteracting the attempts of our domestic enemies, exertions of this kind may do more than all the military force you could apply towards the establishment of order. The example may produce the best effects in other parts of the kingdom, and may give you a disposable force to be carried to the South. The sense of danger and the proper spirit which has prompted this combination may dispose those who have entered into it to allow your Excellency to methodise, direct, and bring them into the state ot subordination which may enable you to employ their zeal to the best advantage.'[1]

Had Camden's Administration been actuated by the fanatical spirit of Protestant ascendency which it

[1] 'Portland to Camden, March 24.' S. P. O.

is usually said to have represented, the Viceroy would have caught eagerly at a permission to accept assistance which would have relieved him of all anxiety for the possible success of the rebellion. He had shrunk from the Orangemen, and he shrank from them still, because he held it inconsistent with the duty of the representative of the Sovereign to raise again the banner of the Boyne, or arm Protestants against Catholics. His forbearance was the more creditable to him, because he had cause to know that Catholic loyalty, even where most loudly professed, was from the lips outwards. He was unable to accept Portland's advice on either side.

'As to a provision for the Catholic clergy,' he replied, 'the temper of the country will not bear it at present. There seems much reason to think that the Catholics in general are not hostile to these commotions; that even the most loyal of them wait with some hope that a revolution in Ireland will restore them to the possessions and the consequence that they have lost.' As for the Orangemen, Lord Camden was still under the spell of the remarkable theory that the secret of governing Ireland was to humour the enemies of the British connection and look coldly on its friends. He did not deny that there were among them 'very respectable persons.' Their present numbers were forty thousand; they were likely to increase, and in the event of open rebellion might possibly be useful. He should therefore take no steps to suppress or dissolve their lodges. To encourage them, however, would, he said, 'much increase the jealousy of the Catholics.' In 'the dreadfully disturbed' condition of the South 'he feared to recommend the employing one party in the kingdom to put down another.' 'Many of the Orangemen,' he believed, 'would enter regiments, either in the Yeomanry or the Militia.' 'They are the persons,' he added, with involuntary compliment, 'most to be trusted with arms in either kingdom.'[1]

Lord Camden was rejecting assistance which at that moment would have been of invaluable service. Having drawn the sword, there was no longer room for pause. It was obviously necessary to utilise the confusion which had been created by the arrest of the Revolutionary Committee, and to disarm Leinster and Munster by the same measures which had been found effective in Ulster, before the conspirators could repair the blow and elect a new Directory. For this purpose he was obliged to appeal to General Abercrombie.

The Cabinet had been painfully shocked at Abercrombie's persistence in resigning the command. Portland feared that Camden himself, weary of calumny and sick of so ungrateful and dangerous a service, might himself follow the example.[2] He declared Abercrombie's conduct to be most 'unjustifiable and distressing.' He insisted that Abercrombie should remain at his post till a successor could be provided for him; and as the circumstances admitted of no delay, Abercrombie was called on to undertake the work of disarmament. He seemed to have come to Ireland to

---

[1] 'Camden to Portland, March 20, 1798.'

[2] 'You, at whatever sacrifice, we entreat to remain at your post. I think the existence of Ireland would be endangered, and its ruin would ensue, were you to give up the Government; and, severe as the avowal of such a sentiment undoubtedly is, I should neither do my duty to my country nor to you were I to conceal it, or omit to add that there is not, in my opinion, any person existing who would fill your place.'—'Portland to Camden, March 31.'

effect the utmost extremity of mischief which his opportunities allowed him. Instead of complying, he said that the whole country was totally disaffected. The troops were as disloyal as the people. He could rely neither on the Yeomanry nor the militia, and 'ten thousand additional troops must be drawn from Great Britain' if the disarmament was to be persevered in.[1]

The rebels soon rallied their courage when they saw signs of hesitation in following up the arrest. On the 30th of March Lord Camden reported that another magistrate, Mr. Darragh, of Eagle Hill, of Kildare, had been murdered on his own lawn. A man brought him a petition, and shot him while he was reading it.[2] The plundering of private houses began again. Villages had been attacked at noonday. Large bodies of insurgents had collected and fired upon the troops. On the 28th of March a thousand men, well-dressed and well-appointed, many of them in regimental boots and pantaloons, rode into Cahir, in Tipperary, posted guards at the entrances of the town, examined every Protestant house, Lord Cahir's among them, and carried off all the arms which they found.[3] Mr. Pennefather, who commanded a Yeomanry corps at Cashel, reported himself surrounded by swarms of armed insurgents, and begged for help. Similar accounts came from Tipperary, Limerick, and Cork. The Privy Council unanimously decided that the troops must be put in

---

[1] 'Sir Ralph Abercrombie to Lord Camden, March 27.'

[2] Mr. Darragh had been reported, utterly without foundation, to have 'wished he was ancle-deep in Catholic blood.' For this the secret tribunal had sentenced him to death.

[3] 'Camden to Portland, March 30.' S. P. O.

motion. Even Abercrombie, who was at the meeting, appeared to acquiesce in the necessity, and professed himself 'willing to proceed to the disturbed districts and suppress the insurrection.'[1]

A proclamation was immediately sent out, resembling that which had been issued in Ulster by Lake. The country was declared in rebellion. The people were summoned to give up their arms. The army received instructions to act as might be necessary for the restoration of order, and if the arms were refused to take them by force.

No sooner was the proclamation out than Abercrombie had changed his mind. Letters had reached him from England in which he learnt the Cabinet's displeasure with his conduct. He spoke of himself as 'disgraced and ruined.' If the troops were to go, he said that he could not accompany them. Camden told him that the proclamation had been issued in reliance on his promise. If his objections were so strong as he now stated them to be, he ought to have said so at the Council.

At issue with himself, his sense of honour and propriety contending with some inner feeling which remained unexplained, he seemed to master his unwillingness. 'He said immediately that he would go; that under the peculiar circumstances in which he stood he would act with redoubled zeal; that he would not quit the South of Ireland till it was quiet, and the arms restored.'[2]

With these words Abercrombie left the Viceroy, and left him without further misgiving that his orders would be carried out.

[1] 'Camden to Portland, March 30.' S. P. O.
[2] 'Camden to the Duke of Portland, April 2.'

Abercrombie had scarcely left the Castle than another informer presented himself, whose name was not allowed to transpire, but who, like Reynolds, was a member of the General Committee. This gentleman told the Viceroy that the blow dealt in the arrest had been less effective than he had hoped; that the mischief had been repaired, and the vacant places on the Committee had been refilled. Had Major Swan arrived two hours later, he would have seized fifty of them, and among the rest 'Curran, who was to have been proposed for the Committee of a hundred.' 'The Committee had honorary members, of whom Grattan was one.' 'Grattan had been offered all terms if he would fairly engage, but he looked on.'[1]

Some few further particulars this person added as to the insurgents' present condition and prospects. The French Directory had definitely promised to land an army, which might be looked for before the end of the current month. They were to receive three millions sterling to repay the cost of the expedition, and the money was to be raised by the sale of the property of the nobles and the clergy. Preparations were being pressed forward to receive them. Emissaries were engaged at a guinea a day to debauch the soldiers, of whom the Committee supposed that they had gained a third. 'Almost all the lower priests were bought over, and were ordered at confession to urge the people to stand by the cause of their country.' Abercrombie's order 'had been happily calculated to alienate the soldiers from the Government, when they saw their exertions in repressing the people made a pretext for abusing

---

[1] Information enclosed by Camden in his letter of April 2.

them.' The success of the revolution was to be followed by a wholesale confiscation of estates. Full accounts had been drawn of the lands and their owners, and lists made of those who were to be sacrificed. 'The most dangerous man in Ireland was Emmett, from his zeal, his manners, his address, his eloquence, his ability, and his bloodthirstiness.'[1]

These accounts tallied too exactly with what was known already for any doubts to be entertained of the truth of them. The Viceroy and Council were sitting over a loaded mine, and for all that they could tell the match might be already smouldering which would explode it. Abercrombie had done irreparable mischief. The Viceroy believed himself entitled to hope that he was now exerting himself in earnest, and might not even yet be too late.

Some influence was unhappily at work on Abercrombie behind the scenes, which had enchanted him once more in the same fatal irresolution. He went South, but instead of disarming the people he contented himself with issuing orders that the arms were to be brought in and delivered up within ten days. After wasting a fortnight in inactivity, when time was of all things most precious, he returned to Dublin, to tell the Viceroy that although no pikes or muskets had yet been surrendered, he was convinced that they would be surrendered. His unwillingness had returned to employ the soldiers at all. 'His report to me,' Camden said, in sending an account to Portland of his extraordinary conduct, 'was intermixed with observations on the impolicy of allowing the military to act without

---

[1] Informations, April 2.

waiting for the civil magistrate, and of his opinion of the advantage of resorting to the civil power, with which political remarks it is unnecessary that I should trouble you.'[1]

Camden could no longer have desired to retain a Commander-in-Chief on whom he could rely so little as General Abercrombie. He did, however, once more, though to no purpose, invite him to remain. When he refused he was pressed no further; and after having enormously aggravated every element of danger in the country, he left Ireland, and the command devolved on General Lake.

'Sir Ralph's delay and long notice has done nothing but mischief,' Camden wrote, as soon as he was gone. 'It has cooled the ardour of the well-affected country gentlemen. No arms have been brought in, and now the general officers in command are themselves hesitating. At the assizes in Kildare the juries in general did their duty, but there appeared no good disposition among the Catholics, and the juries which did not act with propriety were of that persuasion. The appearance is of the contest becoming a religious one. All means shall be used to avert this danger, but the alarms of the Protestants are so great, and the hopes of the Catholics are so strong, that it is difficult to repress the violence of the first or make any impression on the latter.'[2]

---

[1] 'Camden to Portland, April 20.' S. P. O.

[2] 'Camden to Portland, April 23.' S. P. O.

SECTION V.

STUDENTS of later Irish history are familiar with the ferocious cruelties inflicted by General Lake's army on the Irish peasantry in the spring of 1798, the free quarters, the burnt villages, the pitch-caps, the triangle, and the lash. To these outrages it has pleased the Irish to attribute the insurrection. England, ever stern in extremities, ever penitent when the danger is over, and inclined to shift the blame upon her instruments, has allowed this legend, like so many others, to pass unrefuted, and has permitted one more illusion to swell the volume of Ireland's imaginary wrongs. An attention to dates would have sufficed to reduce the charge to modest dimensions. Lake did not take the command-in-chief till the 23rd of April. On the 24th of May the rebellion burst. The atrocities which are supposed to have caused it were therefore limited to a single month. The preceding history has been written in vain if it be now necessary to insist that the disarming of the South was no measure of gratuitous severity. For seven years the whole of Ireland had been deliberately preparing for revolt. An invisible authority ruled over the four provinces, with a code of laws enforced by dagger, pike, pistol, and houghing-knife. It had formed an army, negotiated an alliance, and conspired to bring to its assistance the deadliest enemies of England. Its regiments were dispersed over the whole country, ready at any moment for action, yet imperceptible to

CHAP.
III.

1798.
April.

the outward eye. The officers were younger brothers, professional men, adventurers, more or less educated, claiming the status of gentlemen, some of them men of fortune, and even of noble family. The rank-and-file were persons pursuing externally their quiet callings as tradesmen, artisans, clerks, farmers, or labourers. They had concealed depôts of arms ready to be snatched at a moment's notice, whether the object was to murder a magistrate or to take the field against the army of the Sovereign. The long forbearance of the Government had shaken the confidence of the troops and of the respectable inhabitants, who believed themselves deserted. Subtle influences were at work poisoning the loyalty of the soldiers. Things had come to such a point that there was scarce a country-house in any corner of Ireland where a Protestant family could go to rest without a sense that before morning they might be awakened by the yells of assassins. The servants who waited on them at table, the labourers who worked in their fields or gardens, might, for all they could tell, be in secret league for their destruction. Well-disposed at heart they might be, but their wills were under the spell of the general terror; and any magistrate whose loyalty was conspicuous knew that he was doing his duty to his country at the risk of his own and children's lives. The Irish gentry were looking upon themselves as doomed. The English press was ringing with execrations against them. They saw peers and statesmen going into the witness-box, to claim identity of opinion with the avowed advocate of assassination. The responsible governor of Ireland would have shown a craven shrinking from the first elements of his obligations if at such a moment he had allowed an impression to go abroad that he dared not grapple with the deadly organisation which was thus openly setting law at defiance. The ten days weakly granted by Abercrombie were allowed to expire, and then, as not a pike had been surrendered, General Lake set about his work. He had to deal with a temper of which the natural stubbornness was encouraged by the impression that the Castle Government would not be supported by the power of England. Of British troops he had but a handful. The force on which he had to rely to carry out his orders consisted mainly of the loyal Irish Yeomanry, men whose friends had been murdered, who had themselves been marked for murder, whose hands had for years been tied by a law which gave them no protection, while to their enemies it was a convenient shield. There was little cause of surprise if now at last, when they were permitted to show a people who had laughed at courts of justice that there were other modes by which they could be compelled into obedience, the poison-fangs were not drawn with the gentlest hand. It is true that during three weeks regiments were sent to live at free quarters in districts where the inhabitants combined to resist the disarmament. It is true that when other means failed the lash was freely used to compel disclosures, though only where sure and certain information had led the officers to know that there was something to be disclosed. It is true, also, that the lash proved the most efficacious of persuasives, that under its pressure the labours of the Revolutionary Committee were rendered futile, that the army of insurrection was deprived of half its means of injury, that the rebellion when it broke out was confined to districts where the process had been imperfectly carried out, and that General Lake's determination, though it could not prevent infinite horrors, did at least prevent a massacre on the scale of the precedent of 1641.

In so rude a scene there were doubtless instances of unnecessary harshness. Passionate indignation had been roused by the long catalogue of unpunished crimes, and passionate indignation is seldom temperate, and sometimes cruel.

The United Irishmen had affected the fashion of short hair. The loyalists called them Croppies, and if a Croppy prisoner stood silent when it was certain that he could confess with effect, paper or linen caps smeared with pitch were forced upon his head to bring him to his senses. Such things ought not to have been, and such things would not have been had General Lake been supplied with English troops; but assassins and their accomplices will not always be delicately handled by those whose lives they have threatened. Occasionally, not often, men suffered who were innocent, so far as no definite guilt could be proved against them. At such times, however, those who are not actively loyal lie in the border-land of just suspicion. Jurymen who would not convict on clear evidence, peasants who had looked on upon murder, yet in court found their memory fail them, those who knew of intended outrages yet spoke no word of warning, are not innocent. Society demands the active help of all its members to prevent or discover crimes, and men who leave these duties unfulfilled are confounded naturally with the actively guilty, when society thus treated falls in pieces and military severity is compulsorily substituted for law.

Among the gentlemen whom history has been pleased to gibbet for his share in these transactions was Mr. Thomas Judkin Fitzgerald, the High Sheriff of Tipperary. It was in Tipperary, the old home of the Whiteboys, that the intending insurgents had shown their colours with the most daring effrontery. When Abercrombie was seen to be hesitating, a town in Tipperary was occupied and plundered of arms in open day by a thousand rebel horse. In another town there a regiment of Yeomanry had been surrounded, and had been driven to apply for succour to save it from destruction. No slight courage was required to disarm Tipperary, nor was the disarming an easy matter when there was courage to undertake it. The High Sheriff was a Uniacke by birth. His father took the name of Fitzgerald. He is likely, therefore, to have been a relation of Mr. Uniacke, who had just been assassinated, with his wife and Colonel St. George. This gentleman did, by decisive measures, effectually break the insurgent organisation in Tipperary, so that when the rebellion came the most dangerous county in Ireland lay motionless. They were not gentle measures. He used the whip freely, and he made one mistake which was not forgotten. A man named Wright, at Clonmel, was suspected of connection with the United Irishmen. The suspicion in all likelihood was well-founded. On searching him a letter was found in his pocket, in French. Fitzgerald did not understand the language, but his mind, like that of everyone else, was full of the expected French invasion. The letter, though utterly innocent, was treated as an evidence of guilt, and Wright was severely flogged. He prosecuted the High Sheriff afterwards, and recovered 500*l.* as damages.

Fitzgerald has been rewarded with a black name in Irish legend and with the scorn of foolish historians. He was rewarded, also, by the knowledge that by his general nerve and bravery he had probably saved at least ten thousand lives; and the English Government, though generally too proud to remember good service in Ireland, yet so far acknowledged Fitzgerald's merit that they paid his fine and created him a baronet.

Had Abercrombie acted at once when first required by Camden to set the troops in motion, there would have been time to have made the disarmament complete, and Irish history would have been unstained by the bloody scenes which will have immediately to be described. Lake, however, had but a month. He succeeded in crippling the rebellion. He could not prevent it. His progress was attended, of course, by renewed outcries from the English Opposition and by yells from the incendiary press of Ireland. Grattan accused the Ministers of sounding the horrid trumpet of carnage and desolation, of encouraging the army to murder the Irish; of being in league with the Orange boys, and at war with the people. It might have been happier for Ireland and for England also if Camden had taken Portland's advice, and frankly adopted the Orange boys. He had himself confessed that of all subjects of the Crown they were the most to be relied upon. He stopped short of the measure which would have given him the absolute command of the insurrection. Within the limits which he had prescribed to himself he went on upon his way undiverted by clamour. By the 3rd of May he was able to report that large quantities of arms had been given up, and an evident impression made on 'the deluded wretches' who had infected the kingdom.[1] A week later he could say that there was a cessation of murders. Before the proclamation of the 30th of March 'not a mail had arrived without accounts of savage cruelties or extensive pillage;' 'now he had the satisfaction to think that at least the lives of the loyal and well-disposed had been protected.'

'But there is still,' he added, 'much to be done. There are great combinations to break. General Dundas has made much impression in Kildare, where the treason was more organised than elsewhere.[2] After the first measures of severity were adopted there was an appearance of contrition; but messages came from Dublin advising them to hold out ten days, when they should have help. Great numbers of arms, however, have been delivered up. In Queen's County and Tipperary there is great improvement. Wicklow is very extensively and very formidably organised. The mountains are depôts of arms and ammunition. The active and severe measures pursued in the country have driven many persons into Dublin. The fear of detection, the delay in the arrival of the French, together with the ill-disposition of those who have been obliged to fly the country, many imagine will induce the rebels to attempt an insurrection in the city. Orders have gone round to the people to be ready.'[3]

---

[1] 'Camden to Portland, May 3.'
[2] Owing, as Lord Cornwallis afterwards admitted, 'to the fostering hand of Lord Edward Fitzgerald, *and the countenance which it received from his weak brother of* *Leinster.'*—'Cornwallis to General Ross, July 13.' — *Correspondence,* vol. ii. p. 363.
[3] 'Camden to Portland, May 11.' S. P. O.

SECTION VI.

BOOK IX.
1798.
May.

THE revolutionary chiefs understood the temper of their countrymen. They knew that whenever authority asserted itself the disposition of the Irish people was to submit. The arms, so carefully collected, were being swept away. Confidence was failing. If they waited longer, their boasts that they could bring into the field hundreds of thousands of men might turn to scandalous nothingness. Lord Edward Fitzgerald had never left Dublin. Neilson, Tone's friend, one of those who had registered the vow on McArt's Hill, was in Dublin also. The vacant places on the Committee had been filled with other daring and desperate men; among them were two young barristers, named John and Henry Sheares, sons of a merchant at Cork, who had been at Paris in the early days of the Revolution, and had been infected with the prevailing enthusiasm. They resolved to act, and to act at once, and Edward Fitzgerald designed a plan.

The Government was watching their movements. Another informer had now tendered his services—a Captain Armstrong, an officer in a militia regiment quartered outside the capital at Lehaunstown. Captain Armstrong happened one day to enter a bookseller's shop in Grafton Street. The bookseller, whose name was Byrne, led by Armstrong's loose talk to suppose he was on the insurgent side, told him that something of consequence was immediately to be done, and offered to introduce him to two of the leaders. Armstrong consulted his Colonel, who ordered him to affect sympathy, accept the introduction, and learn what he could. On the 10th of May, the day preceding the date of Camden's last letter, Armstrong met John Sheares and his brother in the back room behind Byrne's shop, and the reason immediately appeared for their anxiety to secure his help. They told him that Dublin was about to rise. Dublin Castle, the camp at Lehaunstown, and the artillery barracks were to be simultaneously surprised. Many men in Armstrong's company were prepared to desert to the insurgents. He was entreated to use his influence with the Catholic non-commissioned officers to spread the spirit, and was told that if he could bring over the regiment he would be called the saviour of his country.[1]

With the help of Armstrong the Castle was exactly informed, and the conspirators were suddenly astonished by the announcement that Dublin, like the provinces, was to be disarmed, and by an offer of a thousand pounds reward for the discovery of Lord Edward Fitzgerald. Major Swan, who had arrested the Committee, with Major Sirr and Captain Ryan, instituted an instant search for pikes and muskets. Five cannon were taken in a brewer's yard in King Street, four others at a house in Townshend Street. Stores of arms of all kinds were found concealed about the Custom-house Quay. A blacksmith and his journeyman were caught forging pikes. The journeyman, threatened with the whip, told where pikes already made had been hidden, and many cartloads were thus seized. Still Dublin was too well pro-

---

[1] 'Trial of Henry and John Sheares.'—*State Trials*, vol. 27.

vided to be easily stripped of its means of mischief. These measures only determined the conspirators the more to be prompt in their work, and the order went out for all Ireland to be ready to rise at an early day.

For many reasons the Government was specially anxious to discover and secure Lord Edward. A Fitzgerald in the field would be a rallying cry to the insurrection of which more than one Viceroy of Ireland had felt the power. Reynolds, whose treachery was unsuspected, was still admitted to the secrets of the confederacy, and was satisfied that Fitzgerald had never left the city. Fitzgerald, he knew, had been anxious to see Talleyrand. He wanted the French to send two or three frigates to the Wexford coast, which could be done on the instant, merely as an encouragement; and Lady Edward, who was now in Dublin, told Reynolds that her husband had slipped away to Paris to hasten matters.[1] Reynolds, however, did not believe it. On the 18th of May Major Sirr received communications from a quarter unhinted at in the most secret letters of the Viceroy, telling him where Lord Edward would be found; and on Saturday, the 19th, between five and six in the evening, Swan, Sirr, and Ryan, with eight soldiers, in plain clothes, went quietly and without attracting attention to the house of a featherman in Thomas Street, named Murphy. As they approached the door a woman, who had observed them, was seen to rush in and up the stairs, to give the alarm. Major Swan was too quick for her, and running close behind her, entered a room at the stair-head, when

[1] Information of Thomas Reynolds, May 11.

he discovered Lord Edward, lying on a bed, in a dressing-jacket. It was still full daylight. Major Swan told him quietly that he had a warrant for his arrest; resistance would be useless, but he would be treated with the respect due to his rank. Lord Edward cared nothing for his rank. He had abjured his title six years before in Paris, and in Dublin among the initiated he was called Citizen Fitzgerald. But below his citizenship ran the fierce wild blood of the Geraldines. Springing from the bed, he levelled a pistol at Major Swan's head. The pistol missed fire, and he leapt on him with a dagger, and stabbed him through and through. It was the work of a moment. Captain Ryan had followed at his best speed, and when he came in he found Swan bleeding on the ground, and Lord Edward striking at him. Ryan, too, snapped a pistol. The flint-lock failed him. He had a sword-cane, and made a lunge with the blade, which bent on Lord Edward's side, and forced him back upon the bed. In an instant he was up again. Ryan closed with him. Lord Edward, naturally a powerful man, and now with the added strength of rage and despair, hurled him to the ground, rolled upon him, plunged his dagger into him again and again and again with such fury that in a few seconds he had given him fourteen wounds.

He then sprang to his feet and attempted flight. Major Sirr, now entering, met Lord Edward struggling towards the door, endeavouring to extricate himself from the grasp of the two officers, who, though lying on the floor, with the blood streaming from them, still clung to his legs.

Major Sirr's pistols were in better condition than his comrade's. He fired. Lord Edward fell struck heavily in the shoulder, and surrendered. A guard of cavalry was sent for, and he was conveyed to Newgate through a silent, sullen crowd. Major Swan recovered. Captain Ryan died of his wounds in a few days.

In Lord Edward's room were found a green uniform and the official seal of the Irish Union. In a pocket-book was the sketch of the plan for the surprise of Dublin, in which he was himself to have taken the command. The wound was thought at first not to be dangerous. It proved otherwise. Violent spasms came on, attended with delirium. At the end of a fortnight he too died, to the confessed relief of the Government, who were spared the necessity of bringing him to trial.[1] 'Alas!' said Tone, when he heard of the capture, 'Lord Edward Fitzgerald is taken. I knew him little, but I honour and venerate his character. He is not the first Fitzgerald sacrificed to his country. There is a wonderful likeness between him and Lord Thomas, who lost his head on Tower Hill for an attempt to recover Irish independence.'[2] Individuals are known by their friends, nations by their traditionary idols. Silken Thomas, who murdered an Archbishop of Dublin with his own hand; Lord Edward, who for a dream of ambition would have drowned his country in blood, and when caught in his lair fought with the ferocity of a wild beast, are surrounded in the Irish imagination with the aureoles of heroes; while England in an indolent dream of con-

[1] 'Lord Edward died at two o'clock this morning. I know not whether to consider this event a very unfortunate one. The state of his health must have postponed his trial, and prolonged the excitement.'—' Camden to Portland, June 4.' S. P. O.

[2] *Journal*, June 1708.

ciliating Ireland by humouring her illusions acquiesces in the amazing verdict.

On Lord Edward's capture the Committee felt that they must give the signal instantly, or that their organisation would dissolve. The day after, Sunday, John Sheares told Armstrong that 'their friends in the country would hold out no longer unless Dublin supported them.' The Executive Committee would meet on the following morning to settle the last details. The general plan, however, had been already arranged. The time appointed was to be the night of Wednesday, the 23rd of May. Five or six determined men had been told off to take charge of each of the Privy Councillors, and kill or capture them in their houses. Especially they were to make sure of Lord Clare, the peculiar object of the Committee's fear and hatred. Strong bodies of men were then to occupy the quays. The Castle was to be attacked in front and rear. The country for fourteen miles round the city had received its orders, and would surprise the camps. The mails were to be stopped after leaving the city, and their non-appearance had been agreed on as the general signal for the rise of the whole island. A further scheme had been formed by Neilson, the character and purpose of which is unknown, but it was something too atrocious even for John Sheares, who recoiled with horror from it, and threatened to denounce Neilson to the Government unless it was abandoned.[1]

---

[1] 'I am acquainted with the destructive design you meditate, and I am resolved to counteract it, whatever it may cost me. Your scheme I view with horror, whether its effects be considered as relating to my imprisoned friends, the destruction of whose property and lives must be the consequence even of your success, or as affecting Arthur O'Connor's existence, the precarious chance for which you thus cruelly lessen; or (which is superior to every other consideration) as en-

BOOK IX.
1798.
May.

The resolution of the Committee was carried by Armstrong to the Castle, and two days before the blow was to have been struck in Dublin the second set of leaders were seized, like their predecessors. On Monday, the 21st of May, at eight in the morning, Alderman Alexander was at the door of the Sheares's house, in Baggot Street; an entrance was forced, and the brothers were arrested. In a writing-case on the library-table was found the draft of an address in the handwriting of John Sheares, prepared for issue on the news that the Castle had been taken, and the Viceroy and the Privy Council either dead or captured. This paper, written as it was by a person capable of strong indignation at acts which overstepped the margin of permitted violence, is a curious evidence how extravagantly the minds of men otherwise honourable can be unhinged or perverted by patriotic delirium:[1]

'Irishmen! your country is free, and you are about to be avenged. That vile Government which has so long and so cruelly oppressed you is no more. Some of its most atrocious monsters have already paid the forfeit of their lives,'

suring the ruin of Ireland's freedom. In short, to be candid with you, the scheme is so totally destitute of any apology, even from the plea of folly and passion, that I cannot avoid attributing its origin to a worse cause. My resolution, and that of my friends, is this:—If you do not, by nine o'clock this evening, give us every necessary and sacred assurance that you will counteract and prevent the perpetration of this plot against all that you ought to hold dear, notice shall be given to the Government without a moment's delay. We prefer that a

few misguided, not to say guilty, individuals should perish, than that every remaining hope of our country's success, and the lives of our most valued friends, should be sacrificed by the accomplishment of a stupid, perhaps wicked undertaking.— John Sheares.' 'The letter was found on Neilson's person at the time of his arrest, May 23, 1798.'—*Musgrave*, Appendix 13.

[1] Showing evidently that the order had been to kill rather than make prisoners of the most obnoxious of the Council.

and the rest are in our hands, waiting their fate. The national flag—the sacred green—is at this moment flying over the ruins of despotism, and that capital which a few hours since witnessed the debauchery, plots, and crimes of your tyrants is now the citadel of triumphant patriotism and virtue. Arise, then, united sons of Ireland! Arise, like a great and powerful people, determined to be free or die! Arm yourselves by every means in your power, and rush like lions on your foes. Consider that for every enemy you disarm you arm a friend, and thus become doubly powerful. In the cause of liberty inaction is cowardice, and the coward shall forfeit the property he has not the courage to protect. Let his arms be seized, and transferred to the gallant spirits who want and will use them. We swear to punish robbery with death and infamy. We swear we will never sheathe the sword till every being in the country is restored to those equal rights which the God of Nature has given to all men. As for those degenerate wretches who turn their swords against their native country,[1] the national vengeance awaits them. *Let them find no quarter,* unless they prove their repentance by speedily deserting, and exchanging the standard of slavery for that of freedom, under which they may share the glory and advantage which are due to the patriot bands of Ireland. Many of the military feel the love of liberty glow in their breasts, and have joined the national standard. Receive with open arms such as follow so glorious an example. . . . Rouse all the energies of your souls. Heed not the glare of a hired soldiery or aristocratic Yeomanry. They cannot stand the vigorous shock of freedom. Their trappings and their arms will soon be yours, and the detested Government of England, to which we vow eternal hatred, shall learn that the treasure it expends on its accoutred slaves, for the purpose of butchering Irishmen, shall but further enable us to turn their swords on its devoted head. Attack them in every direction, day and night. Avail yourselves of the natural advantages of your

---

[1] Grattan, who had joined a Yeomanry corps, retired when he saw what was approaching, declaring that, come what might, he would never fight against his country.

country, which are innumerable, and with which you are better acquainted than they. War, war, alone, must occupy every mind and every hand in Ireland. Vengeance, Irishmen! Vengeance on your oppressors! Remember what thousands of your dearest friends have perished by their merciless orders. Remember their burnings, their rackings, their torturings, their military massacres, and their legal murders! Remember Orr!'

Of the many gifts which nature has bestowed on Irishmen the fatallest is, perhaps, the fluency of speech, the fertility in florid diction, which at once exhausts the energy that in robust nations takes the form of action, and makes them the victims of their own illusions, by clothing their emotions and fancies in the shining dress of rhetoric. Ideas so brilliantly expressed seem too beautiful to be unsound or untrue. It is only when brought in collision with fact that the unsubstantial pageant fades, and leaves its dupes to add their disappointment to the long catalogue of their wrongs.

Were it not for the enormous crimes which these infatuated men confessed that they were deliberately contemplating, the spectacle of Ireland on the eve of the rebellion of 1798 would rise into tragic piteousness. The long era of misgovernment had ripened at last for the harvest. Rarely since the inhabitants of the earth have formed themselves into civilised communities had any country suffered from such a complication of neglect and ill-usage. The Irish people clamoured against Government, and their real wrong, from first to last, had been that there was no government over them; that, under changing forms, the universal rule among them for four centuries had been the tyranny of the strong over the weak; that from the catalogue of virtues demanded of those who exercised authority over their fellow-men the word Justice had been blotted out. Anarchy had borne its fruits. The victims of scandalous misadministration had risen at last to demand redress; but they had risen in blind rage in pursuit of objects which, if obtained, could but plunge them deeper in their misery. They had appealed to England, and England had for bread given them a stone, for a fish a serpent. Instead of practical justice she had given them political liberty, and when political liberty had proved a mocking phantom they had gone mad and had started to arms, and were preparing for universal massacre and ruin.

Their leaders disguised the hideousness of their schemes in patriotic rhapsodies. They compared themselves in fancy to the liberators of America, or the heroes of Jacobin France. They believed, or dreamt that they believed, that they were to enrich the annals of mankind by the achievement of a glorious revolution. Their road to it hitherto had lain through midnight murder, through seduction of honest men from their duty, through the contemplation of crimes so horrible that they shrunk appalled from the ferocity of each other's conceptions. Though engaged, as they supposed, in the most glorious of causes, they had been unable to inspire one another with the fidelity which the pickpocket displays to his comrades. In every Committee there were traitors, one or many. They had generated round them an atmosphere of villany, and when they lifted their hands at last to strike the blow which was to break the chains of Ireland they found themselves in the hands of the police, fallen from the high peaks to which they were in imagination soaring, to the level of common felons.

Two nights after the arrest of John and Henry Sheares the keeper of Newgate saw a man, muffled in a cloak, reconnoitring the prison. He sprung upon him and seized him, and found that he had taken Neilson.

Why, it may be asked again, had the Government, with the threads of the conspiracy so long in its hands, allowed it to go forward? 'They had permitted and encouraged the progress of the rebellion,' says modern Irish opinion, 'in order that the suppression of it might be effected with more *éclat* and terror.'[1]

Lord Camden's letters form a conclusive answer to the charge of encouragement. It is scarcely less unjust to charge him with having looked on passively, since the arrests which he ventured, and his efforts to disarm the disturbed counties, were received with a tempest of denunciation from the friends of liberty in both islands; and his attempts to prevent the rebellion were described as the gratuitous provocation of an innocent well-disposed people. He did what he could. That he did not do more was the consequence of his situation. The common law of England was not calculated for the Irish meridian. The existence of a country where juries would not convict, where witnesses were afraid to give evidence and magistrates to commit, where laws had no terror, because the general sentiment combined to shield a criminal, had not been allowed for when the Constitution was framed which the connection with Great Britain extended to the Sister Island. Until acts had been perpetrated which no art could conceal or palliate, until the ordinary laws were suspended by

Plowden.

open and undisguised rebellion, the Government did but expose itself by interference to defeat in the courts of justice and to reproach for unjust prosecutions; and thus sate spell bound, while the catastrophe was approaching, surrounded by a ring of traitors, whom only at the last extremity it was able to touch.

The Executive Committee were finally disabled by the loss of Lord Edward, the two Sheares's, and Neilson. On them, after the arrest of the 12th of March, the general direction had devolved, and the rebel bodies in the capital and the provinces were left to their local chiefs. The last act of the central authority had been to fix the day for the game to begin. The match had been lighted, and the explosion was certain. How serious it might now be, the result only could show. Dublin at least was secured.

'If there is a rising in the city,' Lord Camden wrote, on the 21st, ' the insurgents will be annihilated.'[1]

[1] 'To Portland, May 21.' S. P. O.

BOOK X.

CHAPTER I.

THE REBELLION.

SECTION I.

The conspiracy of the United Irishmen had departed almost wholly from its original character before it assumed the shape of rebellion. The first lodges had been formed to spread the principles of the French Revolution. The founders of the society were believers in what is now called the religion of humanity. The belief in God they regarded as a worn-out and vanishing superstition, and their dream had been of uniting Catholics and Protestants, to establish a Republic, in which the petty quarrels of the Christian sects would disappear in the light of a more sublime philosophy.

The opinions of Tone and MacNeven were alien to the Irish character, and could never gain permanent influence over it.

The Catholic of the South and the Presbyterian of the North have this in common—that each believes firmly, and even passionately, in the form of Christianity which he professes. The alliance so ardently aimed at proved incapable of realisation. The country population of Ulster became, year after year, more and more Orange, the party of insurrection more and more Catholic. The Protestant politicians of Dublin and the Northern towns adhered to the cause with as much sincerity as they were capable of feeling. But the Irish politician is usually made of weak material. Belfast was disarmed, Dublin was overawed. The Protestant leaders were in Newgate. The Catholics remained alone in the field. But the Catholics were four-fifths of the population, and they were sworn into the confederacy nearly to a man. The patriots of the Parliament had stirred them out of their desponding sleep. Pitt had forced the franchise upon them, that they might help him against the revolution. Powers were immediately after held almost within their grasp which would have made them masters of Ireland, and enabled them, without striking a blow, to undo the Reformation and overthrow the Protestant settlement.

The hand had been withdrawn. Protestant ascendency was again riveted upon their necks. But the fierce Irish spirit, which had lain asleep since Aghrim, was awake again; and whatever became of his republican Protestant allies, the Catholic Celt intended to try conclusions with sword and pike before he would consent to sink down once more into his bondage.

The Irish are the most unchanging people on the globe. The phenomena of 1641 were repeating themselves. In 1641 Puritans and Catholics had combined to demand political concessions. In 1641 they found themselves ill-yoked and ill-mated, and the unnatural coalition was dissolved. The plot for the rising of Sir Phelim O'Neil was identical, even in minute particulars, with Lord Edward's plan for 1798. In the latter, as in the former, the rising was to be simultaneous throughout the island. Dublin Castle was to be surprised, the Privy Council were to be killed or captured. In both instances the intention of massacre was disavowed, but in both it was rendered inevitable by reports ingeniously spread that the Protestants meditated the destruction of the Catholics. In both there was a settled purpose of eliminating the Protestants out of the country. In both was evidenced the infernal element which lies concealed in the Irish nature, and the vindictive ferocity to which it will descend.

In this only there was a difference between the two periods, that in 1798 there was no surprise. Lord Clare understood Ireland too well to mistake the effect which the conciliation policy of Pitt must produce. He knew that it must end at last in demands which could not be conceded, and that rebellion was then certain. He had watched the conspiracy step by step. He was aware of the coming explosion, and all had been done that the circumstances would allow to limit the extent of its destructiveness. Numerically, and on paper, the troops in the island might have seemed sufficient. Of one kind or another the Government had under its command nearly 40,000 men, but they were of doubtful quality. Of British regiments there were scarcely any, the Ancient Britons—a Welsh Fencible regiment, under Sir Watkin Wynn—a Durham regiment, and a regiment or two of Scotch militia, being nearly the whole. The Irish militia, eighteen thousand strong, were all Catholics, and the utmost uncertainty was felt as to their probable conduct. The rest were Irish Yeomanry, most of them, though not all, well-disposed, but untrained as soldiers, and no better than armed volunteers. The Orangemen Lord Camden was still afraid to employ. But taking the men as they were, his force disposable for service was not in proportion to the apparent numbers. A large part of the army was required in the North. Several thousand men were kept in and about Dublin. Quiet could only be secured in Belfast, Cork, Limerick, and Galway by garrisons of overpowering strength. The regiments who were employed by Lake in the disarmament were scattered in sections over Leinster and Munster, many miles apart. For better security, and to prevent combinations, the companies had been broken up. Each party consisted of a score or two of men from one regiment, as many from another, and perhaps as many more dragoons. They were more like divisions of police than parts of an army; and being thus split in handfuls, with some seditious elements less or greater in every detachment, they were dangerously liable to be overwhelmed. United Irelanders had enlisted in the Yeomanry with the purpose of betraying them. To surprise these parties separately, by simultaneous attacks in overpowering force, and destroy them before they could re-combine, was the rebel plan for the opening of the campaign. The Irish are credited for passionate impetuosity of temperament. Nothing is more remarkable in the present instance than the cool, deliberate treachery of their proceedings. The neighbourhood of Dublin was relied on to prevent any of the troops in the environs from going to the assistance of their comrades in the city. An illustration of their position may be seen in an account of the garrison at Rathcool, a town ten miles distant, on the South-western Road. Captain Ormsby had been stationed there with twenty loyal Armagh militia. Mr. Clinch, a Catholic gentleman in the district, in apparent loyalty had raised a company of local infantry to support him. These men were all traitors. Their intention was to destroy Ormsby and his Protestants on the appointed day, and then march into Dublin, with Clinch at their head. The Catholic corps attended their own chapels. To throw Ormsby the more off his guard, the Rathcool priest addressed them on the 20th of May, the Sunday after Lord Edward's arrest, in two eminently loyal sermons, in Ormsby's presence, although he discovered afterwards that this priest had been the instigator of the plot.

Notice happily had been sent to all the officers in the environs of Dublin to be on the alert. A secret friend told Ormsby what was prepared for him. The corps was paraded and disarmed. Clinch and the priest were sent to Dublin, where the former was a few days later tried and hanged; the latter was transported to Botany Bay.[1] As at Rathcool so everywhere such of the troops as were known to be loyal were marked for destruction; but the warning placed them on the alert; and the people finding the surprise fail, waited for the issue of the expected rising in Dublin. Would Dublin venture to rise?—that was the question. On the night of the 23rd patrols went round the country within a radius of twelve miles to gather arms and warn the people to stay at home. The week preceding, Sir Richard Musgrave had watched the beacon-fires night after night on the

---

[1] Musgrave's *History of the Irish Rebellion.*

distant hillsides from his window in the city. That evening the patrols found in the cabins none but women, children, and old men. Every man who could shoulder a pike was off to the rendezvous. In Dublin itself strong bodies of troops were posted along the river and on the bridges. At daybreak notices were seen upon the walls from General Lake informing the people that they must keep within doors from nightfall to sunrise. By the side of the order of the Commander-in-Chief was an order from Mr. Fleming, the Lord Mayor,[1] to every individual to surrender his arms, and to every householder to hang a list upon his door of the persons residing under his roof, under penalty of being sent to the fleet for disobedience. Dublin, in the face of these precautions, preferred to be prudent. Dusky bodies of armed men, several thousand strong, assembled at various points outside the walls on either side of the river, waiting to hear that their friends were up, and that their aid was needed. At noon, when no signal was given, they melted sullenly away. A gathering at Rathfarnham was dispersed by Lord Roden's dragoons. On the north, at Dunboyne and Dunshaughlin, the genuine spirit showed itself. At Dunshaughlin the Protestant clergyman and his family were murdered. At Dunboyne a Protestant revenue officer and three Protestant policemen were murdered. At Ratoath and Westfieldstown small parties of soldiers were surprised successfully and cut in pieces. About Swords Protestant houses were set on fire.. But for the most part within reach of Lake's garrison the

---

[1] Fleming was among those who were marked for murder. His servant had drawn the balls from his pistols, and was to have admitted the assassins.

insurrection missed fire. Martial law had been proclaimed; those who were caught in breach of the law were carried before courts, where justice was dealt out summarily and surely, and for some days in conspicuous portions of the city dead bodies swinging from crossbeams were preaching to the patriot incendiaries the meaning of armed rebellion.

In the outer circle, at a longer radius from the metropolis, where the detachments were more thinly scattered, events assumed a darker aspect. General Lake had been able to carry out the disarmament only where he had received the active support of the country gentlemen. The hostility of the Fitzgeralds to the Government, the open treason of one member of the family, and the refusal of its head to co-operate in enforcing order, had reinforced the disaffection of the county of Kildare with the elements of feudal allegiance, which ought to have been on the side of the Crown. The inhabitants had not only been left in possession of their pikes, but they were led to believe that their natural chief was with them, and that the cause of the rebellion was the cause of the Duke of Leinster.

On the eastern side of the country, where it approaches or touches the County of Dublin, were three towns within a few miles of each other. Naas, once a frontier garrison of the Pale, was now a thriving borough, on the Great Waterford Road. North of Naas, on the Grand Canal, was Clane, or Cluain, little more than a village, which had grown up as an appendage to a Franciscan abbey; and two miles from Clane was a place called Prosperous, whose name indicated that it had once been a scene of enterprise and industry. The opening of the Canal and the abolition of the restrictions on trade had restored life to it. A Mr. Brewer, an enterprising Englishman, had established a large manufactory there, and was finding employment and comfort for a growing population. As commanding the canal and the roads, these towns were important military stations. Lord Gosford held Naas, with a garrison of 200 men. Captain Griffiths was at Clane, with a corps of local Yeomanry and a party of Armagh Militia. Captain Swayne was at Prosperous, with a detachment of the North Cork Militia and twenty-three of Wynn's Ancient Britons— dragoons. Among the officers of the Clane Yeomanry was Doctor Esmonde, a gentleman of old Catholic family, brother of Sir Thomas Esmonde, of Wexford, who had affected loyalty, like Mr. Clinch at Rathcool, for the better service of his country and her cause. He had seduced the majority of his corps. He was in accurate correspondence with the insurgent leaders in the neighbourhood. It was arranged that on the preconcerted signal, the non-arrival of the mail from Dublin on the night of the 23rd, Naas, Clane, and Prosperous were to be attacked at the same moment. Esmonde and the disaffected Yeomen were to assist, and the officers and the loyal part of the soldiers were to be destroyed. Surprise was an essential part of the scheme. At the two latter places many of the soldiers were billeted in private houses. If off their guard they might be found divided, and could then be dealt with easily. Swayne had been directed to collect the arms of the people at Prosperous. On Sunday, the 20th of May, he took his North Cork men to the Catholic chapel. Father Higgins, the priest, like his brother at Rathcool, addressed his congregation on the duty of submission to the authorities, and Dr. Esmonde, who had ridden over from Clane in the morning to support his brother officer, spoke to them as a Catholic in the same tone. A number of peasants, in apparent obedience, surrendered their pikes. In the priest's presence they expressed regret for having been betrayed into the conspiracy, and promised to have no more to do with it.

To avoid recognition by his comrades, Esmonde undertook the attack at Prosperous, leaving his own captain half-deserted to be destroyed by others. On the afternoon of the 23rd, when the hour was drawing near, he paid Swayne another visit, and dined with him at the hotel in the town. Father Higgins was again present, and he and Esmonde told Swayne that the people were really penitent. Very many of them wished to give up their arms, but they dared not bring them in the day, for fear of being recognised by their confederates. They would have brought them at night and have laid them down in the street, but they were afraid of the sentinels. Swayne, credulous and good-natured, suspected nothing. He ordered the sentinels, if they saw men moving in the street after dark, to take no notice of them.

The mails left Dublin that night as usual. They were all stopped on the roads by the country people, according to the general instructions, and the call to arms went out. At two in the morning, when sleep was deepest, before the first streaks of dawn had begun to show, Esmonde, with his Clane Yeomen and an unknown multitude of ruffians, chiefly armed with pikes, came into Prosperous. The sentinels gave no alarm, and were killed, and then at once before a note of warning had been raised the rebel bands flung themselves with a wild yell upon the barracks. The door went down. Swayne's room was on the ground-floor. They plunged in and stabbed him as he was springing from his bed. The soldiers, startled from their sleep, snatched their muskets and rushed out. The mob swung back into the street, barricaded the doors to keep them secure, and then flung fire into the cellars, which were filled with straw and faggots.[1] Beset before and behind, the miserable men were driven from the lower rooms up the stairs. As the flames pursued them they sprung out of the windows, the mob below catching them as they fell on their pikes, and as each victim writhed upon the point receiving him with a fierce 'Hurrah!' The North Cork were Irishmen and Catholics, traitors to both creed and country, deserving no mercy and finding none. All who were in the barracks were killed or desperately wounded.

The Ancient Britons were quartered in a private house. They, too, were hated almost equally, for they had made themselves notorious in the disarming of Ulster. Eight of the twenty-three leapt out of a back window, and escaped across the country in the darkness. The rest were killed. Their horses, arms, and uniforms were taken by the rebels.

As the roof of the barracks fell in, men and women flung themselves weeping in each other's arms. Tears only could express their joy. 'Ireland is ours

---

[1] The first account which reached Camden was, 'that Captain Swayne had been inhumanly butchered, and afterwards put on the fire and burnt to death.' — 'To Portland, May 26.' S. P. O. It is uncertain whether Swayne was killed or wounded in the first attack; but if he was burnt to death it was afterwards, in the conflagration of the barracks.

again!' they cried. 'Dublin is taken—Naas is taken—Ireland is ours!' 'Where are the heretics?' shrieked savage voices. 'Down with the heretics!' The depression of Irish manufactures had been the first article of Ireland's complaints. Manufactures had come back, finding work for the starving and food for the hungry, but the benefactor of Prosperous was an Englishman and a Protestant. The day was breaking. A shout rose, 'To Brewer's house!' A few moments later Mr. Brewer was lying in his shirt on the pavement with his skull cloven by an axe, the mob yelling over the body of 'the heretic tyrant.' The landlord's turn followed. Mr. Stamer, the owner of most of the town, was staying, unluckily for himself, with a lady at a house in the neighbourhood. The alarm had been given. The lady concealed her guest, and when the insurgents came to the door and demanded him, she said that he was gone. The watch had been too good. They knew that he was in the house. They could not find him, and they cried for fire to fetch him out. To save needless destruction, Mr. Stamer, like a brave man, came out of his hiding-place, and was instantly shot.

The work at Prosperous thus happily finished, it was time to see how their brothers had prospered at Clane, and to help them if Jephson was holding out. The rebel leaders dressed and mounted themselves as Ancient Britons with the dead men's horses and uniforms, that they might be mistaken by the soldiers for friends.

At Clane there were no barracks. The troops were billeted about the place in twos and threes, and were thus more dangerously exposed than at Prosperous. The attack, however, had been delayed till dawn. Captain Griffiths, for some reason, was uneasy and awake. Looking from his window, he saw files of armed men coming in along the roads. He gave the alarm in time to enable the Armagh Militia to dress and snatch their muskets. The street was full as they came out, but they fought their way towards one another, formed into line, and charged. Having failed in their surprise, the rebels showed their usual inability to encounter disciplined men. Though fifty to one, they turned and ran out of the town. Outside they were joined by parties coming up from Prosperous. Cheered by the news which their friends brought, they formed again, and returned to the attack. They were received with a steady fire, which they were unable to face. Falling fast, they wavered and broke. Esmonde had carried with him all the Yeomanry but seventeen. These few charged and completed the rout, and the wretches masquerading as Ancient Britons were every one cut down. It was now six o'clock. Details had come in of the frightful disaster at Prosperous. Pursuit with so small a force was impossible. Griffiths recalled his men and reviewed his losses; and unable to account for the shortness of numbers in the Yeomanry, ordered them to parade. Those who had been concerned in the night's work had come back expecting to find as complete a sweep of their comrades as they had made themselves of Swayne and the North Cork. Finding the day gone against them, they either dispersed or stole into their quarters unperceived. Esmonde, especially, contrived to reach his room, to wash, dress, and powder himself, as a dog would do after a midnight orgie among the sheep, and presented himself in his place in the ranks as if he had never been absent.

There was no time for enquiry. A messenger

galloped up at that moment with the news that Lord Gosport was beset at Naas and required instant help.

The men swallowed a hasty breakfast. Griffiths was in the saddle, prepared to start, when a note was slipped into his hand telling him that Esmonde had led the rebels at Prosperous. He thrust it into his pocket and said nothing till he reached Naas, when the treacherous gentleman was placed under arrest, sent to Dublin to be tried by court-martial, and was promptly hanged.

At Naas it was found that the attack had failed, as at Clane, but not till after a sharper struggle. Gosport, more fortunate than Swayne or Griffiths, had received notice to be prepared on the evening preceding. The alarm was sounded at half-past two in the morning. The rebel columns were entering on four sides. They forced their way to the gaol, where they were received with grape from some field-pieces and with a heavy musketry fire. They bore three volleys before they gave way. Thirty of them were found dead in the streets, and as many more in the fields and lanes outside. The troops in turn had suffered severely. The rebels had fought with dangerous courage, and their evidently enormous numbers created just and serious misgiving. For in fact they were everywhere. The same scenes had been going on throughout the country wherever there was a town or village held in the name of the Government, and outside the towns wherever Protestants were to be found. All day long terrified families were streaming into Naas. All day long the smoke of burning homesteads was seen rising from every point of the horizon. Kildare town had been considered secure, so many arms had been surrendered there without resistance. General Walford, who was in charge, had withdrawn on the 23rd to join General Dundas at Kilcullen.[1] He was no sooner gone than Kildare was occupied by 2,000 rebels, with crosses painted on their pikes. General Dundas, irresolute and unequal to the sudden call upon him, was confounded by the sudden outpouring of so many nests of hornets. They were here, they were there, they were on all sides. A few hundreds of them showed themselves near Kilcullen. He sent a party of Yeomen cavalry to ride them down. They threw themselves into line; the Yeomen rode upon the pikes only for their horses to fall and themselves to be pierced as they rolled on the ground. Dundas fell back on Naas, taking the Judges with him, who were on their way to Clonmel Assizes. Kilcullen was left to its fate. The gentry and clergymen were deserted to shift for themselves. Their houses were burnt. Those who failed to escape were piked. The entire country was a scene of ruin, terror, and confusion.

The news of Dundas's retreat spread South. The same night several thousand insurgents gathered in Sir Edward Crosbie's park, outside Carlow, led by a farmer named Roach.[2] The town was held, like Naas, by a company or two of militia. At half-past two on the morning of the 25th the rebel force went in upon them in the darkness, with the wild Irish howl.

---

[1] On the Cork road, where the bridge crosses the Liffey, seven miles south of Naas.

[2] 'Crosbie was tried and executed as an accomplice—Mr. Gordon says unjustly; the extent of his fault being that he was 'an advanced theoretic politician.'—*History of the Rebellion*, p. 92. The distinction, probably, was more apparent than real. The insurgents were only endeavouring to take what the politicians told them England had no right to withhold.

BOOK X.
1798.
Friday,
May 25.

After the defeat of the Yeomen at Kilcullen they expected to carry all before them, and came on with the utmost audacity. They were expected. Part of the garrison were drawn up in the market-place, and received them with a volley which turned the head of their column. They swerved and flung themselves on the gaol. Another volley from the gaol windows was delivered into the middle of them with deadly effect. They reeled, staggered, and then, struck with panic, flung down their pikes and tried to fly or hide themselves in houses. The troops had heard on the previous evening of the treachery and cruelty at Prosperous. Savage in turn, they chased the miserable wretches into the bye-lanes and passages, shooting and bayoneting every man that they found. Four hundred bodies were taken up and buried at daybreak. Many others were carried off wounded and died afterwards. It was supposed that the number of those who lost their lives was at least six hundred.

The intention had been to encompass Dublin with insurrection, to force the Government to relax its grasp upon the city. On the same 25th the Meath insurgents rose and assembled on Tara Hill, the scene of the mythic glories of the ancient Irish kingdom, four thousand strong. On the 26th they were attacked by Captain Preston and Lord Fingal, with 200 Fencibles and as many mounted Yeomen. Their commander, distinguished by his green uniform, was killed. Three hundred and fifty rebels fell with him. The rest were scattered over the country, to venture no more battles, but to confine themselves to private murders, for which they were better fitted by experience and temper.

Finding that Dublin remained quiet, that the camp

at Tara had been broken up, and that the attack on Carlow had failed, the Kildare men, who were in force at Kilcullen, thought it prudent to temporise. If the general insurrection had missed fire, they held it better to save and reserve themselves for another opportunity. They sent word to Dundas that they had taken arms in self-defence, and were ready to return to their homes if they could be assured of pardon. Dundas, who had remained trembling at Naas, listened only too eagerly. He was an officer probably of the mode of thinking of Sir Ralph Abercrombie, and believed that rebellion could be fondled into loyalty. At any rate he welcomed the prospect of escape from his own present situation. He was shut up in Naas with 400 men, sufficient, if boldly handled, to have opened a road through all the rebels in the country. But the Yeomen were out of heart; Dundas knew not whether he could trust them. The disaffection at Clane had been followed by the revolt of almost an entire corps of Yeomanry officers and men at Rathangar after the murder of their captain. The town was crowded with terrified women and children, for whose lives he was responsible. He rode over at the rebels' invitation to parley with them at Kilcullen. He made a speech to them. He took off his hat to them. With their hands red with murder and their faces grimed with the smoke of the houses which they had been burning, 'he thanked them for their good behaviour.'[1]

---

[1] Musgrave says that Camden sanctioned this negotiation. He was evidently imperfectly informed. Camden writes:—

'General Dundas has been negotiating with the rebels at Kilcullen, making terms with them—treating them with civility, taking off his hat to them, and thanking them for their good behaviour. There is infinite indignation among those who have lost their families

BOOK X.
1798.
May 27.

In Dublin, meanwhile, as post came in upon post bringing accounts of the rising, the complexion of feeling varied with the news. At first men drew their breath with a sense of relief. The treason which had hung over them for so many years as an impalpable spectre could at last be grappled with. 'Martial law,' wrote Camden, 'is now established. The sword is drawn; I have kept it in the scabbard as long as possible. It must now not be returned till this conspiracy is put down.'[1] He hoped that the plot in Dublin having failed, the local outbreaks would be easily crushed. The reports of the bloody scene at Prosperous, and of the universal frenzy which had burst over Kildare, showed that the expectation was delusive, and roused a natural and uncontrollable indignation in the country gentlemen which found a voice in the Parliament. The rebellion might be subdued eventually, but meanwhile throughout the whole country their families, their friends, their Protestant tenants and dependents, above all the Protestant clergy, were exposed to the horrors of another 1641. The treacherous assassinations of the past year showed that the Irishman was unchanged. It was no time to consider by whose fault he had become what he was. They forgot their own negligence. They forgot the intemperate majorities by which they had encouraged Grattan in his dreams of independence. They saw only that Ireland

and their children. The rebels have been guilty of the most barbarous and dreadful cruelties. Other propositions of surrender have been made, which I hope can be accepted without loss of dignity or irritating the feelings of the country, which are so exasperated as scarcely to be satisfied with anything short of extirpation.'—'To Portland, May 31. Abridged.' S. P. O.

[1] 'To Portland, May 24.'

was gone mad in the old fashion, and that they and all belonging to them were to be sacrificed. The blame might be shifted from one party to another; but they were all guilty, the careless tyrannical landlord, the scheming politician, the patriotic agitator, the uncertain, vacillating, heedless Government of England. If the guilt rested anywhere with preponderating weight, the individuals most responsible were the great Whig absentee noblemen, the Fitzwilliams, the Moiras, the Devonshires, the Shelburnes, who, by leaving undone every duty which attached to their properties, by consigning the peasantry to whose thankless toil they owed their enormous rent-rolls to the tyranny of the middlemen, and thus exasperating them into madness, had sought to shield themselves and recover a base popularity by advocating the political emancipation of a people among whom Emancipation could only mean civil war and revolution.

But these considerations, if they were to be heeded at all, had to be postponed to calmer times. The present necessity was to meet the immediate danger, and those found readiest hearing who had all along foreseen the inevitable tempest, whose Protestant prejudices were now recognised as wise conclusions gathered from the experience of centuries. The wind had been sown and could not now be recalled, and the whirlwind had come, and they could think of nothing save that those who were dearest to them were left naked to the storm.

Lord Camden became painfully alarmed, not for the horrors only which were hourly reported to him, but for the effects of the anger and fear which they were generating.

'There is too much reason to expect,' he said,

'that the war will be one in which religious animosity will be blended with political enthusiasm, and rendered more desperate from the Irish conceiving that they are fighting for that which they believe to be their own, the estates which were forfeited by the treason of their ancestors. The loyal part of the country are so indignant that I almost tremble that their zeal will drive them to acts of retaliation.' He begged for instant and large reinforcements. He knew the influence which would be brought to bear upon the Ministry, the cry, which he knew to be false, that the rebellion was the fruit of severity, and could be extinguished with gentleness and concession. 'It is my decided opinion,' he declared, with all the emphasis which he could throw into the words, 'that a continuance of vigorous measures can alone save this country. There is no safety in any other conduct than in meeting the rebellion manfully and decidedly. When it is crushed, no man can be more ready than myself to adopt whatever measures may best soften prejudice and restore confidence.'[1]

Dundas was half-believed to be a traitor in disguise. The rebels at Kilcullen had replied to his speeches with laudable promises. He dismissed them with pardons and protections, and they dispersed to burn and murder at their leisure, and despise the imbecility which had trusted them. Wicklow and Wexford were now reported to have followed suit with Kildare. Dublin was filling with fugitives. 'Wicklow, Wexford, and Kildare,' Camden wrote on the 28th, 'are in a dreadful state.' The husbands of the shuddering ladies who were rushing into the city with

[1] 'To Portland, May 26.'

their little ones to tell them that their houses were burning, and that they themselves had hardly escaped with life, were swearing the extermination of the treacherous race whom it was no longer possible to bear with. Of all the advisers of the Crown who surrounded Camden, Clare and Castlereagh, the latter of whom was now acting as Camden's secretary, alone preserved their coolness.

'It is difficult to bring the rebels to action,' Castlereagh wrote on the 31st. 'They commit horrid cruelties, and disperse when the troops appear. But the spirit of the country rises with its difficulties. The result will be to place this kingdom, and of course the empire, in a state of security much beyond that in which it has stood for years past.'[1]

Mr. Edward Hay, the Catholic historian of the rebellion, pretends an ostentatious impartiality, and affects to confess and deplore the atrocities committed by the people. He confesses only what he cannot deny, and leaves half of what is undeniable unmentioned. He attributes the rebellion itself to the harshness with which the Southern counties were disarmed, and in every instance when there was marked barbarity represents it as only revenge for barbarities still greater on the other side. When he denies the right of the Government to deprive the peasants and farmers of the pikes and muskets with which they had provided themselves, he assumes that they had a right to be armed. For what purpose all Ireland had for three years turned itself into an arsenal, and every village into a place of drill, he does not care to enquire. He passes over in

---

[1] 'To Mr. Wickham, May 31.' S. P. O.

silence the correspondence with France, and the series of savage murders which made necessary the Insurrection Act. The Assassination Committee, the plots for the murder of the Council, are events too insignificant for him to notice; nor does he touch on the combination of treachery and ferocity which distinguished the performances in Kildare on the night of the 23rd of May. He assumes that when the Irish took arms, and used them in the manner which has been described, they were entitled to the courtesies of war, and that when punished as murderers and incendiaries they were within their rights when they retaliated in kind. This is the burden of the defence. The worth of it is recommended to the consideration of those who have read the preceding pages. Mr. Gordon, a clergyman, whose history is accepted as the most favourable to the Protestant cause which truth will permit, and shows a real effort at impartiality, yet wrote with the same desire to soothe the wounded feelings of the Catholic party. He professes to believe that the submission to Dundas at Kilcullen was made in good faith; that if the policy thus begun had been followed, the insurrection would have died out without further violence. He attributes the bloody scenes which have next to be related, by the side of which the massacre at Prosperous seems tame and colourless, to an act of outrage on the part of the troops, by which the terms were violated which General Dundas had granted without authority.

Sir James Duff, who was in command at Limerick, hearing that Kildare had risen, and that Lake could not spare a regiment from Dublin, came across the country by forced marches to Dundas's assistance. He was in Kildare in forty-eight hours. There was a large rebel camp on the Curragh, at a place called Gibbet Rath, where the insurgents were said to be willing to lay down their arms on the terms which had been allowed at Kilcullen. When Duff advanced to receive the surrender a shot or shots were fired in the rebel lines. One account [1] says that the shots were aimed at the troops, that one man was killed and three others wounded. Another account says that a musket was fired in the air in foolish bravado. Whichever of these stories be true, the scene which ensued is too easily intelligible. The treacherous massacre of the North Cork Militiamen at Prosperous had created such deep distrust and such savage indignation that the troops believed that they were betrayed. They rushed upon the rebels with their bayonets, and after a sharp fight drove them from the Curragh, leaving three hundred and fifty men dead upon the grass.

The intention of surrender may have been serious for the moment. It will hardly be pretended that it was offered in good faith, or that the men who were then willing to promise obedience for the future would have observed their engagements one hour beyond the time when it had ceased to be dangerous to break them. Even with this reservation the misfortune was serious, yet it was a misfortune only, for which the troops did not deserve to be blamed. If a people choose to arm with the avowed purpose of making a bloody rebellion, if their rising is no sudden movement, but has been deliberately prepared, and has been attended in all its stages by murders, housebreaking, domestic treason, and the forcible disarming

---

[1] Musgrave's *History of the Rebellion*, vol. i. p. 323.

of loyal subjects, their advocates have no right to complain that the police are over-rough in handling them. A more serious cause for regret is that the victims were not the men whose guilt was deepest. The forces which set in motion the Irish rebellion had worked in the dark or behind the shield of the Constitution. Of those who took arms, the noisiest in council were the most careful of their safety in the field. Those who fell were those who fought, and those who fought were the ignorant, the simple, and the brave.

SECTION II.

THE action at Gibbet Rath may have been an ill-timed accident, but whether accident or wanton cruelty it was not the cause of the insurrection of Wexford. That insurrection had already assumed its bloody and desperate character, and the flying rumours of murder and incendiarism beyond the Barrow were among the probable causes which had exasperated and infuriated the troops.

Of all the counties in Ireland Wexford had the fewest grounds for taking arms, and betrayed outwardly the fewest symptoms of intending it. With a fertile soil, a gentry and clergy generally resident, its towns thriving, and a population made unusually dense by the more advanced civilisation of its inhabitants, it had escaped contact by its situation with the revolutionary elements at work in the rest of the island. Bounded on the east by the sea, on the north and north-west by the Wicklow and Carlow hills, and on the west and south by the Barrow, which divides it from Kilkenny and Waterford, it forms a long parallelogram, cut in two by the Slaney, which, rising in the mountains behind Glendalough, pursues its way through a series of rich pasture land past New Town Barry and Enniscorthy to Wexford city, where it runs into the sea. Enniscorthy, to which the tide flows, was, in 1798, a prosperous and growing town, with four thousand inhabitants; barges, lighters, and small coasting craft coming up to it and unloading at its quays. New Ross, on the Barrow, was still more considerable, and was already a place of historic fame, having been besieged by Cromwell. The population of the whole county was a hundred and thirty thousand. There were no Whiteboys among them, and no Orangemen. The landlords, if not superior to the rest of their class, were at least to be found on their estates. Arthur Young describes the land as better cultivated, the cabins and food of the Wexford peasantry as of a higher class, than what he had seen in most other parts of Ireland. He observed what was, perhaps, connected with this superiority, the unusually large Protestant congregations which were to be found in the Wexford churches. The Bishop of Ferns, Dr. Euseby Cleaver, was eminent above all his brethren on the bench for piety and learning, and especially for his kindness and generosity to the Catholic poor. Wexford city contained a population of ten thousand. The harbour was already crowded with shipping; and as a sign of the growing wealth of the merchants there, a splendid bridge had just been erected over the wide estuary on which the town was built.

The county had not escaped the tithe agitation of 1793. A mob of two thousand men had then attempted to capture the gaol and let loose the prisoners. But they had been defeated and dispersed by five-and-thirty local police; and so little was the state of Wexford a cause of alarm to the Government, that the troops stationed there had been withdrawn for service elsewhere, and the county was left to three hundred militia and the protection of its own Yeomanry. Over-confidence had encouraged disaffection. Towards the end of 1797 Wexford was discovered, like the rest of Ireland, to be secretly arming. The lagoons on the coast swarmed with wild fowl. In the cabins adjoining them were generally to be found duck-guns, and the fishermen in winter time made their living by shooting. But besides the fowling-pieces, many muskets had crept in; pikes had been manufactured and distributed in tens of thousands. Those who had guns for lawful purposes were not interfered with; but near Gorey, a town at the north end of the county, on the Arklow road, where the Protestants were most numerous, nineteen parishes were placed in December under the Insurrection Act. The priests of these parishes complained of the precaution as an unnecessary insult to a harmless and loyal people. They swore in the presence of Lord Mountmorris that they were not United Irishmen, and that they never would be; that they would use their best endeavours to prevent or discover any conspiracy which might arise in the neighbourhood; and on the representations of these men, among whom were the two Murphies, John and Michael, who were about to become historical personages, the enforcement of the Act was suspended and the people left undisturbed, until the seizure of Lord Edward Fitzgerald's papers, in which Wexford was mentioned as a place where the French could land with the greatest assurance of welcome.

The extent to which the inhabitants had by this time armed themselves was too notorious to be any longer denied. The magistrates of the Northern baronies met at Gorey on the 27th of April. The county was proclaimed. Orders were issued for the arms to be brought in; and other means failing, the whip was resorted to in a few instances in Wexford as well as elsewhere. Enough was done to exasperate the people, too little to frighten them into submission. On the 23rd of May, after Lord Edward's arrest, when it was known that a rising was intended, the magistrates issued a notice that unless the pikes were given up, companies of soldiers would be sent among the villages on free quarter; and three gentlemen of family and fortune who had made themselves notorious for the violence of their political opinions—Mr. Bagenal Harvey, Mr. John Colclough, of Ballyteigue, and Mr. Edward Fitzgerald, of New Park—were arrested and confined in Wexford Gaol. On the 25th came the news that Kildare and Carlow were in arms, and it fell like sparks on tinder lying ready to kindle. On the 26th began the month of horrors, which has left one more indelible stain on the history of the Catholics of Ireland.

On that Saturday evening, the long May-day falling to twilight, a beacon was seen to blaze into flame on Corrigrua Hill, ten miles west of Ferns. A fire answering to it was seen immediately after on Boolavogue, between Corrigrua and the sea, and by an instinct easily explicable the inhabitants of Wexford felt that the hour was come, and prepared to meet it. If there had been doubt before of the character and aims of the rebellion, that doubt was no longer to exist. Conceived originally by Jacobins, it had become by this time a struggle of the Irish Catholics to get possession of the county. Father John Murphy, of Boolavogue, was the son of a peasant at Ferns, and had been educated for the priesthood at Seville. He had been settled in his own country a few miles from his birthplace, and there he had remained waiting for the salvation of Israel, and had grown into a big, coarse, powerful man of forty, when his country called upon him for his services. It is to be hoped that his action was unpremeditated, for he had recently taken an oath of allegiance and made solemn protests of loyalty. The arrest of Lord Edward had perhaps absolved him.

This man it was that lighted the signal-fire on Corrigrua Hill. The next day was Whit-Sunday, and Father John was about his work betimes. His first move was against his Protestant rival pastor, Mr. Burrows. The Protestant families in the neighbourhood, seeing the fire, had crowded for shelter into the parsonage of the adjoining parish of Kilmuckridge.

Father John, with an army of pikemen, appeared soon after daybreak on the lawn before the door. He demanded arms, and when the arms were refused set fire to the outhouses. From the outhouses the flames spread to the parsonage itself. Mr. Burrows, a harmless gentleman, appeared at a window and begged for mercy for his family and flock. He was told that if they would come out their lives should be spared. He obeyed, and was instantly piked, with his son, a lad of sixteen, and seven of his male parishioners. The women were mercifully spared. Father John was swift, for he had a long day's work before him. Gathering up the muskets and fowling-pieces which had belonged to the house, he was soon in motion again, leaving Mrs. Burrows, with her niece and four children, sitting among the bleeding bodies, beside her dead husband and her dying boy, in front of her blazing home.

Having destroyed the heretic clergyman, the next object was the heretic Bishop. The Palace was at Ferns; and Ferns being Father John's native place, the purgation of it was of special consequence to him. While the day was still early he marched across country, pausing only to fire such Protestants' dwelling houses as lay in his way. Perhaps, too, having begun the Holy War, he was anxious for a blessing on it, and halted to say mass. Arrived at Ferns, he applied the torch in like manner to heretic residences, but his special object was the Palace. Dr. and Mrs. Cleaver with their children had happily escaped. Their servants and their labourers, many of whom the Bishop supported out of charity, gave Father John a hearty welcome. An orphan lad, whom the Bishop had found starving, and had fed and brought up and educated, displayed his gratitude by singular eagerness to assist in the injury of his benefactor. The Palace was plundered. The valuable library was torn to pieces. The vellum bindings of the books of divinity were stripped off and used for saddle-covers. When the spoils were all secured the shell of the house was set on fire, and all that would burn was consumed.

Father John was no longer alone. He found a brother in spirit and in arms in Father Michael Murphy, his neighbour, who now hastened to join him. Father Michael also was the son of a Wexford peasant. He had learnt his Latin grammar at a hedge-school on Oulart Hill. Thence, growing into promising boyhood, he was transferred to the Irish College at Bordeaux; and finding favour with Dr. Caulfield, the Catholic Bishop of Ferns, he had been appointed curate of Ballycanew, a hamlet adjoining Kilmuckridge. The holocaust at Kilmuckridge parsonage had brought him at once to the standard of the Cross. Having finished work at Ferns, the two priests, their army now swollen to several thousand men, spread over the adjoining district, sacking houses and burning them, and killing every heretic man that they were able to identify. By mid-day they had drifted to Oulart,[1] and encamped on the hill, for dinner, five thousand strong.

The news that the people were out had been brought early in the day into Wexford city. All the morning messengers were coming in bringing accounts of the murdering and burning, and praying for help to those who were left exposed. The garrison in the town was scanty, but Colonel Foote was despatched after breakfast with a hundred and ten of the North Cork men and thirty or forty mounted Yeomen, a force considered amply sufficient to subdue any resistance which they were likely to meet with. At four o'clock the same afternoon Mr. Perceval, the High Sheriff, galloped wildly in over the bridge to say that all was lost—that Foote and his entire party had been totally destroyed. Supposing that he had to deal only with a contemptible mob, Colonel Foote had flung himself on a body of men who fifty times outnumbered him, mad with the excitement of a religious war, and armed with a weapon which in determined hands was gradually discovered to be formidable. Father John, seeing that he was to be attacked, had divided his force with extemporised generalship. Finding the rebels stand better than they expected, the troops recoiled, to reform, when they found that they were surrounded and their retreat cut off. Most of the Yeomen deserted.

---

[1] Midway between Enniscorthy and the sea, five miles from each, six miles south-east of Ferns, and eleven north of Wexford.

Panic set in among the North Cork. They broke their ranks and attempted to fly. They were cut down almost to a man. There were no wounded in these battles. Everyone who fell was despatched. The report that Colonel Foote had himself fallen was untrue. The Colonel only, with a sergeant and three privates, made his way back to Wexford. Major Lombard, Captain De Courcy, and four other officers had been killed.

The battle over, Father John rested from his labours, entering in his diary a brief epitome of the first day's work:—

'Began the Republic of Ireland in Boulavogue, in the county of Wexford; commanded by the Rev. Doctor Murphy, parish priest of the said parish, where all the Protestants of the said parish were disarmed, and a bigot named Bookey lost his life by his rashness. Then came to a country village adjoining, where the Republic attacked a minister's house for arms, and was denied. Laid siege to it, and killed him and all his forces. The same day burned his house and all the Orangemen's houses in that and all adjoining parishes in that part of the country. The same day a part of the army attacked the Republic on Oulart Hill, when the military were repulsed, with the loss of 112 men. And the same day took another town and sate of a bishop.'[1]

The effect of Foote's defeat was frightful. The widows and children of the North Cork men who had fallen rushed about the streets of Wexford wringing their hands and shrieking. Their comrades threatened to break into the gaol and retaliate on

---

[1] *Father Murphy's Journal*—Musgrave. Appendix, 18, 1.

Bagenal Harvey and his two companions. Edward Hay, the historian of the rebellion, gave a hint to the gaoler, and the gaoler supplied the prisoners with arms for self-defence. The inhabitants of the city generally were four-fifths of them Catholics, and disaffected. Fierce, gloomy knots of men began to gather about the quays, while the Protestant ladies and clergy took refuge in the ships in the harbour, offering high prices for a passage to Wales. The panic spread through the country. The exposed Protestant families crowded on all sides into the nearest towns; while Father John, reposing for the night on his field of glory, sent out his scouts, calling on the peasants to shoulder their pikes and join him on the following morning.

If the reader will turn to a map of the county he will see on the Slaney, twelve miles above Wexford, the town, which has been already mentioned, of Enniscorthy. The river is here crossed by a bridge. The town itself stands on the west side. On the east, immediately opposite, rises a rounded eminence, known as Vinegar Hill, about four hundred feet high. The summit was then open grass, surmounted by a ruined windmill. The sides toward the river were enclosed in gardens and small fields. Below the town the river could only be crossed at low tide, and made its way to the sea between rich meadows and woods, just bursting at the time of the rebellion into their early summer foliage.

The station, as commanding the passage between the two divisions of the county, was important enough to have retained a tolerable garrison, composed of eighty men of the unfortunate North Cork—so many of whose comrades had fallen at Oulart and

Prosperous—a hundred and sixty Yeomen belonging to Enniscorthy itself, and sixty more from Ferns and the adjoining baronies. Captain Snowe, of the North Cork, was in command. Captain Drury, a local officer of Yeomanry, who commanded under him, had seen service in the American war. Father John's performances had sent every Protestant in the neighbourhood who had escaped his pikemen into Enniscorthy for shelter. Several hundred, the greater part of them women, children, and old men, had crowded into the town in the course of Sunday, where, if their property was destroyed, they believed that their lives would be safe. So it would have been, had the insurrection been no more than a common riot. But Father John, after his victory over Foote, aspired to be the liberator of his country. He required possession of Enniscorthy Bridge, that he might open his way to New Ross and Kilkenny. Oulart was but five miles distant, and Snowe was not long in learning that he must prepare to be attacked in the morning.

The townspeople, with the exception of the few who were enlisted as Yeomen, were all on the rebel side. He had the Yeomen's families to protect, as well as the fugitives from the country. In these hard circumstances he made the best dispositions in his power. He arrested the most dangerous of the inhabitants, and locked them up in the gaol and market-house. The North Cork were posted on the bridge, on the direct road from Oulart. The Yeomen were placed at the back, where the roads entered from the north and west. In this position they lay under arms through the night of Whit-Sunday.

Father John was early astir on the morning of

Whit-Sunday. His call had been well answered. The news of his first triumph had rung a peal through every parish in the neighbourhood. Among the recruits who had come in to him before daybreak were a few score of duck-shooters from the marshes—experienced shots, armed with their long fowling-pieces. He had secured the muskets and pouches of the dead soldiers, and he found himself with 800 men possessed of firearms of one kind or another, besides 5,000 pikemen. To use his numbers to advantage he manœuvred as on the previous day. The Slaney was fordable a few miles above Enniscorthy. Leaving a division to move direct upon the bridge, he marched at dawn with the main body, crossed the river, and gained the road which descends the west bank from New Town Barry. It was now eleven o'clock. He halted for half-an-hour to say mass, and then advanced along the road at the head of his men, while the other division was approaching to attack the bridge. It was a hot, brilliant summer morning. Father John was a born general. The country outside the town was intersected with walls and fences. He threw out skirmishers on either side of him, who availed themselves of the natural cover, and pressed on from bank to bank. According to ancient Irish custom he drove along the road in front of him a herd of wild cattle, goaded into madness, who rushed into the Yeomen's lines. The duck-shooters fired steadily. Captain Drury said that in all his American experience he had never seen guns better handled; the soldiers were raw hands, caught up but a few weeks before, and scarcely better disciplined than the rebels. Outnumbered twenty to one, with the cattle plunging upon them, and losing men fast, the Yeomen sent to

Snowe for assistance. Snowe had by this time his own hands full at the river, and needed rather help himself than was able to spare support to others. They gave way, but very slowly, fighting desperately inch by inch. A Yeoman named Thompson was struck in the neck by a ball. He cut it out, loaded his musket with it, and returned it. Still numbers told. As the rebels advanced they kindled the houses on each side of the street, and the battle went on under an arch of flame. The inhabitants, seeing the soldiers retreating, fired upon them from the windows. Women rushed out among the bullets with whisky-bottles and glasses to cheer the patriots' hearts. The streets were strewed with dead and dying, five rebels falling for each Yeoman; but the rebels still dauntlessly pressed on, till the troops were driven back upon the market-place. There, among stone houses, which would not burn, they recovered their advantage. Themselves under shelter, they sent their volleys with destructive effect into the exposed mass of men who were struggling within ten paces of their guns: and in the afternoon Father John, seeing he could make no further progress, and was throwing away lives unnecessarily, fell back to the fields outside, and prepared to try again at nightfall.

Captain Snowe had held his ground with less difficulty. He had been assailed with equal determination, but his men were better protected by situation. Foiled at the bridge, the rebels had twice attempted to force a passage above and below. They were beaten back at both points. By two o'clock the town was cleared, and Enniscorthy was still in possession of the loyalists.

But in what condition was it left? Half the town

was burning. Five hundred rebels lay about the streets, dead and dying. The prisons were crowded with desperate men, whom there was no force to guard. The Catholic inhabitants were furious. Of the scanty garrison a third had been killed, besides the wounded; and an unknown number of Protestant gentlemen and tradesmen who had given their services had fallen also. Outside was the fast-increasing insurgent army, savage for revenge; within were several hundred unfortunate beings—families of tradesmen and farmers, households of gentry and clergy—all now on a common level of misery. The garrison might maintain themselves in the gaol, but these forlorn creatures, when the rebels broke in again, must inevitably be sacrificed. To prevent a scene which would have rivalled the worst infamies of 1641, Snowe decided on evacuating the town and escorting his charge to Wexford.

It was a frightful alternative. The distance was but twelve miles, and the weather was dry and warm; but there were no carriages, no horses, save the few belonging to the mounted Yeomen, and these, though cheerfully surrendered, were altogether inadequate. There were wounded men to be transported, and delicate ladies and little children, too young to walk, too old for their mothers to carry them; and the infirm and aged, and the sick and impotent.

Yet to leave them behind was to leave them to certain death. Late in the afternoon the miserable march began. The insurgents rushed in as the troops filed out. Women, unable to reach the bridge, waded the river to escape them, with their babies on their backs. The march was rapid. Two miles below, on the Wexford road, they passed a wood, known as

BOOK X.
1798.
May 20.

the Wood of St. John, or Ringwood; and many poor creatures, struggling painfully on, were tempted to fling themselves down among the brushwood, hoping to lie concealed there till morning. The rest, of stronger limb or stouter spirit, pushed on, and soon after nightfall found a brief respite from their sufferings within Wexford gates.

Had the rebels followed they might all have been destroyed. Happily that evening they attempted no pursuit. They were busy in Enniscorthy sacking the Protestants' houses, piking such obnoxious wretches as were found loitering, burying their dead, or in the wild revel of their second victory.

Father John's fast-expanding mind was engaged upon another project, which with the morning he hastened to execute. He conceived it would be desirable to have a standing camp as a rallying-point for the county. For such a purpose no place was more central, more convenient, more appropriate in every way, than the crest of Vinegar Hill.

The insurgents were increasing with marvellous rapidity, and their numbers soon amounted to many thousands. Men in good position in society came—John Hay, of Newcastle, a so-called gentleman; Edward Roche, a wealthy yeoman; Father Roche, his kinsman, and twenty other priests. With men came women, some vagrants, some whisky-selling, some to dress their husbands' or brothers' food, some for the wild enjoyment of the strife. With such organisation as he could extemporise Father John made his preparations for their entertainment. The weather was warm and dry, and well suited for an out-door encampment. The Protestant houses in Enniscorthy and for many miles round were searched and relieved of their contents. Before the evening of Whit-Tuesday the slopes and brow of Vinegar Hill were dotted over with hundreds of booths, of motley colour, shape, and material. Carpets, window-curtains, sheets, blankets, whatever came first to hand, were stretched on poles and made into rude tents. The women appropriated the ladies' wardrobes, and fluttered in silks and feathers. Barrels of wine and ale were rolled up out of the cellars of squire and parson, and mounted on tressels, for all who pleased to help themselves. Pianos were brought for such as had skill in music. Blind minstrels were gathered from far and near, and sounded out the old airs of Ireland on harps which but a few days before were touched by delicate fingers in gilded drawing-rooms. In curious contrast the manners and habits were revived spontaneously of the great days of Erin's ancient chiefs. Cattle were driven in from neighbouring farms and parks. At feeding-times cows and oxen were knocked down, and slices were cut from the unflayed and fresh-bleeding carcases and toasted on the points of pikes.

All sorts were gathered together—men of good condition, traders, farmers, shopkeepers, interspersed with plundering ruffians; all ranks blended harmoniously together in the uprising of the true Irish nature such as when left to itself it tended to become. So little trust had they in each other's honesty that they slept on their faces, with their hats and shoes under them, lest they should wake and find them gone. Two exercises only were discharged with regularity and punctuality on Vinegar Hill. Law might be forgotten, but religion was remembered. Twenty priests said mass each day at different points of the camp. Each day a holocaust of Protestants was offered to the national divinities. The windmill on the brow of the hill and a barn at the bottom were appropriated as prisons, and gangs of ruffians were sent out to scour the country and bring in every Protestant that could be found. Ringwood, where the feeblest of the Enniscorthy fugitives had taken refuge for the night, was drawn in the morning, as hounds draw a fox-cover. Many poor creatures, and those perhaps the happiest, were piked upon the spot. Others were carried captive to the hill, where a council of leaders was held to determine on the treatment of them. Some were for an instant and undiscriminating massacre; others, Father Roche especially, were against murder in cold blood altogether.[1] It was decided finally that those only should be put to death who could be proved to have been actively traitors to the Irish cause. A court-martial was established in permanent session outside the windmill. The prisoners were brought before it in batches, like the aristocrats before Fouquier Tinville, and on receiving sentence were passed out to instant execution on the pikes of the rebel guard in waiting. On the first day, as an inauguration ceremonial for the camp, twenty-four victims were condemned, and were stabbed or shot. As the windmill prison was emptied it was refilled from the barn. The barn was kept supplied from the country. Every day, so long as the camp continued, the bloody work went forward—the crimson blossoming of the tree of liberty which had been planted by Grattan in '82. A large tub of water was daily blessed to

---

[1] See the depositions.—*Musgrave*, vol. ii. Appendix, 19. The general character of the proceedings on Vinegar Hill is not disputed. The difference is only as to the number murdered there. Musgrave's estimate is 500. Gordon reduces it to 400.

sprinkle the miserable assassins and persuade them that they were Christ's soldiers. It is expressly recorded that those most ready with their services on these occasions were not the peasantry, but men who had received what is now called education.

SECTION III.

BOOK X.
1798.
May 29.

FATHER JOHN was too enterprising a general to rest upon his laurels. Others could superintend executions of Protestants. Father John's place was in pursuing the campaign which he had so auspiciously commenced. On Whit-Sunday he had murdered a clergyman and his parishioners. He had burnt a Bishop's palace, and had fought and won a battle. On Whit-Monday he had fought another and more desperate battle, and had taken Enniscorthy. On Whit-Tuesday, having established his camp and left ten thousand men there, he marched the same afternoon to Wexford. Flood, Grattan, Wolfe Tone, O'Connor, Edward Fitzgerald, these all in their way had seemed to pass for representative Irish patriots. But here was the real thing. The politicians were but shadows, Father John was the substance. With pistols in his holsters, his sword at his side, and a large crucifix in his arms, he rode at the head of his army, the true and perfect representative of Catholic and Celtic Ireland. His object now was Wexford city. He encamped that night four miles from it, at a place called Three Rocks, under Mount Forth, on the road from Wexford to Taghmon. When the news spread of the defeat at Oulart, General Fawcett, who commanded at Duncannon, guessing that Wexford might be in danger, sent Colonel Maxwell thither in haste, with 200 men of a Donegal regiment. They arrived on Whit-Tuesday morning, to find the town in a confusion approaching close on panic. Half the garrison had been killed at Oulart, and that first disaster had been followed in less than thirty hours by the news of the battle at Enniscorthy, and the appearance of Snowe with the remnant of his Yeomen and the miserable beings under his charge. Ladies, and such of their husbands and brothers as were unwilling or afraid to fight, were hurrying on board vessels with redoubled speed, offering half their fortunes for a safe conduct to England, the boatmen making a harvest of their fears. Shortly after Maxwell's arrival a report came in that Father John was advancing. Maxwell, finding matters so much worse than he expected, sent a mounted messenger in all haste back to Duncannon, to bid Fawcett come up himself with all the force that he had. Fitzgerald, of New Park, and Mr. Colclough were released and sent to meet Father John and persuade him to leave Wexford alone. Fitzgerald remained with the rebels. Colclough returned to report that they were close to the city, and might be looked for with certainty on the following morning. The fate of the city depended on Fawcett. He started from Duncannon with two regiments, the 13th and the Meath Militia, immediately on receiving Maxwell's message. Two companies of the Meath, which were most speedily in marching order, were sent in advance, with some artillerymen and a couple of guns, Fawcett promising to overtake them at Taghmon. Fawcett loitered on the way. The officer in command of the advanced party, hearing that Wexford was threatened, resolved, after waiting some hours, to push forward; and in total ignorance that Father John now lay on his road, at the foot of the Forth Mountain, went on about midnight. All was quiet till he reached Three Rocks, and was almost within sight of Wexford, when the darkness was lighted by the flashes of five hundred muskets. Above, below, before, behind, the rebels were everywhere, yelling like packs of hyenas. Surprised and surrounded, the half-trained Meath men lost coherence. They had to do with an enemy whose policy was to treat the Irish militia as traitors to their country, and to refuse all quarter, and the savage character of the war added to the weight of the terror. They were killed to a man. The guns were taken. A few of the artillerymen were kept alive, to serve them. One single officer alone survived to carry the tale to Maxwell. Notwithstanding this disaster Wexford might have been saved had Fawcett possessed conduct or courage; but the evil spirit of Abercrombie had unnerved the spirit of too many of the English generals. Fawcett, who had reached Taghmon in the morning, at once turned back and retreated on Duncannon. Maxwell pushed out from the town, hoping to meet him on the road. He arrived at Three Rocks, only to find Father John too strongly posted for his small force to dislodge. The mounted Yeomanry were unsteady and fled. His infantry were driven back with loss; and he was obliged to retreat precipitately.

Wexford, too, like Enniscorthy, had now become untenable. The bulk of the inhabitants were at heart with the rebels, and were kept quiet only by fear. If Father John advanced they would certainly rise and assist him. The troops could no longer be relied upon; and the citizens, Catholic and Protestant, who had property to lose, and feared that the place would be set on fire, entreated Maxwell not to defend it.[1]

[1] Mr. Hay accuses Maxwell of cowardice. He insists that the inhabitants were loyal, and would have supported him, and that the

'I refused to consent,' Maxwell wrote in his report to General Eustace. 'I ordered the troops to their posts; but when I visited the barriers, to my astonishment and concern, I found that the Yeomanry corps [1] had quitted their places. At one post, where I expected sixty or seventy men, there were not three privates. At another, a like number. The men of the North Cork refused to obey their officers, or take further part against the rebels. I could not further oppose or take on myself the responsibility of subjecting the loyal part of the garrison to the resentment of a numerous and sanguinary rabble.' [2]

The North Cork were scarcely to be blamed. Being Catholics, they were reproached as deserters from the national cause. One detachment of them had been destroyed at Prosperous, another at Oulart. At Enniscorthy they had fought splendidly, and had retreated only before numbers enormously superior. The Meath corps had been destroyed. Fawcett had deserted them. Maxwell himself had been beaten in a skirmish, which proved that Father John was too strong for him. The enemy was without and traitors were within. Their own wives and their comrades' widows were shrieking round them. The last virtue which has been honoured and rewarded in Ireland by her English masters is excess of loyalty. The rule has been to conciliate traitors and leave fidelity to be its own compensation.

At midnight, on the 30th of May, Maxwell marched out of Wexford, thirty-six hours after he had entered, unnecessary evacuation of the town was the sole cause of the horrors which ensued. As in an image in a looking-glass, every feature in the story is thus precisely reversed.

[1] Raised in Wexford itself from among the inhabitants.
[2] 'Colonel Maxwell to General Eustace, June 1, 1798.' S. P. O.

and retreated by the sea-road which was still open, to Duncannon. His soldiers are charged with having been guilty of some outrages on the way—burning houses and flogging men. It may have been so; discipline is rarely sustained in the wreck of a beaten army; and the road lay through the Barony of Forth, which had supplied Father John with the duck-shooters, from whose long guns they had suffered at Enniscorthy. Maxwell himself merely says that he reached Duncannon without interruption.

On the morning of the 31st the rebels from Three Rocks moved on to Wexford. They halted outside the barriers for the whole line to kneel and pray; and they then rushed in upon the spoils. For three days there was a saturnalia of madness; the houses of the Protestants were sacked, the gaol was thrown open; the prisoners, Bagenal Harvey among them, were released in triumph, and loyal Protestants were thrust in to take their places. Wild Amazons rode about the streets, with plumed hats and pikes in hand. A man named Keogh, once a captain in the army and a magistrate, was appointed governor, and the green flag of Ireland floated over the barracks. The ships which had been hired to carry the fugitives to England were still in the harbour. Among the largest shipowners at Wexford was a man named Dixon, a tavern and billiard-room keeper on the Quay. This person, having extorted enormous sums for the use of his vessels, had contrived under various pretexts to delay their sailing. When the English flag was hauled down and the Irish harp was blowing out in its place, the Protestants on board prayed the captains to cut their cables and depart. The same sacred emblem of liberty was run up for answer to the mastheads. Boats came off from the quays, led by Dixon in person. The fugitives were invited with mocking courtesy to disembark and return. Some were carried to the crowded gaol, some were forced on board a miserable hulk below the bridge, which was converted into a prison-ship.

To maintain the fiction of a united Ireland, Protestant gentlemen of liberal sympathies were offered the alternative of joining the patriot army. Cornelius Grogan, a gentleman of large fortune in the neighbourhood, took the United Irish oath, as he represented afterwards, 'to save his property.' Mr. Colclough and Bagenal Harvey, who had been imprisoned by order of Government for their revolutionary sentiments, were released and promoted to honour. Colclough drove through the town with his wife, with green ribands flying. Bagenal Harvey accepted high command in the rebel army. At Vinegar Hill the spirit was savage from the first, in consequence of the fight at Enniscorthy. At Wexford, where there had been no resistance, the thirst for blood had not yet been awakened. A few obnoxious gentlemen were piked and shot under special provocation: others were sent out to receive their deserts on Vinegar Hill. The feeling in Wexford for the first few days was chiefly of triumph and exultation. Victorious Ireland desired rather to show her zeal for saving souls than destroying bodies, and frightened heretics were dragged or led in batches to the Catholic chapels, to be converted into Christians.

Father John meanwhile had his eyes on larger objects. Wexford was now secured, but a local rising could not hope for permanent success. If the insurrection was to triumph, it must spread: it must envelope Ireland. Nothing had really been done till Dublin especially had been wrested from the invader. The effect was now showing itself of the organisation of past years. The people everywhere were prepared to rise, and the rebel army had only to show itself to be swollen by the local levies. More extended operations had now become necessary. The object was the deliverance of Dublin. The number of armed men who could be counted upon was practically unlimited. A second permanent camp was established at Three Rocks, and the movable forces were divided into three great bodies. The first, under Bagenal Harvey, with Father Roche as second in command, was directed to take New Ross, force the passage of the Barrow, and raise Kilkenny and Waterford. The second division was ordered to move up the Slaney from Enniscorthy, take New Town Barry, sweep the loyalists out of the north of the county; and then, advancing through Carlow into Kildare, threaten Dublin on the west. The third division Father John reserved for himself and his friend, Father Michael. His intention was to march north through his own county, where his force would grow like an avalanche. After taking Gorey he proposed to force Arklow, and make his way along the sea-road into Wicklow, where the levies of the county were waiting to join him. With Wicklow in their hands on one side, Kildare on the other, and the central plain of Ireland on fire behind them, the rebels calculated, not without reason, that Dublin could not long hold out against them.

SECTION IV.

HITHERTO the defence of Ireland had fallen almost entirely on her own people. Camden had applied repeatedly for reinforcements. The Government had sent a regiment of cavalry, which was comparatively useless. Portland said, in reply to remonstrances, that he understood the insurrection to be too inconsiderable to require a large addition to the number of the troops. He had been taught to believe that the danger was from the North. So long as Ulster was quiet he attached little consequence to disturbances in the rest of the island. The mistake was inexcusable, for Abercrombie had told him that ten thousand British troops would be required if the South was to be disarmed, and now the South was in the field.

Lord Camden's position was thus cruelly difficult. He might hear at any moment that a French army had landed. The Dublin mob were only held in check by the presence of an overwhelming garrison, which by its concentration left the country exposed. At any moment also he might hear of what he dreaded even more than the French—the rising of the Presbyterians. From 1791 to 1797 Ulster had been the chief seat of political discontent. It was at Belfast that the taking of the Bastille had been celebrated with such passionate sympathy. It was among the Scotch-Irish artisans that Jacobin principles had taken earliest root. Down and Antrim had furnished the emigrants who fought at Bunker's Hill and Lexington. It seemed incredible that when the long-talked-of crisis had come Ulster would take no part in it. The Viceroy's friends in the revolutionary committee continued to apprise him of its secret workings. A week had passed since the fatal 23rd. 'The bleach-greens were still strewed with linen,' 'the artisans were still at their looms.' The informers reported that the friends of liberty were less enthusiastic. The doings of France in Switzerland were giving dissatisfaction. There were murmurs at French tyranny in the West Indies. The Orangemen were an alarming feature to the rebel mind. Though the Viceroy had not employed them hitherto, he might be less scrupulous if there was open insurrection, and they confessed to serious fear of the Orangemen. Most of all, 'an alteration had been worked in their minds by the Popish tinge of the rebellion, the Catholics in the South making the rising a matter of religion.'[1]

Still, entire quiet in a part of the country which had been so violently demonstrative was 'unaccountable.' The Ulster men, who were naturally more deliberate and determined than the Southerners, were the less likely to have changed their minds completely and suddenly. Camden could not yet venture to withdraw or even weaken the Northern garrisons. When the news arrived of the capture of Wexford either he or General Lake divined the course which the rebels were likely to take afterwards. It was essential, if possible, to enclose and trample out the insurrection within the limits of the county where it was for the present victorious; and, shorthanded as he was, the Viceroy immediately made such efforts

---

[1] 'Camden to Portland, June 2.' 'Cooke to Wickham, June 2, 1798.' S. P. O.

as his resources allowed. Fresh regiments were enrolled out of the Dublin loyalists to take charge of the city. A portion of the garrison was thus released. General Loftus was sent with 250 additional men to join the garrison of Arklow. Colonel L'Estrange was sent to New Town Barry, with 400 militia and a couple of field-guns, to block the road from Enniscorthy to Carlow. Colonel Walpole was directed to take up a position, with 500 men from Naas and Kilcullen, at a place called Carnew, half-way between the position of L'Estrange at New Town Barry, and that of Loftus at Arklow. The three columns were then to advance in parallel lines towards Wexford. Such a force, the Viceroy calculated, would overwhelm all resistance.[1] The strength, the skill, the resolution of the rebels were still far underestimated, as Camden was bitterly to find. It was too much to expect that a thousand half-drilled militia, men taken hastily from desk and plough, could encounter fifty times their number. L'Estrange was in time to save New Town Barry. He reached the place by forced marches a few hours only before it was attacked. The rebels came up on the 1st of June from Vinegar Hill, on both sides of the river. Their leader was a priest, a huge savage named Father Kern.[2] Other priests acted as officers of their own parishioners. The victories over the troops had by this time furnished the insurgents with artillery; they had a brass six-pounder with them, a howitzer, and some swivel-guns. They came on with the usual Irish howl. L'Estrange

[1] Camden to Portland, June 4, 1708.'
[2] 'A man of extraordinary strength, stature, and ferocity.'— Gordon's *History of the Rebellion,* p. 130.

allowed them to enter the streets, when they begun at once to burn and plunder.[1] He then opened upon them with grape and musketry. When they turned to fly they were pursued and cut up by the Yeomanry. Four hundred fell. Among the bodies were found two priests, in their vestments.

Loftus and Walpole reached their posts on the same day, and so far without accident. Loftus, on the 3rd of June, finding no enemy in front of him, felt his way cautiously out of Arklow, along the Wexford road. Lord Ancram, on the same day, descended the Slaney from New Town Barry. Walpole advanced simultaneously, as he was ordered, from Carnew, parallel to both of them. Had all gone well he would have joined Ancram at Ferns. Together they would have attacked Enniscorthy and Vinegar Hill, and after carrying them have combined with Loftus in recovering Wexford. Walpole, to his misfortune, was confronted by Father John, and Father John proved himself once more a dangerous antagonist. The body of rebels under his command had been moving leisurely, according to the plan which had been concerted, towards Arklow. His camp on that day was on Ballymore Hill, between Ferns and the sea; and as Walpole and Loftus marched on their several ways Father John was at last between them. Bent simply on their object, they were wholly ignorant that he was so near. Walpole had been warned to be careful, but he had neglected the most simple precautions. He had no advanced guard, and

---

[1] Mr. Gordon, who, though a Protestant clergyman, shows a strong prejudice in particular directions, declares that L'Estrange, 'according to the too commonly practised mode of the King's officers,' advised a retreat, and was only brought back into action by the remonstrances of Colonel Westenra.—*Gordon*, p. 130.

had sent out no skirmishing parties on either side of him. His line of march was among lanes and hedges and wooded enclosures, thick with the newly-opened leaves. Suddenly, at a narrow pass, he found the road blocked, and shot poured in upon him on all sides from invisible enemies. He himself, being in full uniform, and conspicuous on a tall grey horse, was killed early in the action. His men fell into confusion. They were in a position where they could neither advance nor retreat, nor reach their enemies. After three-quarters of an hour of hopeless effort, in which more than half of them were killed and their guns taken, the wreck of the detachment contrived to extricate itself, and made its escape to Gorey. The news of their defeat preceded them. In Gorey the houses were lined with sharpshooters, who fired on them from the windows. They were driven through the town; and mingling with a crowd of flying Protestants, struggled on till they reached Arklow.

Loftus was now exposed to a similar fate. The fugitives from Walpole's force had passed behind him, along the road on which he had advanced in the morning. He now had Father John in his rear. Wexford was in his front, but he could not venture upon Wexford single and unsupported. By a dexterous cross-march over Slievebuoy Mountain he contrived to reach Carnew, on which Lord Ancram also had found himself obliged to fall back. The first combined effort to recover Wexford had thus utterly failed; and a yet more serious consideration was, that the Arklow garrison was so weakened by the loss of the force with Loftus as to be incapable of present resistance. Father John, if he used his opportunity, might march to Dublin unfought with.

BOOK X.
1798.
June.

Camden was now for the first time really alarmed. The reports from the North were less favourable, and Walpole's defeat might decisively turn the scale. He felt that he had been unjustly neglected. He was left alone with the Irish Yeomen and militia, a third of whom were unfaithful. The cruelties towards the Irish which he had been accused of encouraging or permitting might too easily become realities, when the scenes which were now recurring daily on Vinegar Hill became generally known. He could now neither oppose the rebels nor restrain the Protestants from savage retaliation, and under the weight of the last blow he addressed a letter of earnest remonstrance to Portland:—

'The aspect of the rebellion becomes most alarming. The North will rise, unless the rebels near Dublin can be crushed. The salvation of Ireland, on which Great Britain as an empire eventually depends, requires that this rebellion should be instantly suppressed. No event but instant extinction can prevent it from becoming general, as it is notorious that the whole country is organised. The Chancellor, the Speaker, all the friends of his Majesty's Government whom I am in the habit of consulting, have this day given it as their solemn opinion, and have required me to state it as such, that the salvation of Ireland depends on immediate and very considerable succours—that a few regiments will perhaps only be sent to slaughter or to loss. This opinion is perfectly well-founded. General Lake agrees. I make this appeal to your Grace in the most solemn manner. My services cannot be useful to his Majesty unless I can restore the confidence of the kingdom, and immediately and effectually suppress the rebellion.'[1]

[1] 'Camden to Portland, June 5, 1798.' S. P. O.

It was quite certain that at this particular moment Father John could, if he had pleased, have reached Dublin with ease. He had twenty thousand men with him at Ballymore. He would have doubled his numbers before he had arrived at Bray, and at Bray he would have been but a day's march from the city. Happily for the country, he had been rendered careless by his extraordinary successes, and for the first time allowed an opportunity to escape him.

SECTION V.

BOOK X.
1798.
June 4.

Two of the great divisions of the rebels were thus accounted for—one had been defeated at Carnew, the other victorious at Ballymore. The third, under Bagenal Harvey and Father Roche, had meanwhile made leisurely approaches upon New Ross. The undertaking was not an easy one, for New Ross was better defended than Enniscorthy. When it was known to be in danger General Johnstone had been sent to take charge of it with several companies of militia, some English artillerymen, a squadron of dragoons, and part of a Midlothian Fencible regiment. A County Dublin regiment, which was pushed forward after Walpole's overthrow, commanded by Lord Mountjoy, arrived late on the 4th of June, and raised Johnstone's force to 1,400 men. The rebels on their side had commenced by making a camp, six miles off, at Carrickbyrne Hill, from which they plundered the adjoining baronies. Having taken many Protestants, they availed themselves for their safe keeping, of Scullabogue, a place belonging to a Captain King, at the hill-foot. They turned the barn into a prison, and they quartered the guard in the dwelling-house. After being thus occupied for a week they pushed forward, and arrived at Corbet Hill, overhanging the Barrow Valley, on the afternoon of the same day on which Mountjoy arrived.

New Ross stands on the slope which rises on the Wexford bank of the river. It was then surrounded by a wall, which had once resisted Cromwell. There were four gates, two at the bottom of the town, by the water-side, through which the high road passed from Dublin to Waterford, and two above. Large vessels of four hundred tons could lie alongside of the quay. Cross-streets and lanes ran up the hill-side to the market-place and the barracks. The Enniscorthy road entered at the top of the town, at the market-gate, at the north-east angle. From the market a long broad street ran parallel to the river half way up the hill, and issued at the Three Bullet Gate, to which the road descended from Corbet Hill and Wexford. The rebel camp was a mile and a half distant. The troops were under arms all night. They were paraded at two in the morning, and as day began to break the peculiar Irish cry was heard rising in gathering waves of sound in the direction of the camp. Nearer and clearer it came through the morning air. The rebels came on slowly and in enormous numbers. Scouts said they were not less than thirty thousand, and General Johnstone considered that, 'from the myriads which came down, they could not be much less.' They marched in order by parishes and by baronies. The Dublin regiment under Mountjoy, the dragoons, and other companies were drawn up outside the Three Bullet Gate, on open ground. The rebel masses bore down the hill towards them.

When a rifle-shot off they halted. Priests were seen moving up and down the lines in their vestments and carrying crucifixes. Mass was said at the head of every column, the men kneeling, with marked and earnest devotion. For the moment Johnstone thought that they were hesitating, but he was swiftly undeceived. It was now a little after three o'clock, daylight being scarcely yet fully established. They rose from their knees; the lines opened, and between them came herds of wild cattle rushing on, amidst shouts and yells which burst from the enormous multitude, the rebels pricking them forward with their pikes. A fourth part of the rebel army had firearms, but their main strength was in the pikemen, who formed in column behind the cattle and charged with a fierceness of resolution for which the English and Scotch officers present were unprepared.[1] They rushed upon the Dublin regiment, which was in some confusion, and drove it back through the gate. Mountjoy fell wounded, and was carried off into the insurgent lines. The dragoons charged, but without effect, and recoiled with loss. A gun was taken, and the rebel pikemen poured into the town after the retreating troops. According to their usual tactics they instantly fired the houses. Cannon had been placed in the long straight street which leads from the market-place to the Bullet Gate, and poured round-shot and grape into their dense masses. Multitudes fell. An entire column was annihilated—not a man escaped out of it. Brave as they were, so terrible a reception startled them. They fell back for a while, and the troops had time to rally and re-form. But soon they came on again through smoke and flame, their courage and their overwhelming numbers compensating for want of discipline and inferiority of arms. Nor was the pike in

---

[1] Colonel Crawford, writing from Ross on the 9th of June, stated that before the action he had the most contemptible opinion of the rebels. He expected that they would be easily hunted together by small columns, and then disposed of. 'I have now,' he said, 'totally changed my opinion. I never saw any troops attack with more enthusiasm and bravery than the rebels did on the 5th. We must proceed against them with caution as well as vigour, and with a much larger force.' S. P. O.

the hands of a strong bold man a weapon to be lightly regarded. With a shaft twelve or fifteen feet in length, a long taper point, with a hook at times attached, which would drag a horseman from his saddle, it was an overmatch under some conditions for the bayonet. Johnstone's advantage was in his heavy guns. The rebels had no artillerymen, and such cannon as they captured they were unable to use. But the daring of the Irish on that day defied even artillery. A spectator from a window close to the spot from whence a gun was strewing the street with piles of dead saw a man rush straight upon it, and thrust his hat into the smoking nozzle, crying, 'Come on, boys; her mouth is stopped!' In another second he was blown to atoms. Careless in their desperate fanaticism,[1] the Irish showed for once in rebellion the contempt of danger which, as soldiers in the army of their sovereign, they never fail to show. Four guns were taken. They forced the troops backwards and downwards to the river, part into the market-place, where, as at Enniscorthy, the stone buildings became a fortress which they could neither burn nor penetrate; part down over the bridge and into Kilkenny.

At one time they seemed to have won the day, and they would have won it, could their leaders have restrained them in victory. But they turned uncontrollably to plunder and incendiarism and whisky, and discipline resumed its superiority. Behind the river the broken troops again formed. Johnstone led them back to the charge; and the rebels, now scattered,

---

[1] Musgrave says that they had taken the following oath before starting, and that copies of it were found on the bodies of the slain:—
'I swear by our Lord Jesus Christ, who suffered for us on the Cross, and by the Blessed Virgin Mary, that I will burn, destroy, and murder all heretics, up to my knees in blood.'

were driven back in turn at the bayonet's point. The guns were recovered, and again began to work havoc in the disordered crowds. The carnage was now dreadful. No quarter had been given by the rebels at the beginning of the engagement—none was allowed them at the end of it. They were driven out through the gate at which they had entered. They attempted a stand within the lines where they first appeared in the morning. Johnstone stormed in upon them and broke them. There Lord Mountjoy's body was found, far from the place where he had fallen, 'mangled and butchered in the most horrid manner.' Mountjoy was the Luke Gardiner of '82, who had wrung from the Protestant Parliament the first concessions to the Catholics, and this was his reward.[1] The sight of their commander thus barbarously mutilated drove the Dublin regiment to fury. Three gentlemen had been murdered near Ross the day before with peculiar brutality. The militia generally had behaved excellently in action, but when the fighting was over could no longer be restrained. Major Vesey says, 'The carnage was now shocking; the troops were exasperated, and could not be stopped.' The scene became too hideous ' to be represented.' The battle had raged for eleven hours. It began at four in the morning. At three in the afternoon, when it was at last over, Vesey

---

[1] The usual story is that Mountjoy was killed at Three Bullet Gate. Major Vesey, who was present, and whose account of the battle I chiefly follow, says that Mountjoy was wounded and taken prisoner early in the morning, and that he himself saw the body, 'mangled' as I have described, a mile from the gate where he fell, when the rebels' last position was stormed. He was fifty-three years old when killed; his name attaching itself to living memories through his son, or rather through his son's second wife, Lady Blessington, of West-End notoriety.

estimated the rebel bodies which lay strewed round him as at least two thousand. Musgrave, on further enquiry, placed the number of those who were killed in the fight and after it at two thousand six hundred.[1]

[1] Compare the accounts of the battle in Musgrave, Gordon, and Hay with the despatches of General Johnstone, Major Vesey, and Colonel Crawford, in the State Paper Office.

SECTION VI.

[BOOK X. 1798. June 5.]

MAJOR VESEY, gazing on the field at Ross, enquired 'if there could be a curse too heavy for the wretches who had brought on Ireland so horrible a war?' Six miles distant there was at that moment another spectacle, of which he was as yet ignorant, still more dreadful than the scene which he was witnessing.

It will be remembered that when encamped at Carrickbyrne the rebels had seized many of the Protestants of the neighbourhood, and had shut them up in Captain King's house, at Scullabogue. A hundred and eighty-four of them, chiefly old men, women, and children, who had been taken because they were too helpless to escape, were confined in a barn thirty-four feet long and fifteen wide.[1] From thirty to forty others were kept in the dwelling-house. With the party in the barn were sixteen Catholics, wives and children of the hated North Cork men, who had fallen somewhere into the insurgents' hands. When the rebel army advanced from Carrickbyrne to Corbet Hill, the day before the battle, the prisoners were left under charge of John Murphy, of Loughnageer, with a guard of three hundred men. At the first check in the street of New Ross a party of rebels, who were cowards as well as savages, turned their backs and

---

[1] Mr. Hay gives the dimensions. He shows that there was barely standing-room for a hundred and eighty-four persons in such a space, and therefore boldly throws aside the evidence of persons present, and reduces the number to eighty. It will be seen that he has involuntarily established the fact which he believed he was disproving.

ran. Before nine in the morning [1] they came panting to the door of Scullabogue, declaring that the day was lost, and that they had brought orders for the prisoners to be put to death, as they might otherwise be dangerous. The officer of the guard hesitated, but a commission was produced, signed by a priest,[2] which was accepted at last as sufficient authority. Those who were in the house were at once brought out and shot on the lawn.[3] The standers-by stabbed them as they fell with their pikes, and licked the blood from the points.[4] Captain Murphy interpreted his orders to extend only to his male prisoners. The savage rabble who surrounded him were not so easily satisfied. While the bodies on the lawn were being stripped for burial a party of the wretches rushed for the barn. The miserable beings who had been pent up there through a summer's afternoon and night must have been in a

---

[1] 'The massacre began in the forenoon. See Richard Grandy's evidence.'—*Musgrave*, Appendix, xx. 7. The hour is important; for Hay, while he affects to deplore and condemn the atrocities at Scullabogue, attributes them, as usual, to the carnage which followed the battle at Ross. 'The fugitives from Ross,' he says, 'communicating accounts of the tortures practised there, and that no quarter would be given to the people, an infinite multitude of men and women rushed to Scullabogue and forced the guards. General Johnstone was blamed, for he was warned to spare the people, or they would resort to retaliation. If giving quarter would have prevented the fatality at Scullabogue, humanity excites a wish it had been given.' Mr. Hay claims more than the permitted license of a partisan when he explains what happened at nine in the morning at Scullabogue as the result of the behaviour of the troops at Ross at three in the afternoon.

[2] 'Father Murphy, of Taghmon.' —*Musgrave*, vol. i. p. 530.

[3] 'Thirty-four were killed in this way... Two brothers were among them, one of whom was married. The wife knelt between her husband and her brother-in-law, holding a hand of each, and praying to be allowed to share their fate. Captain Murphy's scruples obliged him to refuse. "Such a horrid deed," he said, "would make the Virgin Mary blush."'—*Musgrave*, vol. i. p. 529.

[4] 'One witness, who was present, swore to this.'—*Musgrave*, Appendix, xx. 7. Another, who had himself a narrow escape of death, confirmed it privately to Musgrave.

condition in which death would be a relief to most of them. Humanity may perhaps hope that till their murder was resolved on they were allowed the range of the yard. In the barn they were, at any rate, at that moment crushed so close together that their bodies supported each other, and they could neither sit nor lie on the ground. The doors were barred on the outside, and the rebels with their pikes thrust blazing faggots into the thatch. The majority must have been instantly suffocated. Those who were near the walls sought chinks and cracks for air, but were driven back by pike-points thrust into the openings. One little child crawled under the door and was escaping; a rebel ran a pike into it as a peasant runs a pitchfork into a cornsheaf, and tossed it back into the flames. A woman who came four days later to look for the remains of her husband and son found the ruins of the barn full of blackened bodies, 'all in a standing posture'—an unintended confirmation of the received estimate of the number of those who perished there.

For this act the Irish Catholics have affected the same inadequate penitence with which they at once deny and excuse the massacre of 1641. They cut down the dimensions of their crime in defiance of evidence, and explain what remains as the consequence of the cruelties of their adversaries. They fail to recognise that, alike in 1641 and in 1798, no injury had been done to them, and no hurt had been designed against them, till they had either taken arms in rebellion or were preparing for it so openly that the Government was compelled to take their weapons from them. The burglar who kills a policeman is none the less held guilty of murder because the policeman began the quarrel by laying his hand upon his shoulder.

Bagenal Harvey, the nominal commander of the detachment which fought at New Ross, received the news of the massacre at Scullabogue with horror and indignation. He swore that he would shoot any man in future who murdered a prisoner. It was seen instantly that he was not the man to be a leader in an Irish rebellion. The rebels assured him with a howl that they would bear no dictation from a Protestant and a landowner. Father Roche, his lieutenant, preaching a sermon on the defeat at Ross, and endeavouring to explain it, said they would have neither grace nor luck while there was a Protestant in their ranks. Bagenal Harvey was deposed for his interference, and returned to Wexford, better enlightened as to the nature of the people whom he had been so eager to emancipate.

SECTION VII.

AFTER the disaster which befel Walpole, Dublin became with difficulty manageable. Father John promised to be at Bray, with 50,000 men, by the 12th or 13th of June at latest. Letters from the North were less and less assuring, and there was still the same appearance of apathy in England. Though the rebels had been defeated at New Ross, they had shown fighting qualities entirely unexpected. There was no sign and no promise of the so anxiously demanded reinforcements; and so dark was the prospect, that Lady Camden and many other ladies were sent off to Holyhead, to be out of the way of the scenes which were now probably imminent.

On the 9th of June Camden again endeavoured to open Portland's eyes. 'You will be much deceived,' he said, 'if you imagine a rebellion which has been so long in preparing, which is fomented by party spirit and religious animosity, can be speedily put down. The struggle will be violent and bloody, and will shake the connection between the two countries.'[1] Camden thought the Ministry infatuated. The Ministry knew by this time the extent of the danger, but they were in greater difficulties than Camden was aware of. The Irish Protestants since '82 had not deserved the confidence of England, and they did not possess it. O'Connor's acquittal had created an impression in England that the story of the conspiracy was untrue.

---

[1] 'Camden to Portland, June 9.' S. P. O.

The impression which prevailed on the state of Ireland was that a bitterly wronged peasantry had attempted by constitutional means to rescue themselves from their oppressors. In return they had been lashed, pitch-capped, tortured, till they had been driven into arms to protect themselves from atrocious tyranny, and England was now called on to send troops and shoot down those who resisted, and restore the rest to their taskmasters. Every charge against the Protestant Yeomanry received ready credit; every cruel act which was really committed, and a hundred others which were never committed, were trumpeted abroad till nothing else could be heard. The Protestant gentry were doubtless not innocent. They had been careless and dissipated as landlords. They had behaved in Parliament like an assembly of idiots. England, too, had her share of guilt for the condition to which Ireland had fallen, though in her impatience it pleased her not to remember it. She saw the faults of the Protestant gentry: she forgot her own.

Nor could the English mind comprehend how a Jacobin conspiracy could have converted itself into a Popish insurrection. Protestant bigotry might please to call the rebellion Catholic. So far as it was real, it originated in an attempt to assert the great principles of the sovereignty of the people. If the means were too violent, the object was laudable. The great Whig statesmen had for years described the disorders of Ireland as the aggravated results of despotism. In consequence every difficulty was thrown in the way of sending assistance to Camden. The Cabinet might know that Camden was right, but they were still unable to produce evidence which would convince the world, and the world remained stubbornly incredulous.

'I do not wonder,' wrote Wickham to Edward Cooke, on the 1st of July, 'that the indignation you speak of in Dublin should have increased and be increasing. The conduct of certain individuals on this occasion[1] is most extraordinary and unaccountable. They will live to be sorry for what they have done.'[2]

Every day was bringing to the private knowledge of the Cabinet how widely the mischief had spread, as the correspondence which continued with Lord Downshire's friend added to the list of accomplices. Lord Cloncurry's son was no sooner arrested than Stewart of Acton, a young Agar, a young Tranent, young Curran, McGuchin, Dowdall, and twenty others whose names never came before the public, were found to be as deeply compromised as he.

'We know by our private accounts,' said Portland, 'that all these persons are more or less implicated. There are papers found in Mr. Lawless's possession that tend directly to show his connection with some of the most desperate of the Republican party in England, as well as with those who are in habitual communication with the French agents at Hamburgh;' 'and yet,' he continued, 'under present circumstances, and with evidence of the nature of that of which the Government here is in possession, strong and decisive as it is, none of these persons can be brought to trial *without exposing secrets of the last importance to the State, the revealing of which may implicate the safety of the two kingdoms.*'[3]

Meanwhile the explanation of the difficulties of the

---

[1] He was perhaps referring to Abercrombie, who had told Portland, after his return to England, that there was no occasion to send more troops to Ireland.
[2] *Irish MSS.* S. P. O.
[3] 'Portland to Camden, June 8.' S. P. O.

Government did not help Camden. The check at Ross had for the present saved Waterford and Kilkenny. Colonel L'Estrange had blocked the road into Kildare, but Arklow was ungarrisoned ; on that side the approaches to Dublin were uncovered ; and if Father John reached Bray with as large a force as he promised, it was quite certain that a bloody and desperate insurrection would break out in Dublin itself.

At all hazards it was necessary to defend the passage at Arklow. The handful of men who were left there when Loftus advanced had retired, with a crowd of Gorey Protestants, to Wicklow. Major Hardy, who was in command in Wicklow, sent them back to their post, without so much as allowing them to rest and eat. The Dublin loyalists raised four thousand additional Yeomanry among themselves, that the rest of the troops might be made available. General Needham reached Arklow on the 6th of June, with a regiment of Cavan Militia. He gathered up the wreck of Walpole's men, which were drifting about unowned, reorganised the rest of the garrison, and armed a few additional volunteers and Yeomen. With all Needham's efforts, however, the force in Arklow remained inferior to that which had so hardly defended New Ross; while Father John's rebel division was equal, if not superior, to that under Bagenal Harvey and Father Roche, and Father John had as yet succeeded in all that he had tried. Had he come on to Arklow at once, with as much promptitude as he had shown at Enniscorthy and Wexford, he would easily have overwhelmed Needham. Happily, he lingered on the road, burning Protestants' houses; and at midnight, between the 8th and 9th of June, three hundred men belonging to the Durham Fencibles arrived under Colonel Skerritt. The Durham was the most distinguished regiment in Ireland. When it was called out of Ulster for service in Wexford the rebels were so conscious of its value that they placed an ambush of 7,000 men at Balbriggan, in Meath, to intercept and destroy it. Skerritt brought his men safely through. They reached Dublin on the 8th, and were dispatched to Arklow at once on jaunting-cars, carts, and carriages, to gain time and bring them fresh to the scene.

With the addition of the Durham, Needham's force was raised to 1,600 men; of these a hundred and twenty were the survivors of Sir Watkin Wynn's Ancient Britons; the rest consisted of eight hundred Irish Militiamen, three hundred Arklow Yeomanry, a hundred Scotch regulars, and the Durham.

Arklow stands at the mouth of the Avoca, which runs down out of the Wicklow hills and there falls into the sea. At Arklow the river is crossed by a bridge, over which passed the only road available for a large body of men from Wexford into Wicklow county.

The Avoca was fordable higher up, but the tracks were bad, the hills steep, the route in that direction practically impossible. Over Arklow bridge lay Father John's way, if he meant to reach Dublin. He had loitered about Carnew, and it was not till the morning of the 9th that he again set out in earnest. Strategy would have suggested the dispatch of a certain number of men by the mountain-road to turn Needham's position, while he himself attacked in front. Hitherto Father John had been skilful with operations of this kind; but he was confident in his numbers. Success, perhaps, persuaded him that in a holy war the supernatural powers were on his side. He believed that he had a charmed life, and the extraordinary career of a Catholic curate starting up suddenly as the general of a victorious army had intoxicated him. According to the moderate estimate of Mr. Gordon he had twenty-seven thousand men with him (Musgrave says thirty-one thousand). Of these five thousand had muskets and fowling-pieces. He had the guns which he took at Three Rocks, and the artillerymen whom he had saved to serve them. His huge masses had already shown that, under the double inspiration of religion and patriotism, they were more than an armed mob, and had taught experienced officers to respect their resolution.

They approached Arklow on the afternoon of the 9th of June. They formed at the outskirts, in three large columns, each company with its own green flag, with the harp in the centre. The right wing advanced along the shore road, which enters the town by the sands at the mouth of the river. The left swung round upon the road from Gorey, which, striking the Avoca above the town, passes through the middle of it to the bridge. The centre poured down into the gardens, fields, and wooded enclosures which cover the slope at the back of the houses between the two roads, the whole body thus forming one vast semicircle.

So earnest were the rebels in their religious observances that they had halted at every mile of their march to hear mass. It was five in the afternoon before scouts brought word that they were coming on in earnest. But at midsummer there were still five hours of daylight, and on the use made of those hours depended the present fate of Dublin.

Needham's position was simple. Skerritt and the Durhams, with a party of Antrim Militia, under Colonel O'Hara, and three six-pounders, held the Gorey road. A barricade of carts and cars had been extemporised in the street, and the men were thrown out on either side of it, sheltered among the hedges and cabins. The Yeomanry and remaining militia were divided. Two companies, with another gun, covered the back of the town. The rest, with a fifth gun, were posted at the angle between the bridge and the sea. A squadron of dragoons was across the bridge, out of shot-range, on the Wicklow side of the river, to be used as occasion might serve. The fight began on the sea side. The right column of the rebels came plunging along the sands; the green banners waving, the priests with pistols and crucifixes; the Irish cry rising and falling in fitful cadences like the swell and scream of an Æolian harp. They had no cattle with them, but trusted to their own courage ; and, as at Ross, with their first rush they drove the soldiers back. They fired a row of fishermen's cabins at the end of the street. A piquet of Ancient Britons had to gallop through the flames in retreating; and, unable to reach the bridge, swam their horses through the river. The road turns at a right angle as it reaches the town. As the rebels rounded the corner they were received with a fire, which staggered them and drove them back. They formed again and again. They fought their way desperately to the bridge-foot, recoiled, and again advanced, but could never pass that point. On their last retreat the dragoons were let loose on them, and cut them down as they scattered among the sand hills.

The attack on the Gorey road was more determined, and the fighting far more severe. Father Michael Murphy and his brother priests here distinguished themselves. Political lay conspirators in Ireland have been magnificent on the platform, but have been uniformly found wanting in the field. The courage of their opinions was in the Catholic peasantry, and their natural chiefs the clergy. The battery behind the barricade completely swept the road. Twice the priests led on their followers, over the bodies of their falling comrades, through musket-shot and round-shot and grape, to the very mouths of the guns, the priests coming so close that they shot the gunners at their posts with their pistols. Twice they failed; the second time with such desperate loss, that they wavered and sought shelter among the walls. Father Michael seized a standard with a blazoned cross upon it and a motto of 'Liberty or death.' Conspicuous on horseback, he dashed out amidst the shot, and dragged from his pocket a handful of balls which he swore that he had caught as they reached him. 'Come on, boys,' he cried, ' the heretic bullets can never hurt you. You are fighting for your God and Holy Church.'

A third time they charged till they again touched the barricade. With a contempt of death which was really admirable, they seemed determined to take the guns, though every other man might fall in doing it, when a round-shot, against which Father Michael's spells could not avail, caught him and his horse and hurled them into ruin. Sullenly and slowly the rebels then drew back, leaving the ground covered with their dead. Even yet they might have tried once more; but it grew dark, and night rather than defeat ended an engagement more desperate than even the battle of New Ross.

SECTION VIII.

NEEDHAM reported that he had held his ground. He could say no more; and he added that he expected to be attacked again with thrice the number of assailants.[1] At the same moment Camden learnt that the blow which he most feared had fallen, and that the North was in arms. The insurrection in Ulster was in fact confined to the heated centres of philosophical republicanism, where the united Irish spirit had been grafted on the discontent generated by landlord evictions and the long injustice to the Presbyterians. That it would be limited to this area Camden could not possibly foresee. In the eyes of the Established Church, Dissenters still remained the enemy which Ireland had most cause to fear; and the absurd prejudice which might have gone far to realise the Churchmen's alarms, had the Catholics been more prudent in concealing their real purpose, still powerfully influenced the atmosphere of Dublin Castle. A meeting of magistrates was called at Antrim, on the 7th of June, to devise measures for the security of the county. The United Irish Committee saw an opportunity of destroying the leading country gentlemen at a single blow, and, under the impulse of Samuel Orr, the brother of Orr who had been hanged, concluded that Antrim should rise when the magistrates were in session there.

The plot was formed, and was executed. Lord

---

[1] 'General Needham to General Lake, June 10.' S. P. O.

O'Neil, who had made himself peculiarly hated by the Jacobin zealots, was killed, and a squadron of dragoons was almost annihilated. But there the success ended. Another regiment which had been sent for arrived opportunely, and the Antrim insurrection was quelled at its first appearance.

The example spread. On Thursday, the 10th, a party of rebels attacked and carried Newtown Ardes. Colonel Stapleton was driven out with severe loss, and was obliged to take refuge in Belfast.[1] The detached companies which lay in exposed situations were called in and concentrated. The utmost hope of General Nugent, whom Lake had left in command, was to confine the movement to the two counties of Antrim and Down.

General Nugent was agreeably disappointed. The massacre at Scullabogue was worth fifty regiments for the pacification of Ulster. It was not for an Irish nationality headed by the priests, for another 1641, for a war of creeds and races in which the Catholics of the South were to pike and shoot and burn till every Protestant had been destroyed out of the land, that the Presbyterians of the North had joined in a conspiracy for Irish independence. Thousands who had hung back and hesitated now joined the Orange ranks. Thousands followed of those who had quaffed toasts to the heroes of the Bastille at the revolutionary banquets of Belfast. Rebellion in Ulster drifted away to its special home and nursery—the estate of Lord Moira at Ballinahinch. Distrust spread among the remaining adherents of the cause. Two thousand

---

[1] 'Colonel Stapleton's loss has been very severe. Many officers and men killed and wounded.'— 'General Nugent to General Lake, June 10.' S. P. O.

Catholics discovered the companionship of heretics to be sacrilege, and deserted, and the remnant of the once so dangerous Jacobin combination fought and lost their last battle in Lord Moira's park, on the 13th. Five hundred insurgents were killed, and the Presbyterians of Ulster, whose wrongs at bottom were more cruel than those of any other section of the Irish nation, fell back into the place which befitted the descendants of the defenders of Derry, the worst rewarded but the most loyal to the connection between the two islands of all branches of the Irish community.

This happy consequence could not have been anticipated when Lord Nugent reported the loss of Newtown Ardes, and Lord Camden felt deeply indignant at the want of support from England. The Irish Protestant gentry were suspected of desiring to exterminate the Catholics. Innocent before the agitation for Emancipation commenced of the faintest emotion of animosity against them, the Irish gentry were being fast taught that in extermination lay their only hope of preserving their own lives. On them, so long as the Presbyterians held aloof, the weight had fallen of encountering the rebellion. They were called on to defend Ireland. They were doing their duty gallantly, and were abused and maligned for doing it. Well-intending, but with a profound ignorance of the nature of the Irish people, Mr. Pitt and Dundas had excited hopes which they were unable to realise. The Catholics had seen their expected ascendency taken from them when it was almost their own. In revenge they had conspired an insurrection which was following step for step the pattern of 1641. The Irish gentry, after

CHAP. I.

1798.
June 13.

braving assassination for seven years, were now set upon with the ferocious instincts of Phelim O'Neil and Roger Moore. They forgot the share of their own foolish Parliament in provoking the crisis. They saw only that England was the immediate cause of it, and that England was now leaving them to defend themselves and their families from murder, and to preserve Ireland to the British connection.

The war was in consequence becoming savage. When a small minority are contending with the overwhelming numbers of an enemy which is aiming at their annihilation, war is always savage. A hundred men fighting against a thousand cannot afford to make prisoners. Those who find no quarter give no quarter. The Irish Yeomanry were accused of confounding the innocent with the guilty. When the innocent will take no part against the guilty, when eyewitnesses will give no evidence against murderers, when juries will not convict, when an entire population—to the very groom and valet of the magistrate who is marked for assassination—are in league either to assist at his death or to conceal the actors in it, at such a time it is impossible that the gradations of crime should be accurately measured by men so harassed, so excited, so cruelly judged, so unjustly dealt with, and that severity should never be in excess.

After hearing of the loss of Newtown Ardes, Camden felt that unless the state of Ireland was to become a disgrace to the civilised world the Cabinet must be compelled to exert themselves. He sent over his private secretary, Mr. Elliott, to explain the circumstances of a situation which might resolve itself any day into some appalling catastrophe. A letter of which Elliott was the bearer shows how honourably and how profoundly Camden felt his own responsibilities:

'Unless a fresh force is sent immediately you may be assured the country will be lost, and will not be gained again to his Majesty's Crown except by a re-conquest. I cannot conceive from what circumstances his Majesty's Ministers can have imagined that this rebellion can be easily crushed. Mr. Elliott will communicate to you the religious frenzy which agitates the rebels in Wexford: that they are headed by their priests, that they halt every half-mile to pray, that they are taught to consider that they are fighting for their religion, that their enthusiasm is most alarming. He will inform your Grace how violently agitated Protestant feeling is in Ireland at this moment, and with how rapid strides the war is becoming one of the most cruel and bloody that has ever disgraced or been imposed upon a country. He will explain to your Grace how impolitic and unwise it would be to refuse the offer of Protestants to enter into Yeomanry and other corps, and yet how dangerous any encouragement to the Orange spirit is while the army is composed of Catholics, as the militia almost generally is. Neither present and most imminent danger, nor further embarrassment, can be removed but by an immediate landing of very large bodies of troops from England. Every portion of the kingdom is infected with the poison of disaffection. If the rebels, assisted by the French, possess themselves of it, the immediate danger to England will be obvious. The rebel force at Wexford is too strong to be attacked at present. The North has risen. Dublin is in immediate danger of insurrection, and the troops cannot be moved.'[1]

Equally interesting and equally instructive is a letter from Lord Castlereagh to Mr. Wickham, written on the following day. The Cabinet had not waited for Elliott, and had roused themselves at last. The mail, on the evening of the 11th, brought word that

[1] 'Camden to Portland, June 11. Abridged.' S. P. O.

the Guards were on their way, and that other regiments were preparing to follow.

'The intelligence,' Castlereagh said, 'is most welcome. It is of importance that the authority of England should decide this contest, as well with a view to British influence in Ireland as to make it unnecessary for the Government to lend itself too much to a party in this country—a party highly exasperated by the religious persecution to which the Protestants in Wexford have been exposed. In that county it is perfectly a religious frenzy. The priests lead the rebels to battle. As they march they kneel and pray, and show the most desperate resolution in their attacks. The enclosed certificate is curious,[1] as marking the complexion of the rebellion in that quarter. They put such Protestants as are reported to be Orangemen to death, saving others on condition of their embracing the Catholic faith. It is a Jacobinical conspiracy throughout the country, pursuing its objects with Popish instruments, the heated bigotry of their sect being better suited to the purpose of the Republican leaders than the cold reasoning disaffection of the Northern Presbyterians. The number of the insurgents is immense—so great as to make it prudent to assemble in very considerable force before an attempt is made to penetrate that very difficult and enclosed county. The conduct of the militia and Yeomanry has exceeded our most sanguine expectations. A very few of the Yeomanry have been corrupted, but in no instance have the militia failed to show the most determined spirit.'[2]

---

[1] 'I recommend to your protection, for Christ's sake, the bearer hereof, who has voluntarily embraced the Roman Catholic religion, and received the sacraments thereof, who is no Orangeman.—Lachen, June 1.
'RAYMOND ROCHE, P.P.'

[2] 'Castlereagh to Wickham, June 12. Abridged.' S. P. O.

SECTION IX.

SOME days had yet to elapse before the troops could arrive, and the Protestants of Wexford were meanwhile at the mercy of the insurgents. The reverse at New Ross put an end to the good humour which at first had prevailed in the city. Scenes of blood now became frequent. Each day bands of rebels paraded the streets with drums and bagpipes, recovering heretics to the faith, and piking and shooting those who refused to be converted; Protestant prisoners being told off to be the executioners of their fellows, as a preparation for their own deaths. The desire to convert was perfectly sincere—no less determined the resolution to punish the obstinate unbelievers. The Catholic clergy in the town did not encourage ferocity; the Catholic bishop, so far as was consistent with his own security, opposed the bloody method of working conviction. One priest, in a scene to be presently described, succeeded in preventing murder by risking boldly his own life. What one could do others might have done, had they been equally brave, and the reproach cast upon their order by the doings of Father John and his companions might have been redeemed or washed away. It was, perhaps, too much to expect. The bishops and clergy of the Catholic Church would have been more than mortal had they not desired the success of a rebellion which would have restored Ireland to the faith, and they did not care to come to an open

CHAP. I.

1798. June 12.

rupture with men whose fault was but excess of zeal. When the penitents were brought to their chapels they received them with enthusiasm, exhibited them to their congregations in triumph, and exulted from their pulpits over the victory of truth. The 3rd of June was Trinity Sunday. Father Roche, the bishop's chaplain, preached on the enormity of heresy. On the 10th the same reverend gentleman dilated on the penal laws. He condemned the murder of their oppressors, but he exhorted his hearers to be bold in the field of battle, as became the soldiers of Christ. The rebels took such part of his advice as pleased them, and forgot the rest. Keogh, whom they had made governor, was powerless. He was a Protestant, and himself in hourly danger. The hero of the hour in Wexford was Dixon, the shipowner, who had brought back the escaping heretics. Another prisoner had been since captured of unexpected consequence. Lord Kingsborough, Earl of Kingston afterwards, was colonel of the North Cork Militia. He was in Dublin when the insurrection broke out, and he hurried off to join his regiment. Finding when he arrived at Arklow that he could not approach Wexford by land, he took a boat, with two of his officers, and went down the coast to enter from the sea. The town had risen meanwhile. Lord Kingsborough was taken at the mouth of the river, and was detained for the present as a hostage should fortune turn.

It was at Vinegar Hill that 'Irish ideas' were to be seen completely in the ascendant. There, although converts were made, it was not always to save life in this world. To be a Protestant was to be an Orangeman. To be an Orangeman was to be an enemy of Ireland. The day after the battle of New Ross a batch of prisoners was carried out from Wexford Gaol to Vinegar Hill, and piked in front of the windmill. Day by day other gangs of victims were dragged out of their hiding-places in the neighbourhood, carried before the permanent tribunal, and by them handed over to the pikemen. From the 29th of May and onwards these bloody scenes continued without intermittence. Every day saw its allotment of prisoners before the judges. Every day saw its half-dozen or dozen of them delivered over to the assassins who sprinkled with holy water executed the sentence on the enemies of Ireland and the Church. One poor wretch who was piked imperfectly, survived to describe the scene. He was brought out with thirteen others after half-an-hour's confinement in the windmill. He was asked in what religion he would die. He said he would die a Protestant, as he was born. 'You bloody Orange thief,' said one of the executioners, 'you are damned, and will go to hell when we put the life out of you.' He was stabbed in the body and the neck, his clothes were torn from him, and he lay in a pile of bleeding bodies till consciousness returned, when he contrived to crawl into a ditch, where he lay till dusk, and then escaped.[1]

Father John, while he remained on the hill, had his intervals of compunction. After a scene of this kind he called some of the prisoners not yet condemned before him to harangue them into penitence. 'You sons of Belial,' he said, cracking his fingers at them, 'will you withstand our holy religion, which existed eight hundred years before yours began?'

[1] *Musgrave*, Appendix, xix.

'You see how our pikemen will treat you, unless there is great reformation in you.'[1]

'This is the handiwork of God,' said a Catholic of Enniscorthy, attempting to console the wife of a Protestant clergyman whose husband had been murdered. 'There must be but one religion on the face of the earth. Father John catches red-hot bullets in his hand.' A rebel named Beaghan, who was one of the executioners on Vinegar Hill, and was executed a year later, on the scene of his crimes, declared that what he had done had been by order of his superiors. He said that before the rebellion Catholics and Protestants had lived peaceably together, and for himself he had always found the Protestants better masters and more indulgent landlords than those of his own religion. But after the insurrection broke out every Protestant was called an Orangeman, and every one of them was to be killed, to the poorest man in the country.' Even when the people were put down he declared that he never heard one of them express sorrow for what they had done. If they were sorry at all, it was because when the power was in their hands they had not made cleaner work. 'Remember what I tell you,' he said, as his last word before he was hanged. 'If you Protestants are ever in the power of the Catholics again, as they are now in yours, they will not leave any of you alive. Even those who campaigned with them, if things had gone well, would in the end have been killed. I have heard them say so many times.'[2]

Thus through the first weeks of June, the rebels

---

[1] 'Deposition of Richard Sterne.' —*Musgrave*, Appendix, xix.

[2] 'Confession of James Beaghan, executed on Vinegar Hill, August 24, 1799.'— *Musgrave*, Appendix, xix. 8.

after their manner were fighting the battle of Christ. To have killed three Protestants was counted a passport into heaven. One day after an execution there was a thunderstorm; and a humorous spectator observed that 'God was sounding his horn because an Orangeman was killed.' The victims were generally men, but wives were allowed to support their husbands at their death, and more than one poor woman went mad at what she had witnessed.[1]

All things have their appointed times, and so had the horrors of Vinegar Hill. For a hundred years the English and Irish Protestants had been affecting to govern Ireland. They had not governed Ireland. They had left it to ignorance and misery. The funds which should have provided schools had been squandered on royal mistresses and bastards. The Church had been sacrificed to political corruption. The Calvinist colonies of the South had dwindled and disappeared for want of teachers. The Presbyterians and Wesleyans, who would have supplied them with ministers, had been frowned on by the gentry and

---

[1] Women were sometimes killed by their own sex. A Protestant, named Joseph Dale, lived with his wife in the town of Kildare. On the rebellion breaking out there, on the 24th of May, Patrick Dowling, the insurgent leader, sent for Dale, and told him that he and his wife should die unless they went with the people. Dale was frightened, joined Dowling's band, and marched to Athy. As soon as he was gone, Mary Dowling, Patrick's wife, gathered the women of the place about her, and proposed 'to go and kill Catherine Dale, the Orange whore.' Two of her daughters, another woman, named Elizabeth Byrne, James Byrne, Elizabeth's son, a lad of sixteen, and some other boys, went off to Dale's house. They found the poor woman with a Prayer-book in her hand. They knocked her down with the handle of a churn. Elizabeth Byrne dragged her out into the road. The women collected pebbles in their aprons, and the boys stoned her to death. These women were tried and convicted at the Spring Assizes at Naas, 1801. Two of the boys gave evidence; and being asked by the Judge why they had joined in the murder, answered quietly, 'Because she was a Protestant.'

persecuted by the Bishops, and now the bill was presented for payment, and the debt had to be washed out in the blood of innocents. For three weeks the murdering continued, and then deliverance came. The Guards arrived in the middle of June, and Lake found himself able to advance without risk of further failure. A combined movement was again arranged. Additional troops were sent to Dundas, at Naas; to Needham, at Arklow; to Johnstone, at New Ross; to Loftus, at Carlow, to which he had retired. On the 16th of June Dundas was ordered to cross the Slaney at Tullow and advance to Carnew, where on the 18th he was to be joined by Loftus. On the 19th, at three in the morning, Needham was directed to push forward from Arklow to Gorey, when he would be on a level with Dundas and Loftus. On the same 19th the orders to Johnstone were to drive the rebels in from Carrickbyrne, sending parties out north to see that none of them doubled back between New Ross and Carnew. These officers would thus be moving in from different points in a circle of which Vinegar Hill was the centre. To prevent an escape south into Waterford, General Moore was directed at the same time to advance from Duncannon, cross Waterford Harbour at Ballyhack Passage, and proceed thence along the Wexford road as far as Foulk's Mill, at the back of Forth Mountain. Father John had returned, after the defeat at Arklow, to Vinegar Hill. The rebel force was between Carrickbyrne, Vinegar Hill, and Three Rocks. Moore would hold the road to Waterford; Johnstone the road to Kilkenny; Loftus, Dundas, and Needham the roads into Carlow and Wicklow. Wexford Harbour was blockaded, and escape by sea was impossible. The five columns gradually converging, would force the rebels into a mass, and thus it might be hoped extinguish them.

The orders were executed without mistake and without resistance. Lake himself accompanied Dundas as Commander-in-Chief, the entire force at his disposition amounting to 13,000 men. On the 20th the circle was to be contracted further. Dundas and Lake were to descend on both sides of the Slaney to a point three miles above Enniscorthy, Loftus to make for the same point from Carnew. Needham was to advance to Oulart, Johnstone to Ballymackerey, half-way between Enniscorthy and Carrickbyrne, and Moore to Taghmon. Vinegar Hill could then be attacked on three sides at daybreak on the 21st. The Wexford road only would be left open for the rebels' retreat, and at Wexford they would be surrounded, and must surrender at discretion.

The insurgent chiefs had misinterpreted the inaction of the Government. The failure of the first attempt to penetrate the county had persuaded them that at home they were irresistible, and they were almost surrounded before they were aware of their danger. Johnstone's advance on Carrickbyrne first opened their eyes. The last hope for them was to stop Moore, sweep round from Three Rocks in Johnstone's rear, and seize New Ross in his absence. On the 19th of June, when Johnstone's column was seen approaching Carrickbyrne, Father Roche mounted his horse and rode at full speed to Wexford. He called on every man who could handle a pike to follow him, and with the force at Three Rocks marched through the night to look for Moore. He fell in with him on the afternoon of the 20th, as he was coming out of Foulk's Mill. Father Roche's men fought gallantly, and with real discipline and skill. They displayed in excess the same singular religious passion which had throughout distinguished the movement. They knelt so often in the action to pray, that even the priests at last swore at them and used their horsewhips. It was not cowardice, however, but the profound superstition which is the master-spirit of the Irish peasant's heart, and is the source alike of his crimes and his virtues. The rebels behaved none the worse for their prayers, nor for the prayers of the thousands of old men and women who on their knees along the roads and in the village streets were entreating the Virgin Mary to help them. At one time they had almost gained the day. They gave way only at eight in the evening, when their powder failed them. They had then inflicted more loss than they had sustained, and they fell back to Three Rocks in good order. Moore had fought the battle with but a part of his force. The remaining division coming up after the action, he pushed on at once to Taghmon, where he learnt news which led him to press forward to Wexford without waiting for further instructions.

It would have been well for the Catholic cause had Father Roche succeeded in carrying the town rabble with him, as he had intended. A few only obeyed the call. Dixon and the crew of scoundrels who followed him hung back and kept out of sight. They had other work in view. The news that the army was advancing had made them savage, like wolves at bay. On the same 20th of June, when Lake was coming down the Slaney, and Roche was engaged with Moore at Foulk's Mill, a column of pikemen crossed Wexford Bridge into the town, carrying a black banner, with a red cross upon it, which they planted on the Custom-

House Quay. Drink was there served out to them, and the cry was then 'To the gaol!' where three hundred Protestant prisoners had been lying for three weeks. A court of justice was extemporised in a public billiard-room, where Dixon, the shipowner, presided. The prisoners were brought one by one before him. Only a single question was asked—Could it be shown that any one act, which in the estimation of the court could be called good, had been done by the person at the bar? If no witness came forward the sentence was immediate death. The prisoner was passed over to the rebels outside, and surrounded by a yelling mob, in which there were more women than men, he was led out upon the bridge. There, stripped naked, he was placed on his knees in the middle of the road. Two pikemen stood in front of him and two behind. They knelt, said a prayer, then levelling their pikes, rose and ran upon him, held him aloft for a moment writhing on their points, and pitched him over the parapet into the stream. In this way through that midsummer-day ninety-seven men, whose crime was to be of the Protestant religion—country gentlemen, magistrates, tradesmen, merchants, clergymen—were ceremoniously and deliberately murdered. During the afternoon Dixon, weary of his functions in the billiard-room, left the judicial work to others, and sate on horseback with his wife watching the executions. The day wore on. At seven in the evening a fresh batch of victims had been brought out, and were in position waiting their turn for death, when Father Corrin, a Catholic priest, but none the less a noble-minded man, threw himself in the way of the murderers, denounced their infernal work, and insisted that it should end. Throughout the day the Catholic clergy had been invisible. Dr. Caulfield, the Bishop, declared afterwards that he was ignorant of what was going forward till it was over. If the Bishop was ignorant, other priests must have been too well informed; yet none of them interfered but Father Corrin, and he, perhaps, would have failed and been thrust aside. But at that instant an express came in to say that the battle was going ill at Foulk's Mill, that Vinegar Hill was beset, and that every man who was able to fight was needed in the field. Panic-struck, the mob scattered to their dens, as if they already saw the bayonets of the avengers. The prisoners on the bridge, who had taken leave of life, remained on their knees, unconscious of what was passing round them. The guard by-and-bye returned and carried them back to gaol, telling them that they were respited for the night; the next day neither man, woman, nor child among the Protestants should be spared.[1]

As night fell the town began to fill with fugitives from Foulk's Mill, who brought word that Moore was behind them. Just a hundred and fifty years before Wexford had witnessed a too similar scene. Then, as now, a hulk in the river had been converted into a prison for heretics. The hulk had been scuttled without the ceremony of a trial, and all its inmates had perished. In recompense for that deed Cromwell had stormed over the walls of the guilty city, and every rebel found in arms had been put to the sword. General Moore, when he heard of that day's work on the bridge, might prove a second Oliver. Not an instant was to be lost. Lord Kingsborough

---

[1] Narrative of one of the prisoners, named Jackson, quoted by *Musgrave*, vol. ii. p. 24.

was taken from the room where he had been confined and made governor of the town. The bloody wretches gathered at his feet and implored him to save them from the doom which they had provoked. Two emissaries were sent at daybreak to Needham, at Oulart, with a promise of surrender, if their lives and properties might be secured; and the leaders in the town undertook to use their influence to persuade the rebels in the country to submit. Lord Kingsborough added a letter, which he could not refuse to write, though he must have known that it could not be listened to, expressing a hope that, for the sake of the surviving prisoners, who were very numerous 'and of the first respectability,' the offer of the townsmen might be accepted.

SECTION X.

So passed the night of the 20th of June in Wexford. General Lake, meanwhile, had completed his last dispositions, and Vinegar Hill was to be stormed at daybreak. It was creditable to the skill and spirit of the Irish that preparations so elaborate had been found necessary. The rebels of '98 were at least in earnest. They did not, like their degenerate modern representatives, dissolve like a mist at the touch of the policeman's staff. The different divisions arrived duly at their allotted stations. Dundas and Loftus lay that evening at Solsborough, on the Slaney, two miles above Enniscorthy. Needham had reached Oulart Hill. Johnstone was on Ballymakessy Bridge. At dawn they severally advanced; and if the professed design had been carried out, Needham would have occupied the road to Wexford, and the net would have been closed on every side. From an unexplained cause the orders of the day in this one direction were not carried out, and one opening, called afterwards Needham's Gap, was left. It was whispered afterwards that the mistake was intentional, lest too terrible a vengeance might fall on the wretched beings who had been guilty of crimes so atrocious. If this was the reason, it was misplaced leniency. Nothing but some decisive and overwhelming evidence of the consequences of a rebellion carried out in the spirit which had been shown in Wexford would ever convince the Irish of the hopelessness of measuring strength with England, or prevent a repetition of the same folly when opportunity seemed again to offer itself. Never had the villanous elements of the Irish population gathered themselves into form with more deliberation, or could have been taken at a time when the nature of their crimes would have made acknowledgment of sympathy with them impossible. Justice would, in the long run, have been found equivalent to mercy, and a stern example made them on Vinegar Hill might have spared Ireland the scenes of barbarity which for two years continued to disgrace her population, and might have extinguished possibly for centuries or for ever the infatuated dreams of an impossible independence which still work like poison in her veins. Subordinate officers, however, cannot be expected to discharge duties as painful as they are serious and stern when they are uncertain of support from authority. General Lake was well aware of the irresolution of the Cabinet, and, with the natural humanity of a brave man, he was perhaps glad to be spared the necessity of adding fresh horrors to a war already savage beyond modern experience.

At sunrise on the 21st the columns closed in upon the Irish camp. Dundas's and Loftus's divisions came down the east bank of the Slaney, spread over a front of almost a mile, and as they approached the hill formed round it at various points from the north to the south-east. Johnstone came up simultaneously from Ballymakessy. The rebels held Enniscorthy in force, and Johnstone's duty was to drive them out and take possession of the bridge before the general attack commenced. A second time within three weeks the little town of Enniscorthy became the scene of a desperate and bloody engagement. Only after two hours of severe fighting, Enniscorthy was taken, the bridge secured, and the rebel garrison forced back over it to their friends on the hill. It was now seven in the morning. The rebel army, sixteen thousand strong, was drawn up on the open ground on the brow. Their guns, thirteen in all, of various sorts and calibre, were at the windmill. General Lake, with Dundas, attacked on the east side; Sir James Duff, with part of Loftus's division, on the north-west, from the bank of the river; Loftus himself was between them. On these three sides they forced their way simultaneously up the slope. The rebels held their ground for an hour and a half with moderate firmness. Lake's horse was killed under him early in the action. Father Clinch, of Enniscorthy, an enormous man, on a tall white horse, specially distinguished himself. But successive defeats had cooled the courage which had been so eminent at Arklow and New Ross. There was no longer the contempt of death which will make even the least disciplined enemy formidable. Lord Roden singled out Father Clinch and killed him. The rebels were afraid of being surrounded; and seeing the southern side of the hill still open, they fled down it, and escaped through Needham's gap to Wexford, from the scene of their brief and wild supremacy.

The army rested for the day on the ground, burying the dead and examining, with ever-gathering indignation, the traces of the butcheries which had been perpetrated there. The rebels, with their surviving generals, Father John, once invincible, now twice beaten, and savage in his despair, John Hay, Edward Fitzgerald, and Father Kerne, streamed away down the east side of the Slaney. Some crossed the river at Carrick Ferry, three miles above Wexford; some went on to the bridge, and rushed mad and furious into the town, threatening vengeance on every Protestant still in their hands. It would have gone hard with the prisoners there; but on the other side General Moore was coming on from Taghmon. Two hours at most would bring him to the gates. Bishop Caulfield and his priests were energetic enough now to prevent a renewal of the murders. If Moore came up when such work was going forward, the town might pay for it as it paid before. They turned out into the streets, exhorting, praying, threatening, imploring the armed insurgents to leave the town while there was time, and to give no fresh provocation to the soldiers. The cause, they said, was plainly lost for the present. Lord Kingsborough had promised that life and property should be respected, if no more blood was shed. For the sake of Ireland, for the sake of their holy religion, for the sake of all they held dear in earth or heaven, they besought the rebels to spare the city the risk of being stormed and sacked by the bloody Orangemen.

Their prayers prevailed, and in prevailing left them with the less excuse for their apathy on the preceding day. Towards sunset part of the rebels filed back over the bridge out of the town. Dixon and his wife, on horseback, threw themselves in their way, praying them to stay at least till they had despatched the remaining prisoners. They were borne away in the crowd, the woman screaming, 'We shall conquer yet: my Saviour tells me we must conquer.' These wretches went north to Gorey, where they committed a frightful massacre on the unfortunate Protestant inhabitants who, imagining themselves safe in the rear of the army, had returned to their homes. Thence, breaking into smaller parties, they made for the Wicklow mountains. The rest, the remainder mainly of the army which had fought at Vinegar Hill, rallying under the indefatigable Father John, slipped away behind General Moore, who had halted two miles from the town, and made their way over the Barrow into Kilkenny, carrying havoc and destruction along with them. Moore, in the twilight, entered Wexford after they had all left it. The scene was described 'as most affecting.' 'The windows were crowded with women who had been expecting massacre.' The prisoners in the gaol heard, in the noise of the approaching troops, the summons as they supposed to death upon the bridge. When the door was thrown open they saw the King's uniform, and knew that they were saved.

At three o'clock the following morning (June 22nd) the trumpet sounded in Lake's camp on Vinegar Hill. Before the army began its march for Wexford, Edward Hay[1] and Captain Macmanus, the bearers of the proposals of the townsmen to submit on conditions, were brought into Lake's presence. They had failed to find Needham, to whom they were commissioned. They had gone on to Enniscorthy, and were carried before the Commander-in-Chief. It was not then known that Moore was in the town. They delivered their message. Lake replied briefly that he would make no terms with rebels in arms against their Sovereign. He required instant and unconditional surrender. If

---

[1] The historian of the Rebellion.

they hesitated, he said. he would use the force entrusted to him with the utmost energy for their destruction; and the utmost which he held out in the way of hope was, that he would spare the ignorant masses if they would give up their leaders and their weapons and return to their allegiance.

Mr. Hay, unconscious of a difference between honourable enemies and murdering rebels, and considering that both were equally entitled to the courtesies of war, pleaded the promise of Lord Kingsborough. Kingsborough, if he had given a promise, had exceeded his powers, and Lake refused to be bound by it. He marched at once to Wexford, entered it, reestablished authority, and proceeded to the hard but necessary duty of searching for and punishing those on whom rested the chief responsibility for the crimes of the past month. Father Roche, who had commanded at Foulk's Mill, had remained in the town, on the faith, it is pretended, of the conditions of surrender. Father Roche could not have been ignorant that a person in the position of Lord Kingsborough could grant no conditions. Had Lord Kingsborough possessed sufficient authority, there would have been no occasion to send a deputation to General Lake. Father Roche was taken, tried by court-martial, and hanged at the scene of the massacre on the bridge. John Hay, Father John's brother general on Vinegar Hill, was hanged beside him. Special care was taken to make no distinctions on the score of religion. The Protestants concerned in the rebellion, though guiltless of a share in the murders, were more criminal in principle. Cornelius Grogan had an estate worth ten thousand pounds a year. He had misjudged events, and had joined the insurgents to save it. He was found at his own house, brought in, tried by the same tribunal, and hanged also.

Bagenal Harvey and Colclough had disappeared. They had gone off in a boat to the larger of the Saltee Islands,[1] Grogan's property, which Colclough rented of him, and they hoped to lie concealed there till the storm was over. Some one betrayed their secret; and on the 23rd of June Captain Willoughby was sent in the 'Rutland' cutter to find them and bring them back. There was but one house in the island, and there were unmistakable signs of their recent presence, in the sheets upon the bed and the clothes which were lying about the room. The cabin was searched; the island was searched. They were not to be found. A boat had been seen stealing away when the cutter was approaching, and it was thought that they had escaped. As a last chance the cutter's gig was rowed round the island under the cliffs. One of the crew, watching narrowly, observed a place where the earth seemed to have been recently disturbed. They landed and discovered a cave, where the two gentlemen, with Colclough's wife, were lying concealed. They were carried back to Wexford, and sentenced to immediate death. Bagenal Harvey, Cornelius Grogan, and a wealthy citizen of Wexford, named Prendergast, were hanged on the 27th. Colclough suffered the same fate on the following day.

On the 27th General Lake put out a proclamation that, to prevent further bloodshed, every man who had been a leader in the insurrection and would give up his arms should receive a free pardon. If the offer was not accepted, and the late outrages were

---

[1] Small islands off the coast, half-way between Wexford and Waterford Harbours.

renewed or continued, every village, cottage, and farm-house found unoccupied would be destroyed, and every man found with arms in his hands would be put to the sword. The next day he returned to Dublin, where his presence was immediately required, leaving General Hunter to investigate the massacre on the bridge, and to punish as they deserved the chief actors in so horrible a crime.

The insurgents who escaped with Father John over the Barrow, after ravaging part of Kilkenny, and finding the peasants, contrary to their expectation, disinclined to join them, doubled back into Wexford, and thence into the Wicklow mountains, where, divided into roving gangs of murderous banditti, they protracted through the summer the bloody and miserable struggle. Father John, either separated from his companions by accident, or having designedly withdrawn from them, found his way in disguise to Taghmon, where he was recognised and arrested. When seized he struggled like a wild beast, but vengeance had overtaken him. After forty-five years of hitherto inoffensive life, he had become possessed with the ' Irish idea ;' and after one desperate month of murder, triumph, defeat, and ruin, he closed his career on the gallows on the 26th of June.

CHAPTER II.

LORD CORNWALLIS AND THE UNION.

SECTION I.

BOOK X.
1798.

THE delay in sending reinforcements to Ireland was due, as has been already said, to other causes than the carelessness of the Cabinet. The persevering disloyalty of the Liberal party in both Houses of the English Legislature had created a condition of public feeling which could be affected only by the publication of secrets which Pitt was forbidden to reveal.

Defeated in the Irish Parliament, Mr. Grattan, the Duke of Leinster, and the Ponsonbies had transferred their agitation to Great Britain, where they found ardent allies in the new school of politicians, who believed that the overthrow of authority was the condition of human improvement. After the reproof which he had received from Clare, Lord Moira returned to Westminster, where ignorance of Ireland procured him a more sympathising audience. In March 1797 he introduced a motion for the recall of Lord Camden, and the replacement of Fitzwilliam in the Viceroyalty. Could a glass have been held up to Moira which would have reflected his true image, he would have seen that he and Lord Fitzwilliam and their brother-absentees were the persons chiefly responsible for the condition to which Ireland was reduced. There was an ironical appropriateness in non-resident Irish proprietors putting themselves forward as the advocates of political concessions which were but spurious substitutes for measures of genuine reform. Moira insisted that Fitzwilliam must return to the Castle. Fitzwilliam himself declared that had he been allowed to carry out his policy, the Irish would have returned to their allegiance. The great English Whigs echoed the idle cry. 'Give back to the Irish,' said the Duke of Bedford, 'the man whom they admire. Act on the principles on which he acted, and discontent will cease.' 'Let the people have their rights,' said Lord Lansdowne, 'and they will require neither fleets nor armies to protect them.' 'The more Ireland is under Irish government,' said Fox, forgetting his own experience in '82, 'the more she will be bound to English interest.' The Cabinet, tied to secrecy, could give but feeble answers. The Opposition had the best of the debate, and their printed speeches were circulated throughout the two islands, addressing themselves in England to a generous people, ready to believe in freedom and to suspect authority which was compelled to be severe; persuading the Irish conspirators that their treason was undiscovered, that they had no thing to fear from English interference, and that they would be left alone, as Dundas had threatened Westmoreland, to settle accounts with the Castle by themselves.

In the absence of evidence to the contrary, England continued to believe Lord Moira's rhetoric, and to regard Camden, Clare, and Carhampton as a triumvirate of tyrants. The papers contained their daily anecdotes of picketing and flogging, one instance, by trifling alterations, expanding itself into many.

The goodwill of the English nation towards the Irish was only equalled by its ignorance of them. After the arrest of the Revolutionary Committee at Oliver Bond's house, on the 12th of March, 1798, the Duke of Bedford again moved for an address to the King to change his Irish Ministers. He told the Lords that if he was to dwell in detail on the conduct of the Irish Administration, the picture would appal the stoutest heart. Lord Holland demanded especially the dismissal of the Viceroy and the Chancellor. The speeches of both these eminent men contained indignant denials either that any treasonable conspiracy existed in Ireland or any desire for separation from Great Britain, and were interspersed with appropriate commendations of Arthur O'Connor, the advocate of political assassination.

Lord Grenville defended the Government as far as he was able. The lives of magistrates must be defended, he said, and the laws must be maintained. Lord Downshire, fresh from Ulster and his own estates, reproached the Liberals for their heedless encouragement of a spirit which they did not understand. Their 'conciliation,' he told them, might convert Ireland into a province of France, but would never save it to Great Britain. In excited times those orators alone gain the public ear who appeal to sentiment. The motion for dismissal was lost, but a protest was entered in the Journals of the House of Lords, bearing the weighty names of the Duke of Bedford, the Duke of Norfolk, and Lord Holland; and popular clamour, well-intending but utterly uninformed, continued to grow.

The unfavourable opinion was confirmed by the acquittal of Arthur O'Connor at Maidstone. The failure

of the Government was accepted as a proof that they
had no evidence which they could produce, and therefore that the conspiracy was a dream. O'Connor's
second arrest on another charge was indignantly denounced. Lord Holland called it inhuman and
atrocious. Tierney and Sheridan commented with all
their eloquence on the breakdown of the prosecution,
and the Cabinet was unable to clear itself. Finally,
when Lord Edward Fitzgerald was shot and the rebellion burnt out, and the horrid work of murder
and incendiarism had begun, the eloquence of the
Opposition rose to the greatness of the occasion.
They found in Ireland a second America, and they
called on England to support them in refusing to the
Government the means of continuing their oppression.
The Irish, they said, were not in arms against Great
Britain, but against the insupportable tyranny of a
detested faction. If, instead of sending armies to
crush them, they had redressed the complaints of the
American colonists, the American colonies would
have remained attached to the empire. As America
had been in 1776, so Ireland was in 1798—lost, if
the war was persevered in; recovered to a more
sure allegiance, if the claim to self-government was
acknowledged.

The Whigs had been proved right about America.
The English people concluded that they might be
right about Ireland. Public opinion went with them,
and the Parliamentary orators redoubled their exertions.

On the 14th of June, when Lord Camden was
writing that without instant reinforcements all Ireland would be in a flame, Sheridan interposed
with a motion for a Committee of Enquiry, and

out of two hundred members found forty-three to support him. Defeated, he moved once more for an address to the King to dismiss Camden and his Irish advisers, whom he charged with having produced the insurrection. This motion was negatived also, but the speech was published, and did its work; and the next day the Duke of Leinster renewed the accusation in the House of Lords. Lord Edward was just known to be dead. The Duke's appearance in deep mourning gave sensational credibility to his invectives. He too denied that any disloyal spirit existed in Ireland beyond the brain of the Viceroy and Council, who were driving the people to madness. The outside world not unnaturally believed him.

The Duke of Norfolk followed with a demand for the removal from office 'of those persons to whom the afflicted people of Ireland could feel no sentiments save those of anger and revenge.' An unfavourable division was again followed by a protest to which were attached the names of six peers—the Dukes of Devonshire, Leinster, and Norfolk, Lords Moira, Fitzwilliam, and Ponsonby—five of them Irish absentees, who were discharging thus their duties to the poor country which supported their idle magnificence.

Three days later, when Dundas applied to Parliament for permission to send over English militia regiments which had volunteered for the Irish war, these same wise noblemen and gentlemen renewed an opposition as cruel as it was absurd. If their object was to repress the cruelties of the Irish loyalists, it could only be obtained by the presence of English regiments. If they wished the rebels to succeed, they were making themselves parties to high treason.

Yet Lord William Russell was not ashamed to say that English troops should not be sent to subjugate a neighbouring people to a Government which nine-tenths of them abhorred. Sheridan said 'the Irish had been duped, insulted, fooled, disappointed in their dearest hopes. No wonder they were discontented, no wonder they were indignant.' 'If,' said Tierney, 'I could be convinced that the Irish leaders had invited the French into the island, I would consent to send troops to resist them, but I deny that they have invited the French. Lord Fitzwilliam says it is untrue, and I believe Lord Fitzwilliam more than I believe the Government. The Irish people are in arms—no doubt of it. After having been scourged, burnt, and massacred, they are not likely to be in love with their rulers. But I for one will not agree to place the militia of England at the disposition of a desperate Irish faction. The cure for Irish rebellion is to gain the affections of the people. I will vote neither a man nor a guinea till the cause of the rebellion is known.'

Wilberforce came to the help of the Cabinet. To refuse troops, he said justly, would but increase the misery of the people. The force at present in Ireland might subdue the rebellion at last, but only after a bloody and furious struggle. Humanity as well as policy required that the insurgents should perceive the hopelessness of prolonged resistance in arms. The rebellion was not created by Lord Camden's Administration, it was the consequence of long-standing and varied misconduct and neglect. 'I cannot help,' he said, with a bitter glance at the motives of the Liberal faction, 'protesting against the kind of sensibility I see in some gentlemen, who seem not to

BOOK X.
1798.
June.

begin to feel for he wretched condition of the lower Irish until it becomes for party purposes a convenient subject of lamentation in this House.'

Wilberforce could not be suspected of sympathy with tyranny or indifference to human suffering. Leave was given for the militia to go, and regiment after regiment was poured across the Channel as fast as they could be moved to the coast. But the Opposition speeches had their effect notwithstanding. The public did not choose to obstruct the Government in measures necessary to restore peace, but they shared the suspicions which the inexplicable reserve of the Ministers could not fail to generate; and in sending the troops the Cabinet felt compelled to show a certain deference to the general misgiving, and to place a nobleman at the head of the Irish Administration in whose rectitude the nation had confidence. To recall Camden was to admit, at least in appearance, that the charges against his Administration were just, and the Cabinet knew well that he acted throughout with their fullest approbation; but the outcry was too strong to be resisted. Camden's position had long been intolerable to him, and only the highest principle had induced him to endure so long the ungrateful and dangerous burden. An excuse was found to cover the change in the probability of a French invasion, and in the desirableness at such a crisis of the presence of a soldier at the Castle. In justice to a nobleman who had carried himself in his high position with signal uprightness, Mr. Pitt ought to have assumed the responsibility for the parts of Lord Camden's conduct which the public condemned, but which Pitt knew to have been necessary. Portland ought to have confessed that he had recommended the acceptance of the services of the Orangemen, and that Camden had refused on grounds supremely honourable to him. But Cabinet Ministers dependent on Parliamentary majorities are rarely capable of acts of heroic virtue. Enough that Camden was removed, that Cornwallis re-considered his refusal of the past year and consented to be named as his successor.

SECTION II.

The nomination of Lord Cornwallis to the Viceroyalty of Ireland was generally approved in England, as well on account of his reputation as a soldier and a statesman, as because he was known to have disapproved the coercive policy of Lord Camden's Government. He was a nobleman of stainless honour, excellent intention, and commonplace intelligence. He had shared the popular impression that Ireland ought to be conciliated by Catholic Emancipation and Reform. The secret information which the Cabinet laid before him on entering upon his office satisfied him that it was vain to attempt to remodel the existing Irish Legislature. If the Catholics were to be emancipated he saw that the Irish Parliament must come to an end. But Emancipation itself, he was as much convinced as ever, would recall the Catholic population to its allegiance; and he disapproved the existing Constitution, not because it was incompatible with a firm and honest Government, but because it was the instrument and the representative of Protestant ascendency.

Lord Cornwallis's Irish despatches are characteristic of the attitude which English common-sense assumes instinctively towards the Irish problem. They betray a total ignorance of Irish history — an ignorance almost as complete of the country and of the temper of its inhabitants; and at the same time a confidence no less remarkable, which no experience of his mistakes appeared to affect, that the problem itself was perfectly simple, and that the Irish statesmen, by whom the Viceroy found himself surrounded, were blinded by prejudice and passion.

The combination of unacquaintance with the facts and unhesitating trust in his own judgment revealed themselves in a series of errors, which, inasmuch as Lord Cornwallis's opinions affected so materially the subsequent policy of England, it is worth while to notice more particularly.

First, he misunderstood the nature of the rebellion. He found on his arrival that it was generally spoken of as Catholic. He called this account of it 'folly.' He insisted that it was *Jacobin*. Cornwallis might call it Jacobin, but could not make it so. Jacobin doctrines had been industriously sown among the Irish Catholic peasantry, but the soil was unfavourable to their growth. The taint was confined to the clubs at Dublin and Belfast, and had but a faint existence among the rebel bands of Wexford and Kildare. The rebellion was neither Jacobin nor Catholic; it was the revival of Irish nationality: and because the religion of the Irish was connected so closely with the national spirit, the rebellion, like every other Irish rising since the Reformation, assumed a Catholic aspect, and was regarded as a holy war. The aspirations of the native race had been quickened into life by the fantastic pretensions of the Protestant colony to independence. The English Cabinet had played with them in an ignorant dream that they might form a check on the revolutionary temper of the Northern reformers. They had been led on from concession to concession till they had believed, as in Tyrconnell's time, that Ireland was to be their own again—restored to them by the forms of the Constitution. Their hopes had been raised too high to allow them to bear disappointment. The political agitators of Belfast and Dublin, dangerous nowhere but in the press or in debating committees—brave in recommending assassinations, and leaving others to execute them—had cowered down when they had to yield or to fight. The native race had risen from the sleep of a century, and furiously, savagely, and desperately were struggling to break their chains.

Not less Lord Cornwallis had mistaken the character of the Protestant gentry. Their Parliament had been absurd and corrupt. Their Volunteer movement had been ridiculous, their attitude towards England unwise and unbecoming; the conduct of many of them, in private life and towards their dependents, had been reckless and negligent. But they were not, as Cornwallis supposed them, a sanguinary oligarchy overtaken by a judgment on their crimes, and bent on the extirpation of the miserable people whom they were no longer able to oppress. Their faults might be many, but they were due as much to their position as to themselves. The kingdom of Oude is of the same size as Ireland. Seventeen years ago it rose in rebellion, and the entire population was then as bitterly hostile to British rule as Ireland in 1641 or 1798. Thirty Englishmen now govern Oude with perfect ease, and administer its affairs in perfect order. Their salaries are paid by the Government. They have no interest in the country beyond discharging their immediate duties to it. If, after the rebellion in 1857, the estates of the Zemindars had been confiscated ; if the soil had been made over to English settlers, who had been left to govern as they could out of their own resources, surrounded by a swarming population who hated them as aliens and plunderers, they would have found their situation even then more easy in many ways than that of the English colony in Ireland. The descendants of the Scotch and English settlers planted by Elizabeth, and James, and Cromwell, were a garrison in a hostile country. Had they been permitted to develope their resources they might have thriven and grown strong: but England for her own purposes condemned the country to barrenness, and its inhabitants to misery and want. She rejected them when they petitioned to be incorporated in the Empire. She extinguished their manufactures and their shipping, and discouraged them long even from cultivating their estates, lest the value of her own lands should suffer from the rivalry. The settlers were essentially an army of occupation, of which the gentry were the officers; yet half of them were allowed unlimited leave of absence, deserting their special charge, and handing over the people committed to them to be plundered and ground to wretchedness. If those who remained became negligent and careless, England had set them the example and had pointed out the road. If they were politically corrupt, England had begun with prostituting their patronage and misappropriating their revenues. If they were discontented and mutinous, never in the history of the world had any subjects more just ground for complaint. Cornwallis knew nothing of their history. He knew but little of what they actually were. On the roll of the Irish Parliament are long lists of honourable men, untainted by corrupt transactions with the officials at the Castle, landowners who remained on their estates, and fought to the best of their ability their ever-losing battle against vice and misery. To them and their exertions Ireland owed all that she possessed in the form of order and decency. They had given her a language and laws at least better than her own; and even the yoke of the worst of them was lighter on the peasantry than the little finger of their own chiefs. Where the peasantry suffered most, it was under the middlemen and agents of the absentees—under men who were for the most part of their own blood, and those chiefs' lineal representatives. England, not the gentry, was most to blame for the condition of Irish society. The clamours of the colony for self-government, their rant of patriotism, the applauding shouts with which they greeted their Grattans and their Floods become intelligible, and almost pardonable, when studied by the light of England's accursed legislation and yet more unpardonable policy. It would have been better and happier by far had England never confiscated the lands of the Irish, had she governed Ireland as she governs India, and never attempted to force upon her a landed gentry of alien blood. Having chosen the second alternative, having given the land and the Constitution into the hands of men of her own race and creed, principle as well as prudence should have taught her to remember their difficulties, and to encourage them in introducing habits of order and industry, which would have reconciled the people through prosperity to the imposed presence of the stranger among them. The wisdom of England had been to weaken her garrison instead of strengthening it, to make it useless for purposes of government, to saturate it with the elements of disorder, and when it broke into discontent and complaint to hold it in check by elevating and arming as a counterpoise the wronged and resentful race whom it was planted in the island to keep in awe. Ingenuity could not have invented a line of action more certain to precipitate rebellion. When the Protestants at the last moment felt the knife at their throats, when they found themselves threatened with a second 1641, when they found England, which had provoked the insurrection, turn round and charge it upon themselves, and refuse to help them, Cornwallis should neither have been shocked nor surprised when desperate men turned to desperate remedies; and being too few in number to hold in subjection the poor frenzied wretches who had begun a war of extermination, were being driven to write upon their memories a lesson which it should be impossible for them to forget. The Yeomanry were strong enough to destroy the rebels. They were not strong enough to pardon them. Irresistible power alone can afford to be merciful. The Protestants of Ireland, like the scanty English garrisons of earlier times, having to deal with an irreconcileable foe, as fierce as a wolf and as untameable, were being taught, in spite of themselves, that if England declined to stand by them, they and the Irish could not live side by side, and that if they would sleep in peace thenceforward they must give no quarter to enemies in arms. Cornwallis saw the feeling, and was shocked at it. He did not care to enquire into the grounds in which it originated; although, had he cared to reflect, his Indian experience might have enlightened him. In studying Ireland he was thinking, not of India, which would have been full of instruction for him, but of America, which was fatally misleading. He regarded the disposition of the Parliament and Privy Council as a confirmation of the accusations which had been levelled against them by Lord Moira; and, with an insight into Irish history which, if his letters were

BOOK X.
1798.
June.

not unjust to him, extended no further than the preceding year, he attributed the rebellion to the whips and pitch-caps of the Yeomanry, and as such determined to deal with it.

Again, and more fatally, Cornwallis mistook the character of the native Irish. Like every Englishman who becomes first acquainted with them, he found much in their character that interested and attached him. From the impurity which disgraced other nations they were singularly free. To one another they were affectionate and charitable. In the army he had himself experienced the fine qualities of courage and fidelity which reveal themselves invariably when the Irishman is under military discipline. He looked upon them as an innocent, cruelly injured people, who had been driven mad by tyranny, and required nothing but gentleness and kindness to bring them back to their allegiance.

Gentleness and kindness the Irish indeed needed, but the gentleness of inflexible authority and the kindness of even-handed justice. Cromwell had landed in Ireland under circumstances not unlike those of Lord Cornwallis. Cromwell insisted first on absolute submission, and when submission was refused dealt two blows so resolutely, so sternly, and with so clear a meaning, that rebellion turned sick, lay down and died, and peace was restored to Ireland with a loss of life which was as nothing compared to the waste and ruin of a protracted war.

If Cromwell's hand was heavy on the enemy on the field, he was as severely just in repressing disorder in his own army. Two soldiers stole a fowl from an old woman. Cromwell immediately hanged them. He had come to Ireland to enforce respect for the laws. The army was made to set an example of obedience.

Cornwallis found his troops in disorder, living at free-quarters among the peasantry, and making the rebellion a plea for plunder. He was indignant. He wrote despatches and reprimands. But neither on one side nor the other did he venture to imitate Cromwell. He checked indiscipline by combining rebukes which were just in themselves with reflections on the conduct of the Yeomanry in the field, which, after Ross and Enniscorthy, he ought to have spared them. In dealing with the insurrection his chief thought was to win the rebels by forgiveness, to supersede martial law while they were still everywhere in arms, to restore the jurisdiction of the civil courts when it implied impunity for the most horrible crimes, and to conciliate them at the earliest possible moment, by placing them on a political equality with the Protestants. The Irish people had many fine qualities, but they had a lesson yet to learn, that the laws of the land must be obeyed. Cornwallis believed that he could persuade them into it by what he called clemency, and confessed to a foolish pleasure when he had brought the mob to cheer him in the streets.[1] Many times he thought that he had succeeded. As often some fresh spurt of ferocity, some village burnt, some family murdered, checked his ardent expectations. His letters confess his disappointment, but they show no abatement of confidence in the correctness of his own insight; and when he recorded his failures, it was only to reassert with more emphasis that he failed only because the Catholics were not in Parliament.

[1] 'When I passed the people cried, "God bless him! That's he! There he is!" Not unpleasant.'— 'Marquis Cornwallis to General Ross, August 10, 1800.'

And as Cornwallis had misconceived the character of the people with whom he had to deal, so his despatches are searched in vain for a sign that he understood the remedies for the condition in which he found them. Always, when there is anything to be done, the indispensable preliminary is to understand the facts of the case. The facts with which Cornwallis had to deal were these:—

1. The Irish were a conquered people. Had their votes been taken, four-fifths of them would have desired separation from Great Britain. They remained attached to the British Crown by force, and by force only. Cornwallis supposed that if the Catholics were admitted into the Constitution, disaffection would disappear, and that they would become loyal subjects. Nothing but the most complete unacquaintance with the history of the country could have misled him into so perfect a misapprehension. If Ireland was to be incorporated into the empire, the Constitution might be incomplete without a representation of the hostile Irish element; but Emancipation by itself would have as little tendency to remove or qualify the hostility as Home Rule to cure the potato-blight.

2. Had Ireland been a thousand miles distant in mid-ocean, and her connection with the British Crown no longer essential, therefore, to the security of the empire, the Protestant colonists left to themselves would long since have asserted their natural superiority. Either by penal laws they would have compelled the Celtic Catholics to conform, with the alternative of exile, or if the native inhabitants had remained and persisted in rebellion they would have gradually destroyed them. Lord

Camden had refused the assistance of the Orangemen, yet without the Orangemen, and with a large part of the Presbyterians neutral, the Irish Yeomanry were able to stem the first rush of the insurrection in 1798. Had Ireland been unconnected with the English Government, the Protestants would necessarily have formed one united body, and there can be no serious question how the insurrection must then have ended.

England could not permit a war of extermination at her own door. If the past conduct of the Irish gentry had been as blameless as under too many aspects it had been reprehensible—if the rebellion of the native race had been as gratuitous and wanton as it had been in fact provoked by the neglect and oppression of centuries—the continuance of a ruthless and desperate conflict would have been a reproach to her own civilisation. In honour, conscience, and even from mere instincts of humanity, she was bound to interpose her hand. Having interposed, she reassumed her responsibilities for the condition of the Irish people. The one compensation which a conquered people has a right to claim for the loss of liberty is a just and steady government. England had long excused herself for the disregard of her obligations by pretending that Ireland was self-administered, like herself. The fiction had disappeared; the scandal and mismanagement had issued at last in a bloody convulsion. The immediate duty of the superior nation was at once to look to the causes which had brought the country to so miserable a pass, and to set itself in earnest to a task which had been left undischarged from the day of the conquest.

Having taken the conduct of the war out of the

hands of the Irish Council, Cornwallis ought first to have compelled the rebels to lay down their arms. Insurrection under Elizabeth had been patched with compromises, always to burst out afresh. Cromwell laid rebellion prostrate. Charles the Second undid Cromwell's work by concessions, and the battle had again to be fought. William the Third, in false mercy, consented to a conditional peace, and the broken treaty of Limerick had remained as a splinter in the wound. It was essential to convince the Irish that they were part of the British Empire, that they were not to be allowed to separate from it, and that if they persisted in attempts to free themselves England had both power and resolution to crush them. Cromwell refused an amnesty so long as a rebel force remained in the field. He insisted on unconditional surrender, and to Cromwell the Irish submitted as they never submitted to any English ruler. They were not constituted so differently from other men as to refuse to recognise the inevitable.

Rebellion being suppressed, the next necessity was obedience to the law. The most elementary condition of human society is respect for life and person, and not one step could be taken towards improvement so long as soldiers could be houghed and women ravished with impunity, and secret societies could supersede the authority of the Crown, and enforce their orders by midnight assassinations. The landed gentry had proved unable to maintain order by the old-fashioned machinery. If the magistrate was to become a reality, and be feared and obeyed, an effective disciplined constabulary was required in every part of the island. The patriots in Parliament knew instinctively that with the establishment of a police their power would be gone, and they had fought against it with an energy which hitherto had been too successful. A wise governor of Ireland would have seen that without this every other remedy would be a jest.

Among the many institutions which England had attempted unsuccessfully to naturalise in Ireland was trial by jury. To arrest criminals and bring them to the bar was of little use so long as jurymen and witnesses were not afraid of perjury. Where the offences had been of a kind which was regarded as part of the war against the national enemy, Irish criminal trials had been a jest. The protection of a police would deprive witnesses of the excuse which they might at present plead, that if they told the truth they would be murdered. If jurymen continued to play with their consciences, the law should have been modified, unanimity dispensed with, and the Scotch practice substituted for the English.

To check crime was but half the work. The other half was to prevent the wrongs which provoked it. The Irish gentry as a body were not fulfilling the purpose for which a gentry is designed. It was not that he might plunder his tenants to feed his appetite for luxuries that an individual man was allowed to call himself owner of the homesteads of a thousand families. Over half Ireland the relation between landlord and tenant was a money relation only, the landlord using the large discretionary powers which the law allowed him to extort the last penny which could be wrung from the miserable 'earth-tiller'—the peasant worse housed and fed than the master's cattle—the master spending the spoils of the peasant's labour in waste and dissipation. The difficulty was not new. It had been successfully encountered before, and might be successfully encountered again. The villeins under the feudal system held their lands at their lords' pleasure. According to the law the lord could strip them of all that they possessed, and make slaves of themselves and their children. 'But,' says Blackstone, ' the good-nature and benevolence of lords of manors having time out of mind permitted their villeins and their children to enjoy their possessions without interruption, the common law, of which custom is the life, gave them title to hold their lands in spite of their lord. They were still said to hold their estates at the will of the lord, but it was such a will as was agreeable to the custom of the manors.' The Irish peasants, if Great Britain chose to hold them as her subjects, were entitled to at least as much protection as the serfs of the Norman barons. The custom of the well-managed estates in Ireland might justly have been made the law for the whole. Courts might have been established where an injured tenant could have applied for protection, and the people might have been led to see a friend rather than an enemy in the government which they had been taught to detest.

Once more, it was not enough that England had been compelled against her will to remove the monstrous laws which had condemned Irish soil to barrenness, and Irish hands to inactivity. She had created artificially a condition of misery and poverty; she was now called upon to repair artificially the wrong which she had inflicted, and, at any cost to herself, to apply her intelligence, her capital, and her industry, to restore to the Irish what she had taken from them. Materials of prosperity lay undeveloped in the Irish soil and on the Irish coasts. Capabilities of industry lay in the Irish people. But having been nurtured so long in anarchy and idleness, the native inhabitants of the Southern provinces were unable to recover themselves. They required active help, and the help ought to have been given. Cromwell's first step on the completion of his conquest was to order an accurate survey of the area and capacities of the desolated island, and to settle it with colonies of vigorous and enterprising Englishmen. When the rebellion of '98 had been finally subdued, an English Minister aware of his responsibilities would have sent a skilled commission to examine everywhere the neglected wilderness, to which a country where Nature had been prodigal of her gifts had been reduced by the misgovernment of twenty generations; to examine by what means its morasses could be turned to meadow and cornfield; the haunts of smugglers and privateers be opened to lawful commerce; its fisheries in sea and river be made to yield their harvest; its manufactures be enabled to thrive by English capital; and penury and barrenness be exchanged for order and prosperity.

The public service of Ireland had been conducted hitherto on the principle of rewarding the unworthy, and neglecting and throwing aside the loyal and the able. From the Peerage downwards, through all branches of the State, promotion had been the recompense of dishonesty. Employments under the Crown had been either bought and sold in open market, bartered away for political support, flung as bribes to scandalous agitators, or bestowed on some unworthy member of a powerful family who could not decently be provided for in England. The effect had been universal demoralisation, the encouragement of every tendency which an honest government would most desire to repress, and the ruin of every public department. Almost forty years before, George the Third had protested in vain against the continuance of a system of which he, if no one else, perceived the natural outcome.

The time had come at last when the experiment ought to have been tried of providing Ireland with officials in Church and State whose loyalty could be depended upon, and who were qualified by character and ability for the duties of the post which they were chosen to fill.

A government strong, just, and impartial, with honest men to administer it, was Ireland's sovereign necessity. It was the one remedy which, except during the nine years of the Commonwealth, had never been applied. Lord Cornwallis's Correspondence shows disgust with the tone of public policy in Ireland, and indignation at the wretchedness of the people. He nowhere seems to have recognised the only measures which could elevate the one or relieve the other. He could think of nothing but the extension of political liberty. Had he looked below the surface, he would have seen that political liberty was the cause of the corruption which he abhorred; and that to lead the Irish people to look to political reform as a cure for poverty and disorder was to teach them over again the fatal lesson which had plunged them into their existing misery.

SECTION III.

WITH his mind preoccupied by false impressions, and fortified against a possible correction of them by the conviction that he, with his English common-sense, understood the country better than those who had lived in it from their childhood, Lord Cornwallis landed at Dublin on the 20th of June. On the following morning the rebel camp on Vinegar Hill was stormed by General Lake. Wexford was occupied by Moore. The insurgent force was broken up, and from that moment made no more attempts to encounter the troops in the field. The rebellion, however, did not cease to be dangerous. Rather it became more dangerous, for it assumed a form with which it was infinitely more difficult to deal. From being concentrated it became dispersed; from being local it became universal. Wexford, Wicklow, and the midland counties were overspread with detached parties of banditti, who no longer showed an open front, but appeared in their more congenial character, as 'cruel robbers, housebreakers, and murderers.'[1] In every direction, on a reduced scale, the atrocities of Wexford were repeated. Houses of Protestants were set on fire. The inhabitants, the men at least, were piked or shot. The perpetrators of these infernal deeds were savagely slaughtered in revenge; and Cornwallis found himself in a scene of horror the like of which he had never witnessed in America, in India,

[1] 'Cornwallis to General Ross, July 13.'—*Cornwallis Correspondence.*

or anywhere. His pity was for the rebels; his indignation was for the severity with which they were treated by the Yeomanry.[1] With the support of Lord Clare, whom, to his confessed astonishment, he found 'by far the most moderate and right-headed man in the country,' he endeavoured to arrest the spirit which was manifesting itself, by an act of amnesty. In a general proclamation he promised pardon, protection, and free permission to return to his home, to every insurgent who would lay down his arms, and had not been guilty of deliberate murder in cold blood. To the originators and organisers of the political conspiracy he refused, and so far most properly, to allow the excuses which he could imagine for the Catholic Celts. There was still a want of evidence against the Committee who had been arrested on the 12th of March. Addys Emmett, Arthur O'Connor, and MacNeven, the most guilty of the whole party, were protected by the unwillingness of the informers to appear against them. With others who had been seized on the eve of the outbreak there was not the same difficulty. On the 12th of July John and Henry Sheares were brought to the bar to take their trial for high treason. Captain Armstrong swore to their conversations with him. The address to the people of Ireland found in Henry Sheares's desk, and in the handwriting of his brother, was fatally corroborative. When sentence was pronounced they fell into each other's arms in court.

---

[1] Yet Cornwallis admitted that the atrocities committed by the rebels were greater than the retaliation inflicted upon them. 'The deluded wretches,' he wrote, 'are still wandering about in considerable bodies, and are committing still greater cruelties than they themselves suffer.'—'To Portland, June 28, 1798.'

Henry, the younger, said he had a wife and six children, and prayed for a respite, to arrange his affairs and provide for them. His sobs choked him as he spoke. John Sheares endeavoured gallantly to shield him by taking the blame upon himself. But the pleading of neither could avail. Their guilt was as plain as it was gratuitous. Rebellion in Ireland was too terrible a thing for theoretic politicians to be allowed to play with it with impunity. They were both executed on the 14th.[1]

The next to be tried was John MacCann, a gentleman of private fortune in Dublin. He had been a member of the Revolutionary Committee. Reynolds, the informer, appeared in evidence against him. A treasonable paper was found in his handwriting when he was taken. Curran used his skill in torturing Reynolds; but though he could display his own power as an advocate, he could not obtain a verdict

---

[1] Henry Sheares, after his sentence, wrote an agonised letter to Jonah Barrington, imploring him to save his life. The Chancellor whom he had wished to murder was now his only hope.

'Tell the Chancellor,' he said, 'that I will pray for him for ever, and that Government shall ever find me what they wish. Oh! my family! my wife! my children! my mother! Go to them. Let them throw themselves at the Chancellor's and Lord Shannon's feet. I have been duped, misled, deceived, but with all the wishes and intention to do good.'

'It is only justice to Lord Clare,' writes Barrington, in relating the story, 'to record an incident which proves that he was susceptible of human feelings. By some unfortunate delay the letter was not delivered to me till eleven o'clock of the morning after the trial. I waited on Lord Clare. He read it with great attention. I saw he was moved. He said, "What a coward he is! But what can we do?" He paused. "John Sheares cannot be spared," he said. "Do you think Henry can say anything, or make any discovery which can authorise the Viceroy in making a distinction? If so, Henry may be reprieved. Go to the prison. See him. Ask him this question, and return to me." I hastened to Newgate, and arrived at the moment when the executioner was holding up the head of my friend and saying, "Here is the head of a traitor."'—*Historic Memoirs*, vol. ii. p. 266-7.

for his client. MacCann was found guilty, and suffered five days after the brothers Sheares.

William Byrne, a Wicklow gentleman, was tried and convicted on the 20th. On the 23rd, Oliver Bond, at whose house the Committee sate, was convicted and sentenced also. The rapidity of the proceedings, and the unexpected readiness of the juries to find verdicts for the Crown, began to startle the remaining prisoners. They knew their guilt. They knew that the Government was aware of it, and they could not tell what evidence might not now be producible against them. Samuel Neilson, who had been taken outside Newgate, had reason to expect the worst. Arthur O'Connor remembered his near escape at Maidstone, and feared that another time he might not be saved by evidence to character. Byrne and Oliver Bond were to have been hanged on the 25th and 26th of July. Life was usually granted in return for valuable information, and the prisoners in a body —there were seventy of them in all—sent word to Cornwallis that if their own lives and the lives of their two friends might be spared they would make a full and free confession. Cornwallis had been in the deepest embarrassment about these men. He had no desire to show them mercy.[1] The leaders among them he was well aware were the persons really responsible for the rebellion, and deserved the severest penalties which the law could inflict. Public witnesses, however, were not to be found, and to try them would end probably in their acquittal. On the other hand, a confession of the circumstances of the conspiracy, of which the existence had been so fiercely denied, an

[1] 'He says this pointedly. See Letter to the Duke of Portland, October 20, 1798.'

acknowledgment from Arthur O'Connor himself of his negociation with General Hoche, of which so many eminent Whig statesmen had appeared in court to declare him incapable, would not only be a political triumph, but would be materially useful in tranquillising English opinion. It was not that the Government wanted information. They already knew as much, perhaps, as the prisoners could tell them. They wanted to be able to satisfy the world; and no question could any more be raised when the chief actors had admitted their guilt.

The Chancellor was in the country. Cornwallis consulted the Chief Justices and the Attorney and Solicitor-General. They were unanimous in objecting to a compromise with men whose guilt was of so dark a dye. They said that if Byrne and Bond were not executed no Irish juries would find again for the Crown in a trial for treason. When the Viceroy objected that under no circumstances was there a hope of a verdict against O'Connor and his companions, he was answered that more than one might perhaps be convicted, and that others could be proceeded against in Parliament.[1] An attainder had much to recommend it. If the proceeding was exceptional, the circumstances were exceptional which called for it. It was extremely desirable to show Irish traitors that the cowardice of witnesses and the perjury of jurymen could not always secure them from the consequences of their crimes. But such a measure could be ventured only by a body whose purity of purpose was above possibility of sus-

[1] 'Lord Carleton said that several of those who signed the papers, and particularly Dr. MacNeven, might possibly be convicted, and that others might be liable to pains and penalties by proceeding against them in Parliament.'—'Cornwallis to Portland, July 26, 1798.'

picion. The reputation of the Irish Parliament was not of this unblemished kind, and any high-handed overriding of the forms of justice would only confirm the suspicions already too prevalent in England.

Cornwallis consented that the law should take effect on Byrne, who was hanged on the day appointed. The execution, however, instead of inducing the prisoners to withdraw their proposal, led them to renew it with increased eagerness. The Chancellor came back at the moment to Dublin. His opinion coincided with that of the Viceroy, and on the approval of Lord Clare the Judges withdrew their opposition. O'Connor and MacNeven were informed that the offer would be accepted; and Cornwallis, before he knew what they intended to write, could scarcely contain his satisfaction. 'What,' he wrote, 'will the gentlemen who appeared at Maidstone say to this? It is the most complete triumph, both in England and Ireland.'[1] His exultation was diminished when the confession was placed in his hands. The prisoners had stipulated for the publication of it. The composition was O'Connor's. Secure behind a promise of life, they had paraded their treasons before Ireland and the world in a tone of bold bravado. They admitted that they had conspired to raise a rebellion and to introduce a French army, and they declared that they were justified in what they had done. They threatened the British Government with the perpetual enmity of the Irish race, and informed Government and the public either that Ireland must be allowed her own way, or that they must extirpate the population. Cornwallis treated this remark-

[1] 'To General Ross, July 30, 1798.'

able production as a deliberate insult. He sent a copy of it to the Cabinet. He told the prisoners that they must alter it, or it would not be received as a discharge of their engagement. They refused to make any changes, anticipating that it would be published as it stood. But a Committee of the House of Lords was sitting to enquire into the causes of the rebellion, and as an alternative they agreed to give evidence before it. They answered every question which was put to them with adequate frankness. The tone of insolence remained, but the rhetorical declamation was escaped. The publication of the Committee's report answered the end which Cornwallis desired, and at least exposed with sufficient completeness the value of the insight of the English Liberals into Irish character and Irish affairs.

The Cabinet meanwhile had considered the document which Cornwallis had sent over to them, and on the perusal of it were so justly indignant, that before they were aware that the Viceroy had allowed the prisoners to appear before the Committee they had resolved to refuse their sanction to negociation in any form whatever. Even Cornwallis himself they were inclined to blame for his excess of anxiety to excuse and pardon traitors.

'We consider,' the Duke of Portland wrote to him,[1] 'that the proposal should not be listened to. The memoir, beyond admission of the writers' criminality, contributes nothing to what we already knew. On the contrary, an air of presumption, arrogance, insolence, and superiority so pervades the whole, that I cannot but feel their conduct to be a great

---

[1] 'Portland to Cornwallis, August 15, 1798. Secret and confidential.' S. P. O. Endorsed 'Not

aggravation of their former crime. I ought not perhaps to wonder that men who, in the act of expiating the greatest of all crimes, permit themselves to tell you that you must extirpate or reform, should not see the behaviour of which I complain in the light in which it strikes me. But I cannot but observe that such an opinion, uttered at such a moment, if it is to be received as a testimony of honesty and good faith, is not less so of those dangerous and destructive principles to which the present convulsion of Europe is to be attributed. And so much I fear that nothing but a system of continued unremitting and active opposition can overcome it, that I cannot believe it can be softened by any concession or operated upon by any lenity, unless it is exercised under a conviction on the part of those who experience its benefits that those who use it are able to crush and annihilate the objects on whom it is bestowed. Your Excellency, therefore, must excuse me if I doubt the advantages which your natural disposition inclines you to hope for, from the establishment of a character for extraordinary lenity. I must, though I am sorry to say it, give it you as my opinion that the most desirable idea to establish in Ireland, and that which will lead most readily and surely to the object we have all in view, is that you are possessed of an overwhelming and irresistible power, which can neither be overturned nor shaken, and which is able and ready to punish impartially alike, all offenders against the law. Then I think you may show mercy, and indulge the feelings which are so well known to be congenial to your nature. But till then I fear that acts of lenity must be done with a sparing and distinguishing hand. In the temper which unhappily prevails in Ireland the most amiable motives will be misrepresented and misunderstood, and a conduct suggested by the finest and best of feelings will be attributed to pusillanimity and fear, and be productive of contempt and licentiousness instead of gratitude and attachment. Such, I fear, is human nature in the state of civilisation which it has acquired in Ireland, and such, I fear, it will remain until it is forced to conform itself to a more rigorous and austere observance of civil institutions and the laws of the country.'

Had the resolution of the Cabinet been formed more expeditiously, Cornwallis would probably have resigned, and the policy of conciliation would have been suspended. But before the despatch could leave London the faith of the Government had been pledged to the prisoners. Their evidence had been given and printed; it remained only to abide by the agreement, and to inform O'Connor and his friends that if they published their manifesto they would be considered, one and all, as parties to a fresh crime, and be excluded from the benefit of the pardon. The original intention was to allow them to emigrate to America. Mr. Rufus King, the American Minister, after reading the report of the Secret Committee, protested, in the name of the United States, against the introduction there of such pernicious and dangerous miscreants.[1] They were sent to Fort St. George, in Scotland, where they were detained till the Peace of Amiens, and were then released, on condition that they should never return to Ireland. O'Connor went to France; America consented after all to receive Emmett and MacNeven; and in their several places of refuge they continued their implacable animosity against the Government of Great Britain, which had rescued them from the justice of their countrymen.

[1] 'The principles and opinions of these men are, in my view, so dangerous, so false, so utterly inconsistent with any practicable or stable form of government, that I feel it to be a duty to my country to express to your Grace my earnest wishes that the United States may be excepted from the countries to which the Irish state prisoners shall be permitted to retire.'—'Mr. Rufus King to the Duke of Portland, September 13, 1798.' S. P. O.

SECTION IV.

BOOK X.
1798.
August.

Too late to render effective help, not too late to aggravate the exasperation of the Protestants and inflate the hopes of the rebels, their French allies now appeared upon the scene. Napoleon's indifference to Ireland had prevented any fresh attempt for an organised invasion in force. But the scheme of flying squadrons to hover on the coast, and make local descents wherever opportunity offered, had continued before the minds of the Directory; and as soon as it was known in Paris that the Irish were in arms, orders were given to prepare detachments as quickly as possible to be sent to their assistance. General Humbert, who had been with Hoche at Bantry, was commissioned to organise a force at Rochelle; General Hardy to collect another at Brest. They were designed to sail together, and to act in concert, if not in union. Hardy's division was the largest, and Humbert was ready before him. August came, and Admiral Bompart's squadron, which was to convey Hardy, was still behindhand. The Irish exiles were wild with impatience, and Humbert at last started alone, with no more than 1,100 men, accompanied by Barclay Teeling and Matthew Tone, Wolfe Tone's brother. He landed at Killala, on the north coast of Mayo, on the 22nd of August, distributed five thousand stand of arms among the Irish peasants who came to join him, and marched at once into the interior. On the 25th he was at Ballina. Unless he could be met and checked immediately, it was feared that the whole country would be again in flames, and General Lake and General Hutchinson, who were at Galway when Humbert arrived, hurried up to intercept him. They reached Castlebar on the 26th, with 2,000 men, militia chiefly, and a battery of field artillery. Humbert advanced in the night by a difficult mountain-road, which had been thought impassable and had been left unguarded, and came on Lake by surprise at daybreak. He had left part of his small force in garrison at Killala. He had but eight hundred French with him, something over a thousand armed Irish peasants, and three small guns. The Kilkenny and Longford militia, who formed the principal part of Lake's force, were Catholics, and many of them United Irishmen. They were said to have been tampered with. If not tampered with, they were unwilling or unable to encounter disciplined troops. They ran at the first advance of the French. The Galway Volunteers followed. The few artillerymen and Lord Roden's Fencibles from Ulster attempted to stand, but were overborne. Lake was totally defeated, and his guns were taken. Now or never was the time for the Irish patriots to show what they were made of. Had they been in earnest, their regiments, so long organised, would have started out of the earth as at a trumpet-call. But they preferred to wait, and let their allies fight their battles for them. Their zeal showed itself only in an effervescence of murder and robbery, which Humbert himself had to check. To his surprise he found himself, notwithstanding his victory, substantially alone, or joined only by a miserable rabble who were worse than useless to him. Had he been left unmolested, the Irish would probably have gathered heart. General Hardy was expected hourly from Brest. If Hardy landed while Humbert was still at large and successful, the consequences would, no doubt, be serious. Cornwallis took the field in person, with the troops in Dublin, while Lake collected his defeated regiments.

Perplexed at a reception so different from what they had been taught to look for, the French turned into Sligo with no definite purpose. They gained a second small success at Colooney Bridge; and hearing that the insurgents were up in Longford they struck across Leitrim, and passed the Shannon at Ballintra. Lake was close behind them. Cornwallis, in superior force, was in front. Before he could reach Longford, Humbert found himself surrounded; and seventeen days after his landing he closed his brief adventurous career by surrendering at Ballinamuck. The French became prisoners of war, and were treated courteously. Teeling and Matthew Tone, who were taken with them, were immediately hanged.

Napper Tandy, Lewines, and others of the Irish party at Paris, hearing that Humbert had sailed, had followed in a separate vessel, hoping to be in time for the revolution which they expected to follow. At Rathlin Island they learnt that all was over, and they made their way out of reach of danger to Hamburgh.

A month after Humbert had been disposed of, Bompart and Hardy arrived on the coast. Hardy had three thousand men with him. The French squadron consisted of the 'Hoche,' a seventy-four-gun ship, and eight frigates. On board the 'Hoche' was Wolfe Tone himself, not this time buoyant with hope as before, but with the shadow of his approaching fate upon him and resolute to meet it.

They had sailed from Brest on the 20th of September. To avoid Sir John Warren, who was known to be on the watch for them, they made a long circuit into the Atlantic. They were separated in a storm; and on the 10th of October the 'Hoche' and three frigates found themselves alone at the mouth of Lough Swilly, with Warren in pursuit of them, and already in sight in the offing. The frigates, drawing little water, were able to escape through a shallow channel. Tone was entreated to fly with them, but he chose to remain. The 'Hoche' fought for six hours against four ships each as large as herself, and did not strike till she was sinking. Tone distinguished himself greatly in the action; and in his French uniform was not immediately recognised when the survivors of the crew were brought on shore as prisoners. He was known to have accompanied the expedition, but he was reported to have been killed, or he might have escaped in one of the frigates. Curious enquiries were perhaps purposely avoided. The French officers were politely and hospitably received. They were invited to a breakfast by Lord Cavan; and Tone, who accompanied them, would have passed unnoticed at the table, had he not himself rashly spoken to an old acquaintance whom he encountered there. He was instantly arrested by Sir George Hill. He professed to expect that his French commission would protect him. He was painfully undeceived, and was ordered into irons as a traitor.

Not with dignity, but with the half-sincere heroics of its Irish counterfeit, he tore off his coat. ' These fetters,' he said, 'shall never degrade the revered insignia of the free nation which I have served. For the cause which I have embraced I feel prouder in my chains than if I was decorated with the Star and Garter of England.'

He was taken to Dublin, under an escort of dragoons, and was consigned to the soldiers' prison. If the forms of law had been observed, Wolfe Tone should have been tried at the King's Bench; but his rank in the French army, though not allowed to shield him, was held by a violent construction to place him under military jurisdiction, and on the 10th of November he was brought before a court where General Loftus sat as president.

He appeared in the full dress of a French officer, wearing the tricolour cockade. At first he was much agitated, but after calling for a glass of water he became more composed. He had been taken in the act of bearing arms against his Sovereign, and his conviction was a matter of course. He therefore read for his defence a political effusion which he had composed as a justification of his conduct. He said that from his earliest youth he had regarded the connection with Great Britain as the bane of his country. He had laboured to break it, and had sought assistance wherever it could be found.

The president told him that his language was irrelevant, and would rather injure than serve him.

'In a cause like mine,' he continued without attending to the check, 'success is everything. Success in the eyes of the vulgar is the test of merit. Washington succeeded. Kosciusko failed. I have forfeited my life. The Court will do its duty. I shall not be wanting to mine.'

Having been tried as a soldier, he begged that he might have a soldier's death. With an inconsistency which it would have been more seemly to avoid, the request was refused. He was sentenced to be hanged on the following morning, in front of the New Prison. He did not care to figure in a scene which was merely ignominious. There was no time for an appeal, and in the night he cut his throat with a penknife. The wound, though severe, was not immediately mortal. It was dressed, and sufficient life was left in him to permit his being carried to the scaffold. The cart was prepared. The escort was already mounted at the prison-door. A spectacle which could not have been other than revolting was prevented by the interference of Curran, who rose in the King's Bench, and declared that Tone, having held no commission under the British Crown, was not within the cognisance of a court-martial. The Judges agreed. The Sheriff was sent to the barracks, with a writ of Habeas Corpus, to claim possession of the prisoner. The Sheriff returned to say that he was too ill to be moved; but Curran's end was gained: the execution was put off; Tone lingered in pain for a week, and then died.

SECTION V.

BOOK X.
1798.
November.

THE ignominious story draws towards an end. The chief leaders of the insurrection were either dead or banished. Napper Tandy was arrested at Hamburgh at the instance of the English Minister, sent to Ireland and tried, but was spared as too contemptible to be worth punishing. The other actors in the drama were cleared away, and their brief notoriety was ended. But the insurrection itself did not clear away. It had cost by this time many thousand lives.[1] But the agrarian murders continued unabated. The peasantry, savage in their misery, were unable to understand the Act of Amnesty, and, as Portland expected, attributed it to fear. Again and again the Viceroy flattered himself that he had gained his end. Again and again he bewailed his disappointment. The frenzy slackened only to burst out again with renewed and more widely-spread destructiveness. The courts-martial were suspended, but he was compelled to revert to them; and a system of alternate blows and caresses—the least promising which could be pursued either with the Irish or any other human beings—was the chief outcome of the humane efforts of Lord Cornwallis.

'The rebellion in Ireland,' said Lord Clare, speaking, in 1801, in the British House of Lords for the further continuance of martial law, 'is of a nature unparalleled in the history of the world. It did

---

[1] Plowden estimates the numbers killed on both sides as nearly 70,000, but this is probably a great exaggeration.

not proceed from mistaken loyalty, religious zeal, or party difference; all principle had been corrupted, every laudable feeling had been extirpated, and nothing prevailed but treason, blood, and cowardly assassination. Though vanquished in the field, it was not subdued. It existed long before. It exists still. Lord Cornwallis did all that could be done by man; but to think of repressing such a spirit by coaxing, concession, and indulgence, is absurd.'

Cornwallis found his life as Viceroy 'his idea of perfect misery.' His failure to restore quiet never led him to mistrust his own judgment. He was confident as ever that Clare and Kilwarden and Toler and Carleton were blind, and that he alone saw clearly. He discerned the cause of the ill-success of conciliation to be the want of completeness in Catholic Emancipation; and as it was clearly impossible to introduce Catholics into a separate Irish Legislature, he now directed all his energies towards carrying the Act of Union.

The Parliamentary Union was indeed most necessary, but not chiefly or at all for the sake of Catholic Emancipation. The remedy which Ireland required was not additional liberty, but a firm and just Government; and the admission of the Catholics to the united Legislature would be useful or mischievous so far only as it did or did not conduce to that indispensable end. A Constitution professing to be national and representative from which four-fifths of the nation was excluded, was an intolerable absurdity; but the error lay in having inflicted such an instrument of government upon Ireland at all, rather than in having refused to remodel it upon conditions which would have rendered it only the more unendurable. The argument for a Union was the proved impossibility of so much as commencing the reformation of Ireland so long as a separate Legislature existed there. From the moment at which the Irish Parliament discovered its power of embarrassing the Administration, it became the fertile mother of every kind of disorder and demoralisation. The inconvenience of an adverse vote compelled Government to corrupt the members, and led the members to insist on being corrupted. The public departments were sacrificed to jobbery. Public morality was debauched and poisoned. The scandal and shame gave point to the declamations of agitators, and a show of seeming reason to the periodic explosions of patriotism. An Independent Parliament kept alive the dream of an independent nationality, and the result had been an eruption of the Irish volcano in a stream of horror and ferocity.

So long as the cause continued the same effects must necessarily repeat themselves. In 1704 the Irish Parliament had petitioned for incorporation. The request had been refused on unworthy and dishonourable grounds; and reluctance afterwards on both sides had prevented the renewal of the suggestion as a question of practical politics, till the rebellion had made serious men on both sides of the Channel feel that Ireland was too dangerous a subject to be any longer trifled with.

A Union would not of itself secure good government, or prevent Ireland's interests from being sacrificed to Parliamentary manœuvres. Unprincipled ministers playing on the ignorance of the public might still make a party cry of justice to Ireland, and carry measures which they knew to be mischievous, to maintain themselves in power by the Irish vote. A Union would not necessarily put an end to the scandalous misappropriation of patronage, or prevent the appointment to offices of trust and consequence of men whose fitter place would have been a penal settlement.[1]

But at least it would remove an institution the continuance of which in any shape was fatal to the possibility of amendment. So long as an Irish Parliament controlled the Irish finances the Administration would remain at its mercy, and could only carry on the Government by means as disgraceful to one country as ruinous to the interests of the other.

The influences by which the Act of Union was carried are notorious, and there is no occasion to dwell upon a subject on which too much stress has

---

[1] So little had the lesson of the rebellion been laid to heart, that for some years after the Union Irish preferments continued to be so bestowed as if Ministers desired to prove Wolfe Tone's assertion true, that Ireland could never prosper till she had shaken off the English connection. In 1802 a bishopric fell vacant in Ireland. Mr. Addington nominated a young man to it whose name I do not mention, lest I should inadvertently wound the feelings of persons at present alive. But the attempt was the occasion of a letter of a very remarkable kind, from the Archbishop of Armagh to the Prime Minister:—

'I affirm, on my honour,' the Archbishop wrote, ' that I object to —— upon public grounds only. Emolument is the only object of this young man, whose character is indisputably infamous. His promotion would, in my opinion, be fatal to the Church Establishment. It exposes us to ridicule and contempt. It encourages that profligacy of manners already too prevalent in Ireland, and it holds forth to the young men of this country that morals are of no estimation in the opinion of the English Minister. My understanding suggests no surer method of destroying the Church than by placing irreligious and profligate men in those situations where the people have a right to expect examples of piety and virtue. I will not pursue the subject further, but beg the favour—if the appointment is persisted in—to lay my humble request before his Majesty that he will allow me to resign a situation which I can no longer hold with advantage to the public or credit to myself.

. . .

'W. Armagh.'

been laid. For fifty years a seat in the Irish Parliament had been regarded either as a passport to promotion and rank, or as securing to its occupant a lien on the Irish revenues in the form of a pension or sinecure. The Noble Lords who returned nine or ten members to the Lower House received, as the price of support to the Crown, the patronage of their respective districts; and either provided by means of it for needy members of their families, or sold the appointments in their gift to the highest bidder. The system had been carried on so long and so unblushingly, it had been so completely sanctioned by the successive Administrations who had been parties to the bargain, that the sense of disgrace had disappeared. When they were called on to consent to the suppression of two-thirds of the Irish representatives, and the transfer of the remaining third to the Imperial Parliament, the Irish patrons were in fact required to surrender not only their consequence in the State, but a considerable part of their fortunes. The seats for their private boroughs entered into the value of their estates, and had been paid for by themselves or their fathers; and the sacrifice of them to men already embarrassed, as most of them were, by extravagant expenditure, was equivalent to ruin. They had the control of the situation in their hands, and it was not to be expected that persons who had risen into weight and influence mainly by corruption should ascend suddenly into a nobler sphere of patriotic self-devotion. They insisted on compensation for the destruction of their property, and they fought against the Union till their respective claims had been weighed and admitted. Cornwallis laboured patiently at a work which he detested. At one time he hoped to overcome or weaken the opposition by the help of the Catholics, but the Catholics would not listen to his blandishments. They trusted if the separate Parliament was maintained to make their way into it eventually; and though England had saved them from extermination by their Protestant countrymen, yet, as long as there was a hope of success, they preferred to join the Protestant opposition in defence of their national independence.[1]

The demands of the borough patrons increased with the eagerness of the Government. 'I long,' wrote the unhappy Viceroy, 'to kick those whom my public duty obliges me to court. My occupation is to negociate and job with the most corrupt people under heaven. I despise and hate myself every hour for engaging in such dirty work, and am supported only by the reflection that without a Union the British Empire must be dissolved. Nothing but a conviction that a Union is absolutely necessary could make me endure the shocking task which is imposed upon me.'[2]

The 'dirty work,' after two years' defilement with it, was at length completed, mainly through the exertions of Lord Castlereagh; and the Irish Parliament, which had been barely tolerable when controlled by Poynings' Act—which, under the Constitution of 1782, became the most mischievous parody of a representative Legislature which the world has ever seen—closed its dishonoured existence.[3] One only remark-

---

[1] 'The opposition to the Union increases daily. I was too sanguine when I hoped for the good inclination of the Catholics. Their dispositions are so completely alienated from the British Government, that I believe they would even be tempted to join with their bitterest enemies, the Protestants of Ireland, if they thought that measure would lead to a total separation of the two countries.'—'Cornwallis to Portland, December 12, 1798.'

[2] 'Cornwallis to General Ross, May 20 and June 8, 1799.'

[3] Act of Union finally passed through the British Parliament July 2, 1800.

BOOK X.
1800.

able feature gave interest to the debates which preceded and accompanied its fall. Let statesmen who dream of reviving, under any pretence, a separate Parliament for Ireland study the speech of Lord Clare, delivered in the Irish House of Lords, on the 10th of February, 1800. It lasted for four hours. The substance of it was a summary of Irish history from the Reformation to the present rebellion, and was distinguished, like all else which came from Clare, by keen, unsparing truthfulness. Ireland had been fed too long upon illusions. 'We have for twenty years been in a fever of intoxication,' he said, 'and must be stunned into sobriety.' He delineated alternately the negligence and tyranny of England,[1] 'the insanity of the English colony, which in an evil hour separated itself from the English nation;' the blind but not unnatural rage of the old inhabitants, who saw the stranger in possession of their inheritance, and sullenly brooded over their wrongs. He passed to the Constitution of '82, described its origin, and explained its workings. He showed that in peace it made corruption a necessity, that in war it led inevitably to rebellion. There are those who imagine that a Union between Great Britain and Ireland might be formed on the same principle which connects Great Britain with her larger colonial dependencies, on the principle of 'unity of the Executive with complete independence of the Legislature.' Our self-governed colonies remain attached to us because

---

[1] Clare strongly condemned the whole of the past English policy to Ireland, and the chief credit which he allowed her was her interference to save the Catholics in 1798. Speaking of the rebellion of 1641, he called it a war of extermination. 'The rebellion of 1798,' he said, 'would have been a war of extermination also, if it had not been for the strong and merciful interposition of Great Britain.'

they are willing to remain. If through their Legislatures they expressed a desire to part from us, both parties know that the connection might be dissolved without vital injury to the empire. If the majority of the inhabitants of the Canadian Dominion were of the same disposition as the majority (numerically) of the inhabitants of Ireland, the connection would be dissolved; or if maintained would be maintained by force only, with the suspension or overthrow of the Colonial Constitution. The vicinity of Ireland forbids us to contemplate separation as a possibility. Great Britain cannot sacrifice the integrity of her existence to the pleasure of a numerical majority of the Irish people. We are compelled to retain them as subjects of the Crown, whether they consent or object; and therefore to restore an independent Legislature in Dublin is to bring back the necessity of controlling it by the same methods which prevailed before the Union. The experiment has been tried. Let Lord Clare describe the results:—

'Between two countries equal in power such a connection could not exist for an hour. Its existence must depend on the admitted inferiority and marked subordination of one of them. Ireland is that inferior country; and call the Constitution independent, dignify it by any other high-sounding title in the Irish vocabulary, hers must be a provincial government, and of the worst description—a government maintained, not by the avowed exercise of legitimate authority, but by a permanent and commanding influence of the English Executive in the Councils of Ireland, as a necessary substitute for it. If there be not an implicit concurrence by Ireland in every Imperial Act of the Crown which has the sanction of the

British Parliament, and in every article of British legislation on Imperial subjects, there is an end of our connection with the British nation; and I repeat that the only security which can by possibility exist for their national concurrence is a permanent commanding influence of the English Cabinet in the Irish Council. Such a connection is formed, not for mutual strength and security, but for mutual debility. It is a connection of distinct minds and distinct interests, generating national discontent, and perpetuating faction and misrule in the inferior country. The first obvious disadvantage to Ireland is, that in every department of the State every other consideration must yield to Parliamentary power. Let the misconduct of any public officer be what it may, if he is supported by a powerful Parliamentary interest he is too strong for the King's representative. A majority in the Parliament of Great Britain will defeat the Minister of the day. A majority in the Parliament of Ireland against the King's Government goes directly to separate the kingdom from the British Crown. If it continues, separation or war is the inevitable issue; and therefore it is that the general Executive of the Empire, so far as it is essential to retain Ireland a member of it, is at the mercy of the Irish Parliament. It is vain to expect, so long as man continues to be a creature of passion and interest, that he will not avail himself of the critical and difficult situation in which the Executive Government of this kingdom must ever remain under its present Constitution, to demand favours of the Crown, not as the reward of loyalty and service, but as the stipulated price to be paid in advance in discharge of a public duty. Every unprincipled and noisy adventurer who can achieve the means of putting himself forward commences his political career on an avowed speculation of profit and loss; and if he fails to negociate his political job, will endeavour to extort it by faction and sedition, and with unblushing effrontery will fasten his own corruption on the King's Ministers. English influence is the inexhaustible theme for popular irritation and distrust. Our present connection, therefore, must continue to generate national discontent and perpetuate faction and misgovernment.'

Let me close this book with one more extract from the same speech. It contains a promise which still waits to be completely fulfilled—which will be fulfilled only when English statesmen of all parties shall have at last awakened to a remembrance of their responsibilities, and shall have determined that Ireland shall be excluded henceforth and for ever from the sphere of permitted party politics.

'If we are to pursue the beaten course of faction and folly, I have no scruple to say it were better for Great Britain that Ireland should sink into the sea than continue attached to the British Crown on the terms of our present connection. Our difficulties arise from an Irish war—a war of faction, a Whig war, a United Irishmen's war. It has been demanded, how are we to be relieved by a Union? I answer, we are to be relieved from British and Irish faction, which is the prime source of all our calamities. When I look at the squalid misery of the mass of the Irish people I am sickened with the rant of Irish dignity and independence. I hope I feel as becomes a true Irishman for the dignity and independence of my country. I would therefore elevate her to her proper station in the rank of civilised nations. I would advance her from the degraded post of a mercenary province to the proud station of an integral and governing member of the greatest empire in the world.'

INDEX.

ABB

ABBEYS, suppression of, i. 40
Abbott, iii. 318
Abduction made felony, i. 418
Abercrombie, Sir Ralph, iii. 306-310, 327, 329, 331, 332, 335, 418
Aberdeen, Lord, ii. 362
Abjuration Oath, i. 315, 333, 336, 337
Abraham, Heights of, ii. 52
Absenteeism, i. 26, 163, 216, 218, 454; ii. 22, 28, 214, 450, 453; iii. 75
Absentee rents, ii. 177
Absentees, i. 40, 277-279; ii. 149, 152, 155, 193, 224, 469, 511; iii. 450
Absentee tax, ii. 59, 62, 67, 151, 153, 160, 372, 394, 305; iii. 231, 232
Adair, Sergeant, ii. 375
Adet, M., minister of the French Republic, iii. 190
Adrian IV., Pope, i. 16
Agar, Archbishop of Cashel, ii. 261
Agar, Charles (afterwards Lord Somerton), iii. 41
Aghrim, battle of, i. 199; iii. 353
Agitation, trade of, i. 609
Agrarian riots of 1762, ii. 27
Agrarian laws, ii. 481
Agricultural Bill, ii. 105
Agriculture, i. 398
Aix-la-Chapelle, Peace of, ii. 71
Albany, ii. 203
Albemarle, Earl of, i. 220, 222
Alexander the Great, iii. 198
Allegiance, oath of, i. 311
Alnager, duties of, ii. 169
America, battle of, ii. 83; compared with Ireland, 83, 84, 125, 133, 163, 174, 204, 221, 275, 320, 330, 340, 430; iii. 16, 22, 159, 190, 254, 295, 348, 453, 463
American army, ii. 281, 284
American colonies, ii. 132, 133
American fleet, ii. 206
American Independence, ii. 205
American privateers, ii. 255
American question, ii. 181

ASS

American Revolution, iii. 3, 6
American war, iii. 235, 384
Amherst, Lord, ii. 215, 216 note
Ancient Britons, iii. 354, 359, 361, 420
Ancram, Lord, iii. 402, 403
Anderson, a smuggler, i. 493
André, Major, ii. 281
Andrews, Dr., Provost of Trinity College, ii. 169
Anglican system, i. 156
'Annals of Lough Cé,' i. 31
Annaly, Lord, ii. 223, 224
Anne Queen, i. 284, 304, 353 note, 360
Anti-Popery Act, ii. 216
Antrim, Earl of, i. 86, 88, 181, 182, 404
Antrim, i. 69; ii. 131, 488; iii. 19, 151-153, 177, 188, 303, 399, 425, 426
Appeal, final court of, ii. 350
Arbuthnot, Admiral, ii. 280, 282
Archdall, Mervyn, iii. 20, 145, 181
Ardglass, iii. 317
Aristocracy, English, iii. 3; of Ireland, iii. 5
Arklow, iii. 398, 401, 402, 403, 419, 420, 421, 436
Armada, i. 57
Armagh, ii. 131, 436; iii. 153, 162 note
Armstrong, Mr., i. 420
Armstrong, Captain, iii. 340, 474
Army, state of the, i. 98, 99, 358; ii. 42, 190
Army Bill, ii. 66
Arnold, General, ii. 281, 284
Arran, Isle of, i. 134
Artois, Comte d', ii. 338
Asgill, Mr., i. 300, 356
Ashton, Sir Arthur, i. 123, 124, 195
Ashton, Mr., i. 169, 170
Ashton, Sir William, Chief Justice of the Common Pleas, ii. 26, 27
Assassination, iii. 167, 270, 320, 368
Assassination Bill, iii. 170
Assassination Committee, iii. 250, 289
Assassination Plot, i. 250, 254, 259

K K 2

INDEX.

ASS

Assembly, National, iii. 76
Athanasius Secundus, ii. 81 *note*
Athenry, Lord, i. 256, 404
Athlone, i. 57, 194, 198; ii. 126; iii. 258
Athlone, Lord, iii. 171 *note*
Athlone Parliament, iii. 112
Atkinson, Mr., iii. 154
Attainters, i. 216
Atterbury, Bishop, i. 559
Augmentation Bill, ii. 68
Aunger, Captain, i. 166
Austrians, ii. 127; iii. 198
Avoca, the, iii. 420, 421
Avonmore, Lord. *See* Yelverton

BACK LANE PARLIAMENT, iii. 70
Bagenal, Mr. Beauchamp, ii. 147, 148, 343, 348, 358, 359
Bagwell, Mr., i. 576 *note*
Baker, Major, i. 183
Balbriggan, iii. 420
Bale, John, Bishop of Ossory, i. 42
Ballina, iii. 482
Ballinahinch, iii. 426
Ballinamuck, iii. 484
Ballinskellig's Bay, ii. 235
Ballycarew, iii. 360
Ballyhack Passage, iii. 436
Ballyhige House, or Castle, i. 478
Ballymore Hill, iii. 402
Bandon, emigration from, ii. 126
Bank of England, i. 559
Bantry Bay, i. 156, 186, 204, 200, 230, 262, 263, 287
Barclay, Alexander, iii. 20
Barclay family, iii. 152
Barnewell, Mr., i. 580, 581
Barnwalle, Robert, ii. 15.
Barré, Colonel, ii. 133, 134
Barrington, Sir Jonah, i. 510; ii. 357, 359, 448 *note*, 475 *note*, 515 *note*
Barrow, the, iii. 375, 398, 406
Barry, Sir James, Lord Chief Justice, i. 144
Bathurst, Lord, ii. 77
Bastile, ii. 519; iii. 10, 11, 17, 19, 399
Beaghan, executioner at Vinegar Hill, iii. 434, and *note*
Bedford, Duke of, iii. 230
Bedford, Duke of, Viceroy, i. 422, 613, 614, 619, 621, 623, 625, 626-627; ii. 12, 45; iii. 451, 452
Beef, salt, ii. 22 *note*
Belfast incendiaries, ii. 454
Belfast Committee, iii. 179
Belfast, i. 319, 623; ii. 77, 105, 119, 132, 141, 232, 292, 368, 410, 419; iii. 17, 18, 22, 50, 59 60, 69, 71, 75, 95, 105, 106, 135, 153, 157, 160, 162, 174, 175,

BOS

179, 183, 187, 190, 196, 217, 225, 235, 237, 245, 255, 258, 280, 353, 355, 399 426, 459, 460
Belfast Committee, ii. 201, 265
Beling, Richard, i. 103 *note*, 125 *note*
Belleisle, ii. 15
Bellingham, Sir Edward, i. 42
Bellew, Christopher, iii. 70
Bellew, Lord, at Aghrim, i. 221 *note*, 256
Bellew, Walter, i. 221 *note*
Bentinck, Duke of Portland, i. 222; ii. 351
Bere Island, iii. 205, 210, 212
Beresford, iii. 26, 41
Beresford, Mr. John, ii. 104 *note*, 107
Beresford, John, Chief Commissioner of the Customs, iii. 126, 129, 141
Beresford, William, ii. 107
Beresfords, the, ii. 5
Berkeley, George (afterwards Bishop of Cloyne), i. 507-509; ii. 449
Berkeley, Lord, Lord-Lieutenant, i. 165
Bernstorff, Baron, i. 519
Bessborough, Earl of, ii. 46, 47, 150, 152; iii. 232
Bill of Rights Battalion, ii. 393
Bingham, Sir Charles, ii. 111, 156
Binns, iii. 314
Birch, Robert, ii. 109 *note*
Bishops, i. 323; iii. 62
Bishops of Ireland, ii. 449, 452
Black Dog, prison so called, i. 592 *note*
Blackrock, ii. 520
Blake, Martin, i. 374 *note*
Blake, Sir Walter, i. 410, 415
Blakeney, Mr., ii. 181
Blaquiere, Sir John de, Colonel, ii. 145, 153, 154, 176 *note*, 178, 179, 187, 394, 490 *note*; iii. 29, 30, 137, 150, 240, 243 *note*
Blasters, Society of, i. 510
Blood, William, i. 513
Bodkin, blind Dominick, i. 442-445
Bodkin, John FitzOliver, i. 445
Bodkin, Mr. Dennis, ii. 448 *note*
Bodkin murder, the, 441-445
Bodkin, Oliver, of Carnbane, i. 441
Boffin, Inis, priests confined in, i. 134
Bolingbroke, Lord, i. 358-360
Bolton, Duke of, Viceroy, i. 388, 401, 555
Bolton, Sir Richard, Chancellor, i. 91
Bompert's squadron, iii. 482
Bonaparte, iii. 192, 197, 265, 282, 287, 302, 482
Bond, Oliver, iii. 105, 283, 315, 317, 452, 476
Boolavogue, iii. 378
Bophin, Lord, i. 325
Borlase, Sir John, i. 82, 85
Boston, ii. 135, 136

BOS

Bosworth Field, i. 29
Boulter, Hugh, Archbishop of Armagh, i. 376, 393, 403, 493, 519, 542, 577, 600 note; ii. 449
Bourbon, Duc de, ii. 338
Bowes, Lord, Chancellor, i. 625; ii. 56
Boyle, Speaker of the Irish House of Commons, i. 612, 616 note; ii. 5, 6
Boyle, Michael, Primate, made Lord Justice, i. 166
Boyle, Richard, second Earl of Shannon, i. 632. *See* Shannon
Boyle, Roger, Lord Broghill, third son of the Earl of Cork, i. 143
Boyles, the, ii. 5
Boyne, battle of the, i. 194; ii. 22
Brabant, iii. 149
Bramhall, John, Bishop of Derry, i. 91, 154, 158
Brandywine, the, ii. 202
Bray Head, ii. 219
Bray, ii. 237; iii. 419
Breadstreet, Recorder of Dublin, ii. 295
Brehon laws, i. 18, 28
Brest, iii. 201, 202, 230, 248, 263
Brewer, Mr., iii. 362
Bridges the informer, ii. 29, 30
Bridport, Lord, iii. 214, 230
Bristol, iii. 23, 201
Bristol, Earl of, Viceroy, ii. 44, 380, 382, 383, 386, 392, 393, 398, 390
British Fencibles, iii. 306
British fleet, iii. 195, 198, 200, 201
British regiments, ii. 471
Brodrick, Alan, Solicitor-General, i. 232; Speaker of the Irish House of Commons, 301, 309, 354; becomes Lord Middleton, 389
Brodrick, Alan, son of the last, i. 389, 524
Broghill, Lord, i. 143, 144; created Earl of Orrery, 147
Brooke, Sir Arthur, ii. 109 note
Brooklyn, ii. 201
Brown, Dennis, ii. 439, 405; iii. 26, 31, 80, 102
Brown, General, ii. 127
Browne, Mr., member for the University, ii. 479, 481, 486; iii. 170
Brownlow, Colonel, ii. 387
Brownlow, Mr., member for Armagh, ii. 423, 424, 428, 430, 434, 435, 468, 510
Bruff, village of, iii. 110, 111
Brunker, Captain, ii. 141 note
Brunswick, Duke of, iii. 64
Bruton, Colonel W., ii. 109 note
Buckinghamshire, Earl of, Viceroy, ii. 207, 217, 222, 224, 232, 233, 242, 246, 250, 253, 269, 270
Buckingham, Marquis of, Viceroy, ii.

CAM

487, 489, 490, 493, 494, 504, 504 note, 505, 509, 511, 513, 515, 516, 517, 520; iii. 26
Buller, Sir Francis, iii. 318
Bunker's Hill, ii. 141 and note, 174; iii. 11, 399
Bunler, Captain, ii. 214
Burdett, Sir Francis, iii. 227, 228, 310
Burgh, Hussey, ii. 178, 181, 183, 237, 238, 244, 245, 317, 318, 324
Burgh, Hussey, ii. 223, 227; Prime Sergeant, 227
Burgh, Mr., ii. 477
Burgoyne, General, ii. 202, 208, 374, 392
Burke, Edmund, i. 442-445
Burke, Right Hon. Edmund, ii. 214, 215, 247, 414, 338, 493; iii. 10, 14, 23, 33, 42, 46, 53, 65, 110
Burke, Hubert, i. 576
Burke, Richard, iii. 33, 34, 37, 38, 49, 50, 58, 61, 62, 111 note, 114, 115 note
Burkes, origin of the, i. 24
Burke of Clanrickarde, i. 87
Burrows, Mr., iii. 379
Burrows, Mrs., iii. 379
Burrowes, Peter, iii. 10
Bushe, Gervase, Provost, ii. 310
Bushe, Mr., ii. 155, 185, 258, 261; iii. 102
Bute, Lord, ii. 34
Butler, Mary, ii. 33
Butler, Mr., iii. 299
Butler, Simon, iii. 20, 105, 109, 117
Butler, Sir Theobald, i. 314
Butlers, the, i. 30, 34, 52, 53, 55
Byrne, Elizabeth, iii. 435 note
Byrne, Mr. Edward, iii. 52 note, 56, 62, 70, 135, 144, 246
Byrne, James, iii. 435 note
Byrne, the bookseller, iii. 340
Byrne, William, iii. 476, 478

CAHIR, Lord, iii. 328
Cahir, iii. 328
Calvinism, i. 628
Calvinists, i. 238; ii. 488
Cambridge, ii. 139
Camden, battle of, ii. 206
Camden, Lady, iii. 416
Camden, Lord, ii. 247, 265; viceroy, iii. 137, 138-140, 141, 143, 144, 155, 163, 164, 167, 170, 177, 179, 183, 184, 186, 202, 211, 215, 216, 226, 234, 236, 240, 244, 245, 248, 252, 255, 256, 266, 267, 270, 271, 272 note, 274, 275, 287, 289-291, 293, 300, 304, 305, 308, 315, 316, 324, 327, 331, 338, 350, 367, 360, 399, 400, 404, 416, 417, 425, 427, 429, 451, 453, 455, 456, 457

CAM

Campbell, Lord Frederick, ii. 66, 146
Camperdown, battle of, iii. 265
Canadas, ii. 14, 132, 133, 274
Cane, Mr., ii. 181
Capel, Sir Henry, created Lord Capel, i. 231, 232
Capel, Lord, i. 233, 237, 250
Carey, Edward, ii. 109 *note*
Carey, the printer, iii. 69]
Carhampton, Lord, iii. 161, 162, 167, 177, 188, 250, 251, 261, 288, 451
Carleton, Sir Guy, ii. 202
Carleton, Lord, iii. 477 *note*
Carlingford, ii. 457
Carlingford, Lord, i. 256
Carlisle, Earl of, ii. 204; Viceroy, 286, 311, 315-319, 320, 322, 327, 331
Carlow, iii. 110, 303, 365, 378, 398, 401, 436
Carlow Hills, iii. 375
Carmarthen, Lord, ii. 412
Carnew, iii. 401, 403, 420, 436
Carnot, ii. 412; iii. 194, 195-197
Carolina, ii. 206
Carolina, South, ii. 284
Carolinas, ii. 280, 283
Carr, Charles, i. 283 *note*
Carrick, iii. 110
Carrick, Lord, ii. 29, 32
Carrickbyrne, iii. 412, 436
Carrickbyrne Hill, iii. 406
Carrickfergus, i. 81, 97, 192
Currin, Father, iii. 439
Carteret, Lord, Viceroy, i. 493, 497, 533, 535-537, 541, 574
Curton, ii. 518
Carysfort, Lord, ii. 257
Cashel, ii. 268
Cashel, Archbishop of, ii. 33, 404, 503; iii. 41
Castle Martyr, ii. 46
Castle, the, ii. 495, 502; iii. 16, 21, 34, 69, 116, 163, 165, 179, 223, 227, 233, 354, 277, 303, 307, 310, 345, 346, 425
Castlebar, ii. 381
Castlecomer, iii. 110
Castlehaven, Lord, i. 86, 118, 128
Castlereagh, Lord, iii. 18, 119 *note*, 137, 179, 371, 429, 493
Catherine II. of Russia, ii. 274
Catholics, the, i. 46, 47, 74. 86, 89, 94, 101, 115, 133, 134, 147, 164, 167, 191, 209, 210, 212, 225, 235, 250, 252, 257, 259, 271 *note*, 273, 274, 281, 296, 306, 307, 312, 314, 316, 317, 318, 319, 323, 329, 332, 336, 337, 362, 367, 370, 372, 378, 381, 566, 568-573, 576, 578, 583; ii. 11, 13, 16, 18, 42, 176, 193, 209, 214-217, 276, 277, 278, 303, 304, 311, 312, 314, 325, 350, 354, 356, 386, 407,

CHI

409, 419, 428, 430, 433, 446, 450, 451, 453, 459, 461, 470, 476, 480, 488, 489; iii. 6, 7, 16, 18, 20, 21, 24, 25, 33, 35, 40, 44, 45, 47, 50, 52, 56, 59, 61, 68, 70-73, 76, 79, 80, 84, 85, 86, 87, 90-92, 94, 96, 98, 100, 101, 108, 109, 111, 125, 127, 131, 134, 136, 146-148, 149, 150, 153, 154, 156. 169, 171 *note*, 178, 180, 181, 183, 214, 223, 225, 226, 230, 244, 247, 248, 250, 261, 273, 283, 298, 324, 326, 332, 352, 353, 360, 400, 414, 427, 431
Catholic College, iii. 145
Catholic Committee and Association, iii. 109, 112
Catholic Committee, iii. 135 and *note*, 144, 145, 147-157, 158, 172, 122, 192, 196, 246, 298
Catholic disabilities, iii. 83
Catholic emancipation, ii. 488; iii. 15, 19, 20, 21, 74, 108, 123, 125, 135, 145-147, 150, 175, 179, 181, 222, 239, 244, 261, 292, 458
Catholic Relief Bill, ii. 219, 233, 304, 305, 350; iii. 45, 131, 133
Cattle houghing, i. 410, 414 *note*, 415, 416 *note*, 161
Caulfield, Lord, i. 107
Caulfield, Sir William, i. 411
Cavan, Lord, iii. 485
Cave Hill, iii 160, 175
Cavendish, Sir Henry, ii. 272, 273, 345, 375; iii. 88
Celts, revival of the, ii. 1, 276, 278
Champlain, Lake, ii. 200, 202
Champneys, Mr., ii. 85
Chancellorship, the, ii. 56
Channel Fleet, iii. 230, 262
Chappell, William, Bishop of Cork, i. 91
Charlemont Castle, i. 107
Charlemont, Lord, ii. 257, 264, 277, 292, 298, 303, 308, 309, 323, 324, 357, 370, 386, 392, 434 *note*, 503, 507, 509; iii. 9, 16, 17, 112
Charles, Prince, ii. 32
Charles I., i. 77, 87, 117, 118
Charles II., i. 141, 144
Charlestown, ii. 139, 140, 200, 206, 280, 284
Charlotte, Queen, ii. 493
Charter Schools, i. 514, 517, 520, 521, ii. 11, 450; iii. 187
Chatham, Earl of, i. 614, 622, 628, 630; ii. 14, 54, 73, 132, 133, 137, 344, 502
Chesapeake, ii. 202, 285
Chesterfield, Lord, i. 587
Chichester, Lord, i. 102 *note*
Chichester, Sir Arthur, ii. 118
Chief Remembrancer, ii. 490 *note*

INDEX.   503

CHO

Cholmondeley, Lord, ii. 77
Church, i. 243, 374, 379
Church, Anglo-Irish re-established, i. 154
Church catechism, ii. 451
Church day schools, i. 512
Church, Established, i. 342
Church, Irish, ii. 446, 449, 450, 454
Church theories, i. 77
Civilization, iii. 2
Civil List, ii. 209; iii. 103, 112; condemned, ii. 38
Claims, Court of, i. 270
Clane, or Cluain, iii. 358
Clanrickarde, i. 128
Clare, iii. 109
Clare, Lord, ii. 100, 330 *note*; iii. 96, 183, 270, 345, 354, 371, 391, 394, 404, 451, 474, 478, 488, 494. *See* Fitzgibbon
Clarendon, Henry, Earl of, i. 157 *note*, 158; Lord-Lieutenant of Ireland, 167, 173, 174
Clarendon, Lord, i. 106 *note*, 111
Clarges, Sir Thomas, i. 219
Clarke, General, iii. 196
Clear, Cape, ii. 219; iii. 204
Cleaver, Dr. Euseby, Bishop of Ferns, iii. 376, 380
Clements, Mr., i. 621
Clergy, ii. 457, 469, 481, 483
Clifden, Lord, ii. 404, 515, 516
Clifford, Lord, iii. 17
Clinch, Mr., iii. 359
Clinch, Father, iii. 441
Clinton, Sir Henry, ii. 202, 203, 206, 281, 282, 284
Clive, Lord, ii. 43
Cloncurry, Lord, iii. 287, 418
Clonmel, ii. 26, 27
Clonmel, Earl of, Mr. Scott created, ii. 395
Clonmel, Lord, iii. 120
Clover, Adam, i. 108
Coalition Government, ii. 362, 395
Cockayne, the attorney, iii. 117–120
Coghlan, Th., ii. 109 *note*
Coghlen, Mr., ii. 181
Colclough, Mr. John, iii. 377, 397, 448
Cole, Sir William, of Fermanagh, i. 103
Coles, the, of Fermanagh, i. 98 *note*
Coleraine, pestilence in, i. 109
College Green, ii. 242, 428
Collins, Mr., iii. 117 *note*
Collis, Mr., vicar of Tralee, i. 486
Culpoys, Admiral, iii. 230
Colville, iii. 109
Commons, House of, i. 348–348; ii. 420, 430, 436, 439, 476, 482
Commons, Report of the Secret Committee of the Irish House of, iii. 248
Commercial propositions, iii. 123

COW

Committee, Revolutionary, iii. 315
Comyn, Mr., iii. 233
Concord, ii. 136, 138
Condorcet, iii. 64
Congress, proposed, ii. 410, 416, 418
Coningsby, Thomas, becomes Lord Coningsby of Clanbrassil, i. 195 *note*, 219, 231, 271 *note*
Connaught, i. 57, 80, 133, 136
Connaught, Eyre, i. 410; iii. 161, 188, 197, 233, 303
Connecticut, ii. 206
Connell, Maurice, i. 476
Conolly, Mr., i. 382; elected Speaker, 383; Lord Justice, 535
Conolly, Tom, ii. 109 *note*, 156, 239, 294, 370, 388, 498, 507; iii. 80, 113
Conspiracy Act, ii. 475
Constabulary, ii. 459
Constitution of '82, ii. 274, 394, 420, 421, 458, 494, 498, 512; iii. 6, 75, 147, 196, 239
Convention, the, ii. 354, 386, 395; iii. 69, 71, 75, 83, 296
Convention Bill, iii. 113, 115
Convocation, address of, i. 349
Cooke, Edward, Army Secretary, iii. 45
Cooke, Edward, iii. 92, 418
Cooper, Captain, i. 280
Cooper, Mr., iii. 110
Coote, Sir Charles, of Castle Coote, i. 113, 128, 143; created Earl of Montrath, 147
Coote, Sir Eyre, ii. 282
Cootes, the, ii. 127
Corbet Hill, iii. 406
Corby, Mr., of Stradbally, created Lord Corby, ii. 69 *note*
Cork, ii. 11, 17, 77, 219, 232, 292; iii. 174, 207, 212, 213, 291, 328, 355
Cork, Bishop of, ii. 33
Cork, Dean of, ii. 147
Cork Harbour, ii. 96, and *note*.
Cork Squadron, the, ii. 389
Corn Bill, Irish, i. 400
Cornwallis, Lord, ii. 206, 283, 284, 286, 290, 320; iii. 306, 339; Viceroy, iii. 457, 458, 461, 466, 489
Corrigrua Hill, iii. 378, 379
Corruption, ii. 106
Corry, James, i. 222
Corry, Mr., ii. 512; iii. 81
Cotter, James, i. 418 *note*, 432
Cotter, Sir James, i. 354, 431
Council, Irish, ii. 301, 425; iii. 43
County Police Bill, ii. 489
Cove Fort, ii. 96
Cowkeepers, ii. 22 *note*
Cow Pens, defeat of Gen. Tarleton at, ii. 283

504 INDEX.

COX

Cox, Sir Richard, i. 198, 373; Chancellor, 302
Cradock, Colonel, iii. 155 note
Craik, Mr., of Arbigland, ii. 212
Crawford, Colonel, iii. 408 note
Creighton, John, ii. 109 note
Crichton, Abraham, created Lord Erne, ii. 69 note
Crillon, Duc de, ii. 338
Croix, M. de la, Minister for Foreign Affairs at Paris, iii. 190-193, 194, 200, 246, 281
Cromwell, Henry, i. 143
Cromwell, Oliver, i. 118, 119, 122, 124, and note, 126, 127, 132, 133, 137, 149, 285; iii. 376, 406, 440, 464, 468
Cromwell, Richard, i. 143
Cromwell's troopers, ii. 130
Croppies, iii. 336
Crosbie, Mr. Arthur, Clerk of the Crown for Kerry, i. 480, 481, 484, 497
Crosbie, Sir Edward, iii. 365, and note
Crosbies of Ballyhige House, or Castle, i. 478
Crosby, Bridget, or Widow Maghee, i. 467
Crosby, Sir Maurice, of Ardfert, i. 467
Cuffe, Mr., iii. 148
Cullimore, Isaac, i. 416 note
Cummins, Mr., iii. 300
Cunningham, Colonel, i. 616 note; ii. 109 note
Cunningham, General, iii. 52
Curragh, iii. 373
Curran, ii. 389, 419 note, 441, 444 note; iii. 28, 116 note, 120, 121, 150, 168, 243, 252; Master of the Rolls, 301, 330, 475
Curry, Dr., ii. 13, 479, 480 note
Cusack, Adam, i. 372
Cusack, Robert, i. 372, 373
Cusacks, case of the, i. 372
Customs duties, ii. 161

DALE, Catherine, iii. 435 note
Dale, Joseph, iii. 435 note
Dallas, iii. 318
Dalrymple, General, iii. 177, 204, 209, 210, 211, 214, 230
Daly, Bowes, ii. 388, 389
Daly, Denis, ii. 178, 237, 359
Daly, Mr. Justice, i. 168
Damer, Mr., i. 419
Dandaels, General, iii. 262, 265
Danmanus, iii. 209
Darlington, Lady, i. 519
Darragh, Mr., iii. 328
Darrynane Abbey, the O'Connells of, i. 463
D'Auvergne, Captain, iii. 287

DOP

Dawson, Joshua, i. 280, and note, 282 note, 283 note
Dawson, Richard, i. 283
Dawson, Thomas, created Lord Dartry, ii. 69
Dawson, W. H., created Lord Portarlington, ii. 69
Day, Mr., ii. 330 note
Deal, iii. 313
Declaration of Independence, ii. 200
'Defenders,' ii. 489; iii. 104, 105, 110, 152, 154, 162 note, 165, 168, 175, 192, 298
Delafaye, Secretary, i. 384 note
Delaware, the, ii. 202
Delegates, iii. 257
Democracies, iii. 3
Denmark. Queen of, ii. 149
Dennis, Mr., i. 549 note
Dennis, Mr. James, made Prime Sergeant, ii. 147 and note,155, 169
Derry, i. 181, 183, 319; ii. 130, 131; iii. 19, 151
Derry, Bishop of. Frederick Augustus Hervey, Earl of Bristol, ii. 370, 371, 380, 382, 383, 386, 392, 393, 398, 399, 418, 449
De Ruvigny, Earl of Galway, i. 250
Desmond, i. 24
Desmond, Earl of, i. 52, 53, 56
Desmond, house of, i. 52, 53
Devereux, John, iii. 71
Devonshire, Duke of, Viceroy, i. 422, 451, 585; ii. 46, 55 note, 150; iii. 232, 454
Diamond, battle of the, iii. 154
Dickson, Dr., Bishop of Down, iii. 294
Dignam, Garrat, ii. 411
Dillon, Count, ii. 585
Dillon, General, i. 559
Dillon, Gerard, Prime Sergeant, i. 186
Dingle, i. 280 note; iii. 110
Directory, French, iii. 112, 159, 192, 193, 198, 260, 278, 287, 298, 302, 314, 339
Dissenters, i. 335, 359
Dissenters' Relief Bill, i. 384, 387; ii. 217, 407; iii. 47, 261, 248, 249
Dixon, iii. 396
Dixon, the shipowner, iii. 432, 438, 439, 445
Dobbin, Elizabeth, i. 421
Doddington, George, i. 320, 321 note, 323
Donegal, iii. 66
Donegal Arms, iii. 19, 60
Donegal, Lord, ii. 141, 478; iii. 151
Donegal, Marquis of, ii. 120
Donoughmore, Earl of, ii. 61 note
Donoghue, the, i. 477
Dopping, Anthony, Bishop of Meath, i. 188, 189, 224

Dorchester, Catherine Sedley, Countess of, i. 301 note
Dorchester Heights, ii. 200
Dorset, Duke of, Viceroy, i. 497, 498, 574, 581, 582; again Viceroy, 610, 611; ii. 5
Dowdall, iii. 418
Dowling, Mary, iii. 435 note
Dowling, Patrick, iii. 435 note
Down, i. 69, 152; iii. 131; iii. 10, 18, 67, 151, 245 note, 303, 399
Downshire, iii. 179
Downshire, Lord, iii. 278–281, 284, 304, 305, 314, 418, 452
Downshire men, iii. 214
Drapier's Letters, i. 531, 533–535, 536, 537, 539
Drennan, Dr., iii. 10, 119
Drogheda, i. 118, 123, 124, 195; iii. 258
Drogheda, Lord, ii. 29, 32, 75
Drumlannon, ii. 33
Drunkenness attacked by the Irish House of Commons, i. 593
Drury, Captain, iii. 384, 385
Dublin, Archbishop of, ii. 33
Dublin, Artillery corps of, ii. 382
Dublin Castle, i. 97, 100; iii. 341
Dublin Committee, iii. 270
Dublin incendiaries, ii. 454
Dublin merchants, ii. 9
Dublin Police Bill, ii. 484
Duelling, ii. 194, 447
Duels in the Phœnix Park, ii. 148
Duff, Sir James, iii. 372, 373, 444
Duigenan, Dr., iii. 86. 94, 147, 181
Dumourier, iii. 65, 106
Dunboy Castle, i. 457
Dunboyne, iii. 357
Duncan, Admiral, iii. 263, 265, 287
Duncannon, iii. 392, 436
Duncombe, Mr., Lord Justice, i. 241
Dundalk, i. 118, 126
Dundas, General, iii. 339, 365, 367 and note, 370, 372, 436, 443, 444
Dundas, Mr., iii. 25, 34, 37, 38–40, 42, 43 and note, 58, 64, 66, 71, 76, 83, 85, 108, 110, 113, 122, 133, 248, 253, 261, 427, 451, 454
Dunleckny, ii. 359
Dunluce, Lord, son of the Earl of Antrim, ii. 109 note
Dungannon, ii. 96, 307, 309, 311, 360, 380; iii. 83, 95
Dungannon, Baron, i. 43
Dungannon Convention, iii. 100
Dungannon resolutions, ii. 317, 355
Dungannon Volunteers, ii. 488; iii. 1, 3. See Volunteers
Dunkerron, barony of, i. 452

Dunmanway, iii. 209
Dunmore, i. 90 note
Dunn, the blacksmith, iii. 250–252, 270 288
Dunning, Mr., ii. 155
Dunshaughlin, iii. 357
Durseys, ii. 219
Dutch, the, ii. 267, 275, 282, 337
Dutch army and fleet, iii. 262
Dwyer, Captain, ii. 24, 28
Dyson, Jerry, ii. 108

EAGER, George, i. 469 note, 470 note
East Indian monopoly, iii. 123
Echlin, Robert, Bishop of Raphoe, i. 77
Eden, Mr., afterwards Lord Auckland, ii. 204, 286, 290, 312, 316, 320–322, 327
Education Act, foreign, ii. 312
Education, ii. 450, 451; industrial, 451
Edward I., i. 8
Edward VI., i. 42
Egan, Mr., iii. 26, 46, 50 and note, 116 note, 241
Egremont, Lord, ii. 17, 26
Egremont, Wyndham Earl of, Secretary of State, ii. 6, 8
Egypt, army in, ii. 61 note
Elizabeth, Queen, i. 45, 48, 50
Elliot, Admiral, i. 624
Elliot, General, ii. 280, 338, 339
Elliott, Mr., iii. 428
Ellis, Wellbore, ii. 55 note
Elphin, Bishop of, i. 515
Ely, Lord, ii. 218; iii. 231
Emmett, Robert, iii. 10, 41 note, 259, 331
Emmett, Thomas Addis, iii. 10, 120, 288, 317, 474, 481
English settlers, i. 499
Enniskillen, i. 182, 184
Enniscorthy, iii. 110, 375, 383, 384, 386, 401
Enniskillen, i. 98, 103
Enniskillon, Lord, iii. 251
Ennisworthy, iii. 434
Erris, iii. 110
Erskine, Captain, ii. 119
Erskine, Lord, iii. 173, 320
Esmonde, Dr., iii. 359, 360, 363, 364
Esmonde, Sir Thomas, of Wexford, iii. 359
Essex, Earl of, i. 53, 61, 62
Established Church of Ireland, i. 157
Estaing, Count d', ii. 205
'Evan,' i. 411, 412
Exodus of the Irish, i. 393
Eyres, the, ii. 127

EYR

Eyre, Colonel Stratford, Governor of Galway, i. 326, 598, 599 and *note*, 601
Eyre, John, created Lord Eyre, ii. 69 *note*

FAIRFIELD, ii. 206
Falkland Isles, seized by Spain, ii. 96
Farnham, Lord, ii. 370
Fawcett, General, iii. 392, 393, 395
Felons, i. 593
Fencibles, Durham, iii. 420
Fencibles, Midlothian, iii. 406
Fenn, Edward, i. 433
Fergusson, Mr., iii. 318
Ferns, iii. 378
Ferns, Bishop of, ii. 364
Ferris, James, iii. 250
Fetherstone, Mr., ii. 181
Few mountains, iii. 196
Fingal, Lord, i. 86, 404; iii. 25, 35, 244, 366
Fitton, Sir Alexander, Lord Chancellor of Ireland, i. 177
Fitzgeralds of Kildare, ii. 5; iii. 358
Fitzgerald, Edward, iii. 283, 340; of New Park, iii. 378, 444
Fitzgerald, George Robert, of Turlow, ii. 381 and *note*, 382 *note*, 386
Fitzgerald, Lady Edward, iii. 278, 280, 283, 342
Fitzgerald, Lady Lucy, iii. 281, 283
Fitzgerald, Lord Edward, ii. 46, 422; iii. 3, 82, 168, 173, 174, 199, 216, 277, 278, 282, 287, 288, 304, 312, 314, 316, 317, 339 *note*, 340, 342-344, 351, 377, 392, 454
Fitzgerald, Lord Henry, ii. 408
Fitzgerald, Lord Thomas, i. 39, 40; iii. 344
Fitzgerald, Mr., ii. 181
Fitzgerald, Mr. Austin, i. 422, 423
Fitzgerald, Mr. Thomas Judkin, iii. 337
Fitzgerald, Sergeant, ii. 431; Prime Sergeant, iii. 41, 240
Fitzgibbon, John, Attorney-General, ii. 47
Fitzgibbon, the Right Hon. John, son of the last, afterwards Earl of Clare, ii. 40, 48, 50, 104, 181, 294, 303, 305, 311, 312, 314, 317, 318, 389-391, 395, 399, 400, 417-419, 428, 429, 431, 436, 441-444, 460-464, 470, 475, 476, 477, 480, 482, 484, 486, 496, 498, 501 *note*, 503, 505, 510, 515 and *note*; iii. 39, 41, 52, 57, 68, 69, 87, 89, 95, 112, 115, 125, 128, 131, 143, 144, 163, 194, 226, 253, 294, 303, 312
Fitzherbert, Mr., ii. 496
Fitzmaurice, Lord, i. 470 *note*, 472, 475, 476, 493
Fitzpatricks, the, i. 373

FRE

Fitzpatrick, Colonel, ii. 345, 380
Fitzpatrick, Mr., 599 *note*
Fitzpatrick of Upper Ossory, ii. 150
Fitzsimon, Henry, i. 461
Fitzsimon, Walter, i. 461
Fitzwilliam crisis, the, iii. 75
Fitzwilliam, Lord, i. 560
Fitzwilliam, Lord, Viceroy, iii. 122; 124, 125, 128, 133-135, 141, 145, 152, 156, 232, 239, 241, 450, 454, 455
Flax manufacture, ii. 162
Fleetwood, General, i. 129, 151
Fleming, Mr., Lord Mayor, iii. 357
Flood, Henry, ii. 46, 47, 59, 61, 67, 78, 84, 92, 102, 107, 108, 111, 146, 155, 156, 158, 168-174, 178, 183, 223, 224, 238, 295-297, 300, 301, 303, 304, 306, 308, 315, 317, 333, 345, 347, 348, 351, 352, 361, 375-379, 387, 389, 392, 418, 419 *note*, 431, 435, 440, 441, 460, 462, 477; iii. 218, 296, 392
Flood, Warden, Chief Justice of the King's Bench, ii. 49
Fontenoy, battle of, ii. 34, 127
Foote, Colonel, iii. 381, 382
Forbes, Edward, i. 331, 340, 357
Forbes, Mr., member for Ratoath, ii. 462, 463, 468, 513; iii. 81
Foreign Education Act, i. 307
Forfeiture, Act of, ii. 305, 310
Fortescue, James, ii. 109 *note*
Forth, Mount, iii. 302, 436
Foster, Right Hon. John, Speaker of the House of Commons, created Lord Oriel, ii. 238 *note*, 261; iii. 29, 94
Fostering, i. 25
Foulk's Mill, iii. 436
Foundling Hospital, the, iii. 20, 30, 243 *note*
Four Masters, i. 31
Fox, Right Hon. Charles James, ii. 323, 334, 335, 341, 342, 353, 362, 373, 374, 376, 425; clerk of the Pells in Ireland, ii. 219 *note*; iii. 173, 239, 320, 322, 451
France, i. 622; ii. 204, 211, 252-254, 274, 280, 282, 338; iii. 5, 6, 16, 22, 64, 135, 158, 161, 170, 177, 193, 229, 262, 289, 349, 372, 400
France, King of, ii. 32
Franklin, Dr. ii. 136, 204, 208; iii. 18, 106
'Freeman's Journal,' ii. 512
Free Trade, ii. 167, 263, 375, 399
French, the, ii. 132, 133, 283; iii. 110, 257, 339, 377, 399
French fleet, ii. 205, 280, 282, 304, 340; iii. 51 217, 233, 252
French Invasion of Ireland, iii. 120, 320
Frenchmen, ii. 430

INDEX.

FRE

French, James, ii. 32
French, Nicholas, i. 103 *note*
French Revolution, the, iii. 3, 5, 23, 76, 491
French, Sir Thomas, iii. 71, 84 *note*
Friends, persecution of, i. 433

GAGE, General, ii. 136, 138, 139
Gallowglass, iii. 217
Galway, Articles of, ii. 42
Galway, Earl of, De Ruvigny, i. 250
Gardiner, Luke (afterwards Lord Mountjoy), ii. 216, 303, 305, 311, 312, 351, 417, 430, 431, 434; iii. 410 *note*
Gates, General, ii. 206
George, Dr., i. 193 *note*
George I., 6th of, ii. 336, 341, 347
George II., i. 518, 559
George III., ii. 40, 42, 118, 149, 191, 328, 343, 410, 491, 492, 495, 508, 509, 511; iii. 131, 157, 165, 171 *note*, 124, 290, 292, 472
Georgia, ii. 206
Geraldines, the, i. 24, 30
Germaine, Lord George, ii. 282
German linens, ii. 423, 443
German troops, iii. 306
Germans, iii. 197
Germany, ii. 149, 163
Geylin, Samuel, ii. 25 *note*
Gibbet Rath, iii. 373
Gibbon, Edward, iii. 241
Gibraltar, ii. 274, 280, 208, 338, 339
Ginkel, Baron Godard de, i. 196; Earl of Athlone, 196 *note*, 201
Giraldus Cambrensis, i. 15 *note*
Glamorgan, Earl of, i. 116
Glass, tax on, ii. 134
Glendalough, iii. 375
Glentworth, Lord, iii. 293
Gloucester, Duke of, i. 283
Godolphin, Lord, i. 313, 343
Godwin, Bishop of Elphin, i. 535
Godwyn, Dr., Bishop of Kilmore and Ardagh, i. 353 *note*
Goldsmith's Corps of Volunteers, iii. 84
Good Hope, Cape of, ii. 338
Gordon, Mr. iii. 372, 421
Gorey, iii. 377, 398, 403, 419, 421–423, 436, 445
Gorges, Ric., ii. 109 *note*
Gormanston, Lord, i. 86, 580, 581
Gormanstown, Lord, iii. 25, 35
Gosford, Lord, iii. 359, 364
Grafton, Duke of, a Lord Justice, i. 382, 384, 523, 525, 529, 559, 561
Granard, Lord, made Lord Justice, i. 166
Grandy, Richard, iii, 412 *note*
Grantham, Lord, ii. 77

HAM

Grasse, Count de, ii. 283, 284, 285, 338
Grattan, father of Henry, Recorder of Dublin, ii. 50, 51
Grattan, Henry, ii. 50, 183, 185, 209, 237, 238, 243–245, 256, 258, 266, 277–279, 289, 295, 297, 298, 300, 304, 308–310, 315–318, 320–322, 324, 326–329, 330 *note*, 331, 334, 335, 340, 342–344, 347, 352, 354, 350, 373, 376, 378, 379, 386, 387, 388, 390, 401, 424, 425, 431, 438, 439, 441, 449, 463, 467, 468, 477, 480, 481, 482, 486, 491, 495, 496, 497, 502, 504, 505, 507 508, 509–511, 512, 519; iii. 5, 6, 16, 18, 26, 29–31, 44, 61, 76, 77, 80, 81, 89, 92, 102, 112, 116, 122, 123, 125, 126, 128, 130, 131, 143, 144, 145, 147, 149, 167, 168, 180, 196, 218, 222, 233, 224, 232, 233, 236, 239, 240, 243, 252–254, 261, 267, 271, 206, 297, 320, 330, 346, 368, 392, 450, 462
Graves, Admiral, ii. 285
Graziers, ii. 22 *note*
Great Britain, ii. 355, 420, 435
Green, Mr., member for Dungarvan, ii. 433, 434
Greene, General, ii. 284
Gregory XIII., iii. 198
Grenville, Lord, ii. 34, 133, 361; iii. 9, 275, 296, 452
Greville, Mr., iii. 267
Grey, Earl, iii. 173, 321
Grey, Lord, Viceroy, i. 55
Griffiths, Mr. ii. 495
Griffiths, Captain, iii. 359, 362
Grogan, Cornelius, iii. 397, 447, 448
Grouchy, General, iii. 202, 204, 205
Grove, Miss Susannah, i. 421
Guildford, ii. 284
Guinness, iii. 120
Gunpowder Plot, i. 66; Act, iii. 197
Gurney, iii. 318
Guyon, Hugh, i. 499 *note*

HABEAS CORPUS ACT, ii. 163, 164, 295; iii. 179, 180, 226
Hacket, Bishop of Down and Connor, i. 158, 243, 244
Hackney, Darby, i. 437, 438
Hale, Bernard, Chief Baron, i. 536
Haliday, Dr., iii. 60
Halifax, Earl of, Viceroy, ii. 6, 8, 15
Hamburgh, iii. 173, 278, 280, 281, 282, 292
Hamilton, Dr., iii. 234
Hamilton, General, i. 180
Hamilton, Mr., iii. 109, 299
Hamilton, William Gerard, Chancellor of the Exchequer, ii. 55 *note*

HAM

Hampden, iii. 181
Hanover, House of, i. 361, 366
Harbourers, i. 280 *note*
Harcourt correspondence, ii. 185 *note*
Harcourt, Earl of, Viceroy, i. 447; ii. 145, 186, 187
Harden, John, ii. 24 *note*
Hardwick, Lord, iii. 181
Hardy, General, iii. 482, 483
Hardy, Major, iii. 419
Harrington, Lord, Viceroy, i. 606, 608
Harris, Dr., ii. 480
Hartington, Lord, Viceroy, i. 612, 613; ii. 46
Harvey, ii. 197
Harvey, Mr. Bagenal, iii. 377, 383, 396, 397, 398, 406, 415, 419, 448
Hassett, Mr. Thomas, perhaps Blennerhassett, i. 489
Hastings, Warren, ii. 282
Hawke, Admiral, i. 623; ii. 15
Hay, Mr. Edward, iii. 371, 383, 394 *note*, 413 *note*, 446
Hay, John, iii. 388, 444, 447
Hayes, Catherine, i. 435 *note*
Healey, John, i. 435 *note*
Hearts of Steel movement, ii. 164, 120, 488
Heath, Sir John, iii. 318
Hedge schools, i. 511
Heitmann, Captain, i. 490, 497
Hemp, ii. 162
Hennessey, John, i. 550 *note*
Henry VIII., i. 37; King of Ireland, i. 41; ii. 127
Heron, Sir Robert, Irish Secretary, ii. 238, 287
Hertford, Lord, Viceroy, ii. 39-44
Hervey, Frederick Augustus, Earl of Bristol and Bishop of Derry, ii. 380, 382, 383, 386, 392, 393, 398, 399
Hessian troops, ii. 179
Hewett, a Judge of the Court of King's Bench, created Lord Lifford and Chancellor, ii. 58
Hewetson, Mr., ii. 30, 32
Higgins, Mr., ii. 512
Higgins, Father. iii. 359, 360
High Church party, ii. 131
Hillsborough, Lord, ii. 244, 246, 247, 253, 254, 288, 289, 315, 318, 404
Hill, Sir George, iii. 188 *note*, 485
Hindostan, ii. 274
Hoadley, Archbishop, i. 610
Hobart, Major (afterwards Earl of Buckinghamshire), ii. 520; iii. 37, 38, 42, 45, 46, 48, 58, 65, 66, 69, 71, 72, 83, 85, 88, 89, 91-93 and *note*, 104, 108; created Lord Hobart, and sent to Madras, 114, 115 *note*

IVE

Hoche, General, ii. 412; iii. 173-175, 192, 199-202, 230, 248, 262, 265, 278, 281, 282, 283, 477
Hogan, John, called Shan Roagh, i. 442, 445 *note*
Home rule under the Normans, i. 29
Hopkins, Ezekiel, Bishop of Derry, i. 181
House of Commons, Irish, ii. 365, 388
House of Lords, Irish, ii. 401
Howe, ii. 208
Howe, Lord, Admiral, ii. 349; iii. 51
Howe, General Sir William, ii. 139, 140, 200
Humanity, religion of, iii. 352
Humbert, General, iii. 482-484
Hunter, General, iii. 449
Hussey, Dr., iii. 63 *note*, 184-186, 187
Hutchinson, Colonel (afterwards General Lord Hutchinson), iii. 51, 483
Hutchinson, Francis, iii. 51, 52
Hutchinson, Hely, i. 335, 447, 632; ii. 47, 60, 61 *note*, 65, 81, 90, 108, 168, 223, 228, 238, 261, 268, 301, 305, 313, 314, 326, 328, 344, 388, 404, 515
Hutchinson, Henry, Lord, ii. 61 *note*
Hutchinson, Richard, Earl of Donoughmore, ii. 61 *note*
Hutton, Mr., iii. 59
Hyder Ali, ii. 282

INCENDIARIES, ii. 454
Inchiquin, Lord, i. 153
Indemnity, Act of, iii. 162, 165, 171
Independence, ii. 502
Independence, declaration of, ii. 290, 291, 322, 328
Independence, ii. 309
Independents, i. 154, 156
India, ii. 14, 274, 282
Indies, East, ii. 438
Indies, West, ii. 438
Informers, i. 373; iii. 163, 237
Innocent X., iii. 198
Insurrection of 1641, i. 89, 99, 114, 154
Insurrection Act, ii. 479; iii. 197, 242, 275, 299, 372, 377
Insurrection Bill, ii. 483
Intermarriage Act, iii. 35, 48
Inquisition, iii. 295
Ireton, his Irish estates, i. 151
Irish Brigade, iii. 87
Irish in America, ii. 141
Irishman, the, i. 7, 8, 10, 22, 39, 193, 324
Irishman, the modern, ii. 127
Italy, Bonaparte's campaign in, iii. 197; Protestants of, iii. 23
Iveragh, barony of, i. 452

JAC

JACOBINS, iii. 22, 59, 64, 79, 108, 153, 157, 183, 302, 378, 399, 417, 425, 430, 459
Jacobin clubs, iii. 298
Jacobin institutions, iii. 298
Jacobitism, i. 232
Jackson, Mr., of Armagh, iii. 20, 66, 117, 118, 120, 121, 147, 158, 316, 317
Jamaica, ii. 283, 338
James I., ii. 276
James II., i. 170, 178, 182, 186, 194, 365; ii. 306; iii. 98
Jamie, Captain, i. 7, 8
Jenkinson, Mr. (afterwards Earl of Liverpool), Clerk of the Pells in Ireland, ii. 219 *note*
Jephson, Mr. Donham, ii. 147; iii. 362
Jew brokers of Spain, iii. 176
Johnson, Mr., iii. 27
Johnstone, Edward, of Carroe, i. 434
Johnstone, General, iii. 406-409, 436, 437, 443
Jones, Colonel Michael, i. 117, 118
Jones, Dr., Dean of Kilmore, i. 95 *note*
Jones, Dr. H. (afterwards Bishop of Meath), i. 139, and *note*
Jones, Mr. Todd, ii. 431, 505; iii. 109
Jones, Paul, i. 362; ii. 212, 235, and *note*, 236, 255
Joycuse, Admiral, iii. 201, 202
Juan de Aguila, Don, i. 62
Juan de Langara, Admiral Don, ii. 280
Judges Tenure Bill, ii. 53, 54, 57, 59, 62, 105, 184, 249, 290
Jury, trial by, iii. 467
Justice to Ireland, ii. 218

KAOLLY, Doctor Laughlin, titular Archbishop of Tuam, i. 89 *note*
Keating, Chief Justice, i. 180, 187
Keating, Mr., i. 169; ii. 30
Kelly, Pat, i. 469, 470
Kelly, Roger, i. 443-445
Kendal, Duchess of, i. 518, 522; ii. 77
Kenmare Bay, i. 455
Kenmare colony, i. 245
Kenmare river, i. 451
Kenmare, smelting furnaces at, i. 245
Kenmare, Lord, i. 404; ii. 18, 385, 473; iii. 25, 35, 244
Keogh, John, iii. 25, 33, 52 *note*, 56, 57, 63, 69, 70, 71, 73, 77, 78, 83, 108, 135, 144, 158, 159, 165, 178, 179, 183, 190, 197, 259, 396, 432
Keppel, Van, Lord of Voorst, created Earl of Albemarle, i. 221 *note*
Keris, Honor, i. 423
Kern, Father, iii. 401
Kernes, iii. 217

LAW

Kerry, i. 470, 473; ii. 455, 473; iii. 109, 303
Kerry, Earl of, i. 256, 493, 495
Kerry, Knight of, in 1740, i. 451
Ker's dragoons, i. 353
Kilconnell, i. 90 *note*
Kilcullen, iii. 365, 367, 370
Kildare, Earl Gerald of, i. 34
Kildare, Earl of, i. 30, 516, 617, 618; ii. 107, 146
Kilfinnan, iii. 111
Kilkenny, i. 25, 115, 116, 120; iii. 110, 375, 398, 419, 446
Kilkenny and Kildare Militia, iii. 246
Killarney, i. 469 *note*, 470
Killala, iii. 482, 483
Killala, Bishop of, iii. 65
Kilmakilloge, i. 245, 249
Kilmuckridge, iii. 380
King, Archbishop, i. 313, 389, 535; ii. 449
King, Bishop of Derry (afterwards Archbishop of Dublin), i. 252, 285
King, Captain, iii. 406
King, Charles, i. 449 *note*
King, Mr. Rufus, iii. 481
King's County, i. 377 *note*; iii. 74
Kingsale, i. 113, 182, 184
Kingsborough, Lord (afterwards Earl of Kingston), iii. 432, 440, 441, 445, 447
Kingsmill, Admiral, iii. 210
Kingston, Duchess of, iii. 117
Kingston, Lord i. 256
Kirkcudbright Bay, ii. 213
Kirwan, Mr., i. 271 *note*
Knipe, Mr., iii. 299
Knox, Mr., iii. 94
Knox, Sir George, iii. 148

LACY, General, ii. 127
La Fayette, ii. 205, 281, 284; iii. 87
Lake, General (afterwards Lord Lake), iii. 234, 235, 255, 258, 268, 269, 270, 274, 291, 300, 329, 332, 333, 335, 336, 355, 357, 358, 400, 404, 436, 438, 444, 446, 447, 448, 473, 483
Land, i. 130, 507 *note*
Landlord exactions, ii. 53, 120-124, 469, 481, 482
Landregan, David, ii. 32
Lanesborough, Earl of, ii. 85 and *note*, 90
Langrishe, Sir Hercules, ii. 436; iii. 42, 45, 47, 49, 53, 86, 148
Lansdowne, Lord, iii. 451
La Touche, Messrs., ii. 212
La Touche, Peter, ii. 269, 294
Lauderdale, Earl of, iii. 321
Lawder, Rev. Francis, Vicar General, i. 470, 471, 473

LAW

Law, Doctor, iii. 95
Law, Irish Courts of, ii. 325
Lawless, Mr., iii. 287, 312, 418
Lawrence, Sir Soulden, iii. 318
Lee, Mr., ii. 155; iii. 247
Légion Noire, iii. 201
Legislature of Ireland, iii. 5
Legislatures, ii. 197
Lehaunstown, iii. 340
Leinster, ii. 328, 355
Leinster, Countess of, i. 518
Leinster, Duke of, ii. 45, 46, 65, 78, 92, 93, 146, 187, 238, 239, 275, 261, 264, 357, 396, 404, 411, 413, 503, 504, 507, 509, 511, 516-518; iii. 112, 136, 173, 199, 224, 245, 267, 270, 287, 339 *note*, 358, 450, 454
Leinster House, iii. 46, 82, 312, 317
Leitrim, iii. 109
Lent, i. 370 *note*
Leslie, Bishop of Raphoe, i. 158
Leslie, John, Bishop of Down, i. 77
L'Estrange, Colonel, iii. 401, 419
Levinge, Sir Richard, i. 270, 354
Lewin, Mr. Ross, i. 424
Lewines, iii. 283
Lewines, Ed., iii. 117, 259, 262, 266, 267 *note*
Leixleap Castle, i. 125 *note*
Lexington, ii. 139, 174; iii. 399
Liberation, Acts of, ii. 375
Liberty, i. 604; ii. 366
Lifford, Lord, Chancellor of Ireland, ii. 58, 59, 223, 225, 503, 519
Limerick, Articles of, i. 202, 204, 255; ii. 42
Limerick, defences of, ii. 77
Lindsay, Archbishop, i. 384
Lindsay, Dr., Bishop of Killaloe, i. 252
Linen Hall of Belfast, iii. 18, 59
Linen manufacture of Ulster, ii. 71
Linen trade, ii. 124, 162, 421, 423, 443
Lisburn, ii. 368
Lismore, Lord, Mr. O'Callaghan created, ii. 405
Lloyd, Wm., Bishop of Killala, i. 252
Loftus, General, iii. 401, 402, 403, 405, 419, 436, 443
Loftus, Lord, ii. 91, 92, 100, 102, 106, 515, 516; created an Earl ii. 519
Loftus, Mr. ii. 401, 405
Londonderry, i. 75 *note*; iii. 151; house of, ii. 519
Longfield, ii. 155
Longford, iii. 152
Long Island, ii. 201
Longueville, Lord, iii. 173, 225
Lords Justices, government of the, ii. 35
Lords, House of, i. 346-348
L'Orient, ii. 235

MAG

Lorraine, Duke of, i. 128
Longhborough, Lord, iii. 275
Louis XIV., i. 197, 198
Louis XV., ii. 14
Louis XVI., ii. 430
Louth, iii. 66 *note*, 105
Louth, Earl of, ii. 85 *note*
Lowry, iii. 265
Lowry, A., iii. 282, 283
Lowth, Lord, i. 256
Lowther, Chief Justice, i. 91
Loyalty, spontaneous, iii. 170
Lucas, ii. 65, 78; iii. 218
Lucas, Charles, i. 606, 607, 608
Lucas, Mr. Thomas, i. 423
Ludlow, General, i. 128, 151
Lundy, Colonel, i. 183
Luttrell's Town, iii. 178
Luttrell, Colonel (afterwards Lord Carhampton), ii. 322, 395, 417; iii. 161, 455, 460, 471, 472, 474. *See* Carhampton
Lysaght, Mr. ii. 147

MACARTNEY, Sir George, ii. 93, 103, 104; iii. 232
MacArt's Fort, iii. 160, 165
McCabe, iii. 106
McCann, iii. 316, 317
McCann, John, iii. 475, 476
MacCarty, i. 473
MacCarty, of Newry, ii. 255
McCracken, iii. 62
McCormick, Richard, iii. 57, 65, 135, 159, 316, 317, 125, 283
MacDonnell, or MacConnell, Sir Randal, Earl of Antrim, i. 69
Macdonnell, Alaster, i. 106
MacDonnell, Dr., iii. 59
McGuchin, iii. 411
Mackay, i. 198
McKenna, Dr., iii. 39
MacMahon, i. 440
Macmahon, Emer, afterwards Bishop of Clogher, i. 89, 96, 128
MacMahon, Hugh, i. 96, 97, 100
Macmanus, Captain, iii. 446
Macmorris, Captain, i. 7, 8
MacMorrough, ii. 340
McMurdoch, Mr., iii. 175 *note*
MacMurrough, Dermot, Prince of Leinster, i. 16
MacNally, iii. 117, 120
MacNeven, iii. 125, 229, 260, 262, 278, 283, 317, 352, 474, 478, 481
MacTier, iii. 61
Maddin, Dr., i. 412
Madras, iii. 114 *note*
Magee, Island, i. 103, 104

INDEX.

MAG

Magennis, Sir Con, i. 97
Magistrates, ii. 447, 484; iii. 168
Magna Charta, iii. 17
Maguyre, Lord, of Fermanagh, i. 96, 97, 100
Mahony, Mr. Daniel (or Donell), i. 452, 454, 477
Maitland, iii. 283
Maidstone, iii. 315
Malby, Sir Nicholas, i. 57
Malone, ii. 57, 108
Malone, Mr. Anthony, Irish Chancellor of the Exchequer, i. 621; ii. 6, 82, 109 note
Malone, Mr., nephew to Anthony, ii. 109 note, 181
Manchester, ii. 104
Mansfield, Lord, ii. 360, 361
Marcray Castle, in Sligo, iii. 109
Margate, iii. 313, 318
Marino, ii. 386
Marlborough, Duke of, i. 344
Marseillais, iii. 69
' Marseillaise,' iii. 191
Martin, the member for James Town, ii. 352
Martin, of Ballinahinch, i. 477
Martin, Dick, ii. 381 note
Martin, Robert, i. 598
Mary, Queen, and Philip II., i. 42
Mason, Monk, ii. 460
Massachusetts Chambers, ii. 134, 136, 141, 206
Massereene, Lord, ii. 180
Massey, Hugh, ii. 100 note
Mathews, Dr., Archdeacon of Down, i. 239, 243, 244
Matthieson, Mrs., of Hamburgh, iii. 283
Maude, Sir Thomas, ii. 32
Maxwell, Colonel, iii. 302, 394
Maxwell, Henry, i. 288, 290, 387
' May Flower,' ii. 129
Mayne, Sir William, ii. 85 note, 92
Maynooth College, iii. 146
Mayo, iii. 109
Meath, iii. 66, 74, 303, 366
Meath, Bishop of, i. 379
Mervyn, Colonel Audley, i. 102 note
Meskell, Joanna, ii. 24, 25 note, 28
Methodism, i. 628
Methuen, Chancellor of Ireland, i. 250
Middleton, Lord, Lord Justice, i. 524, 535, 542
Milan, iii. 198, 256
Militia Act, ii. 232
Militia, Antrim, iii. 422
Militia, Armagh, iii. 359
Militia Bill, ii. 78, 211, 210, 428, 434; iii. 89, 359, 419, 483
Militia, regiments of, formed, i. 164

MUR

Milton, Lord, iii. 141
Minorca, ii. 338
Mirabeau, iii. 18, 106
Mitford, iii. 318
Mizen Head, iii. 203
Moira, Lord, iii. 9, 17, 18, 63, 64 and note, 71, 114, 115, 224, 229, 237, 244, 261, 268, 270, 274, 275, 291, 292, 294, 299, 301, 300-311, 320, 426, 450, 451, 454, 463
Molyneux, iii. 18
Molyneux, Mr., ii. 394
Molyneux, Sir Capel, ii. 370
Molyneux, William, i. 269
Molesworth, Robert (afterwards Lord Molesworth, i. 356, 386
Monaghan, ii. 67, 306
Monckton, General, wounded, ii. 53
Money Bill, a short, ii. 57, 58
Money Bills, ii. 78, 80 note, 82, 102, 108, 110, 111, 160, 161, 162, 239, 240
Monroe, the American minister, iii. 193
Monro, General, i. 115, 117
Montgomery, Colonel, ii. 200, 370
Montgomery, George, ii. 109 note
Montgomery, Mr., of Donegal, ii. 345
Moore, Captain, ii. 392
Moore, General, iii. 436, 438, 440, 445, 446, 473
Moore, Roger, i. 96, 100; iii. 24, 428
Moores, the, ii. 127
Morgan, Major, i. 135
Mornington, Lord (afterwards Marquis Wellesley), ii. 396, 404
Morris, Mr. Lodge, ii. 517, 518 note
Mount Alexander, Lord, i. 181
Mountjoy, Lord, i. 62; iii. 406, 407, 410
Mountmorris, Lord, iii. 377
Mountrath, Earl of, i. 147
Mountshannon, John Fitzgibbon's estate at, ii. 48
Moylan, Dr., Catholic Bishop of Cork, iii. 70, 214
Muir, Thomas, iii. 115
Mullingar, iii. 258
Mulshinoge, Noe, i. 540 note
Munster, ii. 22, 23, 455, 471, 485; iii 233, 355
Munster, the Geraldines of, i. 56
Munster, President of, ii. 172
Murder, ii. 400
Murphy, iii. 342
Murphy, Father John, iii. 377, 378, 382, 392, 398, 402, 403, 419, 420, 431, 432, 444, 446, 447, 449
Murphy, Father Michael, iii. 377, 380, 398, 423
Murphy, Father, of Taghmon, iii. 413
Murphy, John, of Loughnageer, iii. 412, 413

MUR

Murray, Lord Henry, iii. 188 *note*
Musgrave, Sir Richard, ii. 473 *note*; iii. 421
Muskerry, Lord, i. 128
Mutiny Act, British, ii. 261
Mutiny Act, perpetual, ii. 266
Mutiny Bill, ii. 258, 260, 264, 265, 287, 290, 295, 297, 320, 325, 335, 342, 499,
Mutiny at Portsmouth and at the Nore, iii. 195
Mylne, a prebendary of Kilrush, i. 244

NAAS, iii. 164, 358, 359, 362, 364, 436
Nagle, Sir R., i. 173, 197, 256
Nantes, Edict of, iii. 23
Napiers, the, ii. 127
Napoleon, iii. 192, 265
National Assembly, iii. 82
National Congress, iii. 109
National Guards, iii. 80, 82, 157, 298
National independence, i. 2–13
Nationalist leaders, iii. 76
'Nationality,' ii. 340
Nationality, Irish, iii. 459
Navigation Act, i. 161
Navigation Laws, ii. 215, 438, 439
Nayler, Peter, i. 551 *note*
Needham, General, iii. 419, 422, 436
Needham's Gap, iii. 442
Neilson, Samuel, iii. 62, 160, 175, 179, 190, 340, 345, 350, 351, 476
Nenagh, iii. 273
Nepean, Mr. Evan, ii. 413–415 *note*
Neville, Arthur, i. 612
Nevile, the miniature painter, iii. 245 *note*
Newcastle, Duke of, i. 393, 394
Newdigate, Captain Mark, i. 436
New England, ii. 134, 202
Newenham, Sir Edward, iii. 148
Newgate, i. 592 *note*; iii. 190, 353
New Haven, ii. 206
New Ross, iii. 375, 398, 406, 412, 419, 436
Newton, Sir Isaac, i. 210, 530
Newtown Arden, iii. 426–428
New Town Barry, iii. 375, 385, 398, 401, 402
Newry, i. 97
New York, ii. 134, 201, 206, 281, 283
Nonconformists, i. 155, 156, 209, 215, 236, 319, 354, 385, 391; ii. 216
Nonconformity, ii. 130, 175
Nore, iii. 246, 248, 262
Norfolk, Duke of, iii. 173, 320, 452, 454
Normans, i. 14, 16, 17, 18, 20, 24, 28
'Northern Star,' iii. 208
North, Lord, ii. 108, 111, 114, 137, 145,

ONE

149-151, 154, 160, 171, 179, 181, 184, 187, 207, 215, 217, 218, 289, 310, 318–320. 354 *note*, 362, 364; iii. 295
Northington, Robert Honley, Earl of, Viceroy, ii. 362, 363, 373, 375, 380, 334, 385, 394, 395, 416; iii. 137
Northumberland, Earl of, Viceroy, ii. 36, 39
Nottingham, Lord, i. 229
Nugents, i. 374 *note*
Nugent, General, iii. 426
Nugent, Lord, ii, 214, 220
Nutley, Sir R., i. 353 *note*

OAK BOYS, ii. 116, 447
O'Brien, ii. 448 *note*
O'Brien, Sir Donogh, i. 414
O'Brien, Father, co-adjutor of the Archbishop of Cashel, ii. 31
O'Brien, Michel, vicar-general of Kilfenore, i. 551 *note*
O'Brien, Sir Lucius, ii. 223, 224, 232 342, 497
O'Briens, the, i. 30
O'Callaghan, Mr., created Lord Lismore, ii. 405
O'Coigly. *See* Quigley
O'Connor, a United Irishman, iii. 164
O'Connor, Arthur, iii. 28, 32, 173, 174, 199, 216, 224, 227, 229, 258, 281–283, 288, 312, 314–315, 318, 321, 345, 392, 416, 431, 452, 453, 474, 477, 478,
O'Connell, Daniel, i. 403; iii. 218
O'Connor, Roderick, ii. 458, 460
O'Conolly. Owen, i. 99
Octennial Bill, ii. 59, 65, 66, 224, 363
O'Decies, Marcus, his townlands, i. 130 *note*
O'Dogherty, Sir Cahir, i. 67
O'Donnells, the, i. 30
O'Donnell, General, ii. 127
O'Donnell, Hugh, i. 63 and *note*
O'Donnell, Rory, becomes Earl of Tryconnell, i. 67
O'Donoghue, the, i. 469 *note*
Ogle, Mr., of Wexford, ii. 344, 460, 469; iii. 52, 88, 137
O'Leary, Father, ii. 33, 34 *note*, 413–415
Oligarchy of the Shannons and Ponsonbies, ii. 43
Oliver, Mr., ii. 155
O'Hara, Colonel, iii. 422
O'Hara, Mayor of Galway, i. 598, 599 *note*
O'Hara, Mr., iii. 47, 48 and *note*
O'Loghlin, Captain Charles, i. 414
O'Loghlin, Connor, i. 414
O'Neill, Con, Earl of Tyrone, i. 43

INDEX.

ONE

O'Neill, Sir Henry, i. 97
O'Neill, Hugh, Earl of Tyrone, i. 59-63, 67
O'Neill, Shan or John, i. 43, 252
O'Neill, Lord, ii. 18, 425
O'Neill, Owen Rory or Owen Roo, nephew of the Earl of Tyrone, i. 96, 116, 119
O'Neill, Sir Phelim, his underplot, i. 96, 97, 107 and *note*, 129; iii. 24, 285, 353, 428
O'Neill, Tirlogh, i. 57
O'Neills, the, i. 30
Orange Association, iii. 325
Orange oaths, forged, iii. 273
Orange, Prince of, i. 178
Orangemen, iii. 154, 155, 168-171, 175, 178, 180, 188, 233, 250, 273, 306, 322, 325, 327, 338, 353, 355, 376, 382, 400, 426, 430, 432, 433, 445, 467
Orators, Irish, iii. 6
Oratory. iii. 44, 45, 348
Orde, Mr. (afterwards Lord Bolton), ii. 396, 397, 413, 414, 424-425, 439-441, 457, 468, 469
Ordnance Department, ii. 35, 106
Oriel, Lord, Right Hon. John Foster created ii. 238 *note*
O'Reilly, Philip, i. 96
Orkney, Lady, i. 223, 270
Ormond, Duke of, i. 24, 52, 53, 82, 86, 115, 117-119, 128, 166, 148, 151-153, 295 *note*, 299, 343, 344, 345, 348, 360, 553, 550; iii. 178
Orr, Samuel, iii. 425
Orr, William, iii. 174, 175, 179, 269, 283
Orrery, Earl of, Lord Broghill created, i. 147
Osborne, Mr., iii. 149
Osborne, Sir William, ii. 107
Ossory. Bishop of, ii. 364
O'Sullivans of Berehaven, i. 455; iii. 209
O'Sullivan, Morty Oge, i. 455, 456
O'Sullivan, Sylvester, i. 465, 466, 469, 471, 475
Oulart, iii. 381, 382
Outlawries, i. 177
Outlawries Bill, i. 252, 253, 255

PAINE, Tom, ii. 288, 412; iii. 10, 19, 47, 76, 110
Pale, the English, i. 27, 30
Pallisers, the, ii. 127
Palmer, Mr., i. 240
Pamela, daughter of Madame de Genlis, iii. 168 *note*, 173
Panderus, i. 30-33
Papal power, iii. 149
Paper, tax on, ii. 184

PIT

Papists, Lord Clare on, iii. 100
Paris, Peace of, ii. 34, 133
Paris, iii. 16, 159, 191, 266, 302
Parker, Sir Peter, ii. 200
Parker, the informer, ii. 413-415
Parliament, British, ii. 438, 501, 402, 420
Parliament, the Back Lane, iii. 70
Parliamentary opposition, iii. 220
Parliamentary reform, ii. 372, 420, 435, 43 ; iii. 44
Parliaments, annual, ii. 372
Parnell, Sir John, ii. 388, Chancellor of the Exchequer, iii. 41, 89, 94, 116, 122
Parsons, Sir Lawrence, ii. 439; iii. 27, 90, 91, 94, 136
Parsons, Sir William, i. 99
Patriots, Irish, ii. 325, 433, 435. 467; iii. 28, 224-228, 145, 241, 243 *note*, 289, 353, 392
Patriots, consciences of Irish, i. 632
Peasantry, Irish, iii. 107, 113, 217, 230, 244, 320, 438
Peel, Sir Robert, iii. 148
Peep-of-Day-Boys, ii. 120, 489; iii. 18, 154
Peers, Irish, ii. 404, 503
Pelham, Mr., iii. 137, 141. 142, 144, 145, 147, 174, 180, 186, 253, 270, 271, 274, 287, 289, 290, 303. 304, 316
Pembroke, Earl of, Viceroy, i. 320
Penal Bill, i. 331, 332
Penal Laws, ii. 216 ; iii. 306
Pennefather, Mr., ii. 181, 328
Pennsylvania, ii. 202
Pension Bill, ii. 495; iii. 116, 297
Pension List, i. 301, 510, 612, 614 ; ii. 7 *note*, 35, 36, 55, 65, 77, 143, 149, 167, 100, 209, 462 and *note*, 486, 511, 513; iii. 103
Pepper, Colonel, i. 350
Perceval, Mr., iii. 381
Pery, Sexton, afterwards Lord Glentworth, ii. 64, 78, 84, 90, 102; Speaker, 103, 104, 112, 155, 156, 187, 223, 226, 239, 243, 261, 326; iii. 52, 293
Petersburgh, ii. 284
Petty, Dr., i. 111, 113, 132, 133, 152, 153, 245, 451
Philadelphia, ii. 136, 190, 202
Philip II., i. 42, 48 ; iii. 198
Phillips, a priest, iii. 161
Phipps, Sir Constantine, Chancellor, i. 348, 353 *note*, 355, 357
Phœnix Park, Artillery Companies of, ii. 355
Pie powder, court of, i. 280 and *note*
Pitt. *See* Earl of Chatham
Pitt, Right Hon. William, Chancellor of the Exchequer, ii. 353, 364, 368, 395,

VOL. III. L L

PLA

396, 410, 414, 420, 422, 427, 438, 444, 492, 501 *note*; iii. 9, 21-23, 24, 25, 35, 37, 43, *note*, 44, 56, 58, 64, 67, 68, 75, 76, 77, 81, 94, 95, 103, 104, 113, 117, 120, 123, 133, 144, 145, 158, 184, 229, 233, 239, 244, 248, 253, 261, 266, 270, 279, 281, 283, 284, 305, 427, 450, 456
Place Bill, ii. 495; iii. 116, 297
Plantagenet, Harry, ii. 290
Plowden, Mr., ii. 491
Plumer, iii. 318
Plunket, Captain, i. 116
Plunket, Father, i. 135 *note*
Plunket, Sir Nicholas, i. 144
Pluralists, ii. 469.
Pluralities, ii. 450
Police, ii. 100, 486.
Police Act, ii. 464-468, 497, 511; iii. 6, 131
Policemen, Irish, iii. 218
Political reform, ii. 368
Rooley, Bishop of Raphoe, i. 327, 328 *note*
Pope, the, iii. 16, 148
Pomeroy, Colonel, ii. 109 *note*
Ponsonby, Colonel, i. 237
Ponsonby, George, ii. 47, 30, 296, 495, 496, 516, 517; iii. 9, 27, 51, 81, 82, 92, 93 *notes*, 116, 120, 121, 122, 149, 159 *note*, 180, 201, 224, 232, 242, 243; iii. 450, 252, 253, 267
Ponsonby, John, Speaker of the Irish House of Commons, i. 616, 618, 632; ii. 6, 36, 39, 40, 47, 57, 60-64, 90, 103, 156, 158, 404
Ponsonby, William, son of the Speaker, ii. 65, 100, 388, 507, 509, 516, 517; iii. 20, 80, 116, 122, 224, 232, 241, 252, 450
Ponsonbys, the, ii. 5, 76, 101, 110, 111, 144, 146, 177, 181, 187, 329; iii. 454
Popery Acts, i. 273, 374
Popish colleges, ii. 317
Portadown, Peace of, iii. 154
Porter, Sir Charles, Lord Chancellor, i. 167, 177, 195, 219, 231, 233, 237, 260
Porter, Sir Stanion, ii. 240
Portia, ii. 502
Portland, Duke of, ii. 200, 321, 323, 324, 325, 328, 331, 332, 334, 336, 343, 345, 353, 362, 376, 378, 499, 515, 516; iii. 122, 124, 126, 129, 132, 134, 138, 141, 165, 166, 184-186, 211, 214, 244, 248, 270, 293, 305, 309, 324, 325, 327, 331, 390, 404, 416, 418, 457
Portsmouth, mutiny of the fleet at, iii. 240
Portugal, help to, ii. 17
Power, Mr., iii. 272 *note*
Poynings' Act, ii. 5, 81 *note*, 256, 289, 290, 295, 299, 325, 332, 336, 349

RAP

Poynings, Sir Edward, appointed deputy, i. 35
Prendergast, Mr., i. 134 *note*
Prendergast, Sir Thomas, i. 11
Presbyterian marriages, i. 319, 594; iii. 151
Presbyterians, i. 154, 284, 329, 335, 342, 347, 382, 408, 623; ii. 122, 130, 131, 177, and *note*, 211, 216, 217, 249, 288, 365, 446, 453, 488; iii. 6, 18, 50, 259, 352, 399, 425-427, 430, 435
Press, the, ii. 106, 409
Preston, Captain, iii. 366
Preston, General, i. 117
Pretender, i 325, 357, 365, 408, 451, 553, 559, 598; ii. 21
Priests, i. 317, 547-649 and *note*, 552, 560, 562; iii. 246
Prim, Mr. Joshua, ii. 421
Princeton, battle of, ii. 201; iii. 190
Pritty, Henry, ii. 109 *note*
Privateers, American, ii. 280; in the Irish Channel, ii. 219
Privy Council of Ireland, ii. 254, 380, 492, 499, 518 *note*
Privy Councillors, iii. 345
Profligacy, political, i. 631
Progress, philosophy of, iii. 4
Prosperous, place so called, iii. 358, 359, 361, 362
Protection of Irish manufactures, ii. 399, 400, 470
Protestant ascendancy, iii. 53
Protestant families, i. 107
Protestant gentry, iii. 459
Protestants, Irish, ii. 275-277, 325
Protestant revolt, ii. 3
Protestants of Ulster, ii. 116, 117
Pulling, Lieutenant, iii. 210
Puritans in Londonderry, i. 75 *note*; ii. 133, 151
Puritanism, i. 159; ii. 130
Puxley, John, the revenue officer, i. 456, 458, 459-461

QUAKERS, i. 433, 434
Quebec, colony of, ii. 136, 200; capitulation of, ii. 52
Queen's County, iii. 110, 339
Quiberon, i. 623; ii. 192, 193
Quigley, a priest, iii. 312, 314, 317, 318, 321, 322

RABY, Lord, i. 221
Rack-rents, iii. 74
Radcliff, Sir George, i. 91
Rapparees, iii. 217, 236, 277, 280, 309, 435 *note*, 556

INDEX. 515

RAT

Rathangar, iii. 367
Rathdowney, ii. 98
Rathfarnham, iii. 357
Ratoath, iii. 357
Ravishers, iii. 217
Ravishment, ii. 447, 460
Rawdon. *See* Moira
Rawley, Mr., ii. 32
Rebels' oath, iii. 409 *note*
Reform Bill, ii. 386, 388, 389, 399, 410, 495; iii. 15, 76, 81, 102, 103, 108, 111, 116, 123, 130, 133, 222, 234, 239, 292, 296, 458
Reformers, Northern, iii. 244
Regan, Ned, ii. 448 *note*
Regency, ii. 498, 509; iii. 59, 76, 297, 492, 493, 494
Registration Act, ii. 29
Regium Donum, i. 239, 241, 284, 313, 342, 347, 382
Reilly, Mr. Stephen, High Sheriff of Dublin, ii. 400, 416, 418, 419, 429
Relief Bill, iii. 42
'Renunciation Bill,' ii. 361, 362, 364
Republicanism in Ireland, iii. 219, 282
Responsibility Bill, iii. 112, 297
Restoration of the Stuarts, i. 141
Restriction Acts, ii. 247
Resumption Bill, i. 272, 273
Revenue, the, ii. 149, 190
Revenue Board, ii. 91, 106, 110, 144
Revenue, Irish, ii. 4; hereditary, iii. 103
Revolution, French, iii. 532
Revolutionary Committee, iii. 209, 255, 290, 293, 298, 303, 327, 330, 335, 345, 349
Reynolds, Thomas, iii. 304, 342
Rheinart, Minister of the Directory, iii. 253
Rhine, the, iii. 197
Rhode Island, ii. 205
Rice, Sir Stephen, Chief Baron, i. 173, 177, 107, 314, 404
Richard II., i. 26
Richards, Dr., Dean of Tralee, i. 246, 248, 249
Richmond, Duke of, ii. 46
Rigby, Irish Master of the Rolls, ii. 55 *note*, 404
Right, Captain, ii. 455-457
Rights, Declaration of, ii. 326, 328
'Rights of Man,' Tom Paine's, iii. 10
Ringwood, iii. 388, 390
Rinuccini, John Baptiste, i. 116, 118; iii. 198
Riot Act, ii. 483
Riverstown, Lord, i. 374 *note*
Roach, the farmer, iii. 365
Robinson, Mr., ii. 289, 316

SAI

Rochambeau, de, ii. 283
Roche, Edward, iii. 388
Roche, Father, iii. 388, 390, 398, 406, 415, 419, 432, 437, 438, 447
Roche, Sir Boyle, ii. 307, 384, 385, 398; iii. 52 *note*
Rochelle, iii. 482
Rochefort, Robert, i. 232
Rochford, Mr., ii. 401, 402
Rockingham, Marquis of, ii. 39, 150, 160, 319, 320, 323, 345, 353
Roden, Lord, iii. 357, 444, 483
Rodney, Sir George, ii. 280, 282, 285, 338, 343; iii. 51
Rolleston, Mr., of Green Park, Youghal, iii. 272 *note*
Romney, Lord, iii. 318
Roscommon, county of, i. 409; iii. 109, 152
Roscommon, Lord, i. 153
Rosen, Marshal, i. 182, 192
Roses, Wars of the, i. 28
Ross, i. 127
Ross Castle, on Killarney, i. 127
Ross, General, ii. 298
Rotunda in Dublin, ii. 382, 388, 428
Round-robin, ii. 509, 514, 515; iii. 9
Rowan, Mr. Hamilton, ii. 520; iii. 54, 65, 66, 69, 83, 114, 118, 119, and *note*, 158, 100, 281
Rowley, Right Hon. Mr., M.P. for Meath, ii. 469
Rowley, Sir Hercules Langford, ii. 85 *note*; iii. 10, 17
Royal Exchange in Dublin, ii. 382
Rupert, Prince, i. 118, 128
Russell, Ensign, iii. 9, 11, 19, 20, 160, 165, 179, 195
Russell, Lord, iii. 181
Russell, Lord John, iii. 173, 320
Russell, Lord William, iii. 455
Russia, ii. 163, 274, 423, 443
Rutland, Duke of, Viceroy, ii. 395, 396, 404, 405, 410, 412, 416, 419, 425, 445, 460, 461, 473, 485-487, 518 *note*
Ruvigny, Henri de, i. 222
Ryan, Captain, iii. 341, 342-344

SACKVILLE, Lord George, Irish Secretary, i. 611
St. Alban's, Duke of, i. 301 *note*
St. Eustatius, ii. 282
St. George, Colonel, ii. 475; iii. 291, 293, 294, 300
St. George, Lord, i. 415
St. John, Henry, i. 343, 347
St. John, Lord Bolingbroke, i. 352
St. Leger, St. Leger, ii. 147

SAI

St. Mary's Isle, ii. 213
St. Patrick, Order of the Knights of, ii. 362
St. Ruth, French general at Aghrim, i. 198, 199
St. Vincent, Cape, ii. 280
Saltee Islands, iii. 448
Sanders, Nicholas, i. 54, 55, 56
Sandford, Mr., ii. 181
Sandwich, Earl of, ii. 137
Sandy Hook, ii. 201
Saratoga, surrender at, ii. 204, 206
Sarsfield, Patrick (afterwards Earl of Lucan), i. 201, 256
Savannah, ii. 206
Schism Act, i. 347, 350
Schomberg, Duke, i. 192
Scot, the, i. 7, 8
Scotland, i. 8, 9, 286, 340
Scots partly occupy Antrim and Down, i. 69
Scott, iii. 318, 388
Scott, Attorney-General (afterwards Lord Clonmel and Chief Justice), ii. 238, 242, 243, 262, 263, 395
Scott, Robert, ii. 109 note
Scullabogue, iii. 406, 426
Security Act, 261, 269
Selkirk, Lord, ii. 213
September massacre, iii. 64
Septennial Act, ii. 7, 10
Septennial Bill. 54, 55, 57, 59
Settlement, Irish Act of, i. 148, 150, 190; ii. 22, 305, 310, 506
Shannon, Henry Boyle, first Lord, i. 537, 632; ii. 30, 46; Richard Boyle, second Lord, ii. 46; third Lord, ii. 57, 60, 85, 90, 114, 144, 146, 147, 169, 187, 218, 404, 509, 515, 516; iii. 231
Shannon, Mount, ii. 417
Sheares, Henry, iii. 340, 346, 351, 474
Sheares, John, 340, 341, 345, 346, 351, 474
Sheehy, Father Nicholas, parish priest of Clogheen in Tipperary, ii. 29, 30
Sheehy, Buck (Edmund), ii. 30, 31
Sheep farming in Ireland, i. 397
Sheffield, Lord, iii. 241
Shelburne, Lord, i. 453; ii. 54, 58, 221, 246, 247, 320, 321, 332, 335, 341, 353, 361, 362, 462 note
Sheridan, Charles, ii. 49, 53, 322, 325, 498, 509
Sheridan, R. B., iii. 173, 320, 355, 453
Shrewsbury, Duke of, made Viceroy, i. 352, 354, 358
Shylock, ii. 502
Sidney, Sir Henry, i. 52
Sidney, Lord, brother of Algernon Sidney

STO

(afterwards Earl of Romney), i. 195, 198, 219, 222; Viceroy, 225, 228, 229, 231, 239; ii. 79, 258, 422 note, 471
Simms, iii. 61, 160, 175, 179
Simms, Robert, iii. 283
Simuel, Lambert, i. 29, 34
Sinclair, iii. 19
Sinecures, Irish, ii. 55
Sirr, Major, iii. 341–343
Skeffington, Hugh, ii. 109 note
Skeffington, Major, ii. 180
Skeffington, William, ii. 109 note
Skerritt, Colonel, iii. 420, 422
Slaney, the, iii. 375, 383, 385, 398, 402, 436, 445
Slieveboy Mountain, iii. 403
Sligo, iii. 109
Smerwick, iii. 198
Smith, Ch., ii. 109 note
Smith, Colonel, ii. 138
Smith, Dr., Dean of St. Patrick's, i. 251, 252 note
Smith, Mr., iii. 232
'Smoke money,' ii. 454
Smugglers, ii. 190, 255; iii. 166
Smuggling, i. 446, 447, 440, 450, 506; ii. 76 note, 486
Snow, Captain, iii. 384, 386, 387
Soldiers, Irish, 218
Solicitors and Barristers Bill, i. 577
Somers, Lord, iii. 181
Somerville, Sir James, i. 607
Sons of the Shamrock, ii. 430
Southwell, Secretary Sir Edward, i. 245 note, 295, 295 note, 299 note, 315, 345
Spain, i. 585; ii. 205, 252–254, 274
Spain, fleet of, iii. 51, 340
Spencer, Lord, ii. 495, 497, 503, 504, 508; iii. 122
Spithead, iii. 230
Stack, Mr., iii. 10
Stackpoole, Catherine, i. 421
Stamer, Mr., iii. 362
Stamp duty, ii. 133, 134
Stanhope, Lady, i. 519
Stanhope, Lord, i. 390, 401
Stanley, Mr., i. 251 note
Stanley, Sir John, i. 354
Stannard, Recorder of Dublin, ii. 6
Stapleton, Colonel, iii. 426
Steel, Hearts of, ii. 447
Sterne, Richard, iii. 434
Stewart, A., iii. 10
Stewart, Colonel, (afterwards Marquis of Londonderry), ii. 370
Stewart, Robert (afterwards Lord Castlereagh), iii. 10, 17, 28
Stock, Edmond, i. 423
Stokes, Whitly, dean of Trinity, iii. 10, 59

INDEX. 517

STO

Stone, Archbishop, i. 610, 612, 618; ii. 30, 197, 449
Stone, Primate, ii. 197
Strafford, Earl of, Viceroy, i. 72, 78, 79, 81, 82; ii. 276
Strangford, Lord, Dean of Derry, ii. 401-403
Stuart, A. J., of Acton, iii. 283, 418
Sugar Bill, ii. 267
Sunderland, Earl of, i. 320, 321, 343, 382
Supply Bills, ii. 266, 395; iii. 167
Supremacy, Oath of, i. 311
Swan, Major, iii. 316, 330, 341, 342
Swayne, Captain, iii. 359-361
Swayne, Mr., a magistrate, iii. 272 *note*
Sweetman, iii. 317
Swift, Dean of St. Patrick's, i. 328, 329, 352 *note*, 365, 385 *note*, 500, 501, 531, 536-538, 539 *note*, 546, 605; ii. 196 447
Switzerland, iii. 173, 400
Synge, Dr. Chancellor of St. Patrick's, i. 563, 567; ii. 449

TAAFE, General, i. 127
Taafe, Lord, i. 118, 127
Taghmon, Mount, iii. 392, 445, 449
Talbot, Colonel Richard, known as Lying Dick (afterwards the Duke of Tyrconnell), i. 165, 168, 171
Talbot, Mr., ii. 210
Talbot, Peter, Catholic Archbishop of Dublin, 164
Talbot, Sir William, of Cartown, i. 165 *note*
Talleyrand, iii. 281, 304, 312, 342
Tandy, Napper, ii. 358, 382, 409, 412, 415, 429, 520; iii. 20, 33, 37, 42, 50 *note*, 53, 54, 55, 59, 66, 69, 170, 190, 266, 267 *note*, 281, 283, 488
Tara Hill, iii. 366
Tarleton, General, ii. 283
Tate, Colonel, iii. 201
Taylor, Jeremy, made Bishop of Down, and afterwards of Dromore, i. 156, 158
Tea, tax on, ii. 134
Teeling, Barclay, iii. 281, 283, 316, 317, 482, 484, 485
Temple, Lord, Viceroy (afterwards Marquis of Buckingham), ii. 353 360, 361, 362, 380, 487
Temple, Sir John, Master of the Rolls in Dublin, i. 90 *note*, 104 *note*, 109, 111
Temple, the, iii. 8
Tenants' Protection Bill, ii, 118
Tennent, iii. 265, 283
Tennison, Mr., iii. 109
Ternay, M. de, ii. 280, 281

TUR

Test Act, i. 381, 384, 389; ii. 136, 217, 365
Texel Fleet, iii. 287
Thanet, Lord, iii. 321
'The Press,' O'Connor's publication, iii. 288
Three Rocks, iii. 392, 394, 396
Thurot, M., i. 622-624
Ticonderoga, ii. 202
Tierney, Mr., iii. 453, 455
Tighe, Mr., ii. 181
Tillage Act, ii. 26 *note*
Tillage Bill, i. 400, 501, 590
Tipperary, ii. 22, 23, 26; iii. 328, 337, 339
Tipperary peasant, ii. 20
Tisdall, Philip, Attorney-General, i. 57, 64, 81, 90, 106, 108, 155
Tithes and Tithe-Proctors, ii. 453, 454, 455, 470, 481, 483, 489; iii. 376
Toler, Mr. Daniel, ii. 34 *note*; iii. 26, 54, 126, 129; Solicitor-General, 49, 146
Toleration, i. 563, 566
Toleration Act, i. 240, 359
Tollendal, Lally, his name, ii. 127
Tone, Matthew, iii. 482, 484, 485
Tone, Theobald Wolfe, iii. 8-11, 19, 53, 54, 56, 57, 59, 60, 63, 64, 65, 70, 71, 83, 84, 100, 118, 119, 144, 151, 153, 157, 158, 165, 174, 175, 190, 191, 192, 193-195, 196, 197, 199, 200, 201, 205, 206, 214, 218, 247, 250, 262, 263, 266, 283, 292 *note*, 302, 322, 323, 352, 392, 487
Tories, bands of outlaws, so called, i. 135, 164, 237, 280, 360
Tories, English, iii. 314, 321
Tower of London, i. 559
Townshend, Charles, Chancellor of the Exchequer, ii. 44, 52, 133, 134
Townshend, George, third Viscount, Viceroy, ii. 44, 52, 53, 72, 79, 84, 89, 94, 104, 106, 112, 144, 146, 221, 222, 488, 510
Townshend, Lord, i. 525, 527, 542, 593
Townshend, Marquis, ii. 513
Tralee, Bay of, i. 478.
Trenchard, i. 270
Trenton, battle of, ii. 201
Trim, surrender of, i. 126
Trimleston, Lord Robert Barnewalle, ii. 15, 17-19, 22
Trinity College, i. 331; ii. 503; iii. 6, 289
Troy, Dr., Catholic Archbishop of Dublin, iii. 70, 83, 84, 100, 149, 246
Tuam, diocese of, i. 89 *note*
Tuam, Archbishop of, i. 353
Tubman, Jane, i. 427

TUL

Tullamore abandoned, ii. 126
Tumultuous Assemblies Bill, ii. 483
Turnpike Bill, ii. 502
Two Mile Bridge, near Youghal, iii. 271
Tyrannicide, iii. 270
Tyrconnell, Earl of, Richard Talbot, i. 171, 172; Lord Lieutenant, 174, 177, 180, 182, 196, 197, 201, 256; ii. 276
Tyrone, Lord, ii. 75, 104 *note*, 106, 436, 472; iii. 80
Tyrone, Earl of, i. 256; ii. 107

ULSTER, i. 57, 68 70, 98, 100, 107, 115, 117, 156, 160, 319, 326; ii. 53, 71, 115, 141, 163, 471, 478, 438, 439; iii. 18, 28, 155, 178, 188, 233, 235, 239, 240, 257, 259, 266, 267, 268, 291, 325, 329, 361, 399, 400, 420, 425, 426, 452, 483
Ulster corps of Volunteers, ii. 292, 307, 309, 369
Ulster linen, ii. 423
Ulster, Protestants of, ii. 125, 129
Ulster Puritans, iii. 151
Ulster Republicans, iii. 200
Ulster Revolutionary Committee, iii. 270
Ulster settlement, iii. 98
Uniacke, Mr., iii. 291, 293, 294, 300, 337
Uniformity, Act of, i. 46
Uniformity, second Act of, i. 155
Union, i. 285, 287 *note*, 288, 297, 303, 304; iii. 79, 103, 113, 123, 144, 298, 439, 489-493
'Union Star,' iii. 269
United Irishmen in 1797, ii. 27; iii. 11, 21, 22, 33, 53, 64, 64, 67, 76, 84, 104, 109, 110, 111, 115, 116, 135, 146, 152, 155, 160, 162, 165, 167, 172, 174, 192, 196, 200, 223, 228, 233, 234, 239, 245, and *note*, 247, 248, 255, 256, 257, 259, 267 *note*, 277, 280, 283, 298, 299, 305, 325, 336, 351, 355, 377, 379
Universities, iii. 21
Upton, Mr., ii. 119; made a Viscount, 120
Ushant, iii. 201
Utrecht, peace of, i. 358

VALENCE, General, iii. 280
Valencia, i. 466
Vallancey, Colonel, ii. 77
Valmy, iii. 65, 69 *note*
Vandeleur, Mr., iii. 231
Vane, Sir Harry, i. 89 *note*, 91 *note*
Verner, Mr., iii. 169
Vesey, John, Archbishop of Tuam, i. 158, 502

WES

Vesey, Major, iii. 410
Viceroys of Ireland, ii. 35
Vigo, the Duke of Ormond at, i. 295
Villiers, Sir Edward, i. 223
Vinegar Hill, iii. 393, 388, 389, 397, 401. 402, 432, 435, 436, 443, 473
Virginia, ii. 134, 206, 281, 284, 285
Voltaire, iii. 15
Volunteers, ii. 211, 235, 236, 239, 241, 264, 265, 269, 287, 288, 291, 292, 303, 307, 308, 310, 315, 316, 322, 328, 347, 356-359, 361, 366, 368, 369, 371, 372, 373, 375, 380, 388, 389, 392, 393, 395, 399, 409, 411, 420, 428-430, 432, 433, 434, 445, 447, 459, 460, 461, 485, 488; iii. 1, 5, 6, 11, 17, 63, 67, 79, 83, 84, 89, 95, 105, 106-108, 178, 227, 298

WALDEGRAVE, Lady, ii. 77
Wales contrasted with Ireland, i. 289
Wales, Prince of, title of, i. 10 (afterwards George IV.); ii. 491-493, 495, 497, 500, 501, 504, 508, 511; iii. 229, 239
Walford, General, iii. 365
Walker, Dr., at Derry, i. 183
Wallace, English Attorney-General, ii. 273
Waller, Mr., iii. 234
Walpole, Colonel, iii. 401, 402
Walpole, General, iii. 402, 403, 406
Walpole, Horace, English ambassador in Paris, i. 465; ii. 34
Walpole, Sir Robert, i. 380, 496, 514, 524, 525-527, 541, 581
Walsingham, iii. 181
Walsingham, Lady, i. 519
Wandsworth, Sir Christopher, Deputy i. 52
Warbeck, Perkin, i. 34
Ward, Dean of Connor, i. 244
Warren, Sir John, iii. 485
Washington, General, ii. 200, 201, 281, 283, 285, 478; iii. 18
Waterford, i. 17; ii. 27, 28, 96, 219, 232, 256; iii. 375, 398, 419, 436
Waterford, Bishop of, ii. 33
Waterford, Lord, iii. 231
Waterford road, great, iii. 358
W. D., i. 551 *note*
Welfare, Committee of Public, iii. 162
Wellesleys, the, iii. 127
Wesley, or Wollesley, Arthur, iii. 28, 80, 112
Welsh, i. 9
Welsh Fencibles, iii. 354
Welshman, i. 7, 8
Wesley, John, i. 626

INDEX. 519

Wesleyans, iii. 435
Westenra, Mr., ii. 109 *note*
Westfieldstown, iii. 357
West Indies, ii. 342, 338; iii. 400
Westmeath, Lord, i. 128
Westminster, a commission sits at, to consider the Irish claims, i. 144
Westmoreland, Earl of, Viceroy, ii, 520; iii. 15, 25, 26, 35, 37, 39, 41–43, 49, 50 *note*, 57, 67, 68, 71, 73, 77, 80, 124, 144. 145
West Point, ii. 281
Wexford, i. 17, 113, 126; iii. 110, 342, 370, 375–377, 429–431, 432, 440, 459, 473
Wexford city, iii. 375, 381, 387, 392, 394, 397, 400, 403
Wexford Harbour, iii. 436
Weymouth, Lord, named as Viceroy, ii. 39, 72, 74, 94, 223, 233
Wharton, Earl of, Viceroy, i. 114, 328, 329, 334, 343, 381
Whiddy Island, i. 455; iii. 205
Whig Club of Dublin, ii. 519; iii. 9
Whig Club, Northern, iii. 9, 15, 16, 17, 18, 54, 59, 343, 344; ii. 310, 314, 322, 323, 491; iii. 82, 95, 122, 177, 318, 453
Whisky Bill, ii. 105
Whisky shops in Ireland, ii. 105, 460
Whitbread, Samuel, iii. 321
White, Mr., of Seafield, iii. 209, 213
White, Mrs., iii. 209
White, Rebecca, i. 425
Whiteboy disturbances, i. 500; ii. 22
Whiteboys, the, ii. 24, 25 *note*, 27, 28, 31, 32, 39, 53, 71, 96, 97 *note*, 115, 190, 447, 455, 459, 461, 467, 470, 471, 473, 476, 484, 485, 489, 510; iii. 23, 66, 87, 376
Whitehaven, ii. 214
Whitshed, Chief Justice, i. 503
Whyte, General, iii. 105, 106
Wickham, Mr., iii. 418, 429
Wicklow, i. 113; iii. 303, 339, 370, 398, 419, 473
Wicklow, petition from, ii. 221, 222 *note*
Wicklow Hills, iii. 375, 420, 445, 449
Wilberforce, Mr., iii. 455, 456
Wildgeese, the, i. 365, 451, 456, 585

William the Conqueror, i. 8
William and Mary, 4th of, ii. 498
William III. i., 193–195, 196, 197, 201, 205, 237, 241, 250, 254, 259. 272, 283, 339, 341; ii. 131, 306; iii. 322
Willoughby, Captain, iii. 448
Wilmington, ii. 284
Wilson, Lord, i. 256
Wilson, Mr., iii. 110
Winchester, Paulet, Marquis of, i. 250
Winter, Admiral de, iii. 262, 263, 265
Wogan, Sir Charles, i. 197
Wolfe, Attorney-General (afterwards Lord Kilwarden), iii. 41, 159, 167, 240, 324
Wolfe, General, ii. 52, 126, 129; iii. 198
Women, abduction of, i. 417
Wood's patent, i. 522, 523, 524, 530, 531, 543, 544, 560
Wool, i. 160, 265, 267, 290, 446
Woollen cloths, ii. 228, 229; iii. 297
Woollen weavers, ii. 35
Workhouses established in Dublin, i. 591
Wright, of Clonmel, iii. 337
Writ of Error, ii. 342, 350, 401
Wrixon, Major, ii. 97, 98
Wych, Sir Cyril, Lord Justice, i. 241
Wynn, Sir Watkin, iii. 354

YARMOUTH, Countess of, ii. 77
Yelverton, Barry (afterwards Attorney-General and Lord Avonmore), ii. 238 *note*, 243, 256, 295, 299, 301, 308, 310, 311, 316, 318, 324, 348, 387, 391, 392, 395, 478, 479
Yeomanry, iii. 128, 178, 179, 187, 202, 210, 224, 230, 233, 236, 238, 256, 273, 303, 306, 328, 346, 354, 355, 359, 363, 367, 376, 381, 384–386, 394, 417, 419, 422, 428, 430, 463–465, 474
Yonge, Sir George, ii. 345
York, Cardinal of, iii. 100
York, Duke of (afterwards James II.), i. 151, 153
York river, ii. 285
Yorktown, ii. 285, 293, 307, 338
Youghal, ii. 96
Young, Arthur, i. 406, 418 *note*, 595; ii. 21, 46, 71, 119 *note*, 447 *note*, 479 *note*; iii. 376

THE ENGLISH IN IRELAND

IN THE

EIGHTEENTH CENTURY.

BY

JAMES ANTHONY FROUDE, M.A.

IN THREE VOLUMES.

VOL. I.

LONDON:
LONGMANS, GREEN, AND CO.
1872.

All rights reserved.

www.ingramcontent.com/pod-product-compliance
Lightning Source LLC
Chambersburg PA
CBHW031947290426
44108CB00011B/712